A Peaceable
Psychology

A Peaceable Psychology

Christian Therapy in a World of Many Cultures

Alvin Dueck

Kevin Reimer

BrazosPress

a division of Baker Publishing Group
Grand Rapids, Michigan

Published by Brazos Press
a division of Baker Publishing Group
P.O. Box 6287, Grand Rapids, MI 49516-6287
www.brazospress.com

Printed in the United States of America

Library of Congress Cataloging-in-Publication Data
Dueck, Alvin C., 1943–
    A peaceable psychology : Christian therapy in a world of many cultures / Alvin Dueck,
    Kevin Reimer.
        p.   cm.
    Includes bibliographical references and index.
    ISBN 978-1-58743-105-0 (pbk.)
    1. Christianity and other religions. 2. Ethnopsychology. 3. Psychotherapy—Religious
aspects—Christianity. 4. Psychology and religion. 5. Psychology, Religious. 6. Christianity—
Psychology. I. Reimer, Kevin S., 1968– II. Title.
BR127.D84 2009
261.5′15089—dc22   2009023399

09   10   11   12   13   14   15   7   6   5   4   3   2   1

For Anne and Lynn

Contents

Introduction

. . . .

Let us suppose that you are a Christian psychologist invited by a colleague to consult with a relief agency in Afghanistan. You are assigned to a clinic outside Kabul, the capital city. Red Cross workers are in contact with several Muslim families who recently moved back into their homes after the American overthrow of the Taliban. You are asked to give professional assistance for children who survived the conflict and who are now in need of help. Soheil is a nine-year-old boy who was slightly injured in a terrorist bombing. Through a translator, his parents anxiously report that he can be found on some nights hiding in his sister's closet. At times he will sleep there. Soheil struggles to focus on his parents' instructions when he withdraws and stares vacantly into space for minutes on end. During these episodes he is unable to interact with others around him. Soheil used to love soccer, praying at the mosque, and attending the local elementary school but now shows little interest in these activities. He has lost five pounds since the conflict, even with nutritional supplements from the Red Cross. Aid workers inform you that Soheil was unable to make eye contact during an initial meeting, even when presented with toys, markers, and paper. In your first encounter with the boy, Soheil's oldest sister Anahita stays to translate. During your time together, Soheil sporadically engages in rapid-fire conversation with his sister. When you ask her what he is saying, she shrugs and states that Soheil is feeling sad.[1]

This case seems daunting. Soheil needs help but what do we know about healing within his ethnic tradition? Should Americans even be the ones to assist given our presence as occupiers? Can a Christian therapist provide comfort to a Muslim boy given the long history of animosity between our religions? Would our presence as therapists symbolize and effect peace in some small way? Our response to these questions, we hope, will move the conversation forward on the following interrelated issues: healing, politics/ethnicity, and religion. Jesus's political proclamation of a new world order (the reign of

God), and his empowerment of the poor and voiceless is for us the point of departure for healing.

Some rough definitions are in order. First, psychological healing in the West is dominated by the scientific paradigm. However, we will view healing through the eyes of clients and professional therapists, whether Western or indigenous non-Western. Second, in the tradition of Aristotle,[2] we consider the structuring of relationships in traditions to be a political phenomenon. We also include in this rubric the distribution of power and the empowering of minority voices. Politics, ethnicity, and tradition are, in our opinion, linguistically related. Finally, we bring our theological convictions to bear on contemporary psychology/psychotherapy. We are cognizant of our own limitations in addressing these issues but hope our thoughts will stimulate further reflection.

Over the past century, psychology has been practiced in the manner of medical science working from an objective, universal perspective that assumes one can transcend particular traditions. We have little doubt that some good has come from this brand of psychological practice. However, in this book we will explore a different paradigm. Our hope is to generate conversation emerging from a theologically, culturally, and politically sensitive psychotherapy.[3]

In the Western model, Soheil's suffering would be identified with psychological terms such as "trauma," "depression," and "self." These psychological concepts have respectable histories in Western practice. Beyond their immediate value to clinical psychologists who wish to treat Soheil, each term is freighted with political and cultural meanings. Psychological jargon is heard back home on the evening news, in public school classrooms, in graduate programs, and from the Sunday pulpit shorn clean of its political import. Millions of North Americans worry about their mental health, take pills to enhance it, and write books promoting it. An individualistic psychological vocabulary dominates contemporary definitions of human nature, and with it we diagnose and treat pathology. These are words of enormous utility, but they are seldom understood politically or from within the particular semantic universe of the client.

For Soheil's sake, we believe that facile use of Western psychological concepts is problematic. We do not dispute that Soheil may be traumatized, depressed, and dissociating. But we are concerned that these words, applied in the objective manner of Western psychology, may trample and even violate cherished dimensions of the boy's tradition and forget the political context in which care is given. Soheil is a Muslim from a conservative religious family in a war-torn country living under the powerful presence of a superpower. In his world, "trauma" reflects suffering directly related to moral, religious, and military conflict. There is nothing neutral about it. The world belongs to God (Allah), reflecting cosmic spiritual conflicts between good and evil. Suffering is ultimately subsumed within an understanding of Allah's will. Soheil's religious world is at a linguistic loss to describe "depression." People experience sadness, but from their perspective it is not necessarily a mental disorder like post-traumatic stress disorder (PTSD). Sadness, for Soheil, becomes a companion to the loss and mourning living amid American military forces. It is typical of a place where sin is considered an everyday reality, requiring expiation through obedience to Qur'anic teachings. The notion of a monadic, apolitical "self" is ludicrous. Religion and politics are inextricably connected in his world. Everything attributed to Soheil's selfhood in actuality is directed toward his soul, his Muslim religion, and his relationships with others. Neither Soheil nor his parents are concerned with an autonomous self in a Western sense. The boy's obligations are directed first to Allah, then to his parents and family, and finally to the hopes of his religio-political community. In spite of the well-meaning intentions of the psychologist who sits before him, the assumptions of Western psychology basic to Soheil's treatment are foreign—and potentially destructive—to his tradition. The great risk is that an objective, apolitical Western psychology may undermine Soheil's ethnic and religious narratives, extending the damage of terrorist bombs. Further, if the therapist is from the United States, he or she may assume that the American presence in Afghanistan can be justified as liberating the Afghans from the Taliban. If Soheil feels otherwise, would the therapist recognize the politicized nature of his or her therapy?

At first blush the Western psychologist may find these concerns preposterous. The past twenty years have witnessed a renaissance in clinical sensitivity to ethnic and religious issues. Psychological training departments across the country have adopted thorough training programs for diversity. A gold standard in clinical education, the American Psychological Association (APA), has pulled out the stops in an effort to sensitize the practice of psychology to the needs of persons with diverse ethnic, religious, and sexual orientations. Western psychologists traveling to places like Afghanistan are presumably better equipped to deal with Soheil and his local tradition than at any time in the history of the profession. For these critics, our concerns may be much ado about nothing.

Additionally, the growth of cross-cultural psychology as a discipline continues to change the field for the better. Psychologists have become conversant with anthropology and other related disciplines.[4] As a result, clinicians are sensitized to diversity in a way that permits them to effectively build on Soheil's beliefs toward recovery from even the most severe stressors. We would agree that these trends have made the Western psychology of the present day more effective and appropriate than in the past. However, our sense is that despite these advances, we continue to export our psychological vocabulary and syntax, assuming it is generalizable.[5]

Our objection is that ethnicity and religion in the diversity framework effectively reduces traditions such as Soheil's from the sacred to the instrumental. We hope to demonstrate that ethnicity and religion too often become functional, useful techniques for therapeutic change determined by the psychologist's own definitions and priorities. Soheil's notion of healing, whatever it may be, remains on the shelf. References to Allah or the Qur'an are then only useful instruments applied in the interest of establishing rapport with the boy. Using Soheil's language becomes a clinical advantage when it makes his pathology a little clearer, his language of relationship a little more intelligible.

Diversity in this sense serves the central mission of the clinician to objectively treat pathology within a landscape that fixes human nature in essentialist, Western terms. Soheil's understanding of these issues may be circumscribed to the point where he is no longer a participant in the therapeutic conversation. Like a potted plant, references to indigenous religion and politics are kept at the margins—quietly inhabiting the office corner and collecting dust. Soheil's ethnic and religious tradition in this instance has no life or sacred character; his political context has no relevance.

We acknowledge that the collision between Western psychological universals and particular ethnic traditions may mean little for Americans who lack defined ethnic or religious identities. But for those who have them, the implications are unsettling. As an example, instrumental treatment of African-American identity and spirituality may erode the sacred memory of generations who sought a way out of the darkness of slavery. "Trauma," "depression," and "self" may be more recognizable to African-American clients than to Soheil, but the meaning of these words is not necessarily the same as in the universalistic lexicon of Western psychology. The suffering behind each term invokes a uniquely African-American cachet of idiom and metaphor. The apolitical psychologist who blithely links these concepts with an instrumental approach to African-American ethnicity and spirituality may be socializing the client into a foreign mold. Ironically, no one is immediately aware of what is happening. At the termination of therapy the client lives with a thinly contrived understanding of healing that unconsciously adopts the ahistorical psychologist's words and meanings. The client may find it odd that the new psychological vocabulary doesn't resonate with family and friends but instead creates subtle suspicion. The client may live with a muted sense of "progress" made away from the presenting psychological problem, but in a direction that doesn't seem consistent with African-American spirituality.

We believe that this process belies a subtle insult to the dignity of human beings created in God's image. Rather than recognizing and affirming the client's traditioned sense of healing, the instrumentally trained psychologist unwittingly creates an individual fashioned in the image of Western ideals. Perhaps Christians are aware of this danger. While adopting the training standards of the APA, many Christian psychology programs have also implemented "integration" curricula designed to help psychologists understand the meaning of concepts like trauma, depression, and self at a theological level. Yet this may not be enough. The hegemony of Western psychology is rapidly eroding the remnants of indigenous Christian understanding of the self, community, politics, and tradition. Social thinkers like Philip Rieff have noted that the triumph of therapeutic vocabulary is sufficiently complete that even clergy have come to redefine their roles principally in psychological terms.[6]

We are concerned that psychological ideology is rapidly eliminating ethnic and religious traditions, one person at a time. For Soheil's sake we are morally compelled to consider the complex issues beneath this process. Because we are Anabaptist Christians with a specific religious identity, we write with self-conscious recognition that our analysis and proposed solution is particular and confessional.[7] We extend the argument, developed by the first author in a previous publication, that Jesus is a political figure and that by implication Christian psychologists are to be sensitive to the political nature of their work.[8] From this vantage point we contend that the Christian psychologist must treat Soheil with attention to the particulars of his political situation and his ethnic and religious tradition.[9] The concepts of trauma, depression, and self must wait for qualification on Soheil's terms. To do this respectfully, the Christian psychologist must be self-conscious of her or his own social location. At its most basic level, psychotherapy with Soheil is an encounter between local narratives where two people, each with their particular traditions, are engaged in conversation. With critical reflection on the Western liberal tradition and respect for Soheil's tradition, the clinician may win the trust that encourages Soheil to lead with his own story, permitting an exchange that embraces local definitions of pathology and that anticipates healing. We contend that the universal objectives of psychology are themselves a tradition capable of being imposed on the ethnic or religious client.

We are challenging the Christian psychologist to be cognizant not only of the client's political and cultural narrative, but also the role of her or his own Christian story in the therapeutic dialogue.[10] The incorporation of particular, local traditions into the clinical conversation gives witness to our conviction that to uncritically employ generalized psychological constructs risks imposing a psychology that is practically atheistic, undertaken as if God doesn't exist.[11] Since the psychologist holds in her or his hands the delicate psychic fragments of another human being, maintaining one's Christian authenticity does not mean imposing our Christian story on Soheil. Sitting across from him, we are confronted with a particular individual of inestimable worth to the God who makes healing possible in the first place. Our approach is premised upon incarnation—an encounter between two human beings who each live within stories of existential and transcendent significance.

Briefly, the outline of our argument is as follows. The suffering of the innocent is our point of departure, and Juanita, a Guatemalan, will be our companion through the book. We view her suffering as a continuation of the suffering of Christ who was crucified by the Roman Empire. In her face we see the face of our suffering God. Her suffering, like Christ's, occurred in a political context. Unfortunately, Western psychologists have been complicit in the suffering of the innocent in their collusion with military projects, their presence at hostile interrogation of prisoners of war in Afghanistan and Iraq, and their presumption that their psychological findings are universal. The attempt to build an empire with a common language failed at Babel. We suggest that it is precisely an empire mentality that the apostle Paul critiques. The antidote to universalism is to focus on the local, and so we valorize ethno-religious particularity.

We are not entirely convinced that Western liberal societies prize ethnic and religious indigeneity and differences. Americans tend to value individual rights more than communal rights. Our argument is that differences in ethnic communities are a gift to society. Pentecost points to the goodness of ethnic particularity in that persons who had come to Jerusalem from all over the ancient Near East heard the gospel in their own tongue! However, we will note the push toward linguistic homogeneity in the public sphere. Instead of marginalizing other voices, we hope for a public space in which a range of voices would be heard. Given the hegemony of secularity, clients tend not to bring their native ethnic or religious voice into therapy.

Because language so powerfully shapes identity, we will encourage therapists to empower clients to use their mother tongue, should they wish to do so. Honoring a client's local language and providing tradition-sensitive therapy seem to make the good gifts of his or her community accessible for healing. We recognize that at times the logic and vocabulary of faith and psychology are very different from each other. We must learn which language is most appropriate at a given moment in therapy. However, we must be cautious when we affirm religiosity in therapy, as we may find ourselves affirming a religiosity shaped by individualism, secularity, and pragmatism rather than the indigenous spirituality of our clients. We will examine a model of therapy appropriate for sacral cultures that seek to live by the love and grace of God.

Rather than imposing a general conception of personality or religiosity, the peaceable therapist relinquishes such power, being open to working from a position of weakness and transparency. Internationally, our task is to empower local mental-health practitioners to mine their own traditions for gifts of healing. The tradition-sensitive psychologist would, accordingly, seek to empower local practitioners to explore the contours of a psychology sensitive to the best values of their culture. Then there is the issue of morality in therapy. We will make a distinction between traditioned and abstract forms of morality. Our focus is on a peaceable Christian approach to psychotherapy, and hence we point to the concrete life of Jesus as the foundation upon which we wish to build our therapeutic ethic and our norm for what it means to have human identity. He who is the Prince of Peace seeks reconciliation of enemies within and beyond our communities. When we appropriate the story of his life, it is a narrative that brings healing. Jesus's continuing presence in the body of the church is the context in which healing and ethical discernment can occur.

Before we proceed, we wish to make a comment about our intended audience. First, we write to those engaged in work as psychologists and psychotherapists who desire to have their work reflect their commitment to being followers of Christ. Secondly, we wish to challenge those pastors and mental-health workers who think integrative conversation between theology and psychology is between a domesticated Jesus and a depoliticized psychology. Third, we would hope to empower non-Western Christian therapists who are disenchanted with psychotherapy as practiced in the modern world to find their own psychological voices and to bring their indigenous Christianity to the practice of indigenous psychotherapy. Fourth, we are writing to religious psychologists, international mental-health workers, pastors, and theologians concerned about the negative impact of Enlightenment modernist psychology on ethnic and religious groups. Those who are weary of secular objectivism and fundamentalist triumphalism are our conversation partners. This book is for those who wish to see indigenous psychologies flourish—whether in Guatemala, Kenya, or Sichuan—according to the best in their traditions. Given an increasing concern about globalization, this book is for anyone interested in ways one can engage in a conversation between Christian mental-health practitioners from diverse cultural and political contexts.

Our audience is not only the living, but also those who have preceded us. Annie Dillard reminds us that the soil we walk on contains the dead, those who have made it possible for us to go on.[12] For us this includes the faithful saints through the centuries who have sought peace, who lived patiently, actively waiting for the peaceable reign of God, and who were willing to die rather than submit to the story that was imposed upon them. We come from a tradition that has known suffering. During the Reformation our leaders were burned, tortured, and drowned by civil and religious bodies. In our homes, on the shelf beside the Bible was *Martyrs Mirror*,[13] a book which recounted the testimonies of those whose lives were snuffed out by oppressive ecclesiastical and political authorities from the time of the early church until the time of its first printing in 1660. Then there were our Mennonite grandparents who fled the Ukraine in the 1920s to avoid the random violence. Some fifty thousand were killed. Those deaths were a central theme in the story of our Mennonite people, and, in writing this book, we seek to honor them as well.

We write for the future without making assumptions about how long this book will be in print! We see our writing as a witness for peace that perhaps our grandchildren will read. We live in a time of war, and we cannot remain silent. We have no illusions about what our writing will accomplish. We prefer to think of it as an act of faithful witness to our Lord who empowered a Samaritan woman, who healed the ear of an enemy soldier even as they came for him, and who suffered rather than be violent.

1

Suffering, Symptoms, and the Cross

■ ■ ■ ■ ■ ■ ■ ■ ■ ■

Then he began to teach them that the Son of Man must undergo great suffering.

Mark 8:31

But you, O Lord, are a God merciful and gracious, slow to anger and abounding in steadfast love and faithfulness.

Psalm 86:15

The late-night Guatemalan rain has washed clean the morning air, but already diesel fumes from the nearby thoroughfare are drifting through the window.[1] The bougainvilleas along the eastern wall of our domicile are bright red, the color of suffering. Blue petals from the jacaranda tree in the courtyard fall to earth gently, unlike the way power descends on the heads of the innocent. I (AD) hear the crying of children from the San Pedro Negro Hospital next door—the sick are watched over by a black saint. Are the poor, who mourn and are hungry, actually blessed? Will the meek of Guatemala inherit the earth, or simply more violence from expansionist nations?

I have returned again with my students to this land of suffering. The soil is scorched from a civil war lasting thirty-six years, a conflict between government militia and guerrilla fighters. A million people were displaced. Two hundred thousand Indians from the rural highlands were killed. Some 440 Mayan communities were decimated. In 1996 the Guatemalan peace accords were signed, but the cumulative effect of death and emigration is such that 43 percent of the population is now under fourteen years of age.[2] The fires of civil war were fueled by American paranoia of communist sympathizers in the 1950s, along with capitalist interests in the form of conglomerate fruit companies, and prejudice against native peoples.

Our group is composed of mental-health clinicians in training from the Graduate School of Psychology at Fuller Theological Seminary. Back in the relative tranquility of Pasadena, a small bronze statue in the campus court-yard offers a reason for our coming. The statue represents the mission of the School of Psychology—a cross (✝) embedded in the Greek letter *psi* (Ψ). It symbolizes our desire to keep the cross of suffering in the heart of our work as professional therapists. Being in Guatemala is our way of remembering the suffering of the innocent. Perhaps this experience will help us shape the contours of a peaceable psychology. We wish to experience deeply the lives of the Guatemalans we meet and to consider our professional practice from the perspective of the poor, the forgotten, and the wounded.

The concern for a peaceable psychology in this book emerges from the fact that we saw victims of empire-building in Guatemala. In this chapter we outline some of the contours of this psychology. A peaceable psychology privileges the suffering of the poor and the language they use to understand it. Christian psy-chologists who focus on peace affirm a peaceable view of atonement, yearn for reconciliation and depend on the hope that comes with Christ's resurrection.

To flesh out these themes we will meet Juanita, whose emotional life carries the scars of violence. At least a part of a therapist's responsibility is to assist clients' finding meaning for their lives; another part is symptom relief. We wrestle with the problem of viewing troubling experiences primarily in terms of symptoms rather than in terms of suffering. Symptoms point to an underlying cause, while suffering calls for new meanings. We propose that meaning may be evident in local stories. Hence, we encourage the indigenous persons to give voice to their experience. Moreover, there may be meaning for Juanita in the fact that Jesus suffered in the context of political oppression but still advocated a peaceable reign of God. That is, a Christian psychotherapist understands suffering in terms of Jesus's suffering and believes in the resurrection hope for reconciliation.[3]

Our North American psychology presents itself largely as apolitical and religiously aloof, and that implicates the kind of meaning given to suffering.[4] Is our psychology sensitive to issues of power and oppression? Is it possible that some elements of our American psychology are insensitive to issues of justice or local concerns? We wonder what cross of suffering will be placed in the heart of psychology without reflection on these and other questions that emerge from the real suffering of a forgotten people.

Nestled among Guatemala's volcanic mountains lies the small village of Santiago de Atitlán. The serene ambiance, however, belies a violent history. Juanita's[5] experience will serve to illustrate the main themes of this book. This is the story of a Guatemalan woman known to the first author (AD) that we have adapted into a therapeutic context. The experience of Juanita is as she tells it. Contextualizing her story in a therapeutic setting is our way of illustrating a peaceable psychology. In her first session with her counselor she says:

> I am going to tell you my personal history and about my community. It hurts me to tell this story . . . each time I remember it, the feelings come back strong . . . but it is important that you know how we have lived.
>
> In 1979, the violence began here. We heard that there was going to be a civil war, but didn't know what that was. They told us that in a civil war there would be dead people in the streets—but it wasn't that way. First, pamphlets were placed under our doors with the name of the organization, ORPA. The papers said we should protect the members of this organization, open our doors to them and hide them in our homes. I remember the first day the guerrillas walked by my house. When they passed, they greeted us with, "Good afternoon, friends," and I responded by saying, "God bless you." I didn't know at the time if they were guerrillas or soldiers, but they greeted us very kindly. They went to the central plaza and hung a large ORPA banner. They invited the townspeople to a conference in the plaza. Many went to hear them. There weren't any problems that night; some people gave Coca-Cola, bread, and other gifts to this group who had come into the community.
>
> The next day, there were problems. The first thing we heard was that my brothers appeared on a list that was being circulated. It had the names of all the people who had attended the meeting. You see, the military has its commissioners, representatives who spy in the community. It was just a few days later that the army came, and that night we had our first kidnapping. The first to be kidnapped was a distant relative, whom we were close to, and another man. People were afraid. I went to visit the wife of the man. She didn't know why they had taken her husband, but they were armed and wearing white clothing.
>
> The next day there was another kidnapping . . . this time an ex-seminarian. He was asleep in his bed. They kicked the door in, dragged him out of bed and threw him against the wall so many times that his head split open and left bloodstains on the wall. The kidnappings went on and on, not just at nighttime, but in the daytime when people went out to work in their fields and didn't return. The violence became so bad that people didn't even sleep in their own homes. I went to stay with my sister. Only the military had the right to walk in the streets after 5 p.m.
>
> The community joined together by opening the churches and starting a prayer chain. But we couldn't resolve anything, and many people went to sleep in the churches thinking that the violence would end in just a matter of days. There were so many people in the church that we had to sleep sitting up. At that time, the army did not have the right to enter the churches. The violence continued and we couldn't keep staying at the churches. People stopped coming to visit us here, as everyone was afraid to walk around the streets.
>
> I remember a day when things were a little calmer for us when the army left at Christmas time. When they left, we celebrated a peaceful Christmas, New Year's, and also Three Kings Day, all without the military. They left for only two weeks. They returned on January 7 (1980) around midday. Two truckloads of soldiers passed by my house. A few minutes later we heard the first shots . . .

gunshots, bombs, or grenades . . . I'm not sure. A Canadian friend came by and asked me where my husband was working, and I pointed towards the gunfire. I got really afraid—the shooting wouldn't stop. The streets were full of people. We were asking each other, "Where is your husband? Where is your son? Where is your father?" Later that afternoon two helicopters arrived. The doors were open and soldiers were pointing guns down at the community. We were all afraid and I began to cry because I had no news of my husband or my father.

The gunfire stopped about 5 p.m. We saw the trucks coming this way, and we hid in the house. I still had hope that my husband was alive. The community organized a commission to go to the area of shooting and investigate. Some of my relatives were on the commission; I stayed in the house with my children and my mother. The first person they found was a teacher, and he was dead. Then they found another pregnant teacher, also dead. They walked near the edge of the lake and found a man whose whole torso was cut open. Others were tied to coffee plants. The commission returned with some of the bodies and reported what they had found.[6]

> O God, hear the cries of the innocent.
> Are not the poor your people?
> Did you not bring your people out of Egypt?
> Where were you when Juanita's people suffered in Guatemala?
> Hear, O God, the pleas of the downtrodden.[7]

We are often asked why we have come to Guatemala. To hear the stories of Guatemalan people, we say. But stories like Juanita's are beginning to over-whelm us. As clinical psychologists, despair and lament should be familiar territory. But the suffering of the thousands who lived through the Guatema-lan civil war changes the landscape of psychological theory and practice for us. Theirs is a suffering that comes from political and institutional violence rather than occupational stress, marital conflict, or children who act out. Such pain is a product of a larger political problem that often escapes the attention of the North American therapeutic community. Their suffering is partly a consequence of political and economic expansionism. What form of healing is sensitive to issues of injustice, local political issues, and the thickness of Guatemalan spirituality?

Symptomology or Suffering

Our reflections on a peaceable psychology and suffering emerge directly from Juanita's narrative and the plight of persecuted ethnic minorities and religious communities around the world. The welfare of indigenous peoples is jeopar-dized by governments around the world: Montagnards in Vietnam, the Karen in Burma, the Kurds in the four countries they call home, the Copts and Bahais in Egypt, the First Nations in the Americas. It is especially so if religion is part of the ethnic culture. What are the characteristics of a peaceable psychology that responds to the suffering of the marginalized?

A peaceable psychology cannot avoid addressing the *meaning* of suffering for the individual. A Christian therapist can respond to violence with psychological insight and compassion that is theologically informed. Juanita's story points to the integral role suffering plays in human life. We see Juanita's suffering in view of the role violence plays in society to maintain order. How might Christ's life and death shed light on the nature of suffering? Christ's suffering is relevant because he, like the Guatemalan Indians, suffered innocently. Suffering must be understood, as illustrated by Juanita's experience, both ethically and politically. Do Christian psychologists possess such frameworks for understanding suffering?

It is not clear whether mental-health professionals understand profound suffering. They may understand symptoms, but do they understand *suffering*? Ronald Miller points out that while psychology enjoys considerable popularity as a profession, there is a fundamental dissociation between the discipline as a science and the suffering of clients. Despite the fact that his book is published by the American Psychological Association (APA), the opening chapter is entitled "American Psychological Dissociation."[8] The *Diagnostic and Statistical Manual of Mental Disorders* (DSMIV-TR) speaks of distress, disturbance, and suicidal ideas, but it does not address suffering. Perhaps it is because suffering is a moral concept which we have reduced to a catalog of symptoms.[9] Edwin Gantt wonders whether, by its uncritical adoption of the medical model of pathology and clinical practice, contemporary psychology "has robbed itself of the possibility of genuinely understanding the radically ethical nature and significance of human suffering."[10] Viktor Frankl addressed the suffering of the innocent directly from his Jewish perspective.[11] For him suffering is inevitable, but we can choose how to respond. M. Scott Peck opens his book *The Road Less Traveled* with the simple statement, "Life is difficult."[12] In the 1960s, psychologist David Bakan expressed the hope that a psychology of suffering would emerge.[13] We believe this vision remains unrealized. For the mechanistic model implicit in various contemporary psychological theories, suffering is a symptom of underlying psychological or biological processes which, if skillfully addressed, can be alleviated. In the pragmatic paradigm of psychological practice, the larger ethical and political dimensions of suffering are often lost. The client's communal narrative of suffering is forgotten, and the meaning of suffering is privatized. Healing then becomes a matter of locating the correct technique to assuage discomfort.

Juanita's experience demands a moral response. Hers is innocent suffering. If we are open to the possibility, Emmanuel Lévinas tells us, the suffering of the other will interrupt our psychic life, rupture our consciousness, and sear our unconscious sense of stability.[14] It will undermine our quick and ready explanations of suffering. The suffering of the other makes an ethical demand on me; it is not something I simply observe as a neutral bystander. Our tendency is to view the other as the same as ourselves, to possess the same human nature. To do so is to deny the radical otherness of the person in pain. We may rush in to diagnose, interpret, and explain the suffering individual, and in doing so we may evade the full impact of their pain.

If Juanita were our client, would her suffering fully impact us? Or would we be distracted by our need to quickly reduce her sadness? Juanita's face is the face of our suffering God. She is not simply a client to be diagnosed and treated. She represents the innocent who suffer, and we are implicated in such violence. As psychologists trained in North America, apart from theological and political understanding, we could harm Juanita.

Indigenous Meanings of Suffering

The mountains are colored in variations of blue as we ascend and descend the winding roads of the Guatemalan highlands. As we sit on their workbenches, the widows of the Ruth and Naomi Co-op are bringing out plates of beans, rice, and fried chicken. Surrounded by their handicraft, we hear their experiences of the war. They know that their husbands disappeared and that they must now sell what they have created on their saddle looms to care for their children and grandchildren. However, they seem unaware of the fact that our government was deeply embroiled in the conflict that caused them so much pain. With quiet humility they tell their story of suffering to people like us.

A peaceable psychology takes seriously the particular, local stories reflective of an indigenous psychology. We cannot ignore the fact that therapy involves a culturally particular conversation. The local grammar of healing in Guatemala might look different from that of clinical interventions in the United States. It seems to us that a Christian psychology would, given the history of Guatemala over the past four decades and the experiences of victimization by our North American clients, be compelled to reflect emically on the suffering of an innocent people and a theology which addresses this suffering. There, as here, we are confronted with the effects of structural evil—racism against native peoples, the accumulation of wealth on the backs of the poor, politically expedient instead of peaceable solutions. How can one respond theologically so as to comfort and empower the innocent who suffer?[15] A peaceable psychology responds to the effects of such violence with the suffering and resurrection of Jesus. If we wish to avoid the negative political consequences of North American psychological practices, our peaceable psychology would do well to begin with particular, local stories reflective of a commitment to indigeneity.[16]

The Suffering Christ

To understand Juanita's suffering we begin by remembering that Jesus lived in a political world dominated by the Romans. Evidence suggests that there was a long history of Israelite resistance to alien oppressive rule reaching back to the bondage in Egypt. After a Jewish revolt in 4 BCE, Roman general Varus burned the town of Sepphoris and crucified two thousand men. It was the Roman way of eliciting loyalty (*pistis*).[17] The narrative of Jesus's life begins with a registration of all citizens by Emperor Augustus (Luke 2:1-20). Jesus's response to the Roman presence was not to lead an insurrection, but to announce the imminence of the reign of God—that is, a judgment on rulers who usurp God's rule, and a proclamation of a coming peaceful reign. Given a Roman coin, he said: "Give therefore to the emperor the things that are the emperor's, and to God the things that are God's" (Matt. 22:21). To pay tribute to Rome was against Moses's covenantal law, and not to pay it would have been treason. Ancient Near Eastern listeners who did not separate religion from politics would have known that Jesus's response was a veiled way of saying that God has priority over Caesar.[18] Like the Jews of Christ's day, the Guatemalans have lived with political occupation and oppression—a truth Juanita would understand.

Second, our meaning-oriented response to Juanita's suffering builds on Jesus's words. In a violent society, honor is built on hierarchy. But Jesus turns the hierarchy upside down. In the Sermon on the Mount, the poor and oppressed are honored. Jesus's view of the dishonored was subversive of Rome's hegemony. What we translate as "blessed" might be better translated as "honored."[19]

> Honored are the poor in spirit, for theirs is the kingdom of heaven.
>
> Honored are those who mourn, for they will be comforted.
>
> Honored are the meek, for they will inherit the earth.
>
> Honored are those who hunger and thirst for righteousness, for they will be filled.
>
> Honored are the merciful, for they will receive mercy.
>
> Honored are the pure in heart, for they will see God.
>
> Honored are the peacemakers, for they will be called children of God.
>
> Honored are those who are persecuted for righteousness' sake, for theirs is the kingdom of heaven.
>
> Honored are you when people revile you and persecute you and utter all kinds of evil against you falsely on my account. (Matt. 5:3–11)

Those who are meek, poor, hungry, mourning losses, and yearning for justice are honored. The Christians we met in Guatemala were crushed in spirit but remained dependent on the kingdom of heaven. They mourned the loss of life in their communities but were comforted by faith in God's justice. Such people inherit the earth through meekness rather than violence. Their hunger for justice results in death but also participates in the liberating power of God's peace. When they make peace with their enemies they are called the children of God.

We can only conclude that the words of Jesus in the Sermon on the Mount are as descriptive as they are prescriptive. The Beatitudes are not simply ideals which, if fulfilled, ensure well-being and success. Rather, they describe people who are already participating in the reign of God. Their lives already reflect Christ's presence. Glen Stassen and David Gushee point out: "Jesus was saying that we are blessed because we are experiencing God's reign in our midst and will experience it yet more in the future reign."[20] Reflecting on our time in Guatemala, we suspect our experiences were sightings of the honored in the reign of God.

A Christian psychology that seeks meaning in suffering will give attention not only to the political context and the words of Christ, but also to the life of Christ in which he overcame the evil powers of discrimination against Samaritans (John 4), the neglect of the poor (Luke 4:18), the marginalization of women (Luke 10:38–42), and the hatred of the Romans (Matt. 5:38–42). This too is the work of atonement in salvation and healing. There is consistency between the incarnated nature of Jesus's identity and his death on the cross. When Irenaeus was asked why Christ came down from heaven, the answer was "that He might destroy sin, overcome death, and give life to man."[21]

We understand the meaning of Juanita's suffering not only through Jesus's words and life, but also through his death on a cross. But how do we understand the meaning of the cross of Christ? For many Christians the meaning is simple, if familiar. We are saved personally by the death of Christ, who paid the penalty of sin and reconciled us to God the Father. Perhaps, unintentionally, this shifts the focus of suffering from the other to how Christ's death benefits me, to my suffering and my salvation. But is this the only way of understanding the healing work of Christ's death? After all, Jesus's message was so threatening he was crucified by a Roman governor on a Roman cross, a humiliating form of execution used to intimidate a colonized people.[22]

To victims of violence, it might matter that God suffered as Christ died, that Christ is a model for how to suffer, and that reconciliation with one's enemies is one way we can also be healed. The crucifixion of Jesus explicitly mirrors the arbitrariness and stark reality of suffering. Within the Christian tradition there are those who have asserted that the death and resurrection of Jesus should be understood as an expression of self-giving for his followers. We do well to follow his example.[23]

If the cross is integral to our work as Christian therapists, then our theory and practice must be changed by the stories of people like Juanita. If we wish our work as psychologists to be peaceable, our approach to healing will necessarily be framed by the cross of a suffering God. Remaining open to the suffering of others is integral to being a follower of Jesus.[24] To wait for the reign of God to come in fullness requires patience and the willingness to suffer.[25] Jesus tells his disciples that suffering is part of his future role as Messiah. But Jesus goes further. It is not only he who must suffer—those who follow him are asked to embrace the same possibility. "If any want to become my followers, let them deny themselves and take up their cross and follow me. For those who want to save their life will lose it, and those who lose their life for my sake, and for the sake of the gospel, will save it" (Mark 8:34–35). Clearly the cross is at the heart of what it means to be a disciple. When the Guatemalans or other victims of abuse suffer, they suffer in the same way that Jesus suffered—innocently. Indeed, I am my brother's or sister's keeper when my heart is open to their pain. How central to our professional lives as clinicians is the suffering that comes as a result of systemic social sin?

Christ's call to "take up the cross" implies that pain and suffering in life is not an arbitrary or capricious element in human affairs. Nietzsche rejected this admonition as "gutter religion." What psychologist in today's wealthy, comfortable, powerful, predominantly Christian America would want to be reminded that the Christian God is a vulnerable God who hung on a cross?[26] Perhaps, as the apostle Paul reminds us, the cross and cross-bearing are still a scandal for most of us.[27] John Howard Yoder has argued that in the taking up of the cross, Jesus is our model.[28] It is the key to understanding Jesus's life. Jürgen Moltmann has drawn our attention repeatedly to the suffering Christ, the crucified God.[29] The cross implies a peaceable psychology which is in solidarity with the suffering of the poor and oppressed.

We propose that the cross at the heart of psychological practice is the suffering of our clients who have been violated. On the cross God identifies with the victims of violence. God's priority is to identify with those who suffer violence, those who cannot defend themselves. The justice of God is the justice of compassion, the justice of the God of the widows and the fatherless (Ps. 68:4–6). Those who hurt the poor also hurt God. God is then a victim of the violent. A peaceable psychology suffers with the poor, anticipating a healing that places psychological technique within the larger purposes of God's Spirit present in the therapist–client relationship. This is far from a detached position of observation and clinical diagnosis.

We see the suffering of Juanita in the light of Christ's suffering as a political scapegoat. The violence that resulted in the death of Juanita's husband was an attempt by the Guatemalan government to create social order in the face of a threat. When the scapegoat is killed, society experiences a feeling of catharsis and peace. But it is an illusory peace. This is the sacrificial logic of totality, of empire. In Guatemala, highland Indians in general, and Juanita's husband in particular, were the scapegoats.

Neither Guatemalans nor Jews in the Holocaust died like protagonists in a Greek tragedy. They died as Christ did—victims of political violence. A peaceable psychology will not romanticize death. David Bentley Hart comments:

> None of the mystifications of tragic consciousness should be allowed to intrude here, no talk of a conflict of divine necessities or natural forces should divert attention from the truth that these lives were unmade by the quite contingent political arrangements of an unjust order, and by the demonic cruelty of human sin. Their deaths were without meaning, beauty, or grandeur.[30]

Hart views suffering and violence as universal, historical, particular, and demands an act of justice and rescue from God. A peaceable psychology refuses to be reconciled to such loss of good creation and hopes for reconciliation that is redemptive. As Christians we are the people of God with a memory of suffering.[31] Such a memory predisposes us to see a person first, not as living in sin, as guilty, but as one who suffers.

As Christian psychologists who seek peace, we understand Christ's death on the cross as an act of love, a gift given to God the Father. In his death Jesus continues to retell the human story according to a true pattern of loving obedience and humility. Even in the midst of a social order that sacrifices to reinforce the status quo, the sacrifice of Jesus overcomes it by living out his life in obedience to God. The overthrow of violence is accomplished by peaceful self-donation. Yoder states:

> Christ was exactly what God meant humans to be: in free communion with God, obeying God and loving others—even his enemies—with God's love. . . . [P]erfect love in obedience had to be lived in the world of sinners, respecting the liberty of sinners to be unloving. Thus *agape* comes to mean nonresistance, bearing the other's sinfulness, bearing, literally, our sins. . . . The imagery of sacrifice is particularly relevant here. For the ultimate sacrifice, the sacrifice of self, is precisely giving oneself utterly to communion-obedience with God. This is what Jesus did in letting God express *agape* through his "obedience unto death, the death of the cross."[32]

Faithfulness to and love for God cost Jesus his life in a violent world. Our appropriate response to this act of suffering is repentance and faith. Repentance points not only to sorrow, but to ethics, to a changed life. Faith is more than assent; it is a sense of commitment to obedience and union with the death of Christ as a gift of love. Forgiveness is then not so much the lifting of a sentence as it is the removing of obstacles to restored communion with God.

Finally, in the face of the sufferer—Juanita, for example—we glimpse the face of our suffering God. The God of Jesus Christ is one who suffers.[33] After the death of his son in a tragic climbing accident in 1983, Nicholas Wolterstorff, a Christian philosopher and emeritus faculty member of the Yale Divinity School, wrote the following:

> For a long time I knew that God is not the impassive, unresponsive, unchanging being portrayed by the classical theologians. I knew of the pathos of God. I knew of God's response of delight and of his response of displeasure. But strangely, his suffering I never saw before.
>
> God is not only the God of the sufferers but the God who suffers. The pain and fallenness of humanity have entered into his heart. Through the prism of my tears I have seen a suffering God.
>
> It is said of God that no one can behold his face and live. I always thought this meant that no one could see his splendor and live. A friend said perhaps it meant that no one could see his sorrow and live. Or perhaps his sorrow is splendor.[34]

If I am open to the suffering of God, I will be changed. If I sense a deep connectedness to the suffering of my client, her face makes an ethical claim on me since I am, in ways I do not know, responsible for her suffering. She invites me to empty myself, to create a space within me for her.

From his prison cell Dietrich Bonhoeffer wrote that it is "only the suffering God that can help."[35] Following the suffering servant motif described in Isaiah 53, Moltmann goes further and argues that in the death of Jesus there is healing in that the perpetrators of violence are brought to repentance.[36] The Jesus who dies on the cross, who experiences God's abandonment, portrays for us the suffering God. The scandal of the cross is that for the innocent and the obedient, suffering remains their lot.

Peaceable Atonement?

There is considerable controversy over the meaning of the cross and Christ's suffering. Pacifists, feminist and womanist theologians, and therapists have objected to an image of God as condoning violence.[37] As an innocent sufferer in the divine plan, Jesus is portrayed as a voluntary but passive victim of violence. This model suggests that violence can be instrumental for reconciliation and healing with God. However, an abused person may model this passive approach or even accept it as God's will for her or his life. This contrasts with the Jesus who invites us to love our enemies, who makes visible the peaceable reign of God.[38] A theology that emphasizes that "Jesus died for my sins," while a healing balm for the individual soul, has also been used to defend slavery and colonial oppression.[39] The relationship between God and humanity as the resolution of an abstract legal formula occurs beyond history, while the suffering of Guatemalans and our clients occurs within history. One might also ask whether Christians too quickly adopt the model of an angry God who needs to be pacified in order to justify wars to exterminate evil.

As summarized by Gustaf Aulén, in the history of the church there are three classic theologies of suffering and healing.[40] The first is the *Christus Victor* model (held in various forms by the early church fathers); it focuses on the drama of history in which there is a conflict between God and the evil powers of the world. Christ suffers because of the powers and is victorious over them.[41] The second is often referred to as the *penal satisfaction* model of reconciliation and healing. This theory proposes that human sin so offended God's honor and so upset the divine order of the universe that the suffering and death of Jesus the God-human was necessary to avert God's anger. Since the law required that sin be punished, Jesus, in submitting to death, paid the penalty. A third interpretation of suffering comes from Abelard in the twelfth century and suggests that Jesus's death was a *moral act of God* to model for us God's love.[42]

The meaning of Christ's suffering on the cross differs in each of these models. In the Christus Victor model, suffering is a consequence of historical evil; whereas in the penal satisfaction model, death is aimed at restoring God's honor. The latter's approach seems to imply that God foreordains the death of Jesus, while in the Christus Victor model it is the evil powers that kill Jesus. While the Christus Victor model was most common in the first millennium after Christ, the theory that "Jesus died for me" has dominated the West for the past millennium.

Each view of atonement was a response to a particular social and historical context, and we will follow this same hermeneutic.[43] It is significant that the Christus Victor model emerged in response to empires.[44] Perhaps this simple fact justifies its relevance for today—as evidenced by Western political interests in Guatemala or more recently in the Middle East. According to this reading, the cross symbolizes the conflict between God and evil. Christ died as an innocent man in the context of the Roman Empire.

We have reviewed Aulén because of his historic role in discussing these forms of atonement. His treatment has, however, been critiqued as stereotypic, and we agree with James McClendon, who has suggested that we should not be limited to the metaphors described by Aulén.[45] The New Testament, he points out, uses metaphors of war (justice and judgment, punishment and substitution), of military victory, of sacrifice, and of family. Overall, we would agree with John Howard Yoder when he comments:

> We have seen that the satisfaction theories are the most serious answers found in the history of Christian theology in the sense that they answer the question of piety. They make sense in prayer. They call forth praise, gratitude, and commitment. Therefore they are deeply rooted in the life of the common believer. We need to recognize and respect the theory because of that moral strength.

But we have also seen that it is a biblically unsatisfactory theory. It makes systematic assumptions counter to the meaning of the doctrine of the Trinity. If consistently applied in its own logic it would be ahistorical and universalist in its implications. It gives us a vision of God as a judge rather than as a reconciling and loving Father.[46]

Yearning for Reconciliation

A peaceable psychology yearns for reconciliation with enemies: between warring tribal factions, between superpowers and developing nations, between religious minorities and secular democratic liberalism, between ethnic majorities and minorities, and between an angry father and an alienated son. Hence, we wonder how Christ's suffering mediates reconciliation and healing. If we confess the lordship of Christ, then his nonviolent stance should in some manner inform the nature of our therapy. The scandal of the cross is that nonviolence can be transformational in nature. Such peace is inaugurated not through political aggression or therapeutic prowess but through the peaceable reign of God.

Rather than an exclusive focus on individual change, we are concerned with social and historical transformation. Our focus is not on ontology, but rather on ethics and history. In our view the cross is not a result of a cosmic conflict between good and evil or a metaphysical dualism between mind and matter, something and nothing, human and divine. The victory over evil powers in history brings about a new relationship—reconciliation between God and the world. Most importantly, this reconciliation is the work of a peaceable God. If Jesus is the full revelation of God, as is declared by the Council of Nicea, then God must be nonviolent. If Jesus is fully the revelation of God, then God cannot be violent while Jesus is nonviolent.

A peaceable psychology, then, involves reconciliation. How is Christ's death peaceable when its context is so obviously and terribly violent? How is the death and resurrection of Jesus therapeutically relevant in Guatemala or in the American therapist's office? It is Christ who mediates the reconciliation and healing of humanity from a broken existence imbued with suffering. Sanctification means that Christ bound humanity to God's self in and through his own suffering. As an act of solidarity with humanity, Christ's suffering on the cross is a reconciling ministry of grace against brokenness and estrangement. In the act of binding humanity to God's person, Christ permits us to forgive the enemy and to live in reconciliation with those who violate us. Thus in Christ is found the reconciliation and healing of persons with God through the objective reality of the cross.

The reconciling atonement of Christ is not spiritual alone but contains physical, psychological, and social dimensions of human brokenness. The suffering

God is a beckoning God, who in Christ offers the potential of a new beginning. Consequently, a peaceable psychology is an incarnational event whereupon the invisible spiritual reality of God's grace is attached to and bound up in the visible life of both the victim and the offender. A peaceable psychology is concerned that pathology be framed within the larger rubric of the victim's estrangement from God, from others, and from self. Christian psychology takes up the cross, fully aware that the brokenness and suffering of the client is understood by the suffering of Christ, who images the suffering God.

God bears the pain of a world of suffering rather than responding with judgment and violence. Our focus here is not on Jesus's death for our sins, but on God's love for us, which is healing and peace-giving. Moltmann comments:

> So how does atonement reach the people who commit injustice and violence? It reaches them out of the compassion of the Father, through the vicariously suffered God-forsakenness of the Son, and in the exonerating power of the Holy Spirit. It is a single movement of love, welling up out of the Father's pain, manifested in the Son's sufferings, and experienced in the Spirit of Life. In this way God becomes the God of the godless. His righteousness and justice justifies the unrighteous and the unjust.[47]

The focus here is not on a retributive God who demands the death of Jesus as propitiation. God does not demand the death of the perpetrators, but rather bears the suffering.[48] Atonement is God's welcoming of the enemy, of the other. It is an invitation to new life, to freedom from sin. This is the basis of a peaceable psychology.

Resurrection Hope

A Christian psychology rests in the profound message of hope contained in the resurrection of Christ. The resurrection points to the victory of God over the powers of empire. This new life is genuine fellowship—peace with God. Salvation is the preservation and bestowal of life because the victory of God over the powers of evil is a just peace occasioned not by violence but by persuasion. Hart points out:

> Easter unveils the violence of history, its absolute ungodliness, its want of any transcendent meaning; the meaninglessness and tyranny of death is made absolutely clear in the Father having to raise the Son for the sake of his love. . . . In the light of Easter, the singularity of suffering is no longer tragic (which is to say, ennobling), but merely horrible, mad, everlastingly unjust; it is the irruption of *thanatos* into God's good creation. . . . In the light of Easter, all the sacrifices totality makes are seen to be meaningless, an offense before God, disclosing no deeper truths about being; the system of sacrifice is a tautology, a practice that

justifies itself through further practice; what the totality is willing to sacrifice on behalf of metaphysical solace is what God raises up. Because of the resurrection, it is impossible to be reconciled to coercive or natural violence, to ascribe its origins to fate or cosmic order, to employ it prudentially; as difficult as it may be to accept, all violence, all death, stands under judgment as that which God has and will overcome.[49]

The good news is that the powers of evil are conquered nonviolently by the resurrection, the ascension, and the continued presence of a peaceable church in a hostile world. This, it seems to us, is good news to Guatemalans and people oppressed by empires or scarred by familial violence.

The village of Santiago de Atitlan witnessed a peaceable religious faith. On December 1, 1990, when soldiers had shot a local in a skirmish, the village was in an uproar. Ringing church bells brought the townspeople to the village center. In the early hours of the morning, between two and three thousand people marched peacefully to the military garrison, demanding an end to the harassment. They carried no weapons. Reportedly because of confusion in their ranks, soldiers fired into the crowd. In the ensuing massacre, thirteen individuals were martyred for the cause of peace. Three weeks later, then-president Vinicio Cerezo ordered the removal of the military base from Santiago. The kidnappings stopped. This powerful combination of faith and action eventually led to peace accords some six years later.[50]

A peace park now stands as testimony to the courage of the slain villagers. Stones for the park were taken from the barracks as it was disassembled. The park commemorates the deaths (including that of an eleven-year-old boy) with plaques in the exact places where they fell. A letter from the president is engraved on marble as a reminder. When villagers involved in the construction of the park came across a mass grave, Guatemalan military officials warned that further digging would mean the army would return. It was a fragile peace. The villagers complied with the request but left a gaping hole in the ground as a reminder.

Pedro, now a septuagenarian, witnessed the massacre and told the story as he stood proudly beside the monument with the engraved letter of the president. When Pedro was asked why the town of Santiago resisted when other communities had not, he smiled. "Santiago is a religious community," he said. On that day, Catholics, Pentecostals, and various other Protestant groups came together to protest. "It is the hope of our faith," he stated simply, "that gave us strength then and today."[51]

2

Constantine, American Empire, and "Yankee Doodling"

■ ■ ■ ■ ■ ■ ■ ■ ■ ■

In the volatile mix of geopolitical calculation and messianic enthusiasm that is presently shaping America's foreign policy, it is not American realpolitik that the world most resents. It is American universalism.

John Gray, *Al Qaeda and What It Means to Be Modern*

To be a prophetic Christian is not to be against the world in the name of church purity; it is to be in the world but not of the world's nihilism, in the name of a loving Christ who proclaims this-worldly justice of a kingdom to come.

Cornel West, *Democracy Matters*

In the year 312 CE, the Roman emperor Constantine had a vision in which he was to place a cross on the shield of his soldiers. He then attributed his victory to the presence of God. This experience began Constantine's conversion to Christianity. Upon victory, he then baptized his captives under the sign of the cross as Christians. Those who disagreed with the orthodoxies of the established church were killed under the symbol of the Roman tribunal. One truth, one civilization, one voice in the human soul served as the scalpel to excise the Jews, the Donatist heretics, and enemies. This involuntary imposition has come to be called Constantinianism and what today we would call empire.[1]

The mantra that we live in a global era rings hollow. More pertinent now is the hegemony of an empire mentality. Empires are obsessed with conquest, acquisition, and control, whether Rome during and after the life of Christ, Spain in the fifteenth century, or Great Britain in the nineteenth century. And then there were the colonial empires of the French, Belgians, Dutch, Germans, and Portuguese. Each empire marshaled a concentration of power so massive it permeated every aspect of life: intellectual, psychological, economic, religious, and cultural.

Whether in times of growth or recession, global capitalism is a global order that governs global exchanges. This global form of sovereignty is empire.[2] It has no sense of limits, brooks no territorial borders, and rules over the entire civilized world. It encompasses a timeless and spatial totality. It rules not only the economy, but also the production of knowledge and the construal of nature and human nature. In empire, religion is used to justify expansionism and the subjugation of the enemy. Unbelievers are expected to believe and practice like believers. Those who fail to comply are marginalized, exiled, or exterminated. Most empires claimed to promote peace and prosperity while subjugating one populace after another in the name of some god, economic expansion, territorial rights, civility, or religious ideology. Commenting on early empire, Tacitus said: "Alone among men they covet with equal eagerness poverty and riches. To robbery, slaughter, plunder, they give the lying name of empire; they make a solitude and call it peace."[3]

In the last chapter we focused on suffering and sought to understand its meanings psychologically and theologically. In this chapter we explore some of the political reasons why people like Juanita have been tormented. An empire mentality and the coercive universalization of liberalism and psychology as a discipline have their roots in Constantinianism. Specifically, we will argue that the embeddedness of American psychology in military projects and procedures and the exportation of American psychology to the neglect of local traditions are powerfully capable of doing physical and psychological violence. We begin with a discussion regarding what is meant by "empire." We will then consider the ignominious legacy of psychology as a political partner in Project Camelot. Third, we review the controversy regarding involvement of American psychologists in interrogations in Guantánamo and Iraq. Finally, we cite international psychologists who complain that Western psychologies displace indigenous practices in favor of Western liberal values. All these effects are an artifact of a Constantinian impulse implicit in both psychology and its liberal democratic assumptions. Christian therapists cannot escape these issues. We contend that the rise of American empire requires theological reassessment. The apostle Paul trenchantly addresses the issue of empire in the letter to the churches in Rome. Issues from this discussion recall the account of Pentecost, God's fullest affirmation of human diversity.

American Empire?

Michael Hardt and Antonio Negri propose that the turn of the twenty-first century requires renewed reflection on the meaning of empire. They point out that

> Along with the global market and global circuits of production has emerged a global order, a new logic and structure of rule—in short, a new form of sovereignty. Empire is the political subject that effectively regulates these global exchanges, the sovereign power that governs the world. . . . The passage to Empire emerges from the twilight of modern sovereignty. In contrast to imperialism, Empire establishes no territorial center of power and does not rely on fixed boundaries or barriers. It is a *decentered* and *deterritorializing* apparatus of rule that progressively incorporates the entire global realm within its open, expanding frontiers. Empire manages hybrid identities, flexible hierarchies, and plural exchanges through modulating networks of command. The distinct national colors of the imperialist map of the world have merged and blended in the imperial global rainbow.[4]

And what of America? Is it immune to the pull of empire? It is probably premature to state with any certainty that the post- 9/11 environment is one of an American empire that follows historical precedent. Economist Gray notes that in the past, Americans were probably too divided on a definitive role in foreign affairs to uphold an empire-building project.[5] However, subtle changes may be noted in the wake of the Al-Qaeda attacks on the World Trade Center in 2001. A policy of preemptive military action abroad raises the stakes on the question of American intentions. The pervasive influence of the American military on the world stage cannot be underestimated.[6]

American empire is less about the colonization of foreign lands (an interest of empire in generations past) and more about the promotion of its own constitutional vision of what is right for other peoples and nations. The constitutionally ratified "right" in this sense is those principles of democratic liberalism that were used to validate the conflict in Iraq as a just war. Because the universal claims of the Constitution are without constraint, American foreign policy "suspends history . . . summons the past and future within its own ethical order."[7] John Gray calls this a "*Pax Americana*, in which America's global hegemony is entrenched for the foreseeable future."[8] The new order is ambivalent about the imperial mandate in the Roman tradition, given instead to spreading the universal claims of an American Constitution that upholds a tradition of democratic virtue.

These developments do not fit easily into black-and-white characterizations. The values inherent to the American Constitution are good values. Few would argue that liberty, justice, freedom, and equality are evil or morally inadequate benchmarks. More problematic is the universalizing assumption behind the knowledge framed by the Constitution. The collision of universalizing principles in the American Constitution with local particularities (tradition) has a lengthy tenure.

We can identify one example that is easily recognizable for American Christians. Western societies have exported the gospel of Christ for hundreds of years. But even the most conservative theological minds in recent years have come to acknowledge that the results of this exportation were not always positive. Even when persons were introduced to the love of God in their own vernacular, the gospel was nonetheless encased in a culture often radically different from that of the host country. The resulting displacement of local culture at times resulted in negative societal and economic changes. At issue is whether the cultural history of a host country or indigenous ethnic community is taken seriously enough so as to listen for the presence of God—to respect the way a local people construct a language to contain their experience of Jesus Christ.

Psychology and Empire

The ethical standards for American psychological practice prohibit the imposition of a clinician's beliefs and values upon the client. Graduate training programs rightly emphasize diversity training, ethnic sensitivity, and cultural awareness. Gender, developmental disability, sexual orientation, and religious affiliation are all addressed by the psychological profession that seeks an inclusive and dynamic clinical relationship in which mental health issues can be addressed with maximum confidentiality and security. For these accomplishments we are more than thankful. However, in this chapter we explore the disquieting possibility of collusion between American psychology, American culture,[9] and expansionist empire-building.

If it is the case that American psychology is a tradition reflecting liberal forms of democracy, then the discipline of psychology is hardly neutral. Philip Cushman points to a subtle but pervasive enculturation of clinical psychology in the United States.[10] In his argument, American psychology became big business only after the Second World War. The economy needed a push in the direction of enterprise, particularly in the interest of cementing the consumer at the hub of financial expansion. Psychology was quickly adopted as a tool to convince individuals that consumer goods were necessary in the quest for a higher standard of living. So successful was the use of psychology as a marketing tool that it helped create an economy with previously unheard-of living standards and individual freedoms. However, concurrent with this change was the onset of historically unprecedented levels of divorce, displacement, and family fragmentation. In an individualized and fiercely competitive consumer economy, clinical treatment became an increasingly acceptable solution. For Cushman,

American psychology effectively guaranteed its place as a cultural icon by helping to create the pathologies it simultaneously promised to treat.

If Cushman is correct, American psychology is so enculturated that it reflects the same values that characterize the political and economic priorities of the nation.[11] The language spoken in therapy between client and clinician carries liberal democratic commitments that assume value neutrality, but in reality represent a morally significant conversation. This is difficult to determine, however, in the American context, where our own enculturation makes critique more difficult. An alternative test of Cushman's thesis is found in how American psychology influences other cultures when exported abroad. Where the exported psychological "product" promotes liberal democratic values and Enlightenment principles among indigenous peoples, some might conclude that the enculturation proposal is not problematic. However, the issue emerges for the Christian clinician who, in making these observations, stops to reflect critically on the current state of American culture. In the event that American psychology is globally promoting consumption, individualism, and Western models of treatment for pathology, we may be complicit in an expansionist agenda that obscures a more central Christian concern: the conflation of American culture and psychology with the reign of God.

Project Camelot

Our story begins with the relationship between psychology and American political aspirations. Psychologists have been embedded in military enterprises for most of the past century. Alfred McCoy has traced this history and concluded that the psychological discipline was "the most militarized among the social or biological sciences."[12] During the First World War, Robert Yerkes developed the army Alpha and Beta intelligence tests for officer and soldier screening.[13] During the Second World War psychologists served as consultants and wrote extensively on the causes of global horrors unthinkable to previous generations. A year into the war, 25 percent of all Americans holding graduate degrees in psychology were at work in the military as employees of the federal government, screening applicants, producing improved gunsights, helping the Poston Relocation Center for Japanese-Americans to run smoothly, and shaping public opinion toward the war. Psychologists could be found researching psychological warfare, boosting the morale of the troops, studying the national character of the enemy, alleviating postwar trauma, and even increasing the efficiency of cargo handling.[14] As it turned out, the military was an ideal laboratory to study human motivation and behavior. At the war's end, Gordon Allport and some two thousand members of the American Psychological Association signed a statement entitled "Human Nature and the Peace," in which they summarized their findings from the war experience and concluded that "an enduring peace can be attained if the human sciences are utilized by our statesmen and peace-makers."[15] These scholars and practitioners were confident that collaboration between psychology and politics would result in peaceable ends.

From 1945 until the early 1960s, the Department of Defense poured millions of dollars into psychological research and doctoral education in psychology. Psychologists were recruited to diagnose and explain inadequacies in economic and social models from the developing world. Blinded by their commitment to an individual, consumer-oriented psychology, the American psychological community asserted that economic and social problems in developing nations arose from personal or typological factors. David McClelland's research on achievement motivation suggested that economic development was the product of personality.[16] He testified before Congress that US investment strategy should favor those developing countries that demonstrated the "right" kinds of per-sonality. National security advisor McGeorge Bundy testified before Congress regarding the potential of behavioral experts to covertly help win the cold war, singling out psychologists for special mention. The expectation was established that psychologists would help analyze the political culture of enemy nations or those countries that could be influenced as future trading partners.

Building on the work of Erik Erikson, Lucian Pye (chair of the Social Sci-ence Research Council's Committee on Comparative Politics) suggested that "modernizing the political structures of third-world states would require the inculcation of new forms of identity through a revamped socialization pro-cess."[17] At a meeting of the US Army's council for "Limited-War Mission and Social Science Research," military planners were clear: "The kind of underlying knowledge required is the understanding and prediction of human behavior at the individual, political, social group, and societal levels."[18] Methods of controlling indigenous peoples were needed as a hedge against the specter of communist-inspired guerrilla movements. Ellen Herman comments:

> Conference discussion was limited to the fine points of technical assistance. No one ever questioned either the counterinsurgency mission or the appropriate-ness of involving social and psychological experts in it. Attendees agreed that it was their job to provide the military with an objective "technology of human behavior" and leave their own political convictions at home.[19]

Project Camelot was the direct outgrowth of the growing Cold War alliance between psychology and the American political establishment. Camelot was concerned with Soviet-inspired wars of liberation in Cuba, Yemen, and the Belgian Congo. The central goal of the project was the prediction and control of the social and psychological preconditions of Third World revolution. In the words of the planners:

> Project Camelot is a study whose objective is to determine the feasibility of de-veloping a general social systems model which would make it possible to predict

and influence politically significant aspects of social change in the developing nations of the world.[20]

The first phase of Camelot would review existing data on internal wars and the propensity for violence in local (indigenous) peoples. The second phase would produce twenty-one case studies of post-WWII insurgencies in order to develop predictive indicators of conflict and change. The final phase called for a detailed analysis of individual nations based on data from the first two stages. With a $6 million contract Project Camelot was, given the dollar value of the day, the largest behavioral research project ever funded.

An international scandal erupted when the connection between Project Camelot and American political interests was exposed. The project had been explained to Chile as being sponsored by the National Science Foundation, but the research design was leaked to Chilean researchers, and the true source of funding was revealed. The project was cancelled, a congressional hearing was held, researchers were exonerated, and, in the end, the image of American psychology remained untarnished. The scandal was construed as a failure of communication between governmental departments and agencies. In the wake of this breakdown, a small minority of psychologists admitted that behavioral research could serve repressive ends.[21]

In spite of this eruption, psychological projects similar to Camelot continued clandestinely in Brazil, Colombia, Peru, and South Vietnam. In 1965 a former consultant to Project Camelot, Clark Abt, designed a computer simulation game to monitor internal wars in Latin America. He used data on hundreds of social psychological variables to predict and control internal revolutionary conflict. The game's results were eventually used to support a plan to topple Chile's leftist government by murdering its leader.

More recent examples of psychological engagement with American policies are evident in hypothetical political scenarios associated with the falling of the Berlin Wall, covert military action in Central America, and the use of computational linguistics to break code for security agencies worried about terrorism. The military continues to make use of psychological principles and expertise at all levels of conflict, both for the recovery of American personnel suffering with post-traumatic stress, and in support of tactical objectives in foreign campaigns. The complicity of American psychology with its political handlers raises the specter of a hegemonic agenda capable of unsavory or even violent ends.

Juanita's Encounter with Empire

Guatemala was one country that Project Camelot included in its study. It too was a threat. How might the research of psychologists have affected Juanita? She continues her story.

My brother came by my house and didn't say anything; he just hugged me. He couldn't find the words to tell me that my husband was nowhere to be found. At that moment, I could not cry. I lost control and began to scream. People kept coming with more information about others who had been found dead and others who had disappeared. I gathered up all of my husband's clothing and put it in the middle of the floor and cried over it with my children. I spent the whole night wailing. It didn't resolve anything, but the next day I received more news. Someone informed me that my husband had been found on the coast and that he was dead. I don't know how to explain the pain and sadness that I felt.

Unfortunately, that day I did not have even enough money to bring his body back to Santiago. I had 20 quetzals but I thought, "What can I do with 20 quetzals? Can I go get him or not?" I had to pay for a car, buy a coffin, and pay for the paperwork at the funeral home. With 20 quetzals you really can't do anything. But I wanted to see my husband for the last time. "I am going to bring him back even if I don't have a coffin," I thought. "With 20 quetzals, I can pay for a car and I'll buy a plastic bag to put him in." I was the first one to leave the community, and I was not afraid. We had heard that anyone who left would be taken in the road. Not even my brothers would go. My sisters and a 16-year-old niece went with me. I spent the whole trip screaming, "Miguel, wait for me," because we had heard that if the family didn't arrive right away, they would throw the body away.

When we arrived in the hospital in Mazatenango, it was so sad. Every time I tell this story, I have the face and body of my husband in my mind. His death was a horrible one! The soldiers who killed him were merciless. He was a laborer and when I found him he was no longer Miguel . . . he was tortured. He was strangled and they had torn off the soles of his feet. He was slit in the face with a machete and his whole body was lacerated. I began to talk to that body there. I said, "You weren't a guerrilla; you haven't used weapons. You are an innocent man. Why did they kill you? We are a simple family." When I hugged him, he was so full of blood that I covered myself with blood.

Afterward, fear was the worst thing for us. I lost consciousness. I didn't even think about my children. I even thought it would have been better if one of them would have died instead. Even now, I have an emptiness in my heart and no one can fill that space. I was out of control. I took my pencil and wrote a letter. I said in my mind I would like to come face-to-face with a soldier because I knew it wasn't the guerrillas, it was the army who killed my husband. In this letter, I left my two children in the charge of one of my sisters. I made a very important decision. I went walking to the mountains to look for the guerrillas (to join them) and didn't find any. I returned to the cemetery where my husband was buried and began to cry.

From that day on, I haven't been able to stand the army. Every time the army walks by my house, I hate them. I have lost a lot of weight, from 140 to 90 pounds. From all the sadness, I began to lose my hair and even my eyebrows. I could find no solution. I wanted my husband back and I just got sadder and sadder. I couldn't work. I talked with some neighbors and began to wash dishes and clean their house. They gave me food for my children because I could not sell any of my weavings. There were no tourists. This was how my life moved forward, but in my mind it was the same. Every time I had a problem with my children, I went to the cemetery to consult my husband. My friend told me I should try some drugs because I could not calm my mind; so I tried smoking marijuana, but my hands and legs felt really fat. True, I didn't think about my husband nor my father.

❧

It was Juanita's country that was singled out for psychological study and the exportation of American paranoia regarding the "communist" advocates of the poor. We do well, therefore, to explore the implications for a peaceable psychology. What if Juanita's therapist was insensitive to the moral import of psychology's collusion with potential empire-building?

For us there is danger in avoiding moral and theological reflection on psychological practice that is central to our vocational calling as Christian therapists. For this reason we are willing to consider the darker side of psychological union with American purposes. Conservative American Christians harbor a deep moral ambivalence toward government, concurrently fearing politically-driven processes of secular culture and offering vociferous, patriotic support of the so-called war on terror in countries like Iraq. So thoroughly have we become encultured within the American political ethos that we lack a language with which to speak about the possible negative effects of exporting democratic liberalism.[22] The only basis for resolving this problem, in our view, is to find other discourses capable of providing a critical perspective. It may be that political science, economics, philosophy, and theology are better able to critique psychological enculturation. By utilizing the insights of these disciplines we may gain traction on the nature of an enculturated psychology and its global implications.

Torture and Interrogation

The collusion between psychology and empire could not be more significant and relevant right now.[23] Most countries in the world have ratified the Geneva Conventions for the treatment of prisoners of war. However, former President Bush's "war on terror" appears to have violated these conventions, ostensibly because a war on terror is not war in the traditional sense. However, the Supreme Court ruled five to three in Hamdan v. Rumsfeld (June 2006)[24] that the Bush administration could not set up special military commissions in Guantánamo and that detainees were entitled to rights under the Geneva Conventions. The Military Commissions Act, which was passed by both houses of Congress, gave then-president Bush the authority nonetheless to detain prisoners without charging them.

On December 15, 2001, Sami Al-Haj, a cameraman for Al Jazeera, was on his way to Afghanistan when he was arrested by Americans as an "enemy combatant" and detained at Guantánamo. He remained there as prisoner number 345 for more than six years. During that time, with the help of the British human-rights lawyer Clive Stafford Smith, he received international attention as the only detained journalist. Reporters Without Borders repeatedly expressed concern over Al-Haj's detention and launched a petition for his release.[25] On January 7, 2007 he began his hunger strike, and on May 1, 2008, he was released. Two months later he related the following in an interview.[26] Psychologists are directly implicated.

I came to Geneva, the city of the United Nations and freedom, to ask for the law to be respected, to demand the closure of the Guantánamo camp and secret prisons, and to demand that this illegal situation be brought to an end. . . .

Of course, I am happy to be free again. I have been reunited with my family, my wife, and my son. For six and a half years he did not see me, and had to go to school without me. He waited for me and said, "Dad, I have missed you for so long! I was so unhappy, especially when I saw my school friends, with their fathers, and they asked me where my father was. I had no answer to give them. That's why I asked my mum to take me to school in the car, because I didn't want them to keep asking me that question."

I said to my son, "Now, I could take you to school, but you must understand that I have a message to give, a just cause to defend. I want to fight for the cause of human rights, for those who have been deprived of their freedom. I do not want to fight alone. There are thousands of people who are standing up and fighting wherever human dignity is attacked. Do not forget that we are fighting for peace, to defend rights whenever they are denied, for a better future for you. Perhaps one day we will achieve this, and then I will be able to stay with you and take you to school." . . .

In 2001, when I left my son and my wife to film the war initiated by the USA against Afghanistan, I had to expect finding death during a bombing raid. I went there fully aware of the risks. Every journalist knows that he is carrying out a mission and must be ready to sacrifice himself in order to bear witness to what is happening, through his films and writing. And to help people understand that war brings nothing but the death of the innocent, destruction and suffering. It is on the basis of this conviction that my colleagues and I went to countries at war. . . .

[I experienced] all kinds of physical and psychological torture. As all the detainees were Muslim, the camp administration subjected them to many forms of harassment and humiliation linked to religion. With my own eyes I saw soldiers tearing up the Qur'an and throwing it in the toilet. I saw them, during interrogation sessions, sitting on the Qur'an until their questions were answered. They insulted our families and our religion. They made fun of us by pretending to ring our God, asking him to come and save us. The only Imam at the camp was accused of complicity with the detainees and was sent away, in 2005, for refusing to tell visitors that the camp respected religious freedom.

They beat us up. They taunted us with racist insults. They locked us in cold rooms, below zero, with one cold meal a day. They hung us up by our hands. They deprived us of sleep, and when we started to fall asleep, they beat us on the head. They showed us films of the most horrendous torture sessions. They showed us photographs of torture victims—dead, swollen, covered in blood. They kept us under constant threat of being moved elsewhere to be tortured even more. They doused us with cold water. They forced us to do the military salute to the American national anthem. They forced us to wear women's clothes. They forced us to look at pornographic images. They threatened us with rape. They would strip us naked and make us walk like donkeys, ordering us around. They made us sit down and stand up five hundred times in a row. They humiliated the detainees by wrapping them up in the Israeli and American flags, which was their way of telling us that we were imprisoned because of a religious war.

When a detainee, filthy and riddled with fleas, is taken out of his cell to be submitted to more torture sessions in an attempt to make him collaborate, he ends up not knowing what he is saying or even who he is any more.

I was interrogated and tortured more than two hundred times. Ninety-five percent of the questions were about Al Jazeera. They wanted me to work as a spy within Al Jazeera. In exchange, they offered American citizenship for myself and my family, and payment based on results. I refused. I told them repeatedly that my job is a journalist, not a spy, and that it was my duty to make the truth known and to work for the respect of human rights. . . .

We were under the constant supervision of military psychologists. They were not there to treat us, but to take part in the interrogations, observing the tortured prisoners so that no detail of their behaviour would escape them. The interrogations were the responsibility of Colonel Morgan, a specialist psychiatric doctor. This colonel was stationed in Guantánamo from March 2002. He had served at the Afghan prison in Bagram from November 2001. He gave instructions to the officers who were torturing us, studied our reactions, then noted every detail in order to be able to adapt the torture techniques to each detainee, which had profound psychological consequences.

I spoke to them. I told them that the mission of a doctor is an honorable one, to help people, not torture them. They replied, "We are military personnel and we must follow the rules. When an officer gives me an order, it is my duty to carry it out, otherwise I will be imprisoned just like you. When I signed a contract with the army, I realised at the time that I must obey all orders."

. . . If you feel that someone is there with you, especially God, you will be patient and always aware that God is more powerful than human beings. I must pray to God and thank him. I must also thank all those who supported me. I think that even if I spent my whole life saying thank you, I would not manage to thank them all. Now, through my work concentrating on human rights, perhaps I will be able to contribute to making other people's lives happier.

Well before the publicity of this case, while Al-Haj was still imprisoned and as the deaths of Iraqis and American troops continued to climb, a debate on psychologists' roles in interrogations was ensuing. The American Psychological Association met in San Francisco in August 2007, and the issue of psychological involvement in the war on terror was on the docket for the APA Council of Representatives. Earlier, on June 6, 2007, an official letter had been sent to the APA president, Sharon Brehm. The letter began as follows:

> We write you as psychologists concerned about the participation of our profession in abusive interrogations of national security detainees at Guantánamo, in Iraq and Afghanistan, and at the so-called CIA "black sites." Our profession is founded on the fundamental ethical principle, enshrined as Principle A in our Ethical Principles of Psychologists and Code of Conduct: "Psychologists strive to benefit those with whom they work and take care to do no harm." Irrefutable evidence now shows that psychologists participating in national security interrogations have systematically violated this principle. A recently declassified August 2006 report by the Department of Defense Office of the Inspector General (OIG)—Review of DoD-Directed Investigations of Detainee Abuse describes in detail how psychologists from the military's Survival, Evasion Resistance, and Escape (SERE) program were instructed to apply their expertise in abusive interrogation techniques to interrogations being conducted by the DoD throughout all three theaters of the War on Terror (Guantánamo, Afghanistan, and Iraq).[27]

The letter then detailed how psychologists in the SERE program provided training to Behavioral Science Consultation Teams (BSCT), generally composed of and headed by psychologists. SERE psychologists in consultation with the BSCT psychologists and others developed and standardized a regime of psychological torture to be used by interrogators at Guantánamo, and in Iraq and Afghanistan.

The Department of Defense Office of the Inspector General (OIG) report also clearly revealed the central role of psychologists in these processes:

> On September 16, 2002, the Army Special Operations Command and the Joint Personnel Recovery Agency [the military unit containing SERE] co-hosted a SERE psychologist conference at Fort Bragg for JTF-170 [the military component responsible for interrogations at Guantánamo] interrogation personnel. The Army's Behavioral Science Consultation Team from Guantánamo Bay also attended the conference. Joint Personnel Recovery Agency briefed JTF-170 representatives on the exploitation techniques and methods used in resistance (to interrogation) training at SERE schools. The JTF-170 personnel understood that they were to become familiar with SERE training and be capable of determining which SERE information and techniques might be useful in interrogations at Guantánamo. Guantánamo Behavioral Science Consultation Team personnel understood that they were to review documentation and standard operating procedures for SERE training in developing the standard operating procedure for the JTF-170, if the command approved those practices. The Army Special

Operations Command was examining the role of interrogation support as a "SERE Psychologist competency area."[28]

In a *Tikkun* article, Deborah Kory pointed out that the American Psychiatric Association and the American Medical Association declared that any engagement with interrogation methods was a transgression of policy and those involved would be sanctioned.[29] The Pentagon swiftly responded with an announcement that it would replace psychiatrists with psychologists.

In 2005, the APA president, Gerald Koocher, established a ten-member task force (Psychological Ethics and National Security [PENS]) to determine whether the current psychological code of ethics adequately addresses the ethical dimensions of psychological involvement in national, security-related activities. The PENS task force concluded that the current code provided enough guidance and added that it was consistent with the APA code of ethics to serve in a consultative role to interrogation and information gathering. Koocher felt that psychologists were in a unique position to guarantee that the procedures of interrogation were safe and ethical.

However, many of the task-force members were affiliated in some way with the interrogation of detainees at Guantánamo and Abu-Ghraib.[30] Moreover, the report did not build its case on actual data; no cases of psychologist involvement in interrogations were cited, even though they were clearly available. It appears that Major L., a counseling psychologist and member of the APA, was present at the interrogation of Mohammed al-Qahtani and at some points guided the process.[31]

The letter to APA president Brehm closes with the following mandate:

> It is time for the APA to acknowledge that the central premise of its years-long policy of condoning and encouraging psychologist participation in interrogations is wrong. It has now been revealed by the DoD itself that, rather than assuring safety, psychologists were central to the abuse. This remains true even if some psychologists made efforts to reduce such harm during their involvement in these interrogation contexts at some point in time. It is critical that APA take immediate steps to remedy the damage done to the reputation of the organization, to our ethical standards, to the field of psychology, and to human rights in this age where they are under concerted attack.

At the August 2007 APA convention, the APA council defeated an amendment that would prohibit psychologists from providing services in health-related settings that deprived persons of basic human rights (i.e., interrogations). The council approved a statement that condemned fifteen methods of torture that had been used as a way of eliciting information in interrogations. However, psychologists were still permitted to be present at interrogations, and three forms of torture were still permissible—isolation, sensory deprivation or overstimulation, and sleep deprivation. Military psychologist Larry James said at the APA meeting that "if we remove psychologists from Guantánamo, innocent people are going to die." The council of representatives therefore agreed to permit psychologists to be present to monitor the interrogations.[32]

Nevertheless, when psychologists are involved in interrogations or present in a capacity other than as health-care provider in situations where human rights are being compromised, they may be doing much more harm than good. Pointing to the presence of psychologists who are ostensibly able to protect the welfare of the detainees may give legitimacy to a process that remains in violation of human rights.[33] Also, in addition to the possibility that psychologists' monitoring of interrogations may actually prolong the use of coercive techniques, psychologists' involvement may also undermine any future possibility for recovery by instilling a deep sense of confusion or mistrust when the detainee faces the possibility of working with a therapist whose colleagues were a part of their torture process and/or human-rights violations.

The presence of psychologists at the interrogations, then, gives legitimacy to a process not in accord with the Geneva Conventions.[34] APA assumed psychologists should serve in national-security roles. We would argue that psychologists should be absolutely barred from direct involvement in interrogations. To be present is in fact a violation of our current Code of Ethics as psychologists to do no harm. Reflecting on the PENS task-force report, Olson, Soldz, and Davis conclude:

> The truth is that APA interrogation policy has never adequately weighed the radiating international effects of detainee abuse, and their devastating impact on trust. With psychologists actively involved in detainee interrogations, reports of abuse are a threat to the whole profession. The damage to public trust may also be difficult to measure, but it is likely to be considerably more serious than any benefits believed to accrue from this policy.[35]

We are pleased to report that the APA membership has voted on and approved a referendum that stated unequivocally that psychologists not work in settings where persons are held in violation of either international law or the US Constitution.[36] Then-president of APA, Dr. Alan Kazdin, wrote then-president Bush as follows:

> On behalf of the American Psychological Association (APA), I am writing to inform you and your administration of a significant change in our association's policy that limits the roles of psychologists in certain unlawful detention settings where the human rights of detainees are being violated, such as has occurred at the naval base at Guantánamo Bay, Cuba, and at so-called CIA black sites around the world. This new policy, which pertains to detention settings that operate outside of, or in violation of, international law or the U.S. Constitution, was voted on by APA members and is in the process of being implemented.

The effect of this new policy is to *prohibit psychologists from any involvement in interrogations or any other operational procedures at detention sites that are in violation of the U.S. Constitution or international law* (e.g., the Geneva Conventions and the U.N. Convention Against Torture). In such unlawful detention settings, persons are deprived of basic human rights and legal protections, including the right to independent judicial review of their detention. The roles of psychologists at such sites would now be limited to working directly for the persons being detained or for an independent third party working to protect human rights, or to providing treatment to military personnel.

There have been many reports, from credible sources, of torture and cruel, inhuman, or degrading treatment of detainees during your term in office. Therefore, the American Psychological Association strongly calls on you and your administration to safeguard the physical and psychological welfare and human rights of individuals incarcerated by the U.S. government in such detention centers and to investigate their treatment to ensure that the highest ethical standards are being upheld. We further call on you to establish policies and procedures to ensure the independent judicial review of these detentions and to afford the persons being detained all rights guaranteed to them under the Geneva Conventions and the U.N. Convention Against Torture.[37]

It appears a dark chapter is behind us, and hopefully the lessons learned will remain.

American clinicians might quickly dismiss this review of psychologists' complicity in Project Camelot and the interrogations as an exercise in mild paranoia, pointing out that there is no apparent Camelot behind American military action in Afghanistan or Iraq and that the interrogations are necessary for national security. It might be said that our critique is potentially dangerous in that it undermines popular support for American foreign policy. Some psychologists may insist that these issues remain distant and even irrelevant to more pressing domestic concerns—problems with managed health care and counseling options for clients with limited resources. Psychology, they might say, is first about people rather than politics, whether the work is found in outpatient hospital settings, church counseling centers, or religious institutions in Colorado Springs. However, for Juanita's sake and for protection of political prisoners under the rules of the Geneva Conventions, we are morally compelled to consider the psychological and geopolitical impact of American expansionism and the involvement of psychologists.

Displacing Local Cultures

There is a violence that comes as a result of collusion between military force and psychological consultation, but a more subtle cultural violence occurs when psychological knowledge is exported. We are concerned that the uncritical exportation of an enculturated American psychology will displace local traditions in favor of presumed psychological universals. Far from having a value-neutral commitment to mental-health interventions, American psychologists participate in a morally significant discourse capable of displacing other particularities (traditions) in favor of its overarching vision of the human good. At best this encounter will involve some degree of enculturation that leads to greater health for the client. At worst, we will do outright violence to the client. Kenneth Gergen, Aydan Gulerce, Andrew Lock, and Girishwar Misra point out that when the rigorously scientific psychologist proposes a general theory of personality, memory, or perception, culture becomes a variable that is often marginalized. Gergen and his colleagues argue instead for a more particular, culturally engaged psychology.[38] Such an emphasis on the particulars of local tradition "might help to appraise various problems of health, environment, industrial development and the like in terms of the values, beliefs and motives particular to the culture at hand."[39]

The use of American psychology in developing countries raises a fundamental issue regarding the extent to which the discipline is embedded within culture. Gergen and his colleagues comment:

> For many of us, there is no more dramatic form of critical reflection than that stemming from an inversion of psychology's traditional subject–object dichotomy. That is, rather than privileging the psychologist as the scrutinizing subject for whom culture serves as the object of study, we find it most fully liberating to place culture in the vanguard. Let us begin with culture, as variously lived by each of us, and place psychology under scrutiny. In this case, we may ask: to what degree and with what effects is psychological science itself a cultural manifestation? Beginning in this way, it is immediately apparent that the science is largely a by-product of the Western cultural tradition at a particular time in its historical development. Suppositions about the nature of knowledge, the character of objectivity, the place of value in the knowledge generating process, and the nature of linguistic representation, for example, all carry the stamp of a unique cultural tradition.[40]

Non-Western psychologists are questioning whether there should be a universally acceptable conception of psychological science and whether all cultures should emulate psychology as practiced in America.[41] They are troubled by the fact that their journals seem to differ little from American psychological publications in terms of the issues addressed and the methodological paradigms used. These thinkers indicate that when American psychology is imported into their countries, local psychologies are supplanted. Gulerce points out:

> When psychological terminology is translated into Turkish, the local language loses its richness of connotation along with its multiplicitous functioning in the society. It was not until recently that the conceptual validity of the Western

models or theories behind the technology were challenged and a replacement process began.[42]

Misra, Lock, and Gulerce state that in each of their respective countries (India, New Zealand, and Turkey) the discipline of psychology is practiced primarily in the Western tradition. Research problems and theoretical formulations are borrowed largely from the model of American psychology with its liberal democratic trappings. Misra laments:

> The colonial condition of India led to gross neglect and avoidance of the Indian intellectual and cultural traditions that were central to the practices of the Indian people. The academic world maintained a distance from its cultural heritage and looked down at it with suspicion. The colonial incursion was so powerful that although Western concepts were accepted and welcomed without scrutiny, indigenous concepts were denied entry to the academic discourse. Because the discipline was imitative, its growth remained always one step behind the developments in the donor country.[43]

In many non-Western countries, the discipline of psychology appears to be practiced almost exclusively in the Euro-American tradition. Failure to appreciate cultural particularity tends to encourage minority psychologists to imitate American models of psychological research. Chandra Mohanty has referred to the replication of Western psychology by Indian psychologists as "Yankee Doodling."[44]

If exported American psychology carries with it a kind of empire-building mandate, we have reached a moral fork in the road. On the one hand, our work as clinicians might focus on interpreting actions within a cultural context, sensitizing people to a range of actions that are culturally intelligible, and encouraging emancipatory modes of action. On the other hand, it is equally possible that our work, conducted in a universalizing manner, may displace local psychologies. The freight of capitalistic assumptions in a consumer-oriented society and the hegemony of democratic universals are transported to other nations. In some cases the product is met with open arms. In others it foments anti-Western sentiment on the order of Al-Qaeda.

It is instructive to consider just what kind of local psychologies are at stake whenever the language of liberal democracy displaces indigenous perspectives. Misra notes that in his Indian context local psychologies have existed for centuries, based in part on the Hindu religious and ideological sentiments of the people, which include:

> . . . a holistic-organic worldview, coherence and order across all life forms, the socially constituted nature of the person, nonlinear growth and continuity in life, behavior as transaction, the temporal and atemporal existence of human beings, spatiotemporally contextualized action, the search for eternity in life,

the desirability of self-discipline, the transitory nature of human experience, control that is distributed rather than personalized, and a belief in multiple worlds (material and spiritual).[45]

Similarly, Gulerce's work on indigenous psychologies in Turkey reveals the unique stamp of Islam. Particularly in rural locations, people evidence

> coexistent transformations toward both individuation and connectedness, con-tradicting not only Western theory but classical assumptions about human de-velopment, such as unidirectionality, unilinearity, universalism, hierarchical and progressive order, and so on. Additionally, many other theoretical assumptions relying on a view of rational, materialist, pragmatic, functionalist, self-centered, and self-contained human beings fall short in application to understanding of much Turkish behavior. A guiding model is required that leaves room for the irrational, spiritual, altruistic, conservative, other-centered, community-oriented, and interdependent human being.[46]

We have made a case that an American psychology rife with liberal demo-cratic pretexts has the potential to displace indigenous psychologies. We have been steeped in the belief that modern universals are always benign, and that the fruit of our "neutrality" is economic "progress" as exemplified by the post-WWII consumer economy. This is a testimony to the potency of universal foundations in Western philosophy underneath the American Constitution. It is deeply ironic that Western universals were first articulated in order to avoid the displacement of the local particularities of the emerging New World, the same kind of traditions we have argued are endangered by American psy-chology exported abroad. In order to understand the tension between matters universal and particular, we turn now to consider the philosophical basis for universal foundations, how language constrains conversation between differ-ing particularities, and how God's prerogatives for diversity are evident in the Babel narrative.

Psychological Universalism

If psychology is to be sensitive to local psychologies, the universalist rubric for knowledge is inadequate.[47] Universalism fails to understand that political unity is created through conversation (not presumed universality), and only after radical particularity (difference rather than sameness) is recognized.[48]

In the clinical environment, the client is exposed to the language of the clinician. The universality assumed by modernity implies that clinician and client share the same ability to define problems and identify solutions using reason. The difficulty identified by Gergen is that the apparently neutral lan-guage of therapy, born of universalism, is so influential that it will replace a client's native tradition. The primacy of language in this exchange cannot be overemphasized. It is in the language of the therapist that the client learns the meaning of illness and healing. Thus, the potential for therapy to effect positive change significantly hinges upon the kind of language that characterizes the clinical relationship. In subsequent chapters we will argue that an important step toward a peaceable psychology is the recognition that language emerges out of linguistic communities. Juanita's voice is shaped first by her neighbors, her extended family, and the village populace. Her reflections broadly mirror these contexts, providing scaffolding for her interpretations of experience.

We maintain that one moral outcome of reflecting historically on universal foundations in psychology is a willingness to recognize the radical particularity of languages both abroad and at home. We recognize that English-speaking clinicians regularly converse with clients of other ethnic groups and appear to communicate effectively. But it is easily forgotten that the meanings of clinically specific words such as "self" vary, depending on whether defined by the male clinician speaking the language of liberal democracy or the recently immigrated female Chinese-American client. A growing body of empirical psychological literature supports this more finely nuanced critique of universals, noting that "self" is conceptualized in significantly different ways for indigenous Japanese relative to acculturated (English-speaking) Japanese in North America.[49] In the Far East, the "self" is less autonomous or individualized, and this is reflected in the linguistic constructions of everyday Japanese. There are few words for "self," but many that reflect collective responsibility for family, society, and culture. This appears to be the case even for ways in which depressive emotions are expressed in bilingual Chinese-Americans.[50] We fear that the American psychologist who assumes a level playing field for the linguistic comprehension of "self" has already begun a subtle process of imposition upon the client.

Relativizing Empire: Babel and Rome

We have examined several ways in which an empire mentality and the psychological enterprise collude, particularly in military projects and the exportation of psychological ideology. How can Christian psychologists respond to this? Does scripture speak to the issue of empire? Indeed, we see it in the story of Babel and the letters of Paul to the Roman and Philippian Christians regarding the cult of Caesar. In contrast to the claim that the diversity of Babel is a curse, we suggest that the profusion of languages may be a gift.[51] The assumption that all should speak one language reflects Babylonian hubris not unlike the universal claims of more recent empires. But the Babel account follows the realized eschatology of what is already present but not fully. It is only because of Babel that the broader purpose of God's work becomes evident.

Babel anticipates the Acts account of Pentecost where, through the reconciling work of Christ, a diverse group can speak and understand each other using their local languages. Despite their many differences, all are understood. With Pentecost in mind, Babel's commentary on human diversity is deliberate, an eschatological foretaste of the kingdom in Christ.

The human diversification inherent in the Babel story is typically interpreted to refer to God's judgment on human arrogance, resulting in a diverse and often conflicted ethnic landscape. This conventional exegesis of the Genesis text surfaced during former President George W. Bush's brief but controversial visit to Bob Jones University on February 2, 2000. In the wake of the visit, it came to light that the university's commitment to the separation of the races and rejection of interracial dating was based on the confusion of languages and races at Babel.[52] Ethnic and linguistic differences are, in this view, a punishment inherited from the arrogance of the ancient Babylonian architects (Genesis 11). For desiring to connect heaven and earth linguistically, humanity is cursed with a multiplicity of languages and cultures.

This interpretation reflects a popular conservative American religious understanding of the Babel event. However, it is strangely disconnected from historic Christian theological perspectives on the text. Josephus[53] and John Calvin[54] are among various theological interpreters who advocate a different and more hopeful view of diversity. The builders' sin, they argue, was to gather the people into a centralized location to resist God's purpose, namely, that humanity should multiply, fill the earth, and subdue it. The context of the Babel story necessarily includes Genesis 10, where the dispersion of diverse nations is already assumed. Consequently, diversity of languages and ethnicities per se is not the sin. Instead, the Babel story implies a fear of lost identity through dispersal, a fear of becoming restless, rootless wanderers. The Babylonian solution meant that the people would be united around a single enclave of linguistic and ethnic safety. The marks of empire are unmistakable. The tower would become, Miroslav Volf suggests,

> the pillar for a centralized political, economic, and religious system with universal pretensions. . . . When God disapproves, it is because of the inherent violence and godlessness of all imperial projects (Jeremiah 50–51; Revelation 18), their own self-legitimizing accounts of justice and piety notwithstanding. Imperial architects seek to unify by suppressing differences that do not fit into a single grand scheme; they strive to make their own name great by erasing the names of simple people and small nations.[55]

The profusion of languages and cultures is not the vengeance of a jealous God. Rather, diversity is part of God's plan first evident in the created order. Calvin, commenting on this text, notes: "Men had already been spread abroad; and this ought not to be regarded as a punishment, seeing it rather flowed from the benediction and grace of God."[56]

Instead of standing against ethnic or linguistic diversity, God appears to reject Babylonian attempts to universalize human affairs. As a consequence, humanity is *blessed* with the separation and reinforcement of distinct cultures. The scattering is a gift of Yahweh.[57] Jacques Derrida argues that at Babel God responded to "colonial violence" by deconstructing it.[58] In the end, a multiplicity of idioms made uniformity and translation impossible.[59] So Babel always remains an unfinished project, awaiting the full restitution of relationship in the reconciliation and healing of persons through the presence of the Spirit in the body of Christ.

Paul and the Roman Empire

A second set of texts responds to issues of empire in terms of the worship of the emperor in Paul's day. The cult of Caesar serves as the context of his writings to the churches that existed within the Roman Empire. Fundamental to an understanding of Paul's mission is his rejection of the cult of the divine emperor that dominated the far-flung Roman Empire, maintained peace among the gods (*pax deorum*), and controlled its subjects. Statues and coins proclaimed that justice and peace came through the emperor. His virtues (harmony, democracy, righteousness, etc.) were to be worshipped and imitated in order to secure blessing. Both Caesar and Paul mixed religion with politics, but what differed was the nature of the ingredients. For both religion was more than belief; it included the practices of sacrifices, prayers, and offerings.

In Paul's letter to the Romans we have a political manifesto that opens with the gospel of God (Rom. 1:3–4) and ends with the declaration that Jesus came so that the "the nations might glorify God" (Rom. 15:9). For Paul, the word "gospel" (*euanggelion*) had both Jewish and Roman political meanings. Paul's singular gospel was that Jesus was king, a stark contrast to the emperor's announcements of peace (i.e., "gospels"), which were repeated pronouncements of victory, the birth of a son, or personal achievements.[60] Paul took the empire language of gospel and filled it with Christian content. The central theme of political righteousness (*dikaiosune*) in the Roman Empire was, for Paul, the righteousness and justice of Jesus the Lord. Loyalty to Jesus, not the emperor, is salvific. The peace which the emperor proclaimed and demanded was for Paul the peace of our Lord (Rom. 5:1); after all, "the kingdom of God is not food and drink but righteousness and peace" (Rom. 14:17). John E. Toews states:

> Every word, so rich in Christian theological interpretation, is also loaded with political meaning—gospel, son of God, Lord, power, glorify, mercy, faithful (or

loyal) obedience among the nations, rule the nations, hope for the nations, faith, father, salvation, righteousness. The referent for this vocabulary is understood in Rome as Nero Augustus, the Emperor. Paul asserts without qualification that the Romans have misunderstood. The God of the Jewish people and this God's Jewish Messiah Jesus are the referents.[61]

The honorific title for the emperor was *isa theo*, that is, "equal to God." In contrast, Christians viewed Jesus as one who took on the form of a servant (Phil. 2:6–7).

For Paul to argue in this way was to commit treason. Paul's peace was a challenge to the *Pax Romana*; it was a subversive gospel.[62] Romans scholar Jacob Taubes argues that this letter is "a political declaration of war on Caesar."[63] That Paul was imprisoned four times and that his death came at the hands of the Roman Empire is then no surprise. After all, the apostle Paul was martyred by the empire because his politics and religion confronted the religion and politics of the empire. Clement of Rome tells the churches of Corinth about fifty years after Paul wrote his letter to the Romans that the apostle was martyred because he preached a different kind of righteousness (1 Clement 5:7).

The alternative to empire is the political presence of the body of Christ, the church in society. The church can be a threat to the hegemony of the empire mentality by declaring and living its life according to a different loyalty, not simply by organizing voter blocs. The church can be an alternate society in the midst of an empire. Toews states:

> All of Paul's letters are political tracts. He writes letters to build communities of followers of Messiah Jesus. The letters are designed to foster a distinctive identity and communal unity that is faithful to the gospel of Messiah Jesus. They thus propose theological centers, draw boundaries, create structures, organize small house churches, exhort appropriate patterns of relationships and behavior while proscribing inappropriate relationships and behaviors. They are consummate political statements that are intended to build and nurture alternative communities within major urban centers in the Roman Empire. To organize a group of socio-politically disparate people into a unified community is a profoundly political activity. To organize these people in the capital of the Roman Empire into an alternative society that valorizes a crucified Jewish man, that proclaims a lord other than Caesar, that offers a righteousness and peace other than Caesar's is a profoundly subversive activity.[64]

When Paul exhorts the Philippians to be citizens of heaven, it is a political statement, given that Philippi was a Roman outpost. He writes: "But our political identity (*politeuma*) resides in heaven" (Phil. 3:20a). N. T. Wright comments:

> If Paul's answer to Caesar's empire is the empire of Jesus, what does that say about this new empire, living under the rule of its new Lord? It implies a high and strong ecclesiology in which the scattered and often muddled cells of women,

men, and children loyal to Jesus as Lord form colonial outposts of the empire that is to be: subversive little groups when seen from Caesar's point of view, but when seen Jewishly an advance foretaste of the time when the earth shall be filled with the glory of the God of Abraham and the nations will join Israel in singing God's praises (Rom. 15:7–13). From this point of view, therefore, this counterempire can never be merely critical, never merely subversive. It claims to be the reality of which Caesar's empire is the parody; it claims to be modeling the genuine humanness, not least the justice and peace, and the unity across traditional racial and cultural barriers, of which Caesar's empire boasted. If this claim is not to collapse once more into dualism, into a rejection of every human aspiration and value, it will be apparent that there will be a large degree of overlap. "Shun what is evil; cling to what is good." There will be affirmation as well as rejection, collaboration as well as critique. To collaborate without compromise, to criticize without dualism—this is the delicate path that Jesus' counterempire had to learn to tread.[65]

We suggest two implications for Christian mental health practitioners: ecclesial identity and, when appropriate, subversive clinical practice. The Christian psychologist in his or her work represents this alternative community.[66] One's identity is shaped by this membership in a community that seeks to live faithfully to its confession that Jesus is Lord.[67] Such membership precludes the idolatry of individualism and professionalism. It affirms fundamentally that our work as Christians in mental health is political in nature.[68]

Paul's gospel of Jesus Christ was different from the gospels proclaimed in his day. Is the gospel assumed by the clinician to be simply a reflection of a larger culture, or is it different? Sometimes one is hard-pressed to see the difference between modernist models of psychotherapy and Christian approaches.[69] The Christian dimension appears to be a gloss. The work of the Christian psychologist may well be subversive of empire when the latter oppresses the stranger, women, and the helpless. Laura Brown has proposed that feminist psychotherapy is subversive in patriarchal society.[70] She states:

> Feminist therapy is the practice of a genuinely revolutionary act, in which both lives and society are changed. It is a discourse that subverts patriarchy, which it identifies as a major source of damage in human lives. Subversion best describes a process in which the power of the patriarchy is turned upon itself, to revolution and healing, a revolution that, because it is subtle and not frontal, can be effective even in the face of formidable obstacles. Feminist therapy, as one aspect of the feminist revolution, functions to subvert patriarchal dominance at the most subtle and powerful levels, as it is internalized and personified in the lives of therapists and their clients, colleagues, and communities.[71]

Consistent with our thesis and the concerns of this chapter, the gospel subverts projects that undermine the voices of the poor, the prisoner, or the forgotten minorities.

We have considered the possibility that American psychology is so deeply enculturated that it is complicit with an American empire. Local psychologies have been displaced in favor of Western psychology and liberal democracy. We have pointed to implicit universalistic political and linguistic commitments in this chapter. Rather than uncritically embracing modernist claims of universality or the postmodern call for recognizing difference, we note that in both cases, the competing epistemological paradigms eschew God's overarching purpose for a diverse human creation. The moral upshot is that God's purposes for human diversity, when taken from within the biblical narrative of our own Christian tradition, are both already and not yet realized in harmony among all peoples through the reconciling and healing work of the cross.

It is our hope that the moral implications of this discussion support what we are calling a *peaceable psychology*. This is a psychology of christological commitment that recognizes the radical particularity (tradition) of both clinician and client. Because it is christological, a peaceable psychotherapy embraces suffering in the hope of Christ's work of reconciliation and healing in the client. We turn now to this tradition-laden work of the Christian therapist.

3

Boutique Multiculturalism

■ ■ ■ ■ ■ ■ ■ ■ ■ ■ ■

Our civil rights have no dependence on our religious opinions, any more than our opinions in physics or geometry.

> Thomas Jefferson, "A Bill for Establishing Religious Freedom"

All men are caught in an inescapable network of mutuality, tied in a single garment of destiny.

> Rev. Dr. Martin Luther King Jr.,
> "Keep Moving from This Mountain"

From political collusion and universalism, Guatemala and Babel, we move now to Boston, Massachusetts, for the annual meeting of the American Psychological Association (APA) in 1999. Where we might have expected an empire mentality, we encounter instead an unusual example of particularity, of ethnic and religious languages spoken simultaneously in a public context. With more than one hundred fifty thousand members and affiliates, APA is the largest psychological association in the world, widely regarded for its commitment to ethnic diversity and to a hard-nosed science of human behavior. For the annual conference, some five thousand researchers, clinicians, and students from around the world crowd local hotels and a major conference complex. The keynote speaker is the Rev. Jesse Jackson, noted civil rights activist and pupil of the late Rev. Dr. Martin Luther King Jr.

It is Rev. Jackson's plenary moment at the conference. Thundering from a secular pulpit, he condemns discrimination in the field of clinical psychology, pointing to the managed-care assault on equitable and accessible mental-health resources in America. He appeals for a just, sensitive reclamation of genuine healing in therapeutic practice. He recalls American democratic principles that form the basis for human rights and the obligation of clinicians to uphold those rights in practice. Jackson is eloquent and passionate, able to weld the collective affect of the audience to his convictions as they are applied to psychology with a characteristic sense of urgency.

Then, in his concluding remarks, Jackson does the unexpected, changing the entire context of his commentary. He considers Jesus's parable of the lost sheep! It is Jesus the shepherd who acts out of his own sense of call to find one sheep lost out of the ninety-nine. Jesus becomes the foil for Jackson's appeal to a psychology of the margins, an outreach to the oppressed. The lost sheep, Jackson suggests, may not have heard the call of Jesus, because it might have been deaf, asthmatic, abused, female, gay, or poor. Psychologists, like Jesus, are to care for the one lost sheep, to bring it home, to overcome the obstacles impeding its experience of freedom. The failure to embrace the outcast represents a misappropriation of power that in turn suggests the loss of a moral ethos for the profession and a loss of inner character for the professional healer. Jackson's oration ends to waves of sustained and enthusiastic applause.

Why include an African-American clergyman in the program? Is this a carefully crafted move to portray the APA as culturally sensitive and politically correct? Is there a newly apportioned place for ethnic and religious particularity in the public square?[1] If so, will clients from particular ethnic or religious traditions be empowered to express their opinions in the language of their communities without being pathologized? What are the implications for therapists if these forms of expression are present in therapy?

Jesse Jackson's introduction of ethnic and religious multiculturalism into the public forum has major implications for psychotherapy. It is possible that a therapist who refuses to respond to a client's religious concerns becomes a destructive voice in the client's inner psychological sanctum. The prevailing paradigm in psychotherapy training follows the assumptions of democratic liberalism where the principle of "objectivity" reigns supreme.[2] We believe that the democratic liberal must become much more sensitized to particularity, whether ethnic or religious. The enthusiastic response of the APA audience to Jackson's address may suggest that the context-free liberal discourse of public affairs is inadequate as a healing medium. However, in all probability, the virtues of democratic liberalism will remain entrenched as clinicians continue to create an improved context-free environment for therapy. Perhaps we give only lip service to diversity.

In this chapter we propose that historic democratic liberalism is a tradition, an ideology no more neutral than a religious heritage. Among other things, democratic liberalism enshrines individual rights above communal distinctives, privatizes religion, and imposes the language of secularity. The net result is a public square where only a common language can be spoken, that of democratic liberalism. Alternatively, we argue for a public square which recognizes and honors ethnic and religious differences. The diversity of voices will not necessarily result in chaos but rather, we argue, will enrich the public conversation and ultimately will empower clients to use their religious dialects in the context of therapy. Our proposal is constructed not simply on the basis of liberal values of tolerance, respect, and freedom of speech, but on the story of Pentecost, that event in which commonality was premised on the presence of Jesus and the recognition that those in attendance heard the good news in their own tongue.

To negotiate, let alone recognize, the differences from other groups requires that an ethnic community have the ability to articulate its own convictions, describe its own uniqueness, and have the courage to do both. One must come to the table with something to say. We would hope for a vibrant ethnic and religious integrity, a sense of roots and, at the same time, the ability to engage in peaceable, meaningful dialogue with other ethnic or religious communities. Given a clear sense of one's ethnic or religious identity, conversation with others has the possibility of thickening one's own identity.

What then are the implications for psychotherapy? We insist that therapists who begin with the lifeworld of their ethnic or religious clients are not imposing their culture on the client. They do what any competent therapist does—they begin with the client. Conversely, it is precisely a therapist espousing a liberal theory of justice as universal (individual) rights that is imposing a value on the ethnic or religious client rather than encouraging a sense of justice, or any other value, to emerge out of shared meanings in the ethnic community.

To Speak or Not to Speak?

In 1984, Richard John Neuhaus proposed that religion had been effectively banned from conversation in the public square.

> This is the cultural crisis—and therefore the political and legal crisis—of our society: the popularly accessible and vibrant belief systems and world views of our society are largely excluded from the public arena in which the decisions are made about how the society should be ordered. . . . The answer lies in a more public role for religion.[3]

The legitimization of particular voices in the therapeutic conversation requires that attention be given to the larger, political context in which therapy is embedded. For reasons of space we will not provide an extensive analysis of the debate regarding religion in public settings, but rather focus on what influence implicit assumptions about public displays of religious belief have had on the therapeutic enterprise. For our purposes, it may be simply stated that the role of religion in the public square is premised around two opposing poles. Some participants argue for the legitimacy of religious language and reflection in public settings. Others maintain that religion is a private matter.

Underlying the debate about the role of religion in public are, we submit, assumptions about the function of public and private languages. When persons who are Christian, agnostic, Muslim, or Jewish meet to converse in the public square, how will they communicate? If they speak only in a language that all will understand, individual uniquenesses will be lost. Individuals from rich ethnic and religious traditions feel that in public debate their ethno-religious heritage is a liability. They may even be told that it is an imposition on others. In their ethnic embarrassment, they tend to downplay their particularity for the sake of public acceptance. In the public square, religious explanations are eschewed because the demands on the listener are presumed to be excessive.

Richard Rorty, following Thomas Jefferson's principles for an enlightened democracy, argues that private religious beliefs should be excluded from public discourse.[4] Rorty contends that, given the panoply of religious voices, religion cannot be understood in the public square. The language of religion should not be encouraged in public life, even when the speaker may argue convincingly that the will of God is at stake. The religious issue is therefore relegated to the interior space of the personal, much as hobbies or musical tastes are construed individually, protected from the scrutiny and opinion of the larger public. Rorty emphasizes a secular public square that converses about shared issues of interest, purportedly for the greater good. The utilitarian character of public discourse is unmistakable, its political precepts easily recognizable within the constitutional jurisprudence of the United States. The exclusionist perspective precludes any suggestion that interaction between religious or particular language can and should be applied within the public forum:

> . . . the epistemology suitable for such a democracy is one in which the only test of a political proposal is its ability to gain assent from people who retain radically diverse ideas about the point and meaning of human life, about the path to private perfection. The more such consensus becomes the test of a belief, the less important is the belief's source.[5]

Additionally, Rorty believes religious discourse in the public square is a conversation stopper. When religion is introduced in public, Rorty says, "the ensuing silence masks the group's inclination to say 'So what?' We were not discussing your private life; we were discussing public policy. Don't bother us with matters that are not our concern."[6] And like Rorty, John Rawls considered religious expression in public either imprudent, improper, or both.[7] Presumably, to argue from religious premises sends the message that others must accept the religious basis of a proposal in order to debate it. If one does not agree, one is reduced to silence. For Rawls, reasoning in the public forum should be limited to discourse which any reasonable person could understand, critique, accept, or reject. Issues of race, gender, religious convictions, medical condition, intellectual ability, and moral outlook are all hidden behind what Rawls called "a veil of ignorance." The result is a generalizable view of what is morally good and the justification of rights over goods. One fears that what is reasonable is Rawls's definition of reasoning; those persons are unreasonable who speak with a logic learned in particular, unique traditions.

The Liberal Democratic Tradition

In the acrimonious presidential campaign of 2004, candidates sought to distance themselves from the dreaded "L-word." Democratic candidates assiduously courted moderate voters by avoiding reference to "liberal" policies. On the Republican side, George W. Bush shored up his conservative base by moving away from "progressive" references that even remotely hinted at liberal tendencies. Clearly the candidates wanted to avoid negative political fallout related to popular conceptions of liberalism, often quantified in terms of attitudes and policies toward national enemies. Pushing aside contemporary uses for the term, it is a point of fact that both candidates were profoundly indebted to the *democratic liberal tradition*. Both candidates leaned into the nineteenth-century political ideology of the sanctity of the individual, common human rights, and personal freedoms. Does such a tradition empower minority ethnic groups or women to flourish? Does this tradition silence or enliven religious traditions in the public square of politics or therapy?[8]

In a trenchant analysis, Alasdair MacIntyre lays bare the ways in which democratic liberalism functions as a tradition, even though that is not its self-perception.[9]

> Yet it is of the first importance to remember that the project of founding a form of social order in which individuals could emancipate themselves from the contingency and particularity of tradition by appealing to genuinely universal, tradition-independent norms was and is not only, and not principally, a project of philosophers. It was and is the project of modern liberal, individualist society, and the most cogent reasons that we have for believing that the hope of a tradition-independent rational universality is an illusion derived from the history of that project. For in the course of that history liberalism, which began as an appeal to alleged principles of shared rationality against what was felt to be the tyranny of tradition, has itself been transformed into a tradition whose continuities are partly defined by the interminability of the debate over such principles.[10]

MacIntyre concludes:

> Liberal theory is best understood, not at all as an attempt to find a rational-
> ity independent of tradition, but as itself the articulation of an historically
> developed and developing set of social institutions and forms of activity, that
> is, as the voice of a tradition. Like other traditions, liberalism has internal to
> it its own standards of rational justification. Like other traditions, liberalism
> has its set of authoritative texts and its disputes over their interpretation. Like
> other traditions, liberalism expresses itself socially through a particular kind
> of hierarchy.[11]

So then, liberalism is a tradition. The virtue language of democratic liberalism attaches rights to individuals rather than to groups.[12] Human rights are
individual rights rather than communal prerogatives. It affirms what is rationally commensurable between traditions, but not what is radically different.
Because of this, we believe that democratic liberalism undermines ethnic and
religious particularity. As a result, the treatment of ethnic and religious particularity in liberal societies is akin to choosing between various ethnic foods
based on personal preference. The American context upholds particularity
as a curio. Rather than delving deeply into the meaning frameworks intrinsic
to ethnic and religious groups, we feign worldly sophistication in our loudly
proclaimed appreciation for gospel choirs and through our practiced ability
to use chopsticks in upscale Chinese restaurants.

Diversity Lite

In liberal societies we have only a commitment to *boutique multiculturalism*.[13]
It is assumed that there is a common human core, that everyone is essentially
similar in having a foundational capacity for rational choice and thought.
Culture is mere gloss, a suite of differences amenable to superficial cocktail
chat over one's ancestry and summer holiday travel plans. Boutique multiculturalism accepts differences in dress, food, or worship. But the moment the
sacred values of a particular ethnic or religious community become public,
the toleration ends. Talk in public about the life of the human embryo, slavery,
the risen Christ, or Cesar Chavez quickly changes the tenor of the conversation. Liberal democracy is capable of only boutique multiculturalism since it
neglects the communal character of the local communities from which ethnic
and religious individuals and their convictions come.

Pluralism in America is a truism, but encouragement for ethnicity and religiosity to flourish in public is not. That negative legacy is increasingly laid
at the feet of democratic liberalism. Much as we may tout our commitment
to honor the particularity of ethno-religious communities, the reality is different. While the situation for African-Americans has shown some progress

over the past half century, one certainly would be stretching the truth to make the same claim for Native Americans. Distrust of groups is deeply entrenched in American society, as evidenced in the relocation of Japanese-Americans during the 1940s, the reneging on Native-American treaty rights, the blatant discrimination against African-Americans for centuries, and the distrust of Arabic-speaking American citizens.

Therapy in the liberal tradition claims to be sensitive to the individualized language of particularity in the client, but in reality it proceeds to build over that language a new discourse of liberal virtue and individual rights, and to pathologize the ethno-religious individual when his or her core values differ from what is politically correct in the democratic liberal tradition. It is a bitter irony that religious sensitivity in the APA is promoted only insofar as the context-free goal of therapy is advanced. We believe that this is an imposition upon the ethnic and religious client.

Individual vs. Communal Rights

In the modern world, political liberalism upholds the rights of individuals with forceful and persuasive rigor. Freedom of speech, tolerance of differences, and a right to privacy are all rights attached to individuals. Group rights are a different matter. Liberalism emerged out of a reaction to the tradition and authority of European fiefdoms, and protecting the integrity of ethnic groups became, in turn, a low priority. The separation of church and state created a proviso that guaranteed religious groups would not control the secular state, but it did not protect the church from the imposition of another tradition—secularity—in public education or therapy. From the perspective of liberalism, there was no need to defend community rights, since rights were guaranteed to individuals who were members of groups. All that was needed was a tolerance of differences between individuals rather than celebration of group distinctives.

The liberalism of John Rawls and Richard Dworkin focuses on the rights of individuals.[14] Rawls maintains that in a just society our self-respect is secured by our recognition of others as equal citizens, rather than through membership in an ethnic or religious community. Will Kymlicka has wondered how Rawls can argue that the state can protect itself from external interference when no such claim for protection is made for the ethnic or religious community.[15] Liberals tend to assume that the unity of the nation-state is jeopardized by the existence of vocal minorities.

While the citizen of the political community functions as an individual with protected rights, the private individual lives in much smaller collectivities of emotional connection and ritual. Accordingly, we have hyphenated Americans: African-Americans, Asian-Americans, Latin-Americans, Jewish-Americans, and Native-Americans. Publicly they are expected to live to the right of the hyphen, but privately they can choose the left. In public they are expected to speak a common language, but at home they may converse in ethnic and religious dialects. If the ethnic community is assimilated, life is lived as an American. For the political liberal, little is lost. Ethnic and religious uniqueness is melted into the pot of American homogeneity. Ethnic and religious voices are blended into the single voice of the larger populace. The orchestra now plays with a single instrument.

Modern liberalism has not provided the underpinnings for a pluralist society such that it truly honors ethnic and religious particularity. With its emphasis on individual autonomy, liberalism fails to address the communal context in which moral decision-making is learned. The community in which one grows to maturity will determine the range of choices available, depending on the community's status in the larger republic. African-Americans and Native-Americans de facto have a different range of choices within which to exercise individual autonomy than do persons of European descent. Liberalism fails to consider seriously that the ability to make choices is nurtured in the context of communities that provide a language, tradition, practices, and narrative in which particular choices are made intelligible.

This lack of sensitivity to particularity becomes strikingly clear when one compares the American Psychological Association code of ethics with those of other societies. Jean Pettifor compared six codes of ethics for psychologists around the world. She concluded that

> the description of standards for individual consent, confidentiality, professional boundaries and honoring self-determination appear indistinguishable from Western codes. There appears to be little overt recognition [in Western codes] of values of harmony, interdependence, interconnectedness, sense of community, respect for tradition, wisdom of elders, religious beliefs, or denial of self-interest (i.e., selfish or individual interest).[16]

The American code seems anemic in its vague call to "responsibility to society." The International Federation of Social Workers has two major guiding principles: human rights (for individuals) and social justice (for the collective good).[17] The Canadian code fleshes that out in terms of greater inclusivity of diversity: families, organizations, and communities. It extends moral rights to diverse and collective groupings of people. Christine Wihak examined the values of the *Canadian Code of Ethics for Psychologists*[18] to determine how compatible they might be with four fundamental principles of the Inuit: "(1) the concept of serving others, (2) the concept of consensus decision making, (3) the concept of skill and knowledge acquisition, and (4) the concept of collaborative relationships."[19] Wihak found clear compatibility in that both reflect a deep concern for contributing to the collective good of the community.

Celebration of Difference

Canadian philosopher Charles Taylor addresses these issues from the perspective of the importance of difference over sameness.[20] His concern is the right of aboriginal societies and French Canadians to survive. This kind of multiculturalism poses a challenge to the traditional liberal theory of individual human rights. It involves, he suggests, a politics of difference. Individual cultures should be seen as possessing intrinsic worth, be recognized as unique, and have the right to do what enables their communities to flourish. Taylor perceptively connects the private with the public, the individual with society.

Taylor's thesis is built on several premises. First, a sense of individual human worth emerges from being recognized by others. If others reject, ignore, or malign my minority status, I interiorize their misrecognition.

> The thesis is that our identity is partly shaped by recognition or its absence, often by the misrecognition of others, and so a person or group of people can suffer real damage, real distortion, if the people or society around them mirror back to them a confining or demeaning or contemptible picture of themselves. Nonrecognition or misrecognition can inflict harm, can be a form of oppression, imprisoning someone in a false, distorted, and reduced mode of being.[21]

In a racist, patriarchal, ageist, capitalist, or secular society, those who do not fit in tend to adopt a depreciatory image of themselves. This happens in spite of our commitment to the universal dignity of human beings. A superficial recognition (e.g., in a context-free clinical relationship) of the religious client is similarly detrimental.

Second, following the lead of George Herbert Mead[22] and Mikhail Bakhtin,[23] Taylor asserts that human identity emerges in dialogue. We learn who we are through language in the context of significant others, a community of language users. Taylor notes that ancient societies were organized according to a hierarchy based on honor. This, however, meant that one's sense of honor was dependent on someone being dishonored at a lower level. In reaction, a politics of equality recognizes the fundamental dignity and equality of all peoples. A politics of difference, however, proceeds one step further to include the recognition of differences between groups and their fundamental right to survive. Referring to the latter two, equality and difference, Taylor makes a useful comparison:

> These two modes of politics, then, both based on the notion of equal respect, come into conflict. For one, the principle of equal respect requires that we treat people in a difference-blind fashion. The fundamental intuition that humans command this respect focuses on what is the same in all. For the other, we have to recognize and even foster particularity. The reproach the first makes to the second is just that it violates the principle of nondiscrimination. The reproach

the second makes to the first is that it negates identity by forcing people into a homogeneous mold that is untrue to them. This would be bad enough if the mold were itself neutral—nobody's mold in particular. But the complaint generally goes further. The claim is that the supposedly neutral set of difference-blind principles of the politics of equal dignity is in fact a reflection of one hegemonic culture. As it turns out, then, only the minority or suppressed cultures are being forced to take alien form. Consequently, the supposedly fair and difference-blind society is not only inhuman (because it is suppressing identities) but also, in a subtle and unconscious way, itself highly discriminatory.[24]

Third, Taylor differentiates between substantive and procedural rights. Liberalism recognizes that people have views about the ends of life, about what constitutes a good life (substantive), and that there is a commitment to deal fairly between persons regardless of how they conceive their ends (procedural). A liberal society adopts no particular substantive view about the ends of life but is united around a strong procedural commitment to treat people with equal respect. Yet Stanley Fish argues that even a procedural approach is substantive.[25]

If human rights are assumed to be based on what is universally applicable, it is then difficult to assimilate a doctrine of differences. While Taylor affirms a politics of equality, he is concerned that liberalism imposes a false homogeneity. From Kant onward, human dignity consists largely in the freedom of each person to determine for himself or herself a view of the good life. It follows that the liberal society must remain neutral with regard to the nature of the good life. It need only ensure that citizens deal fairly with one another. In contrast, Taylor points to the situation of French Canadians in Quebec:

> Quebeckers, therefore, and those who give similar importance to this kind of collective goal, tend to opt for a rather different model of a liberal society. On their view, a society can be organized around a definition of the good life, without this being seen as a depreciation of those who do not personally share this definition. Where the nature of the good requires that it be sought in common, this is the reason for its being a matter of public policy. According to this conception, a liberal society singles itself out as such by the way in which it treats minorities, including those who do not share public definitions of the good, and above all by the rights it accords to all of its members.[26]

Taylor's concern is that we go beyond providing support to the disadvantaged by helping them "to maintain and cherish distinctness, not just now but forever. After all, if we're concerned with identity, then what is more legitimate than one's aspiration that it never be lost?"[27] Taylor is concerned not only with the potential of an individual to be fulfilled but also with that of a group or culture to survive. We must accord equal respect to evolving cultures within a nation-state. Taylor comments,

Where the politics of universal dignity fought for forms of nondiscrimination that were quite "blind" to the ways in which citizens differ, the politics of difference often redefines nondiscrimination as requiring that we make these distinctions the basis of differential treatment.[28]

Taylor argues that a politics of difference recognizes not only the need for cultures to survive and flourish, but also their need to be recognized as having worth. "The claim is that all human cultures that have animated whole societies over some considerable stretch of time have something important to say to all human beings."[29] With Taylor's proposal, we have presently moved well beyond "boutique multiculturalism."

We think that a politics of difference implies that one would take ethnic and religious identity very seriously in society and therapy. A religious group is like an ethnicity. This is not without historical and linguistic precedent. Christians in the New Testament were considered a people. The Greek word for people, *ethnoi*, is the root for our word "ethnicity." An ethnic community is a community with a historical memory, a unique set of rituals, symbols, beliefs, and traditions. We think that the health of a nation is dependent on hearing and affirming the narratives of a plurality of ethnicities.[30] In this peaceable conversation one develops the critical convictions necessary for democratic societies. The fear of cacophony in public dialogue, the imminent dissolution of the social fabric, and the fragmentation of national unity is, in our opinion, unfounded.

Granted, there will be greater confusion as we learn to hear the ethnic and religious voice—but then democracies are built for such diversity of convictions.[31] The American Bill of Rights encourages the creation of collective and cooperative forms of social action; it asserts "the right of the people peacefully to assemble." Cultural identity in democracy is enhanced when all particularities have a voice. Hence at a public level it would make sense to support the legal defense of collective and individual rights, the provision of tax dollars for bilingual and bicultural education, and the public celebration of more ethnic and religious holidays. In all of this we assume no single community should dominate or be given preference. We think that Michael Walzer is right when he makes cultural membership a fundamental value:

One characteristic above all is central to my argument. We are (all of us) culture-producing creatures; we make and inhabit meaningful worlds. Since there is no way to rank and order these worlds with regard to their understanding of social goods, we do justice to actual men and women by respecting their particular creations. And they claim justice, and resist tyranny, by insisting on the meaning of social goods among themselves. Justice is rooted in the distinct understandings of places, honors, jobs, things of all sorts that constitute a shared way of life. To override those understandings is (always) to act unjustly.[32]

Richard Rorty's immediate antagonist, Stephen Carter, cites the example of religious justifications that were given in the interest of abolishing slavery as a counterpoint to the exclusion of religious language from public life.[33] Proponents for religiously neutral public debate fail to take seriously enough the contribution of religion to the civil rights movement. James McClendon roots Martin Luther King Jr. in the black evangelical movement and notes the profound way that tradition shaped King and the civil rights movement.[34]

Not only has religion been relegated to the margins of social acceptability, Carter maintains that religious language has been trivialized. Aside from rare instances, religion is an unwelcome guest in the political arena, even though the American public is predominantly self-identified as religious. Carter notes that the splitting off of the religious in politics (parallel to the implicit taboo against religion in therapy) hinges on the idea that religion is irrational.[35] Carter proposes the following:

> What is needed is not a requirement that the religiously devout choose a form of dialogue that liberalism accepts, but that liberalism develop a politics that accepts whatever form of dialogue a member of the public offers. Epistemic diversity, like diversity of other kinds, should be cherished, not ignored, and certainly not abolished. What is needed, then, is a willingness to *listen*, not because the speaker has *the right voice*, but because the speaker has *the right to speak*. Moreover, the willingness to listen must hold out the possibility that the speaker is saying something worth listening to; to do less is to trivialize the forces that shape the moral convictions of tens of millions of Americans.[36]

Public discourse—whether in government chambers or in the psychologist's office—should encourage the full range of ethnic and religious languages, and we believe that such conversation can be conducted peaceably.

In therapy, religion is construed as a private resource or a personal illusion. If religion in the public square is seen as peaceable, as a contribution to the republic, then it may be the case that ethnic and religious clients will find the freedom to use their native tongue in therapy. Perhaps therapists will respond by learning the local language, entering into its ethical ethos, and assisting clients to find life purpose from within their tradition, while still helping them to understand the democratic liberalism of their host culture.

A Deeper Democracy

A peaceable psychology will celebrate ethnic and religious tradition in clinical practice. This argument supposes that difference is not a threat—that the perspectives of the other, even when imbued with passionately held religious convictions, are worthy of engagement rather than mere toleration. The greatest risk of religious violence is not through faith expressed in the public square, but rather through the elimination of difference and otherness from that freewheeling forum. This view reflects a truer, deeper democracy than Rawls's approach, which endorsed a view of the modern nation-state as neutral with regard to conceptions of the common good, and which argued for the use of a public reason independent of tradition (especially religious) in public debate.

We would, however, argue that ethnic and religious language should be permissible—even welcomed—in a democratic public forum that honestly comes to terms with its claims about a set of inalienable rights. An emphasis on tradition need not undermine culture and the creation of virtue. Jeffrey Stout recognizes and affirms this possibility with remarkable prescience:

> Democracy, I shall argue, *is* a tradition. It inculcates certain habits of reasoning, certain attitudes toward deference and authority in political discussion, and love for certain goods and virtues, as well as a disposition to respond to certain types of actions, events, or persons with admiration, pity, or horror. This tradition is anything but empty. Its ethical substance, however, is more a matter of enduring attitudes, concerns, dispositions, and patterns of conduct than it is a matter of agreement on a conception of justice in Rawls's sense.[37]

Stout's vision of democracy is quite particular, evoking the pragmatism of Emerson, Whitman, and Dewey. It does not begin with the assumption that all human beings share a common morality or rationality. Stout is not writing from a religious perspective or for a religious community, but for American society as a whole. His basic point is that democracy is not inherently opposed to tradition.[38]

Nicholas Wolterstorff's views are consistent with this revision when he says that "given that it is of the very essence of liberal democracy that citizens enjoy equal freedom in law to live out their lives as they see fit, how can it be compatible with liberal democracy for its citizens to be *morally restrained* from deciding and discussing political issues as they see fit?"[39] In liberal societies, tradition-specific arguments are considered private and irrelevant. Hence, traditioned speakers remain silent in public and therapy. Democratic liberalism fails to understand that religious justifications can be profoundly transformative in the lives of persons for whom these traditions are normative. Certainly, Lincoln's second inaugural speech would be a clear example. Wolterstorff notes,

> It belongs to the *religious convictions* of a good many religious people in our society that *they ought to base* their decisions concerning fundamental issues of justice *on* their religious convictions. They do not view as an option whether or not to do so. It is their conviction that they ought to strive for wholeness, integrity, integration, in their lives: that they ought to allow the Word of God, the teachings of Torah, the command and example of Jesus, or whatever, to

shape their existence as a whole, including, then, their social and political existence. Their religion is not, for them, about *something other* than their social and political existence; it is *also* about their social and political existence. Accordingly, to require of them that they not base their decisions and discussions concerning political issues on their religion is to infringe, inequitably, on their free exercise of religion.[40]

Where Stout breaks new ground is in his proposal that all citizens should feel free *"to express whatever premises actually serve as reasons for their claims."*[41] This especially applies to citizens in the public square. Religious persons should not be expected to bracket their religious justifications for a policy they advocate. The desired result would be a genuine conversation in the public square that recognizes the legitimacy of traditions and their differences. It also demands of parties that, having given idiomatic expression to their point of view, they be open to other perspectives *and* to the critique of their own. Hence, Jew, Christian, Muslim, and agnostic could all speak from within their tradition, with their unique vocabulary and grammar of values, and be held accountable to the ethical charter of *their* tradition.

The justification for Stout's position is grounded in the twin constitutional rights of freedom of religion and freedom of expression. Perhaps, Stout explains, one can show respect "by offering *different* reasons to them, reasons relevant *from their point of view*."[42] Such a conversation does not begin with a previously agreed-upon contract. Commonality may emerge spontaneously from the conversation. What is needed instead of contracts, Stout proposes, is immanent criticism. This means that to respect the position of another does not require agreement, but rather a willingness to listen to the other. The listener considers the speaker's justifications, critiquing why his or her argument results in the stated conclusions or places where the argument is inconsistent with the speaker's own tradition. Commonality based on an assumed social contract comes up short because it fails dialogically to imagine ethical or political exchange. Wolterstorff comments:

> So-called "communitarians" regularly accuse proponents of the liberal position of being against community. One can see what they are getting at. Nonetheless, this way of putting it seems to me imperceptive of what, at bottom, is going on. The liberal is not willing to live with a politics of multiple communities. He still wants communitarian politics. He is trying to discover, and to form, the relevant community. He thinks we need a shared political basis; he is trying to discover and nourish that basis. . . . I think that the attempt is hopeless and misguided. We must learn to live with a politics of multiple communities.[43]

The liberal contractarian position begins with a description of common public reason and normatively expects restraint from those who do not easily fit this mold.

In his book *God's Name in Vain*, Stephen Carter argues that religious freedom is a freedom for persons with religious convictions to do the things that their faith requires.[44] The goal of state regulations, he asserts, is the standardization of people, the creation of sameness. The calls for the recognition of diversity are then merely pious platitudes. Usually this sentiment is phrased as developing a shared sense of meaning as a nation. The state is either neutral or accommodating to diversity. Carter rejects neutrality as merely a theoretical option. In reality, it is an impossibility. *Accommodation* is his preferred strategy. Accommodation nurtures the plurality of ethno-religious communities, communities that often view existence in ways different from the dominant culture.

Religious freedom in an accommodationist model creates space for religions to exercise their faith in a manner capable of resisting the state and, we would add, contrasting with the prevailing culture. In so doing it is possible that the state might learn from the dissenting religion. The extent to which professional organizations (e.g., the APA) truly create the space for religious clients to freely explore their faith, will define the extent of the possibility that the profession may learn from ethnic and religious diversity in a manner that upholds local language and particularity in the healing of the client.

We offer a concluding observation regarding the accommodationist view. The public square of therapy is not a place of objective and neutral encounter. For one thing, clients from ethnic and religious traditions might speak in their native tongues at home, but a more powerful language is spoken in therapy. As we have indicated earlier, Gergen and colleagues maintain that psychological language was and continues to be exported internationally at the expense of local cultures. It is entirely possible that such imposition occurs in North America as well. Second, what kind of religion could speak with integrity in the public square? To privatize religion means that it has no public voice at all. Can a public religiosity be peaceable? Ethnic and religious clients have learned that since therapy is effectively a "public" place, it is best to leave provincial dialects in the waiting room. Our solution is to create a space for religious ideation and language that is central to the healing of the client. Accordingly, our final justification for this argument arises from our own tradition, from Christian scripture interpreted through the ethnic and religious referents of our Anabaptist particularity.

Juanita

Our approach leans toward a politics of difference rather than a politics of identity or universality. We begin, therefore, with a unique ethnic and religious person like Juanita. We now imaginatively continue her story from where we left off in the last chapter. Juanita grew up in the Guatemalan highlands and is of Indian extraction. Her voice was not heard in the political turmoil. The government assumed she and her Santiago neighbors all supported the guerilla movement.

Given the dwindling family income, Juanita left Santiago, the village she loved. After her husband's death she learned to string beads at Chonita's Beadwork, a small business begun by a war widow. Concepción, the owner, took in women, taught them a trade, and gave them a community of hope. Here too she met Miguel, who came regularly to their little business and ferried their goods to markets in Panajachel, Chichicastenango, and Guatemala City. Their courtship consisted of attending revival meetings at Iglesia del Buen Pastor. When a relative from Los Angeles encouraged them to come to the United States, they did not hesitate.

Unable to obtain legal entry, they entered California at a small border crossing with fake papers. Miguel was able to find work immediately in the Los Angeles garment industry, while Juanita provided domestic help. Now, five years later, Juanita is twenty-eight. They have three children and are very active in a charismatic Pentecostal community.

When Juanita enters therapy for depression after arriving in the United States, will her voice be heard? She describes her current emotional state as clinical depression. She sees her coming to the United States as a gift from God and cannot understand her sadness. She attends church faithfully with her family and feels she listens carefully to the voice of the Holy Spirit. Will the therapist who operates out of his or her Western liberal paradigm truly hear her ethnic and religious voice? Will he or she be cognizant of the larger political context of Juanita's sadness? Will our complicity in that story be considered relevant?

A politics of difference recognizes that individuals like Juanita have the right to demand public recognition of their unique identity. Though she may not articulate it, she yearns to be seen for who she is, a Guatemalan immigrant with a Pentecostal understanding of life. She implied that she wants the adjectives *Guatemalan* and *Pentecostal* to have real linguistic and cultural force. Failure to recognize and honor the reality of differences is a form of psychological violence. We will make a case for recovering and empowering the ethnic and religious voice of clients. For that to occur we will need a deeper democracy in which particular traditions are taken with greater seriousness.

Ethno-religious Therapy

Therapists and clients have learned well the lessons of liberal societies. Religion is left in the therapist's waiting room. Clients adjust their language to that of the therapist.[45] The language of therapy is secularized to accommodate anyone—Buddhist, Christian, agnostic, or Jew. While ethnic particularity

continues to occupy a prominent place in the American psychological literature, the religious question is largely divorced from ethnicity. Until recently,
religion was relegated to the furthest margins of psychotherapeutic practice.
The silencing of an integrated, ethno-religious voice contributes to a feeling of
disempowerment for clinicians and clients alike. In North America, therapists
risk the charge of "value imposition" if they explicitly address ethno-religious
ideation, a prohibition common to virtually all training curricula in the mental
health field. While this stance guards against abuses of authority in the clinical
relationship, its unilateral application may carry grave consequences for clients
of therapists who continue to avoid religious issues for fear of being criticized
for value imposition. In a therapy devoid of ethnic and religious sensitivity, the
clinician's silence regarding clients' cherished issues of identity and faith may
be experienced by the client as invalidation. This is not peaceable.

We maintain that there is mutual reinforcement between the trivialization
of religion in public debate and the silencing of the religious voice in psychotherapeutic conversation. Both are predicated on the assumption that religion
is inherently divisive. With silence comes implicit argument for the exclusion
of ethno-religiosity in psychotherapy. In the world of mental health, critical
interaction over issues of ethnic and religious particularity lags far behind
the debate in the public square.[46] In the same manner that the ethno-religious
person has the right to express his or her convictions in the public square, so
also the ethno-religious client has the right to expect that his or her convictions
will be elicited, validated, and integrated into the psychotherapeutic process.
A peaceable psychology does not impose a religious or political ideology. It
begins with the particular web of beliefs the client brings to therapy and elicits
the religious resources the client may possess.

The liberal demand for a common language in the public realm is a response
to the specter of warring religious traditions. But this assumes that religions
are incapable of making space for the other. Religion does not always end with
prejudicial judgments and out-group bias. Jesus at the Samaritan well reaches
across gender, ethnic, and religious differences to effect transformation in grace.
Similarly, a peaceable psychology does not impose a common language on the
"public square" of therapy. It invites the client to bring his or her "private"
religious language into the public setting of therapy. Personal struggles are then
construed in the language of the client's ethno-religious world. A peaceable
psychology responds to the ethical charter of the religious client by radically
affirming that point of departure. The net effect of this approach is not to
undermine the client's charter, but to extend it into new areas of his or her
life and presenting issues. The resources of the client's religious community
are respected and accessed.

A peaceable psychology empowers clients to speak from within their ethnic
culture and to value their ethnic heritage. Ethnic and religious issues would then
be afforded a privileged status in the clinical relationship, as significant existential

precursors to the client's healing. Given the experiences of Guatemalan Indians, Iraqi Sunnis, Tibetan Buddhists, Ukrainian Catholics, Ethiopian Christians, and other persecuted minority ethnic and religious groups around the world, a peaceable psychology advocates for the voiceless and recognizes the gifts that they possess. In subsequent chapters we will continue to make the case that clients need to be empowered to use their native tongue in therapy and that therapists be encouraged to create a therapeutic setting where ethnic and religious language is honored. North American clients, whether women, evangelicals, African-Americans, Hindus, or Native-Americans, have whispered their fear of not being heard if they speak of their concerns in their religious dialects.

To respond to the religious or ethno-religious background of a client is sometimes rejected as a form of countertransference. We argue that *not* recognizing the integrity of ethnic and religious particularity is countertransference, if not violence; to *not* validate the communal convictions of clients is to do psychological harm. We seek a multicultural framework deeper than the boutique multiculturalism so prevalent in the American context. Rather than advocating mere cultural tolerance, however, we believe that deeper cultural understanding is possible only where individuals know and live within their native or chosen tradition.

Following Stout, we argue that one respectful role for religion in therapy is to engage in what he calls immanent criticism. We would refer to this as empowerment. The point is not to help a client address his or her problems in the neutral ethical language of the secular therapist. Rather, the therapist would first create a space where the client can bring into therapy his or her whole ethnic and religious world. Implicit in their narrative, customs, rituals, and language is an ethic, a normative way of living. The task of the therapist is to elicit that charter, explore its meaning with the client, and discover whether the client endorses its implications or wishes to be held accountable to that charter. This is a tradition-specific therapy that is also peaceable.

Pentecost and Paul: God's Constructive Diversity

Do the scriptures speak to the issue of multiculturalism? We think so. Issues of diversity and unity appear in the New Testament account of Pentecost and of the apostle Paul's ministry of reconciliation among Jews and Gentiles.

In the story of Babel, humanity spoke different languages without mutual understanding. At Pentecost, however, men and women spoke different languages but were able to understand one another. In Babel, those who gathered to seek the hegemony of one culture were scattered. In the New Testament account of Pentecost, people came from the far reaches of the ancient world and created a new culture unified by the Spirit while retaining ethnic differences. As if reading from an astrological chart of all the nations under heaven,[47]

Luke listed them: "Parthians, Medes, Elamites, and residents of Mesopotamia, Judea and Cappadocia, Pontus and Asia, Phrygia and Pamphylia, Egypt and the parts of Libya belonging to Cyrene, and visitors from Rome, both Jews and proselytes, Cretans and Arabs . . ." (Acts 2:9–11). They lived in different cultures, they spoke different languages, and yet at Pentecost they had something in common. Unlike the builders of Babel, they came together not to create a human center, but to celebrate a different one—God in Christ. They didn't try to reach heaven; they pointed to the possibility of unity among all the cultures and languages on earth. This is the basis of a peaceable psychology.

In the Genesis account of Babel, the Babylonian empire builders sought to pierce heaven. By contrast, the account of Pentecost in Acts indicated that the Spirit came down from heaven to a receptive people. On the plains of Shinar they all spoke one language through coercion, but at Pentecost they spoke many languages and were united peaceably by the outpouring of the Spirit. This was not the unity of cultural conformity reinforced by the power of the state, but the harmony of cultural diversity constructed upon the common confession that Jesus is Lord. In the context of the Pentecost miracle Peter pointed to Jesus. He stated, "Jesus of Nazareth, a man attested to you by God with deeds of power, wonders, and signs that God did through him among you, as you yourselves know . . ." (Acts 2:22). With Christ as center, we do not begin with our spoken words. Rather, we begin with the incarnate Word who is the source of life. It is not the abstract universal word or symbol that is absolute or peaceable, but the concrete, particular Word made flesh.

When the church reflects the Pentecost community, we will embrace plurality. We will have the freedom to use many languages.[48] We will understand when other languages are spoken, whether by an Asian feminist, a Palestinian church leader, a Chinese theologian, or Brazilian lay leader. It will mean that in the context of therapy, the African-American woman, the Scandinavian father from Minnesota, and the wealthy young New York lawyer will hear truth in a voice they can understand.[49] Miroslav Volf comments:

> The Lukan claim that "all" spoke contains a critical edge: even those who had no voice have been given a voice. Whereas the tower seeks to make people "not see" and "not speak" and sucks the energies out of the margins in order to stabilize and aggrandize the center, the Spirit pours energies into the margins, opens the eyes of small people to see what no one has seen before, puts the creative words of prophecy into their mouths, and empowers them to be the agents of God's reign. At Pentecost all receive a voice and all are allowed to sound it in their native language. The miracle of Pentecost consists in universal intelligibility and unhindered agency in the midst of social and cultural heterogeneity.[50]

The Pentecost account mirrors the issues addressed by Jesse Jackson at the APA. Fractiousness and exclusion threaten to disrupt human purposes in the Jerusalem of history and in the America of the present.

The Pentecost lesson is a model for a peaceable psychology. Ethnic and religious differences can be accommodated in a manner that anticipates the reconciliation and healing of persons in a suffering Christ. This is not, however, satisfactorily addressed as a function of diversity education for a context-free clinical environment. Pentecost upholds a peaceable psychology where differences are celebrated around God's purposes in and through God's people.

Not only in the account of Pentecost, but also in the work of Paul, there are cues to the way the Christian community can address the issue of multiculturalism. As a result of Pentecost a community of practices emerged. It was a community that appeared able to transcend differences. We know that both Greeks and Jews were members of the community. As a reflection of this communality, the early Christians sold their possessions. They ate together. A concrete historical community with ethnic diversity was created where God was worshipped, Christ was the center, and the Spirit was present. Such an ethnically diverse community, which reflects our Triune God, is the context from which we speak. It is a communal context which is limited neither by our differences nor denies them: Greek and Jew, male and female, master and slave, black and white, rich and poor, old and young.

The test of this new harmony appears in Acts 6 when Greek-speaking Jewish widows of the Diaspora are neglected in the distribution of food by the Aramaic-speaking Jews from Palestine—an example of ethnic exclusion entirely opposed to the Pentecost experience. The practice of sharing goods had broken down along ethnic lines: Hebrew and Hellenist. However, the disparity does not result in total incommensurability. The whole community gathered. What was enforced was not an abstract principle of justice. Instead, seven Hellenists were selected to oversee food distribution to the entire community.

The apostle Paul's mission was the reconciliation and empowerment of Jewish and Gentile communities. Not all would agree. Traditionally, Paul has been viewed as primarily focused on resolving the problem of guilt and sin, law and grace. Krister Stendahl's writing shifted the emphasis from personal salvation to social harmony.[51] He proposed that Paul's "conversion" experience was more a call to serve the fledgling Christian community than it was a resolution of guilt and a justification by personal faith (Gal. 1:13–16). That early church community was ethnically diverse and divided. Paul's response was pastoral. He affirmed each community. The Jewish community was to continue its social life bonded by dietary laws, circumcision, and observance of the Sabbath. The Gentile Christian community was affirmed in its uniqueness and not expected to follow the Jewish customs. J. D. G. Dunn comments:

> It was the attempt to enforce a uniform *Jewish* understanding of the gospel in *Gentile* Galatia which roused Paul to furious indignation. Integral to the freedom of the gospel is freedom to express it differently, with different emphases in different contexts.[52]

While affirming differentness, Paul did not absolutize each tradition. Each is relativized by the truth of the gospel (Gal. 2:14). John Barclay points out that Paul does not present the gospel "as if it carries a whole new cultural package, designed to eradicate and replace all others. . . . Commitment to Christ can simultaneously *encompass* various cultural particularities."[53]

The Pentecost account and Paul's ministry suggest that individuals and groups together are of inestimable value to God. With clients of different religious traditions, the Christian therapist who participates in a peaceable psychology will seek to recognize God's presence in the life of the client's community and learn her or his language of particularity. In so doing, the therapist empowers the client who would otherwise be marginalized by differences in translation, when linguistic and ideological particularities might result in exclusion. Where God is central to the clinician's purposes, we anticipate that the client will experience authentic healing that reveals God's purposes within that individual's context.

4

Secularese as Lingua Franca

■ ■ ■ ■ ■ ■ ■ ■ ■ ■

Secularization is not a zeitgeist but a process of conflict.

> Randall Collins, *The Sociology of Philosophies*

I had baptized the whole Christian tradition in the waters of psychological empiricism, and was vaguely awaking to the fact that, after this procedure, what I had left was hardly more than a moralistic ghost of the distinctive Christian reality. It was as if the baptismal waters of the empirical stream had been mixed with some acid which ate away the historical significance, the objectivity and the particularity of the Christian revelation, and left me in complete subjectivity to work out my own salvation in terms of social service and an "integrated personality."

> Charles Clayton Morrison, "How My Mind Has Changed"

In the West, English is spoken with a secular accent. The language dominating the public square and psychology is *secularese*. It is our lingua franca, the trade language of Western cultures. Secularese is the primary medium through which modern psychology is communicated, and the language spoken most often in psychotherapy. In the last chapter we critiqued the notion that the public square is a place where the only language to be used is one any other reasonable person can understand, and that local dialects should be left at home. In this chapter we extend that critique with the observation that secularism is the privileged public language and that it is precisely this dialect that marginalizes religious voices.

79

In an avowedly secular society one survives by learning to speak a language that reflects prevailing culture—secular discourse. Like any other language, secularese has a vocabulary, syntax, implicit meanings, and biases. If the language of secularity is spoken as one teaches or counsels, the next generation may well construct reality through the lens of that language. Fluency in secularese means that one may be able more effectively to negotiate secular culture. If one is never fluent in the lingua franca of secularity, one may well feel marginalized, misunderstood, or inferior. A society that speaks secularese unconsciously socializes its members into a reality consistent with its assumptions. Only if one can speak the language of the secular is one freely permitted to speak in public.

In this chapter we examine the nature of secularese in modern culture. But first, what do we mean by secularism? Definitions abound. We view secularism as a language and set of practices shorn clean of transcendence, which serves state power and which assumes the autonomy of the individual.[1] There was a time when "there was no 'secular,'"[2] but with the rise of the modern liberalism the religiosity of the medieval era was transferred to the emerging state.[3] Secularity is a paradigm where ordinary time is not qualified by a higher time.[4] As such, secularism is an imagined social project, a political revolution[5] in which traditional religion is no longer public but private. The meaning of history now lies outside the church. Religious practices are removed from public view. The university is pressed to serve this larger secularizing project, and religion becomes simply one more department among many. As the university serves a pluralistic, but increasingly less religious society, secularity becomes a social arrangement, a cultural vision. It is then a sui generis tradition.

Psychology as a discipline emerges in the modern university that shapes the modern state and secular society. The language (vocabulary and syntax) of therapy reflects then a culture that does not need the transcendent for psychological explanations. A discourse describing human behavior in terms of social forces, environmental reinforcement, significant introjections, splitting, archetypes, boundaries, behavior, systems, or hot cognitions seems to have no need for spiritual categories—much less a Creator God or a crucified Christ. The secular psyche stands on its own. A psychology that has no place for the language of evil will focus on "dysfunctionality" or "pathology" in diagnosis and treatment. If secularity has no room for transcendence, then spiritual yearning will hardly be recognized, much less legitimated. It may even be pathologized. Psychotherapy in secular society socializes its clientele into language of secularese. It is not a neutral enterprise; it serves a secular culture. Psychology as a science exists as a secular discipline in the same way that secular society has no need that "the church exist as an alternative to the state."[6]

Is the integration of religion and psychology really only a matter of adding a religious vocabulary to secular discourse? Adding religion to psychotherapy is not simply a matter of replacing what is missing in secularism. Secular psychology and a Christian psychology may well have different cultural visions. A psychology that presumes to be Christian envisions a Christian culture as its goal and is constructed on the confession of the early church and its evolving tradition.[7] Granted, a Christian psychologist will know how to speak this language fluently, but she or he is not monolingual. A peaceable psychology is committed to recovering the local dialects of ethnicity and religion.

A Secular Society

Most commonly, secularism is defined as a set of beliefs and practices that exclude religious discourse. The separation of the religious and the secular is a thoroughly modern phenomenon. Neither time nor space was secularized in medieval civilization:

> The medieval period is generally regarded as one of outstanding achievement in the history of religion. It is looked upon as an age of universal faith, when western Christendom flourished, secure in its beliefs and united under the authority of the supra-national papacy. An age in which long strides were taken in the outward organization of the Church into provinces, dioceses, and parishes; one which raised awe-inspiring cathedrals, monasteries and many parish churches, still surviving among us as monuments to the beliefs and aspirations of medieval men and women. An age which witnessed the creation of an ordered body of Canon Law and its general acceptance and enforcement; and which saw the construction of a superb intellectual synthesis combining the testimony of faith and reason and the enthronement of theology as the queen of all knowledge. An age when the Church dominated the content and conduct of education in the universities, grammar schools and other institutions. An age which looked to the Church as the creatrix and nurse of the crowning achievements of art and civilization.[8]

We make this comparison not to rehabilitate medieval history as the gilded era of Christian culture, but rather to point out that the emergence of secularity is hardly inevitable, that actual historical and cultural processes make for a secularist context that many contemporaries take for granted.

When the government is secular, it is run neither by the pope nor by the imam. Education, health-care institutions, and the helping professions tend to reflect the pluralism of the culture and thus assume a position of neutrality toward any particular religious community. Public education cannot be sectarian if students come from Lutheran, Unitarian, Muslim, or nonreligious homes; prayer to the God of one religion is not permitted. Prisons are run by the state to contain the violent perpetrator; they are not the places of penitence Quakers had once imagined. In secular cultures, individuals engage in religious talk in the home or synagogue, but less, or not at all, in public. Professions are accountable to state-run regulatory boards, not religious bodies. Textbooks for social workers and psychologists are written in the generic manner of secularese to help the reader understand any of the citizens in this society regardless of ethnic or religious origin.

Secularism is a shift in beliefs and practices. Charles Taylor suggests secularism was a way of finding the lowest common denominator among conflicting religious groups and an attempt to define a political ethic independent of religious particularity.[9] There is empirical evidence to support the assumption that the West is increasingly secular, and it is assumed that as other nations modernize they too will become secular. Brierley presents the following as evidence from England:[10]

- Church attendance dropped from 3.9 million in 1979 to 2.4 million in 1999.
- Church membership dropped from 27% of the population in 1900 to 10% in 2000.
- Sunday school attendance dropped from 55% of the population in 1900 to 4% in 2000.
- The percentage of professional clerics dropped 25% in the last century.
- In the Anglican Church 67% of all weddings were performed in the church in 1900, but 20% in 2000.
- Belief in God dropped from 43% in the 1940s to 26% in 2000.

What is the pattern for the United States? The US is viewed as an anomaly: a presumably secular state with a religious populace. Through the past century church attendance has consistently hovered around 40 percent.[11] (However, if all who say they attended church actually attended, churches would be bursting at the seams!) Nonetheless, there are some trends toward increasing secularity. If people are asked how their church attendance has changed, the percent saying "less frequently" is greater than those who say "more frequently."[12] Notions of the Bible as literally true dropped from 65 percent in 1964 to 37 percent in 1984.[13]

A similar picture emerges for professionals in the US. In a 1969 survey, 43 percent of physical scientists attended church, while 38 percent of economists, 20 percent of psychologists, and 15 percent of anthropologists did so.[14] In a 2006 study conducted by Neil Gross and Solon Simmons, and reported in *Inside Higher Education*, professors at elite doctoral programs are most likely to be atheist or agnostic (37%) and, in general, psychology and biology professors are least likely to believe in God (61% atheist or agnostic).[15] They also found that 26 percent of the college-educated population believed that the Bible was an "an ancient book of fables, legends, history, and moral precepts," compared with 52 percent of college professors who agreed with this statement.[16]

Secularity as Tradition

Secularism is not simply the absence of religion, as described above; it is a tradition in its own right, an evangelical, social project. Democratic liberalism is an imaginative invention that emerged from, and was legitimated by, the nation-state, the rise of science, industrialism, urbanism, capitalism, and pluralism. The lingua franca of this tradition is secularese. As an ideology, it is not simply the loss of religiosity; it is the rise of an alternative ideology with its own history, tradition, and discourse. Secularism serves the liberal ideology that emerged out of the Enlightenment and is enshrined in Western political and institutional arrangements.

Secularism as a political doctrine emerged in modern Europe and redefined the meaning of religion, ethics, and politics. A tradition labeled as secular focuses on the rights of individuals; it is uncomfortable with the use of local dialects in public and is biased toward universalizable knowledge. It embraces a particular ontology and epistemology. Contrary to its own self-perception, liberalism and its secularist language did not emerge out of nowhere. It is a result of decisions made in history that resulted in a set of practices and beliefs that constitute a tradition.[17] Secularism allows for any conception of the good except when that involves reshaping the rest of society in accordance with this ideal of the good. Human goods are now preferences that are defended in public in nontraditioned, that is, secular, ways. Liberalism is then a social project, and the normative language is secularese.

The proponents of modern secularism are not as neutral as they assume. They hope that individuals will learn to speak the language of secularity in public. As a culture secularism possesses a socially constructed narrative, unique rituals, and powerful symbols. It is the narrative of the Constitution, the ritual of town hall meeting, and the prominence of the flag as symbol in the post office. Secularity is a tradition just as a religion is a tradition. Each has a narrative to explain its respective history and convictions, and each of them couched in a unique language with a distinct grammar.[18] The religious and the secular are a learned variety of behaviors, concepts, practices, and sensibilities. And, we will argue later, each constructs a view of the other.

Sociology and much of the current psychology of religion accepted a view of seventeenth-century Christianity which was privatized, spiritualized, and transcendentalized, and which concurrently imagined nature, human nature, and society as autonomous. John Milbank argues that secularism invented nature, the state, and private religion.[19] The genesis of a discourse is intertwined with the genesis of a new practice, and secular social theory only applies to the secular society which it helps to sustain. We do not view the story of the West as simply the emergence of secularization, but as the rise of two divergent traditions, secularity and religion, that came to exclude each other.

Secularity and Christianity are not only two traditions, they are *competing* social projects with different cultural aims and practices. While the former is a product of modernity, Christianity emerges from the ancient world. Secularization is the displacement of Christendom with another tradition—democratic liberalism. The emperor Constantine had assumed that an entire culture could be Christianized and that its character should be legislated by the power of the state. The relativization of Christian Constantinianism by the secular tradition we affirm. Religious groups such as the Anabaptists viewed with suspicion the Constantinian marriage of religion, culture, and power. However, secular Constantinianism is not as pluralist or as peaceable as it presumes.

So then, secularism is not simply the process of desacralization such that when the superfluous religious element is removed we have the residue of the human, the natural, and the self-sufficient. No, what we have are two traditions. The secular therapist is then no less neutral than the religious therapist. Both are capable of imposing values, a worldview, and a set of practices.

The Hegemony of Secularese

In contrast to the view of competing traditions is the view of secularism as a tradition that develops sui generis. Steve Bruce's sociohistorical explanation of secularism as resulting from a range of social forces is typical.[20] The narrative usually begins with the Reformation. Catholicism, with its centralized authority, was able to control schism, but Protestantism allowed the individual freedom to choose faith unmediated by the church. This contributed to the rise of individualism, where faith is individual and private, rather than political or public. Capitalism and economic growth encouraged the process of secularization, in that personal means obviated the need for divine provision. With increased wealth, some prohibitions (divorce, drinking) were relaxed. Other forces such as social differentiation also supported secularization. Older religious societies were hierarchical, juxtaposing peasant with king or parishioner with pope. Newly discovered social mobility meant that individuals could move up the social ladder, relativizing authority, even though an older culture with a unified moral universe required that people know their place. In a secular culture, social groups developed religious views more suited to their interests.

Structural differentiation meant, in the standard sociological account, that the development of specialized roles of work were separated from the home. Work became rationalized and pragmatic. Health care, education, and social welfare, once controlled by the church, shifted to a cadre of specially trained professionals. The pastor became a trained professional, and the priest was transformed into a psychologist. Now the therapist is accountable to the state—

not to the church—and functions with secular, universalizable values. Spiritual values may inspire people to become professional helpers, but in a secular society these values are the not the substance of healing.

Secularist ideology, it is argued, emerged as a result of cultural diversity, with its attendant issues of pluralism and relativism. This occurred as social groups immigrated to the New World and modernity created new social classes. In modern secular society we live and move in different worlds. Given this social diversity, the public square is increasingly expected to be neutral—less religious and parochial. Such cultural diversity makes a religious government impossible. The church is marginalized in relationship to the critical political concerns of society. With pluralism also comes competing ideological systems that weaken the power of a single voice, once each voice is treated equally. Relativism means that there is no single truth, but many truths. Moreover, multiple truths are equally acceptable, true, or right. When the secular nation-state garners more loyalty than the local church and its religious commitments, secularism increases. The neutral secular state takes over when religion fragments into warring factions.[21]

Science is usually considered to be the primary engine driving secularity. It functions autonomously and eschews religious explanations. Science is so powerful, so salient, that it displaces religion. It possesses the near-total authority once possessed by the medieval church. As nature has been proven to be rule-governed, the need for religious explanations has abated. God is then called upon to explain what science cannot, a "God of the gaps." The material world as an amoral series of invariant relationships of cause and effect makes us less likely than our forebears to entertain the notion of the divine.[22] Bruce, however, argues that science in itself may not cause secularism and loss of faith as an alternate system of beliefs. What may undermine faith instead is the implicit logic of secularese. Religion is compartmentalized and made an addendum.

Technology and technological consciousness also drive secularity. Technology reduces the occasions when which one need rely on religion. We pray less for health if we know there is a medication for illness. We pray less for wisdom if we can predict occupational success based on a battery of psychological tests. Technological consciousness, according to Jacques Ellul, includes componentiality, linearity, cause and effect, pragmatism, and reproducibility.[23] We can master the universe by calculation.

This is the standard story of how secularity emerged to replace religion, how we were freed from religious provinciality, and how the state freed us from religious violence. Consistent with its own internal logic, there is a determinist element in the narrative. Many sociologists who authored this narrative assumed that secularization was a necessary part of modernization and that as the world modernized, it would automatically secularize. The secularization hypothesis is that in time secularity will naturally triumph. Eventually, Iranian mullahs, Latin Pentecostal preachers, and Tibetan lamas would all think and act like professors of political science, philosophy, psychology, or literature in Western universities.

Christian Smith has argued an alternative thesis. Secularization "of American public life was in fact something much more like a contested revolutionary struggle than a natural evolutionary progression."[24] This revolution replaced the Protestant establishment of the nineteenth century with what we now know as a secular society. He states:

> Thinking through the revolution analogy in the American context, we should understand the overthrown regime in this secular revolution as what we commonly think of as the nineteenth century's mainline Protestant establishment. The rebel insurgency consisted of waves of networks of activists who were largely skeptical, freethinking, agnostic, atheist, or theologically liberal; who were well educated and socially located mainly in knowledge-production occupations; and who generally espoused materialism, naturalism, positivism, and the privatization or extinction of religion. They were motivated by a complex mix of antipathy toward the Protestant establishment's exclusivity and perceived outdatedness; by their own quasi-religious visions of secular progress, prosperity, and higher civilization; and often by the material gain that secularization promised them, for example, with the professionalization of a field that seemed to require the exclusion of religion. In different times, places, and ways, these insurgents enjoyed limited alliances with activist Protestant liberals and certain other excluded religious groups, including Roman Catholics, Mormons, Adventists, and separationist Baptists. As with most successful political insurgencies, the secular revolution was decisively abetted by a complex of distracting and debilitating internal divisions within mainline Protestantism and by other unintentionally facilitating structural forces and historical events, such as expanding capitalism, state expansion, and so on. It was also aided by the intellectually thin character of mainstream nineteenth-century Protestantism, which tended to emphasize populist common sense, subjective experience, and mass-based emotional revivalism and so failed to develop a defensible theological approach to knowledge and society that could withstand the attacks of elite challengers in the late nineteenth and early twentieth centuries.[25]

Smith argues that the secularization of American public life can be thought of as a revolution because before the revolution there existed an established Protestant regime that sought to homogenize, that is, to protestantize Catholics, Jews, and others. First, the institutional privilege of this regime provoked increasing grievances among excluded groups. Second, the aggrieved groups sought to depose the established group from control. Third, the insurgent activists overthrew the established regime. Fourth, in the shift from the old to the new regime a profound cultural revolution occurred which transformed cultural structures of thought and practices. We believe these shifts to be most evident in the university, and they further support Smith's argument.

The University as Temple of Secularity

In the university the language of secularese is spoken, taught, and assumed. In academic forums religious perspectives are largely ignored, disparaged, or suppressed. In contrast to the received academic narrative that secularism will triumph, Peter Berger maintains that religion is alive and well in the world.[26] However, he suggests that the one major exception to the desecularization hypothesis is academic culture:

> There exists an international subculture composed of people with Western-type higher education, especially in the humanities and social sciences, that is indeed secularized. This subculture is the principal "carrier" of progressive, Enlightened beliefs and values. While its members are relatively thin on the ground, they are very influential, as they control the institutions that provide the "official" definitions of reality, notably the educational system, the media of mass communication, and the higher reaches of the legal system. They are remarkably similar all over the world today, as they have been for a long time (though, as we have seen, there are also defectors from this subculture, especially in the Muslim countries). Again, regrettably, I cannot speculate here as to why people with this type of education should be so prone to secularization. I can only point out that what we have here is a globalized *elite* culture.[27]

This contrasts sharply with the picture usually drawn of the nineteenth century, where university education was a function of the church. The sixteenth-century Reformation resulted from the insight of a scholar, and for the next three centuries the religiously oriented university trained leaders for the church and society—that is, Christendom. In this country, until the beginning of the twentieth century, college presidents tended to be clergy, the religion was Protestant Christianity, and the curriculum included the Protestant scriptures. Academics were expected to be practicing church members, and chapel attendance was mandatory for students. At Duke University, a massive Gothic chapel stands at the center of the campus, and in 1924 the bylaws stated: "The aims of Duke University are to assert a faith in the eternal union of knowledge and religion set forth in the teachings and character of Jesus Christ, the Son of God."[28] The dominant language in the academy was the language of the Christian community.

In a sweeping study of the American university, George Marsden chronicles the shift from the beginning of the last century, when religion shaped the university, to a time when religion was marginalized. The title of his book states it well: *The Soul of the American University: From Protestant Establishment to Established Nonbelief.*[29] By the end of the twentieth century, most major Protestant universities were no longer religious. Ties to religious denominations were dropped. In fact, Marsden argues, the religious dimensions of scholarship are currently suppressed, and nonreligious perspectives are privileged. The dominant language of academic exchange is secularese.

Changes in the ethos of university education from religious to secular were striking. Religious service was translated into public service. Theology became moral philosophy or moral psychology. Scientific-research findings replaced dogma. Academic freedom for faculty became more important than adherence to confessions or creeds. Competence in a profession superseded Christian character. When the society which sponsors the educational institutions values scientific knowledge, then courses are taught from that perspective, rather than from the perspective of classical philosophers or theologians. As the professions set standards for the education of their members, universities followed suit and provided more specially trained professionals. In the end, religion was irrelevant. Marsden comments:

> Despite the presence of many religion departments and a few university divinity schools, religion has moved from near the center a century or so ago to the incidental periphery. Apart from voluntary student religious groups, religion in most universities is about as important as the baseball team.[30]

In the past century and a half, the purpose of the university and the nature of the broader society changed dramatically. Presidents in the previous century assumed that the university served society, but society was presumed to be Christian. With the influx of immigrants in the early 1900s, and the recognition of the kaleidoscopic nature of American culture, such cultural homogeneity was no longer conceivable, and such religious control no longer possible. In a pluralist culture it seemed the only options for institutions of higher education were to become either universal or sectarian. The religious observances and ethic of any one religious particularity could not be made normative for all. University education became a vehicle for creating a national, nonsectarian culture. It was hoped that a unified and universal science would provide the basis for a united society, and that the university would provide the leadership for such a vision. It was assumed that the methodology of the scientific disciplines required the suspension of religious beliefs. The knowledge a pluralist culture called for was more general, less constrained, more technical—in other words, more secular.

Religion in the secular university is not only considered irrelevant; it is explicitly excluded from the classroom. If religion was included, it was either as part of the humanities or as a product of social-science research, each with their own arcane methodologies and vocabularies. Should faculty have religious convictions, it was assumed that they would keep these to themselves. Strangely, while this rule may not be applied to a feminist or a Buddhist, it is consistently applied to traditional Protestant and Catholic scholars. Traditional Christianity became a toothless counterpoint to the secularization of the university or the professions. The Protestant cultural establishment has been replaced by a dogmatic secularism.

Secularism was not just the result of aggressive secular academics and philanthropists. The crowning of secularese as the lingua franca of the classroom in part resulted from actions by Protestants themselves who capitulated to the onslaught of secularity. It was a voluntary abandonment of the educational enterprise by Protestant leaders. Changes which took place in the university over the last century were condoned by liberal Protestant leaders on the grounds that traditional Christian beliefs were nonscientific. The pursuit of scientific truth advanced the culture, and hence the kingdom of God. Scientific rationalism and naturalism were given free reign on the assumption that they would not contradict religious truth but complement it.

In retrospect, it appears that leaders in the Protestant world widely underestimated the power of secularism fueled by naturalistic and materialistic worldviews. Most, Marsden points out, thought the changes they were making to accommodate the changing social situation would strengthen Christianity's contribution to American society. Liberal Protestantism's approach to maintaining the "Christian" influence in the university was to allow the sciences and the professions to define what was taught at the university, and to let higher religious truths be added as an option. However, for many colleges, once this separation was made, the religious heritage lost its power and was eventually dropped. In the end, Christianity and American culture were not identical—and liberal Protestantism during this century responded to this problem not by sharpening but by blurring its identity. Accommodation, rather than prophetic critique or careful discernment, led to the cultural hegemony of an established secularity.

The creation of a democratic, pluralist national culture served to undermine the Christian voice in the academy. While Protestantism may have been the social glue in an earlier era, it could not serve that function from any position of power in a pluralist society. This we affirm—the loss of Protestant hegemony and emergent pluralism of the university we do not view as entirely pejorative. It reflects the demise of the Constantinian synthesis of church and power. However, that religions are not given a voice in the academy is a concern. Now the collusion of naturalism and political power is strong enough to marginalize the religious voice in the academy.

Finally, the question must be raised whether the university was able to fulfill its objective to provide a basis for unified culture with scientifically grounded knowledge. Is a neutral, objective science truly possible? Does intellectual inquiry not take place in the context of communities that shape prior commitments? While it may be the case that naturalism provides the best account of certain realities, it is impossible to demonstrate that this is the case for all contingencies. There are no logical grounds for excluding other perspectives, religious or cultural. Marsden states:

> Today, however, the idea of such objective science no longer seems viable and many critics have pointed out the community-relative character of moral ideals,

including those that limit academic freedom. In the present context it seems much more plausible to view all ideals for the social good as sectarian and the sciences that serve those ideals as equally so. There is little basis for sustaining the illusion that "academic freedom" is part and parcel of an open-minded scientific search for truth that ought to exclude the substantial influence of all religious viewpoints.[31]

The truly open university is truer to its commitment to pluralism and the needs of a pluralist society when a wide range of perspectives is encouraged. However, an establishmentarian mentality prevails. The dominance of nineteenth-century Protestantism is replaced by a secular Constantinianism.

Juanita and Her Psychologist

Before we explore the impact of secularity on the discipline of psychology and the practice of psychotherapy, we will create a therapist for Juanita. Dr. Davidson is a product of the modern secular university. A counselor at the school where her children attend referred Juanita for therapy. She presented to her therapist, Dr. Davidson, as quite depressed. She had shared how difficult the children were and how sad she felt. She reported that she often felt homesick and overwhelmed with parenting and work. She also told of recurring nightmares in which she saw people falling down in cornfields. When Dr. Davidson asked her to talk about her childhood, she said that she grew up with parents who loved her and whom she loved in return. She described her home as a loving home filled with happiness and joy. Her parents were evangelical Christians whose lives were immersed in the church. It was in the purple church with the loudspeakers that Juanita had "gone forward."

The therapist, Dr. Davidson, is a forty-five-year-old white male who grew up in an urban setting, was trained as a clinical psychologist at an American research university, and enjoys hiking and reading novels in his non-working hours. He stated in his tax report for the past year that his income was $127,000. He is married and has two children, ages twelve and fourteen. Both are in private schools and doing well academically. His wife is a lawyer with a local firm.

Dr. Davidson was trained in short-term therapy, and since his work is primarily with clients referred from health-maintenance organizations, the number of sessions is limited. His approach with Juanita was to introduce her to democratic models of parenting, to use cognitive restructuring to address the depression, and to describe stress management techniques. He provided her with literature in Spanish, which summarized in lay terms the meaning of depression and what seems to help alleviate the depression based on current research. He suggested she keep a journal of depressive thoughts.

Since Juanita indicated she had a religious background, and because the research literature indicated a connection between spirituality and mental health, Dr. Davidson encouraged spiritual coping strategies. Juanita was pleased, but his language did not sound remotely Pentecostal. Juanita obediently completed four sessions but did not return for further counseling. She indicated that the counselor was kind and gentle. However, she reported that what he said just did not ring true. It was not that she thought he was wrong, but that she simply could not connect with his suggestions regarding stress, parenting, and inner talk. She felt that the therapist was not really like a pastor and that the suggestions he made were more techniques than convictions.

The Secular Psyche

Dr. Davidson's therapeutic approach reflects his culture. Any discipline, whether American literature or social science, cannot evade the influence of the cultural ethos. The metaphysical assumptions, treatment modalities, epistemological commitments, research methods, and subjects studied are all affected by whether the target culture is religious or secular. A contemporary textbook of psychology does not spring *de novo* from the mind of its author. It is a product of the historical developments of the past half millennium. Western psychology is a product of secularizing historical developments: the Renaissance and the Enlightenment, the Industrial Revolution and American capitalism. As a secular discipline, psychology is tailor-made for a secular society.

Reflecting the larger political context, secular psychology perceives the individual as possessing rights, knowledge as universal and derived from consensual validation, and the public square as religiously neutral. The discursive move in the nineteenth century from thinking of a fixed "human nature" to regarding humans in terms of a constituted "normality" facilitated the secular idea of moral progress as defined and directed by autonomous human agency. It should come as no surprise that secular psychology reflects the needs of a pluralist, capitalist, technological, and ideologically fragmented society.

What process of thinking leads to a secularity capable of constructing an entirely new discourse in secularese? The secular psyche, like the secular state and economy, is a product of imagination. In the modern world the inner self is the locus of religion (i.e., privatized religion). The individual could be constructed as self-contained in something called Nature, which too is autonomous. Natural laws governing the individual override any transcendental/spiritual sources of motivation. It is with little difficulty that we speak of the natural psychological forces that shape individual personality formation. In the medieval world this was impossible. There the individual was seen as participating in a world God created, not as an extension of autonomous Nature where the individual is the maker of his or her destiny. Today our life course is a result of individual decisions made in the context of Nature and society, both secular. Autonomous Nature has replaced a created universe. Nature has its own laws. Such knowledge, carefully collected and tested, is as certain as any heavenly truths.

The hegemony of the secular is apparent in the language psychologists use to write case summaries. When we write a case summary it is shorn clean of particularity, both ethnic and religious. Our summaries unwittingly affirm the deeper naturalistic assumptions of the secular milieu, a world devoid of divine immanence or agency. Here is an example:

> Results of this assessment show that Ms. Smith displays many of the defining characteristics of borderline personality disorder: She shows a pattern of unstable and intense interpersonal relationships, inappropriate and unpredictable anger, identity disturbance, and affective instability. Other defining characteristics of borderline personality disorder (impulsivity in self-damaging behaviors, physically self-damaging acts, and chronic feelings of emptiness or boredom) were not observed or reported during this assessment, but may be present. The answer, then, to the question as to whether Ms. Smith might appropriately be termed borderline is a tentative "yes."
>
> Alternatively, but not mutually exclusive, aspects of her personality function to consider are her history of marriage to an abusive alcoholic husband. Her ongoing attachment to an abusive man presents the possibility of dependent features in her personality functioning, and the types of difficulties she experiences in relationships with others suggest passive-aggressive behaviors.
>
> All of these can coexist within the general rubric of borderline personality disorder; mixed features within a disorder are quite common, and it seems most likely that this is, in fact, what Ms. Smith presents. Additional information that emerged from this assessment may be useful in working with Ms. Smith. Assessment of her general intellectual function indicates that she probably functions in the borderline range of general intellectual ability (WAIS-R Verbal IQ = 82; Performance IQ = 84; Full Scale IQ = 82). This level of ability implies that Ms. Smith may not be able to adapt in problematic life situations as easily as might higher-functioning persons. It also has implications for therapeutic strategy because it is unlikely that she will respond to verbal psychotherapy as readily or as positively as might a person who was functioning at higher levels in the verbal domain. This is not to say that verbal therapy with Ms. Smith is useless, but it does suggest that in working with her, vocabulary might be kept simple and that techniques that have concrete and observable aspects (such as behavioral self-recording) might be most successful with her. . . .
>
> Ms. Smith's responses to the Beck Depression Inventory suggest the presence of severe depression. In the context of her overall personality structure, a history of suicidal attempts is likely, though not reported in referring her. If such a history has not been elicited, it is recommended that this issue be clarified with Ms. Smith. If antidepressant medications are used in the treatment of Ms. Smith, repeated administrations of the BDI could be helpful in charting the course of

her response to medication and psychotherapy. Such repeat administrations could be accomplished easily by her staff therapist, if desired.

Results of this assessment suggest that Ms. Smith presents many features of borderline personality disorder accompanied by dependent and passive-aggressive features. She indicates that she is extremely agitated and depressed at the present time; such extreme psychological disturbance may account for the reality testing difficulties noted. The possibility of a history of suicide attempts or overt psychotic symptomatology should be investigated if these issues have not been clarified already.[32]

Note the language of this report. It is a genre unique to secular mental-health culture. We are not told what culture Ms. Smith identifies with or how it has influenced her behavior. The self is assumed to be an autonomous agent influenced by a variety of social, biological, and psychological forces. There is no evidence that Ms. Smith has ever been part of a religious community or whether she practices spiritual disciplines. There is no mention of traditioned religious resources Ms. Smith might possess.

The Religious Psyche in Secular Psychology

In the past century, secular psychology as a discipline has been shaped not by religious institutions but by the secular university. In 1901 William James could still make a case,[33] in the Gifford Lectures, for the relevance of a variety of religious experiences; but contemporary departments of psychology are not constructed on the vision of this early psychologist.[34] With the disestablishment of religion in the university, a religiously informed psychology was replaced with a secular psychology.

We have argued above that a major shift occurs in the ethos of the educational institution with the change in which public is served. The university serves the larger public, while church-related educational institutions serve primarily the Christian community. Which public will be served in the psychology we create? Will it be the Christian community or larger society? If the latter is more important, then the language and content of the curriculum shifts to meet the needs of this society.

The magnitude of the shift from a religious psyche to a secular one is considerable. Introductory psychology textbooks represent a good vantage point from which to weigh the impact of secularese as a narrative reflecting the secular ideology required by a liberal state. Elizabeth Lehr and Bernard Spilka examined forty-eight introductory psychology textbooks published in the 1980s for religious content and compared them with two hundred texts from the 1950s and 1970s.[35] There was a major increase in religious-related material observed for 1980s texts compared with 1970s texts. However, the number of citations and citation lengths were reduced in 1980s texts. Later citations were primarily of a nonresearch nature. Although evaluation of the religious material by text authors was unbiased, the main examples chosen tended to present religion in a negative light. Research on the psychology of religion, a field with a hundred years of publications, was rarely present.

A further example comes from recent analyses of the work of Gordon Allport. Raised in a religious setting, he began his career sensitive to religious issues. His book *The Individual and His Religion* is considered a classic.[36] However, it was also Allport who rejected the morally freighted language of "character" and preferred the neutral language of "personality" to describe the individual.[37]

The argument we wish to make is not simply that religion is ignored in contemporary psychologies but that there is a shift in discourse, an implicit alteration of meaning. As a case in point, our understanding of pain has been secularized. No longer is pain viewed as a punishment of God but rather as a consequence of the laws of nature. Asad comments that more than metaphorical substitution took place; it was a grammatical change in the concept of pain.[38] The discourse of sin and punishment was set aside in favor of a new discourse where pain was objectified and set within a framework of a mechanistic view of nature. This change lay precisely in the fact that (for the physician) the problematical question of pain could be placed outside the problem of sin, evil, and punishment. What occurred not only abandons transcendental language but also shifts to a new language of external stimulus and the experience of pain.[39]

The discourse of the secular self is that of an agent, capable of initiating action. All external power signifies a potential threat to this autonomy. So we are then either agents or victims. To suffer is then to be in a passive state. Pain is seen as passive rather than as embedded in modes of relationship. In the secular model pain is always to be eliminated. But pain is expressed in some way, and the manner by which it is expressed is dependent on relationships. Openness to pain as suffering is precisely part of the structure of agency for Christians. Otherwise, how could one then voluntarily sacrifice oneself for another?[40]

The notion of sincerity also takes on different meaning in the secular self. Asad points out:

> For not only was the idea to be true to oneself construed as a moral duty, it also presupposed the existence of a secular self whose sovereignty could be demonstrated through acts of sincerity. The self's secularity consisted in the fact that it was the precondition of transcendent (poetic or religious) experience and not its product.[41]

It is no small irony that twentieth-century shifts in psychology to the discourse of secularese were closely associated with Protestantism. Keith Meador points to the influence of liberal Protestants such as Charles Clayton Morrison, whose 1908 purchase of the *Christian Century* served as a catalyst for a "therapeutic" gospel that resembled the psychological wisdom of the day.[42] Meador suggests that psychology came to "renarratize" Protestant theology toward a functional study of human nature and behavior. This process included wholesale alignment with the works of Dewey, Freud, Hall, and James. In the case of the latter, religion was effectively fused with psychological inquiry. Matters of salvation became reordered in James to identify the self as the preeminent, autonomous basis for esteem and growth. This became the genesis of self-help literature that, in the name of applied psychology, came to replace theological vocabulary with definitions given to a newly construed scientific psyche. Psychological religion became influential through publications such as the *Christian Century*.

The religion most acceptable to the secular state is one that is most compatible with secularity. From the perspective of thoroughly modern disciplines such as sociology and psychology, religious experience is understood to result from social and psychological processes, rather than transcendent influence or the model of a sacral figure. From a social-scientific perspective, religion is measured in terms of attendance at religious services and the subjective significance of one's religion. Such a view of religion is compatible with a secular state: it is neutral and passive. Some might say it has been domesticated.

Is Secular Psychology Peaceable?

Our hope in this book is to delineate a peaceable psychology. Is secularism, on which modern psychology builds, peaceable? Both secularism and Christianity are faith traditions that claim to be peaceable. In fact, liberal secularism claims to be more peaceable than the religions that wage war in the name of God. The defining event for secularists is the religious war between Protestants and Catholics (1618–1648). Democratic liberalism was to transcend tradition and avoid conflict between traditions. In the subsequent centuries, religious wars have continued between Irish Catholics and Protestants, Jews and Muslims. Religion is then construed as passionate, irrational, and violent. One task of the religionless nation-state is to contain religious fanaticism.

John Milbank argues that secular theories are complicit with an "ontology of violence." That is, secular social theories assume that force is best dealt with by counterforce and that this notion is deeply rooted in Western societies. He does not think secular reason can contain violence. Muslims in a post-9/11 world are accused of being violent, of not embracing secularism, of not entering modernity.[43] Liberal violence is the violence of universalizing secular reason itself. It claims the right to use violence to redeem the world from violence. Liberal politics is constructed on cultural consensus and aims at human agreement. If reason fails, then one must use force. Asad observes:

> In secular redemptive politics there is no place for the idea of a redeemer saving sinners through *his* submission to suffering. And there is no place for a theology of evil by which different kinds of suffering are identified. ("Evil" is simply the superlative form of what is bad and shocking.) Instead there is a readiness to cause pain to those who are to be saved by being humanized. It is not merely that the object of violence is different; it is that the secular myth uses the element of violence to connect an optimistic project of universal empowerment with a pessimistic account of human motivation in which inertia and incorrigibility figure prominently. If the world is a dark place that needs redemption, the human redeemer, as an inhabitant of *this world,* must first redeem himself. That the worldly project of redemption requires self-redemption means that the jungle is after all in the gardener's own soul. Thus the structure of this secular myth differs from the one articulating the story of redemption through Christ's sacrifice, a difference that the use of the term "sacred" for both of them may obscure. Each of the two structures that I touch on here articulates different kinds of subjectivity, mobilizes different kinds of social activity, and invokes different modalities of time.[44]

Is secularism as a project able to contain violence better than ostensibly divisive religions? The secular state assumes it can guarantee toleration and eliminate violence. Secularism, we are told, is inherently peaceful. A religiously neutral state can contain violence. But how is secularism to advance its cause and communicate its message? Peacefully, one would presume. The track record of democratic liberalism, however, suggests otherwise. Constantinian secularism is not peaceable.

Given the secularizing influence described above, there are a number of possible consequences for Western psychology: (a) religion as an object of study for psychologists tends largely to focus on individual private beliefs and experiences, (b) the psychology that emerges must be understandable to any reasonable inquirer regardless of religious or ethnic tradition, and (c) clients learn to speak secularese in therapy at the behest of therapists trained in a medical model of treatment. By contrast, we argue that the therapist who responds to the religiosity of his or her clients is not engaging in an act of imposition, but in one of respect. It is possible for both secularist and religionist to impose their values on the client—whether the issue is hearing the voice of God, religious commandments, or spiritual language, on the one hand; or abortion, divorce, or homosexuality, on the other. A peaceable psychology is one that begins with the client's tradition and determines collaboratively how the tradition is problematic as well as a gift.

Hezekiah's Wall

The tension between secularese and religious particularity plays itself out on an ancient city wall. Returning again to the biblical narrative, we are in the Middle East during the time of the Jewish kings (2 Kings 18 and 19). Hezekiah, a good man and descendant of David, is now king of Judah, the southern of Israel's two kingdoms. Much of the Middle East is occupied by Assyria, an imperial and militaristic empire that dominates regional affairs. Long worried by the Assyrian threat, Hezekiah has managed to avoid direct confrontation with the enemy by giving away the gold adornments of the royal palace and the Jewish temple. But now the inevitable is upon him—Jerusalem is targeted for invasion and conquest.

The Assyrians place the city under siege. After months of severe hardship, Hezekiah finds himself involved in two conversations: one behind the city wall, and the other taking place directly on it.[45] The first conversation is particular to the Jewish community; the second crosses the boundary of ethnicity and religion. The conversation behind the wall takes place in Hebrew, a particular language spoken by a people with a different agenda. The conversation on the wall is in Aramaic, the lingua franca of those in power. The Hebrews honor God and doubt the power of the Assyrian empire. The secular Assyrians question God's existence and assert the universality of their empire.

The Assyrian king sends his field commander to engage in psychological warfare, delivering a stream of propaganda that is audible to the entire city. Speaking in Hebrew on the city wall, the commander openly questions the Judean people about the presence and loyalty of the Lord God. He mocks Hezekiah's deference to the divine, his alliance with Egypt, and his legacy of patronage with Assyria. The commander's purpose is to weaken morale, to force a settlement, and to free up the Assyrian army holding Jerusalem captive to be able to go to other, more profitable fields of battle.

In response to the commander, Hezekiah sends his palace administrator, Eliakim, and several political dilettantes onto the city wall to negotiate with the Assyrians. In Hebrew, the Assyrian field commander loudly warns the entire city to choose life rather than death, for the Assyrian victory is assured. Eliakim pleads with the commander to speak in Aramaic, the international language of diplomacy, so that the conversations can remain confidential between two powers, effectively removed from the people. The commander dismisses the request and resumes speaking in Hebrew.

Eliakim reports the conversation on the wall to Hezekiah. Behind the wall in the temple, Hezekiah tears his clothes and puts on sackcloth. In Hebrew he calls for the prophet Isaiah, who in turn gives an oracle promising that Judah will not fall to the enemy, and in fact it will be Assyria that will suffer defeat. Hezekiah finds himself embroiled in a conflict that involves categorically different levels of discourse. On the wall is a politicized exchange between enemies. The venue is public; the conversation is devoid of religious tolerance. Potent religious and moral meaning in the Hebrew dialect becomes a weapon to discourage the people and open the way for colonization in the trade language of the Assyrians (Aramaic). Behind the wall is an impassioned, vital exploration of faith that includes the most intimate levels of communication, shared weakness, and revelation. Hezekiah's struggle behind the wall takes place entirely in Hebrew.

In the open expanse of the public square, the lingua franca exerts pressure on provincial dialects, minimizing particularity in the interest of universalizing convenience, eliminating particularities that require too much work to learn efficiently. This tension inaugurates potentially awesome moral consequences. Aramaic functions as an early forerunner to contemporary secularese, displacing local religious and ethnic traditions as easily as Bronze Age defenses.

Granted, historically secularism sought to chasten fanatical religion. But as it wages war against religious intolerance, its own blind spots are hidden. We have suggested that we honor secularity for its gifts but at the same time support more religious variety in public life.[46] As secularism seals public life from religious doctrines, it also dismisses orientations to reverence and ethics that deserve to be heard. Secular discourse is too narrow to support the diversity it touts, and theocratic models are too exclusive for a pluralistic society. In this context, Christianity cannot set the authoritative matrix of public life. No one religious tradition can dictate which moral source others should engage in public, but each voice should draw on the moral authority it honors. What is needed is a deeper appreciation of the complexity and ambiguity of pluralistic cultural life.

We believe that the tension over languages in public settings has profound implications for psychotherapy. We think that one reason clients hesitate to use their native tongue in therapy is that it is not welcome in the public square. We argue that ethnicity and religion should be welcome dialogue partners in public, and clients should be empowered to speak their religious language in the context of therapy. This position is foremost to our thinking as we enter the debate about the role of "private" languages in public. Empowering of clients to speak their own language is more difficult given a newfound awareness regarding the ideological force of psychological trade language. The language of Western psychotherapy tends to silence local speakers and remove local dialects, a pattern that mirrors what appears to be happening to non-Western speakers as well. The options are not simply a public religion that is aggressive and violent or a private religiosity that is passive and emasculated. We hope for a public square in which many languages are spoken, and for a therapeutic context where the language of faith is centrally honored rather than passively affirmed as yet one more item to be included in a thin clinical curriculum for diversity education.

Recognizing the complicity of psychology with the ratification and reinforcement of secularity, the peaceable psychologist must reclaim her or his own tradition. This is not about domination of the client—it is rather given to the radical affirmation of the other in that individual's colorful and varied uniqueness. These colors provide clues to the nature of authentic healing that will transform the client's suffering. Recognizing the power of a language metaphor for secularity, we turn in the next chapter to the importance of another language, a mother tongue.

5

A Mother Tongue amid Trade Languages

Our idea of what belongs to the realm of reality is given for us in the language that we use. The concepts we have settle for us the form of the experience we have of the world.

Peter Winch, *The Idea of a Social Science and Its Relation to Philosophy*

The issue of the application of science is a political issue. . . . If it is to be applied, it should be applied locally by local people on a local scale, using the health of the locality as the standard of application and judgment.

Wendell Berry, *Life Is a Miracle*

Lacking a word, I may miss important details. Lacking a language, I may miss a world of nuance and meaning. Without language, I lose my identity insofar as I am known in and through relationship with others. With the proper vocabulary, I might effectively structure personal and social worlds. Knowing a language affords me the opportunity to negotiate relationships with people and objects. This is true when I learn to speak different languages: the church and the world, Christianity and psychology, secular and sacred, and sin and pathology.

Whether as children, or in our training as professional mental-health practitioners, we inherit a language. An older generation teaches a younger generation the language of wisdom regarding adultery, money, and war. Later in the university we are taught the secular language of psychology to understand schizophrenia, mental retardation, and depression. In each culture we are taught, via language, a way of seeing the world.[1] Languages shape the way we construct our biological, social, physical, and spiritual worlds. They also shape the way we negotiate relationships with other communities.

Since cultures are different from one another, it should not surprise us that the languages emerging out of each of them are different. If one lives in only one cultural world, one tends to be monolingual. If one traverses cultures, one perforce becomes a polyglot.[2] In this chapter we explore the similarities and differences between the languages we learn.[3]

The languages we use have profound consequences for psychological healing. Individuals seeking therapy will learn the language and values of the therapist, and that language will shape the way therapists view clients' concerns and respond to their problems. Evidence suggests that clients adopt even the grammatical and syntactic constructions of their therapist,[4] as well as his or her values to some degree.[5]

If the therapist speaks only the language of secular psychological theory and its concepts, clients will learn to use the words they hear. The risk for the therapist is that her or his own clinical language unwittingly displaces the client's moral vocabulary, and consequently the client's hope for a healing which is coherent and comprehensible within his or her worldview. Given the risks associated with the imposition of the therapist's language on the client, we radically affirm the identity of the client through the inclusion of her or his mother tongue in therapy. Ethnic and religious nuances contained within that tongue must be considered, translated, evaluated, and mutually affirmed in the interest of the client's reconciliation and healing. Building on our discussion in the last chapter, a peaceable therapist recognizes that healing is best conducted ethnically, in the client's mother tongue and in his or her local culture. For this to happen, the peaceable therapist must be multilingual.

In this chapter we explore the relationship between "first" and "second" languages. A first language or mother tongue is local, ethnically freighted, emotionally laden, and capable of poetic nuance. By contrast, a second or trade language is more distant, utilitarian, contractual, and general. Both "secularese" and "psychologese" are examples of trade languages, but they can be learned so well they become a mother tongue. We are thinking both literally and figuratively about second languages.[6]

Two caveats. The mother tongue is usually, but not necessarily, the first language one has learned. It can be any second language learned so well that it functions unconsciously, as if it was the first language one learned. Religious individuals can so absorb the language of faith that it becomes a first language. Second, while we suggest that therapists honor first languages, we caution against romantic idealization of mother tongues. As will become apparent in this chapter, first languages can be associated with negative experiences.

The differences in first and second languages raise a nest of issues for the therapist. How well do I know these languages? When do I use them? Which language is more powerful? Do they have relative strengths and weaknesses? Can one translate between them or are they entirely incommensurate? Since first and second languages each have their own syntax, grammar, and vocabulary, at the end of the day, which language is used depends on the wisdom and discernment of the therapist.

We believe that a peaceable psychology empowers native speakers to honor their own mother tongue. Over the past centuries we have slowly learned of the destructive effects of the colonial imposition of language.[7] The violence perpetrated by a therapist who is unable to recognize when a spiritual language is being spoken profoundly shapes the soul of some of our clients. We contend that in a peaceable psychology true multiculturalism will mean that therapy is conducted in the mother tongue—if the client so wishes—and the second language will be used as necessary.[8] In the public square of therapy,[9] it is the client, not the clinician, who decides whether to use his or her mother tongue, the trade language, or to translate back and forth from one to the other.

We begin with exploring the semantic and emotional differences in first and second languages that potentially shape identities and psychotherapy. We return once more to Hezekiah to watch how mother tongue and trade languages functioned in his life. We then explore the languages of faith and psychology as two different linguistic communities and show how that is evident in the case of Monika, who struggles with her parents over adequate food intake. Finally, we will delineate the different logics implicit in our language communities, and we will meet Patricia, a woman who recovers her faith by returning to the spirituality of her mother tongue.

Languages and Identity Formation

Burkina Faso, once a French colony, is today a kaleidoscope of cultures and languages. Foreigners brought their own language, and since they were in power, their language was made official. So the educated Burkinabe speaks French. But French is relatively uncommon in everyday conversation among Burkinabes. The language used by locals moving between villages is Jula, a trade language. In the village, a local language like Nanerge might be spoken as a mother tongue, but in the marketplace it is always Jula. Nanerge is an excellent example of a first language or mother tongue, provincial in nature and local in dialect. Nanerge is used to negotiate relationships within the community, whereas Jula (a second or trade language) facilitates interaction between communities. Trade languages may reflect the colonizing presence of political powers or shifts in meaning association for common words in different contexts.

The differences between mother tongue and trade languages are apparent in émigrés to North America. My (AD) mother's first language was German, the idiom of church and home for the first years of my life. This was the language in which she prayed, dreamed, and read the scriptures. It never became my mother tongue, though I studied it in high school and college. Though mother eventually learned English as her children attended school, the pronunciation was accented, and her grammar Germanicized. Her English was a trade language used to pay bills, deposit checks, get directions, and arrange work schedules. German was the language of faith and family; English was the language used to negotiate Canadian culture.

The importance of linguistic differences is readily evident in the manner by which self-understanding (identity) is framed by words and meaning. If language is related to identity, then recognizing linguistic differences in therapy becomes crucial. Americans and Japanese, for example, vary in their self-descriptions. The research literature suggests Americans tend to provide more detail on their private selves: attitudes, beliefs, and traits. By contrast, Japanese participants tend to describe themselves more in terms of interdependence focused on social roles, group membership, and other people. Westerners are more willing to make positive statements about themselves, while Japanese are typically less self-enhancing.[10] Furthermore, mood (positive or negative) seems to be culturally shaped. Hazel Markus and Shinobu Kitayama found that while Americans reported many more positive than negative emotions, Japanese reported the same number of positive and negative emotions.[11] The language I learn appears unconsciously to shape my identity.

In the following study it was most interesting that simply by changing languages individuals could access the dimensions of Asian identity outlined above. Michael Ross and his associates asked bilingual Chinese-born individuals living in Canada to describe themselves using the prompt, "I am . . . ,"[12] but with one unique condition. They were asked to give their responses in either Chinese or English. The results indicated that those writing in Chinese had self-descriptions that contained more collective statements of identity, more positive feelings about their Chinese heritage, and lower self-esteem scores than those who were Chinese-born but wrote in English! The results suggested "East-Asian and Western identities may be stored in separate knowledge structures in bicultural individuals, with each structure activated by its associated language."[13] This conclusion is reinforced by a study that focused on autobiographical memory. Russian-English bilinguals remembered more events from the Russian-speaking period of their lives when they responded in Russian.[14] When they responded in English, they remembered more experiences from the English-speaking period of their lives. Language and identity seem inextricably linked.

Charlotte Burck has conducted critical research on the effects of bilingualism on the nature of conversation in first and second languages.[15] She interviewed twenty-four adults who were bilingual and also analyzed their autobiographical accounts of growing up and learning two languages. The participants reported that they felt like they were different persons when speaking different languages. A Sicilian woman raised in Britain stated:

> You became quite good at acting because you had to act in a different way in the English-speaking community and then suddenly you're in the Sicilian community, to the point of dress, clothes, language. . . . And you live in no man's land, especially language-wise. You're neither one nor the other. . . . It's quite an isolating factor in your life. You have this dual personality. Only when you get older do you appreciate it.[16]

They indicated that when they spoke in their first language they were more emotionally expressive and felt closer to others. They felt more authentically themselves in their mother tongue. Burck states:

> First languages were commonly attributed with special qualities, described as the language for creativity, for poetry, play and humour. The ease in a first language, in which individuals are positioned unselfconsciously, in comparison to a struggle in a subsequent language, could provide a sense of "being at home" in it. A first language could engender a sense of belonging and a sense of authenticity. These meanings given to first languages were also constitutive of the speaker—individuals saw themselves as expressive, humorous, "themselves" and so on in this language. A first language could also carry a symbolic meaning, of national identity, and could therefore be used to make political claims.[17]

Second languages were viewed as more formal, constraining, and definitely more difficult in which to be humorous. Most common was the observation that second languages introduced distance, not only from the language itself, but also from themselves personally. However, there were some individuals who found greater freedom of expression in their second language, such as in the use of expletives and talking about sex.[18] A Chinese female noted that speaking English helped her to be more aggressive, something that was culturally unacceptable, saying things she could not say in Mandarin, her first language. She states:

> Angry, yes, also in English. Especially in Chinese culture, being angry you should suppress it. So it's much easier to express it in English. So even if I don't need to express it, sometimes I keep it to myself, nevertheless I feel it in English.[19]

Then there are the sociopolitical meanings implicit in first and second languages. A Zimbabwean male who learned English, but whose first language was Shona, stated:

> It had an impact in the sense that personally I began to feel that English was superior to Shona; therefore, there was some degree of cultural imperialism going there, I was aware of that, and also, the more fluent I became in English,

the more I wanted to speak English to people I knew didn't speak it. . . . I would use more complicated words, which I knew they didn't understand, almost as a way of showing off. You know, I can speak English better than you. . . . It becomes very much like internalized racism where you actually become ashamed to speak Shona.[20]

Bilingualism and Therapy: "Playing Pianos with Keys Missing"[21]

Bilingualism has major implications for therapy as well as personal identity. In a city as multicultural as Los Angeles, it is not uncommon to have clients whose first language is Spanish, Cantonese, or Tagalog. Therapy, however, is usually conducted in English. What might be lost or gained in such sessions?

Since there are both positive and negative associations with one's mother tongue, therapists do well to explore both. If the associations to one's mother tongue are negative, therapists may never be aware of them unless the first language is accessed. A number of examples illustrate the possibility of such an ambivalent relationship and the benefits of accessing the mother tongue. In Freud's case of Anna O, she endured complex problems including paralysis, contractions, and expressive-speech disorder. She was often unable to speak in German, her mother tongue, and therefore used words cobbled together from a variety of other languages she knew. She spoke in Italian and French during periods of fewer afflictions.[22] Ralph Greenson reports on an Austrian female patient who immigrated to the United States.[23] She manifested a variety of addictions and was intensely hostile to her mother. She preferred to speak English in sessions, because when she wished to use obscene words she did not feel as dirty. When she spoke German she was more hostile. She stated: "I have the feeling that talking in German I shall have to remember something I want to forget. . . . In German I am a scared dirty child; in English I am a nervous refined woman."[24] Eduardo Krapf observed that a patient could mobilize ego defenses as protection from anxiety and fears in her or his second language.[25] He encouraged therapists and clients to speak in the client's first language. Luis Marcos and Leonel Urcuyo confirmed that patients may split off affective components when speaking a learned language.[26] Kostos Katsavdakis and his colleagues summarize their clinical findings as follows:

First, different defense mechanisms can be specifically tied to the mother tongue or to the acquired language. The acquired language can be used as an auxiliary superego that helps keep unwanted sexual and aggressive impulses at bay. Feelings of sadness associated with loss and shame can also be kept unconscious through the medium of the acquired language. At times, however, the acquired language can serve an adaptive function by keeping intolerable anxiety unconscious. Second, when the mother tongue is invoked, images are vivified and made real because of the rich affective associations, most specifically with obscene words or sexually laden terms/words. A related contribution is that affective shifts can occur when the individual proceeds from mother tongue to acquired language and vice versa. Third, the individual's sense of self and self-in-relation-to-other can shift, depending on the language invoked. Finally, transference and countertransference paradigms can be modified, depending on the language spoken.[27]

Therapists do well to address the experiences and differences related to speaking in first and second languages in terms of race, ethnicity, culture, and colonization. Since certain concerns can be elicited only in a first language, clients can be encouraged to speak in their mother tongue with the help of a translator or co-therapist. It should also be remembered that in some cases clients feel greater freedom of expression in their second language because the topic may be taboo in the culture associated with the first language.

Conversely, the mother tongue may be associated with resources which would not emerge in therapy unless elicited. Ramón Karamat Ali criticizes the pathological associations to language in the psychoanalytic theorists described above.[28] For Ali, language represents culture, and to access a first language is to access the associated cultural resources: normative behaviors, internal narratives, valorized emotions, communal convictions, fantasies, myths, and so on. We concur. If the religion and values were learned in the first language, they may not be expressed in the second language. When the latter is perceived as more sophisticated, religious experiences associated with the first language may be perceived as provincial or irrelevant and hence repressed.

If we apply the research on the identities of speakers in first and second languages to religious clients, the following picture emerges. Those who have grown up in a religious culture with its attendant language and customs may feel like they have a double identity, one presented in the wider public setting (including therapy) and the other for the local religious community. As in native first languages, the religious language as mother tongue may carry considerable emotionality, both positive and negative. The religious person may not feel as close to the therapist when speaking the trade language. Building a therapeutic alliance may be more difficult. The religious client may be less playful, less humorous, more reserved. It is also possible that a religious client may use the trade language of therapy to express concerns unacceptable in the religious community. Most importantly, if the mother tongue of the client is not accessed and legitimated, the rich heritage of narrative and healing resources may not enter the clinician's office.

A Grammar of Faith

For the first seventeen years of his life, former Yale professor of theology George Lindbeck lived with his missionary parents in China before leaving for college during WWII. Growing up in Loyang, he was fascinated with the contrast between the depressing present and the glorious past of this city, once China's imperial capital. He narrates how he learned to love Chinese literature and how he absorbed Chinese culture through the many conversations his highly Sinicized parents had with their Chinese visitors. He discovered it was possible to be warmly Christian in spirit and in manners be Confucian to the core.[29]

It was this experience of living in China, he reports, that was the impetus for his cultural-linguistic view of religion and his grammatical-rule theory of doctrine.[30] Learning theology, he suggests, is like learning the grammar and vocabulary of a language. He includes nonverbal vocabulary, ritual, and moral and other behaviors in what constitutes a form of life. This language, like a mother tongue, interprets and enacts the story of a community.

In this section we build on Lindbeck's indigenous theory of the nature of religion in our understanding of the cultural indigeneity of psychology. The emergence of a literature in indigenous psychology parallels the appearance of more cultural understandings of religion. In both cases there is a significant movement away from individualism and abstract generalization toward what is the contextual, toward what is culturally particular. Lindbeck states:

> In a cultural-linguistic outlook, in contrast, it is just as hard to think of religions as it is to think of cultures or languages as having a single generic or universal experiential essence of which particular religions—or cultures or languages— are varied manifestations or modifications. One can in this outlook no more be religious in general than one can speak language in general. Thus the focus is on particular religions rather than on religious universals and their combinations and permutations.[31]

An indigenous psychology with religious sensibilities would be deeply embedded in local cultures with a local, regulative grammar of cognition, affect, behavior, and relationships. Implicit and explicit psychologies, like religion, are comprehensive, interpretive schemas embodied in myths and ritualized in performative events. When the implicit psychology organizes everyday life, it functions as a religion. Thus, indigenous psychologies and religions are less an array of beliefs and more an a priori set of acquired skills in living. Indigenous psychologies and religions shape the sensibilities from which descriptions of reality, beliefs, and emotions emerge.

Just as doctrines, cosmic stories, and ethical directives are integrally related in ways that resemble a grammar, so too does indigenous psychology involve a distinctive grammar that generates a way of life for an individual and his or her communities. Becoming religious, like becoming human in general, involves the acquisition of a language that shapes how one lives in the world. Lindbeck again:

A comprehensive scheme or story used to structure all dimensions of existence is not primarily a set of propositions to be believed, but is rather the medium in which one moves, a set of skills that one employs in living one's life. Its vocabulary of symbols and its syntax may be used for many purposes, only one of which is the formulation of statements about reality. Thus while a religion's truth claims are often of the utmost importance to it (as in the case of Christianity), it is, nevertheless, the conceptual vocabulary and the syntax or inner logic which determines the kinds of truth claims the religion can make. The cognitive aspect, while often important, is not primary.[32]

Further, this cultural-linguistic understanding of religion helps us understand the incommensurability between different religious traditions. Similarly, indigenous psychologies within disparate traditions may be radically different, making a universal psychology virtually impossible. So then, following Clifford Geertz, we suggest that how one views religion is correlative with how one views indigenous culture.

Richard Steele makes a case for religious emotions from a particularist perspective. He argues that the narratives, customs, and rituals of one's primary community shape the nature of one's emotions.[33]

Theology must be able and willing to show how the authoritative narratives that the Christian church tells, and the congruent rituals, customs, and disciplines that it observes, not only inculcate a highly distinctive set of doctrinal convictions and promote a highly distinctive set of moral virtues, but also elicit an equally distinctive set of religious emotions.[34]

He rejects as universal the view of religion as essentially expressive-experientialist.[35] Steele dismisses the notion that emotions are "value-neutral, tradition-independent, conviction-free bits of experience which just 'happen' to us. They are episodes in our stream of consciousness, not features of our character."[36] Rather, the communities we grow up in or identify with shape the grammar of emotions. When one's thick, primary community is the church, one would expect that the grammar of its convictions would influence one's judgments and emotions. Here is a community that can teach us to love our enemies, experience compassion for the oppressed, give joyfully of our wealth to the poor, and grieve with those who are injured.

Hezekiah's Wall Redux

We have asserted that the languages we learn shape identity, and not only our psychological identity. We also learn a language of faith, what is normative and what is good. When learned well, the spiritual language of our faith tradition can become our mother tongue, our first language. As Christians we intend for that faith language to function powerfully in the way we think and view the world. At times it touches the deepest parts of our soul. Ultimately it can shape what makes our work meaningful.[37] Given its particularity, it is not understood well in the public square, the secular academic community, or in clinical conversation.

Returning to the biblical narrative of the last chapter, Hezekiah is being tormented by the Assyrian king. We indicated before that Hezekiah found himself involved in two conversations.[38] The first conversation is in a mother tongue particular to the Jewish community; the second is a trade language that crosses ethnic boundaries. Two languages are being used to interpret the same reality. Behind the wall Hezekiah engages in a conversation in his mother tongue, Hebrew. Hezekiah's administrators use the trade language of Aramaic to plead with the Assyrian general, making an appeal for him to use Aramaic to create distance between political matters and the sacred religious convictions of the Jewish community. The general is dismissive and speaks in Hebrew. His goal is to take advantage of the potent religious and moral meanings in Hebrew as a weapon to discourage the people and open the way for colonization in the trade language of the Assyrians (Aramaic).

Hezekiah's wall is a meeting place for two different languages, two different interpretations of reality. The religious language *behind* the wall shapes the content of the discourse that takes place *on* the wall, rather than the reverse. The mother tongue of faith behind the wall takes priority. The conversation behind the wall enables Judah to act according to the Lord God's covenantal revelation, a promise for victory. On the wall, Isaiah's prophecy is articulated in the trade language of Aramaic. Thicker ethnic, religious, and spiritual meanings are translated into the public square in a bold act of witness. The conversation behind the wall enables Israel to be suspicious—the empire is acting out of narrow self-interest under the guise of common concern. Israel's response to the Assyrians is an offer, a proposal for the empire to make faith in the living God a relevant factor, to hear the cry of pain and to see that Israel's life embodies an alternative to oppressive power. Had there been no conversation behind the wall, the Hebrew discourse would have been preempted by the universalizing Assyrian discourse. Walter Brueggemann observes

> . . . that people of faith in public life must be bilingual. They must have a public language for negotiation at the wall. And they must have a more communal language for use behind the gate, in the community, and out of sight and range of the imperial negotiators. Such a view may seem harsh or unfair to the imperial negotiators as a type. Perhaps they are not always so hostile, and perhaps more common ground can be found. But the truth is that they speak a language which is for the community behind the wall not only a foreign language but a secondary language in which serious matters are not primarily expressed.[39]

What happens behind the wall effectively authorizes what will transpire publicly on the wall. Hezekiah charts a political course through relinquishment, choosing to reappraise the Assyrian threat in faith rather than by strategic or military design. The king's integrity behind the wall is illustrated by his willingness to live within Judah's identity as the chosen people of God, where that particular identity will shape and form political discourse with other nations. Behind the wall is a disciplined conversation that functions with categories of faith typical of the Jewish community. Without its Hebrew discourse, the Judean nation cannot construct a political scaffold for the future in a manner that is faithful to its origins as an expression of divine covenant.

For the Christian therapist or client, a peaceable psychology is authorized by the acquired religious mother tongue spoken behind the wall. This in no way precludes the use of secular trade language on the public wall of psychotherapy. But for religious clients the force of the client's identity (and, for that matter, the clinician's), with its understanding of healing and change, is ultimately reliant upon the mother tongue. A peaceable psychology is constructed on the model of Hezekiah, who intentionally practiced the mother tongue of faith so that he could effectively translate to the language of the Assyrian empire. This mother tongue included the prophetic oracle and judgment of God. More than this, the king knew when each should be appropriately spoken. It was not assumed that being faithful to Yahweh meant that the language behind the wall should be spoken on the wall. Similarly, the Christian therapist learns when the language of faith is appropriate, and when it is not, in the public context of psychotherapy.

On Different Discourses: Religion and Psychology

Hezekiah had several languages available to him. We as therapists counseling religious clients do as well. The language of faith and the language of psychology are, in a sense, different languages. Both can be first or second languages of the therapist or of the client. Vocabulary, syntax, and metaphors in each reflect different cultures. One speaks the religious language of belief, obedience, and forgiveness. The other speaks the secular language of probability, introjection, pluralism, and behaviorism. With more than one language to describe reality comes a potential Babylonian confusion, when different languages (literally and figuratively) are spoken in the clinical setting. Those clients who speak more than one language can at times translate, while at other times no word comes to mind. Some words that are commonly used in the native spiritual tongue now drop out when using the trade language.

Psychology in Western culture has become so popular that it serves as a mother tongue for many Americans as well as a trade language in many settings. Given the pervasiveness of psychological terminology in American culture, conversations at social gatherings may include referencing the advice of one's therapist or recent psychological research.

Psychology as a discipline is a unique discourse. Scientific psychology is a language with a vocabulary generally limited to the "real world." The grammar of psychology is such that whatever happens is caused by events or stimuli in this real world. As we indicated above, pain is now the result of a known or unknown stimulus, not a moral transgression. Pathology is viewed not in terms of evil but in terms of a dysfunctional environment or problematic genes. The language of character is replaced with that of personality.

As with any other language, the trade language of psychology possesses a unique vocabulary and underlying grammar, and fluent speakers immediately recognize mistakes in that grammar. For example, "Herbert must be schizophrenic because he sinned against the Holy Spirit" violates the grammar of scientific psychology because the latter assumes that an illness is the result of this-worldly causes. By virtue of contradicting these assumptions, the example is nonsensical. Psychology is a language where knowledge of reality becomes unambiguous in a materialist or reductionist framework.

Psychologists in this century have consistently and intentionally replaced the language of the soul with psychological trade language in which religious references are eliminated. As we stated earlier, Gordon Allport preferred the language of personality over character for this reason.[40] When Augustus Jordan and Naomi Meara reintroduced the language of virtue into psychological discourse, there was an outcry by psychologists.[41] However, even though virtue language is more acceptable now among psychologists, the content is not necessarily the same as in the original religious contexts. It is entirely possible that the older religious vocabulary is pressed into the service of the trade language of democratic liberalism.[42] Justice and fairness carry utilitarian definitions far removed from Aquinas's philosophical and theological reflections on these virtues.[43] The ideas of justice and fairness are now applied to individual rights rather than used as expressions of character.

"Psychologese" emerges from a psychological guild that forms American culture. Words take on meaning as they are used and acted upon in a particular professional community. To the extent that human behavior is explained only in terms of empirical science, we secularize our understanding of the self. This was the context of my (KR) early childhood in Vietnam era Berkeley, an incubator for the virtue tradition of democratic liberalism. However, the American populace is generally more religious than this ultraliberal enclave. "A nation with the soul of the church" was the way G. K. Chesterton once described America.[44] Strangely, one would not know it, reading a standard textbook of psychology or the transcripts of psychotherapy. In both, religion seldom appears. The language of the textbook is cleansed of all religious provincialities. Clients seem to have learned that Berkeley-accented secular psychology is the only viable language for therapy.

Juanita

We return to Juanita to illustrate the different languages of religion and psychology. What language does she speak? Not only is there the issue of the quality of her English, there is the bonding of her spirituality to Spanish. When Dr. Davidson asked Juanita what happened after she lost her husband and why she felt the way she did, she answered in her spiritual mother tongue.

> I forgot about God. I didn't go to church for a year. I didn't pray. I kept saying that God does not exist. I believed that because my husband was a peaceful man. He didn't play sports or go to parties. He liked to go to church and visit the sick. His sport was religion. What a pity that God didn't help my husband. I was lost. I sold oranges in the street and tried to change my attitude and raise money to maintain my children. But there was always violence. When there was a death, the funeral procession always passed by my house on the way to the cemetery. I would join the procession and wail and cry.
>
> Finally I was asked to work in a nutrition center, and I began to change a lot. I met other women who were widows and realized that my children weren't the only ones without a father. My attitude was changed and I needed to give care to other children. I really liked that work. I also organized groups of women, and we began to share about the deaths of our husbands. Later, I had to ask forgiveness of God. I had to give this testimony to the other women. We organized visits to the home of widows. We would take food or something to help the family. We suffered in the nutrition center also. The army came and accused the children of being children of guerrillas and said support for the center came from guerrillas. They searched everything. The children were very afraid. The center was closed for a year or two. I was left again without work, and the violence continued.
>
> At that time I worked in a clinic as a health promoter, but the salary was really low. I only earned about $20.00 a month. I began to work with a Guatemalan woman and other widows creating and selling beadwork. I liked to do beadwork, and I was paid well. The mothers of the young women did crocheting. It was easier and not so hard on their eyes (as beadwork). Our goal was to be able to send some of the children to school, to get a little bit of education. There were a number of children who could not go to school.
>
> I was in another group of women, but lamentably the man who was in charge took all the money for himself and didn't share it with us. That is why we didn't want to have men in our groups. Men don't know what the suffering of women is. It isn't a lie, what I am telling you. There are many men who take advantage of women, so I only want to work with women. Women have a special courage!

The religious language that Juanita uses is ancient, emerging from a specific context, the Judeo-Christian understanding of the righteousness of God. It is here that we learn of our own waywardness, the connection between our relationship to God and human alienation. In the Christian view, without acknowledging our fallenness there can be no viable or existential grace, no reconciliation and healing accomplished through the cross. Juanita's tradition includes a vocabulary for demonic possession, spiritual weakness, and separation from God to construe sin.[45] Over the centuries the church has wrestled with the relationship of sin to sickness, of spiritual failure to mental illness. Sin is not a language that makes much sense when extracted from a web of Christian beliefs and the Christian community's commitment to reflect the character of God.

On the other hand, Juanita also uses psychological language to understand her work with her friends, the greed of her boss, and the experience of suffering by women. However, she does not know the specialized language we use to describe and explain pathology from a psychological perspective, which is little more than a hundred years old, with a history dating back only a few centuries more. Its lineage is the modern world, its parentage the Enlightenment. This is the language of deviation, biochemical imbalance, genetic influence, psychic injury, and unconscious conflict. The grammar of this language assumes pathogens surface as symptoms, just as causes lead to effects.

Sin, Pathology, and Monika

We are using the contrast of sin and pathology as markers in the two languages of religion and psychology. Sin is not mentioned in the lexicon of psychology, nor is it implicit in the grammar of psychopathology. In the past there were mental health leaders who objected to this disparity. The legendary psychiatrist Karl Menninger once asked, "Whatever became of sin?" He had little difficulty pointing out the psychological correlates of sin. He commented: "It may do little good to repent a symptom but it may do great harm not to repent a sin. Vice versa, it does little good to merely psychoanalyze a sin, and sometimes great harm to ignore a symptom."[46] Another significant voice from the past, Frank Lake, found biblical characters who illustrated modern pathologies.[47] O. Hobart Mowrer made the point that, on occasion, pathology is the result of unethical conduct.[48] What these three voices had in common was the assumption that the language of sin could be spoken in the same breath as the language of pathology. However, today the language of sin is rarely spoken either in the public square or in the clinician's office.

The primary language of sin and the trade language of pathology are limited by time and space. They are not static, given the changing nature of their practitioners. The community of speakers and their vocabularies expand and contract. Meanings are lost, added, and regained. What was considered a sin or sickness in one era isn't necessarily extended to another period. Generally, Christians tend to view their language of sin as divinely sanctioned and humanly discerned, while clinicians assume their language of psychopathology is empirically validated.

To illustrate, we will consider a clinical case. Soon after her eighteenth birthday Monika,[49] Juanita's niece who had been living in the United States for many years, began losing weight. She seemed to have less energy but at the same time increased her exercise at the gym. At a recent family gathering her uncle, a medical doctor, commented on her gauntness, worrying that she might be suffering from celiac disease given her family history. This inherited disease does not allow nutrients from grains to be absorbed by the stomach and can lead to starvation and death.

Monika's father, a Guatemalan evangelical pastor, encouraged her to eat more. When Monika was reluctant and did not gain weight, it seemed to him that her faith was faltering. His language to describe the situation was that Monika was "under spiritual attack." For her father, issues of sin, lack of faith, and personal emotional problems were inextricably connected. Sin involves lack of trust in God—spiritual unbelief. To him Monika's problem arose from spiritual weakness that could be changed if she redoubled her efforts in the classic spiritual disciplines.

When after several months Monika seemed increasingly listless, her father reluctantly agreed to see Dr. Davidson. After several sessions, he suggested the disorder had a name and that it involved the whole family. Monika suffered, according to the therapist, from anorexia nervosa, and on the insurance reimbursement form the illness has a number—307.51—which can be found in the *Diagnostic and Statistical of Mental Disorders (DSM IV-TR)*. Dr. Davidson indicated that his diagnosis was based on the fact that Monika had lost 15 percent of her original weight, was exercising obsessively, viewed herself as fat, and refused to eat. This is the language of pathology. Parenthetically, Dr. Davidson did not request a medical examination, nor did he explore the religious context of the problem.

As they focused on family dynamics it became apparent that Monika felt unable to meet her father's expectations for spiritual maturity and experienced her mother's overprotectiveness as oppressive. Dr. Davidson encouraged greater autonomy in Monika and that she differentiate from her parents. As a result, Monika moved out of the family home and into the university residence hall. She changed majors from religion to music and began dating.

We have several different languages used to explain Monika's inability to flourish. While her father considered it a spiritual issue, and Monika's uncle focused on medical problems, the therapist considered the family dynamics. The uncle and therapist together incorporated a view of pathology that was wed to a vocabulary typical of psychology as a trade language. The crucial point we wish to make is that both the mother tongue of Monika's family and the secularese of the clinician were valuable to the greater goal of healing. The problem is that these two languages do not "learn" from each other in therapy.

The father's limited view of spiritual weakness does not include sin as a set of practices, emotional attachments, or family loyalties. The therapist's evaluation fails to take into consideration the religious worldview of the family.

In the public square of therapeutic discourse, the challenge is how each party (i.e., clients and clinician) will resource their respective mother tongues in order to create a space for healing.[50] In this new space we transcend language even while different languages are spoken. Creating this space will require more than mere tolerance of different perspectives and values. The father's assumption that sin is limited to unbelief or spiritual warfare fails to take seriously either the concrete acts of specific individuals or the more structural forms of sin, the "principalities and powers of the air" (Col. 1:16; 2:15). The therapist's identification of dysfunctional family dynamics implicated in Monika's diagnosis, while potentially having clinical accuracy, does little to engage the potential deeper theological vocabulary the family possesses as Christians. The gift of healing, we hope, will occur in this transcendent space where multiple languages are spoken, honored, and understood.

The failure of the respective language communities to meet in this case study is larger than the immediate participants. We hope that theologians would help translate what therapists are describing as pathological and thus develop a broader, well-articulated, view of sin for the church.[51] Rather than ignore the religious dimension or treat it as yet another artifact of diversity, therapists would do well to understand a given problem from within the language world of their religious clients. The peaceable psychologist is cast in the role of linguist. He or she recognizes the difference between a religious mother tongue and a psychological trade language, honors these language differences, and is able to shift between language registers.[52] Moreover, the peaceable therapist is able to validate a client's first language and may even learn to understand, if not to speak, the native tongue.

In the interest of a peaceable psychology, we implore caregivers to know both languages well, reflecting upon the limitations of each in order to expand the meanings of vocabularies and explore the linguistic gifts of the other. Therapists would do well to remember that if they are to do no harm, they will need to learn how the religious language shapes the way their clients view pathology. Each language makes reference to—and on occasion creates—a different reality each of which must be considered in the interest of healing.[53]

The Language of Reasons and Causes

In this section we argue that Christianity and psychology speak different languages and dialects, that there is a different logic implicit in religious and scientific psychological explanations.[54] We find the work of Peter Winch most helpful in this regard.[55]

We use language to describe reality. It is in language that we show what counts as belonging to the real. Peter Winch, who constructs a view of social science on Ludwig Wittgenstein's philosophical perspectives, states:

> Our idea of what belongs to the realm of reality is given for us in the language that we use. The concepts we have settle for us the form of the experience we have of the world. It may be worth reminding ourselves of the truism that when we speak of the world we are speaking of what we in fact mean by the expression "the world"; there is no way of getting outside the concepts in terms of the world. . . . The world is for us what is presented through those concepts. That is not to say that our concepts may not change; but when they do, that means that our concept of the world has changed too.[56]

The meaning of a word depends on the context in which it is used.[57] More specifically, the meaning is dependent upon rules exercised in a particular context. For example, Jung's meaning of the word "self" is not the same as the one held by Thomas Jefferson or the one used in the Gospel of John. The meaning of a word is learned in the context of a community of users—and when my actions based on a given linguistic event do not match the specific community's expectations, an error has occurred, a rule has been violated.

Wittgenstein insisted that meaningfulness is dependent on social relations. How a person behaves, he argues, is intelligible only against a background of language users who have developed rules that interpret the behavior. "What has to be accepted, the given, is—so one could say—forms of life."[58] Therefore, if we wish to understand secular psychology, we will need to interpret it in terms of social life that is considered secular, as a tradition which orders social relations. The syntax of the grammar that makes life intelligible within this form of life may not be intelligible when applied to another, whether Burkinabe animism or the piety of Carmelite nuns. It is not as if language comes first and then society; rather, the very categories of meaning are logically dependent on the social interaction of a specific group of individuals.

Winch proposed that the language of science is meaningful because of the relationship between scientists as a community of language users and the rules for intelligibility that follow from experimentation. The language of empirical observation, causation, and effect is the basis of interpreting experimental results. Winch argues that when the language of science is applied to domains such as the individual or society, incredible confusion emerges.

Psychology purports to be a science of human behavior. But since human behavior is complex, we may only be able to make tentative generalizations. Nonetheless, the assumption is that just as there are laws that govern the tides, there are laws that govern human life. Winch argues that the issue of methodology is not a matter of what is amenable to empirical analysis, but what is best addressed using specific linguistic tools. He wants to know not what the data indicate, but what it makes sense to say given the data. He proposes "that the notion of a human society involves a scheme of concepts which is logically incompatible with the kinds of explanation offered in the natural sciences."[59]

Psychologists make explanations of motive and behavior in terms of causality. However, it does not make sense to ask what the motive is for a headache. In this case, the underlying physiological state may be a cause, making it nonsensical to explain the experience of pain in terms of a motive. An explanation of motives is what is needed when a person acts unexpectedly. If a person purchases a lotto ticket and says it is because of a hope to retire early, that person is justifying his or her behavior rather than providing evidence of a cause.[60] The pacifist justifies her behavior on the basis of Jesus's response to his enemies. The behavior is intelligible because there are acceptable or plausible standards for what is being appealed to. "Learning what a motive is belongs to learning the standards governing life in the society in which one lives; and that again belongs to the process of learning to live as a social being."[61] Hence, the explanations of motives would differ in secular society from more religious traditions. For Freud to explain adult life in terms of early childhood requires an understanding of how family life is ordered in a particular culture, but then the explanation is not generalizable. Winch again:

> What in fact one is showing, however, is that the central concepts which belong to our understanding of social life are incompatible with concepts central to the activity of scientific prediction. When we speak of the possibility of scientific prediction of social developments of this sort, we literally do not understand what we are saying. We cannot understand it, because it has no sense.[62]

There is then a logical incompatibility between how we think of social and psychological events, and how we think of concepts belonging to scientific explanation. However, in secular society empirical ways of speaking about individual and social behavior are part of the trade language.

To attempt to understand another culture that utilizes magic (our word for their actions) in terms of science will necessarily be to misunderstand that culture. To say the individuals practicing magic are acting illogically only reflects our prior linguistic commitments. Winch argues

> that criteria of logic are not a direct gift of God, but arise out of, and are only intelligible in the context of, ways of living or modes of social life. It follows that one cannot apply criteria of logic to modes of social life as such. For instance, science is one such mode and religion is another; and each has criteria of intelligibility peculiar to itself. So within science or religion actions can be logical or illogical: in science, for example, it would be illogical to refuse to be bound by

the results of a properly carried out experiment; in religion it would be illogical to suppose that one could pit one's own strength against God's; and so on.[63]

Science and secularity have their criteria for intelligibility, but they are not the criteria for intelligibility in general (though the West has tried to assert that they are). An idea receives its sense from its context. Winch suggests that it is nonsensical to take several systems of ideas, find an element in each that sounds similar, and then claim to have discovered an idea that is common to all systems. It is possible that this is the basic error of Jung's comparative-religions approach.[64]

In this section we have argued for the integrity of different "languages" which reflect different views of human motivation. Failure to legitimate a spiritual language or an ethnic dialect is a way of dismissing the correlative social arrangements. Different languages generate different social relationships. Though languages persist for some time, the death of a language inexorably alters relationships. Conversely, a new idea which is powerful enough to shape one's way of speaking may well entail a new way of relating socially. Enter Patricia.

Patricia's Native Tongue

As we tell Patricia's story, note the primacy and logic of her first language of faith. Would the language of secular psychotherapy have undermined her story? Would a treatment that assumed the logic of cause and effect have been beneficent? Would our approach elicit Patricia's mother tongue? Imagine she is our client.

Patricia, an African-American journalist in her late twenties, reports that she is overwhelmed by her hatred of white people. She grew up in a middle-class neighborhood in Denver, Colorado; her father is an accountant, and her mother a physical education teacher. For the past year the regular column she wrote served as an avenue for her to vent her rage against white people. To no one's surprise, she received a flood of hate mail from around the country. She began to be afraid that the venom of her animosity was destroying her soul. Without warning, the editor suddenly canceled her newspaper column, and she was livid.

If we had overlooked taking a religious history in an initial interview, we might not have known that she deeply loved the missionary sisters at Cleaves Memorial African Methodist Episcopal Church, who punctuated the service by shouting "Thank you, Jesus." It turns out that religion is the deepest part of Patricia's life—the part that she hid, as a child, from white people because of her fear that they would not understand it. It was her first language, her mother tongue. But she might not speak this language in therapy if she lacked a direct invitation to do so, or if she did not feel safe.

What difference would religious language and history make if Patricia were in therapy? If it had not surfaced, then a significant resource for change might have been missed. We might not have heard her confess that forgiveness, prayer, the modeling of Gandhi and Martin Luther King Jr., the memory of her first white friend, and learning to fight, were all part of her healing. What kind of therapeutic context would we need to construct so that this narrative could become a natural part of the process of healing?

Such therapy would require a deep recognition of the inextricable relationship between ethnicity, language, and religion in Patricia's life. The nature of her faith is not incidental to her being black; her faith is her first language. She revealed that she was "trying to get to heaven. A colored and quaint thing. I won't deny it, not even with white folks watching." And again, "Signs and wonders—what a colored thing to ponder, but I can't apologize." Her answer to her own anger emerged out of her black evangelical faith:

> Certainly, as the choir sings and shouts and the sisters rock their heads to the music, I finally see—after months, indeed years of worrying about these matters—that for me this issue of forgiveness is first about making peace with God. That's my little Christian colored woman's matter. Somebody else might reconcile these things differently. But by daring to question not only my father but my God as well, I slowly start to see some things.

If, as therapists, forgiveness were not part of our therapeutic vocabulary, we would have missed the healing role it played in her life. She prayed for the newspaperman, her enemy, and slowly they were reconciled:

> I see the themes of colored Easter plays and children's choirs and sunny Sunday school rooms with linoleum floors gleaming with wax and scented with Avonlady perfumes.

> Father, forgive them; for they know not what they do.

> Through fresh tears, I try to call up the Holy Ghost, that Spirit of the Living God. Fall fresh on me. I want to whirl all over that living room, and find myself again—to fasten myself to that force that established me, as my Daddy's Bible put it, with my maker.

> I want to find Jesus.
> Call him up, and tell him what you want.

> I want to know Jesus because I think in Him I might find answers—a strategy for living inside my brown skin, for coming to terms with white skin, for fixing up my life.

Liberalism speaks abstractly about justice. But justice in Patricia's vocabulary points to real people like Martin Luther King Jr. and Mahatma Gandhi. If the particular sense of justice in Patricia's African-American experience is removed from the clinical conversation, then her healing may be impeded. Justice in Patricia's mother tongue is laden with themes of slavery and the hope for liberation. Theology interprets the character of her pain. It is no coincidence that, by her own admission, Patricia did not find self-psychology books to be helpful. The generic prescriptions of pop psychologists did not activate healing that was animated by words like "forgiveness." She realized that unless she forgave, her anger would consume her. If the encouragement to pray were not an acceptable intervention for a religious client, then our client might still be angry. She says she prayed a simple prayer:

God help me.

A beautiful prayer. I prayed it daily. Upon awakening. At the end of long days. Maybe even as I slept. I breathed this prayer, entreating divine powers. Blatantly, I just asked. God help me to find this way, to walk this path. Even when it's hard. God help me. Even when it's vicious. When the hate mail comes from Grand Rapids, Michigan, and Chicago, Illinois, and Phoenix, Arizona, and Harrisburg, Pennsylvania—"you are a nigger and will never be nothing but a nigger"—and when the cold, suspicious stares follow me down American streets and into American stores and across American highways. God help me to forgive other people's fears. Help me to understand other people's suspicions, not to mention my own. Help me to speak compassion to the malevolent, grant understanding to the hateful, give charity to the spiteful, healing to the hurting, love to the loveless.

By now it may be apparent that this woman is not an imaginary person. Patricia Raybon is indeed a journalist. She describes her journey toward healing in her book *My First White Friend*.[65] The implicit logic of the language that transforms her is not linear or causal. She returns to a language in which there is a web of meanings, a narrative that reinterprets her life.

We have used her story to highlight the themes of this chapter: (1) Her identity is shaped by a language, her religious mother tongue. (2) This language is very different from the trade language of psychotherapy—and racist language. (3) Her story illustrates the powerful role of recovering her mother tongue for healing. Most importantly, it is apparent that Patricia's faith as a first language or mother tongue is a vehicle for healing.

What if we had actually been Patricia's therapist? Would we have recognized the integrity of her mother tongue? Could we interact with her in the register of her own language? Would our therapy address her anger without the help of her emerging faith? How could we communicate to her that in therapy, talking about deeply religious yearnings is entirely acceptable, that she need not filter her concerns through the trade language of secularese?

The tendency of trade languages to displace mother tongues is immediately problematic for clients such as Patricia. Therapists that speak only secularese may consider religion irrelevant, private, or an irrational pathological defense. In all probability, monolingual therapists will not create a sacred space in which clients and therapists are enabled to speak their native tongue. If this is the case, then at least some of the voices that could make for transformation will be muted. We believe that a client such as Patricia will feel free to speak her mother tongue if we clinicians are able to ethically model how to speak our first language in the clinical conversation and that we desire to hear their first language as well.

In the West, the public square is the equivalent of the venue for the town meeting. Here all the citizens have their opportunity to speak their mind. Psychotherapy is like the public square. We insist that all languages are appropriately spoken in therapy—mother tongue, trade language, or even both as a kind of Spanglish. Some of a person's deepest convictions may reside in the register of one's first language, so speaking in that dialect in therapy takes much courage. The multilingual therapist will empower the client to speak, take the time to learn the rudiments of his or her language, and admit the lack of fluency when appropriate.

6

Thick Clients and Thin Therapists

The specifically modern self, the self that I have called emotivist, finds no limits set to that on which it may pass judgment for such limits could only derive from rational criteria for evaluation and, as we have seen, the emotivist self lacks any such criteria.

Alasdair MacIntyre, *After Virtue*

The order of the self is better imagined as a thickly populated circle . . .

Michael Walzer, *Thick and Thin*

The Reverend Jesse Jackson, Patricia, and Juanita all have something in common. They are members of "thick" cultures. A thick understanding of culture assumes that a society can develop elaborate symbolic systems of meaning that serve as the context of speech and action. The structures of meaning are implicit and layered, and, when explicit, make opaque actions familiar or comprehensible. The patterns that provide meanings are not presumed to be universal but are particular to that culture.[1] Culture is not defined by the application of universal laws to specific communities. Instead, Clifford Geertz notes that "it may be in the cultural particularities of people—in their oddities—that some of the most instructive revelations of what is to be generically human are to be found."[2] Thick descriptions of communities are historically particular, symbolically complex, and ethically maximalist. When Rev. Jesse Jackson addressed the psychologists at the American Psychological Association, he employed the image of Jesus the shepherd, and in doing so he embodied the thickness of his particular ethnic and religious community. He was speaking his thick mother tongue.

By contrast, "thin" descriptions of culture are focused more on acontextual explanations of behavior; they assume expression in universal laws and are rationally abstract. Unique symbol systems such as religion are considered to be culturally accidental. Thin explanation is a language of consensus, applicable across cultures and comprehensible to all. Jackson began his address with the thin discourse of the commonalities of mental health care in a sparsely controlled environment of market capitalism. At that point he did not address the moral particulars such as a reduction in fees, the treatment of traumatized families from Chiapas, Mexico, or assistance in the psychic rebuilding of Kosovo.

This chapter extends the argument of the previous chapter. There we suggested that the mother tongue of the client carries powerful emotional and ethical overtones that may well be critical for healing. In this chapter we will expand the argument in terms of culture. We propose that therapists honor the client's thick cultural particularity by eliciting, legitimating, and extending it. This does not mean we are never thin or that we accept the client's tradition uncritically. We do, however, interpret the client's presenting problem emically, from the perspective of their ethnic or religious community. Health is interpreted in terms of the virtue grammar of the client's community. We begin with the case of Avraham to illustrate this thesis. Then we will examine more closely thin and thick construals of personal identity and the corresponding forms of thick and thin therapy.

Avraham

Avraham[3] is a thirty-five-year-old ultra-orthodox Jewish yeshiva[4] student brought to a clinic in North Jerusalem.[5] His father, a well-known rabbi, was killed in an auto accident when Avraham was eight. When his mother was incapacitated with depression, Avraham was placed in an orphanage. Now married for fifteen years to a woman of similar ethnic and religious background, he is the father of five children, living on a small stipend he receives as a student. One day, while he was praying at the Western Wall, terrorists threw three grenades into the crowd—killing one person and wounding many. Avraham was not hurt. Shortly after this traumatic incident, he began to talk to himself in short, incoherent sentences, speaking of bombs and dying people. Two weeks later he began eating enormous quantities of food and gained about forty pounds. In the fifth week he withdrew further, with extensive spells of crying. He slept less, failed to care for himself, and was eventually dismissed from the yeshiva.

Upon arrival at the clinic, Avraham was diagnosed with depression and given appropriate medication. The medication, however, produced little change.

In clinical sessions Avraham continued to act out the terrorist attack. In the context of relating his nightmare, he described an inhuman figure with red eyes and a cock's legs. It threatened him, saying, "I killed your father and now I am going to kill you just as I killed him." Avraham's father appeared in the same dream as overwhelmed with sorrow and unable to assist his son. At the clinician's suggestion, Avraham wrote his father a letter in which he expressed his profound abandonment. His handwriting regressed to that of an eight-year-old. The client began referring to the spectral figure as "the Black." Avraham's clinicians, a Jewish psychiatrist and a Dutch psychologist, interpreted this figure through Jewish folk-religion as being demonic. The clinicians instructed Avraham to announce loudly three times the following mantra whenever the figure appeared: "Go, go, go away because you do not belong to our world." At times this proved helpful. The client was taught relaxation techniques and was additionally instructed to obtain the black figure's name. Again this proved therapeutic. Under a mild hypnotic trance, Avraham was encouraged to go back to where "the Black" had first met him. This turned out to be a desert. Within this landscape the clinicians encouraged him to find a place of safety. Eventually he found on the horizon something that was green and began moving toward it, all the while fending off the attacks of the figure with incantations.

On the day of the celebration of a noted Jewish Talmudist and Kabbalist, Rabbi Chaim ben Attar, Avraham went with a relative to the site of his father's grave. There he wept and prayed that Rabbi Chaim ben Attar would help him conquer the black figure. He returned home feeling better. That night, when the figure arrived in his dream, Avraham asked: "What is your name?" Hearing nothing, he stated boldly: "I am not afraid; Chaim [the rabbi] promised me that I'll destroy you. Here he is with us." Upon uttering the name of the rabbi, the black figure disappeared and his father laughed. This proved to be a turning point. Thereafter, Avraham began reading the Psalms again. In a dream the following night the dark figure returned, but with the help of the rabbi, Avraham sent him packing. In the dream the Book of Psalms lay open where the client could read: "He that dwelleth in the secret place of the Most High shall abide under the shadow of the Almighty" (Ps. 91:1).

The clinicians reinforced Avraham's claim on the rabbi's help in the counseling sessions. One of the therapists commented: "I am very impressed with the work you have done. I think it's very important. . . . This is the first time that I see light in your face after a very long time. It is written: 'Out of the depths I have cried to you, O Lord' (Ps. 130:1). I think that this is the right direction. You must keep going, and we'll work it out together."[6] In the trance Avraham was profoundly moved by the presence of his father and various holy figures, from whose hands he drank refreshing water. After this final session, the client's nightmares and persecutory hallucinations vanished. One year later, the changes had persisted.

Avraham's recovery is in part a consequence of the clinicians' repeated efforts to engage features of the thick ethnic and religious identity that forged Avraham's understanding of pathology, and subsequently of virtue. Medication for depression produced little change. To ask him to chant was a validation of his worldview, including the demonic and its possible effect on his life. The therapists invoked the virtue of courage in facing his tormentors, consistent with the virtue grammar of his Jewish tradition. That a saintly rabbi would support him in his struggle was not considered delusional but, in fact, was validated and extended by quoting relevant scripture. David Greenberg and Eliezer Witztum comment:

> By a process of trial and error, we found that we needed to enter the world of our patients and their families, not just by visiting their homes and meeting their religious leaders but by joining them via their narrative accounts of their religious lives and experiences and trying to understand the meaning of these experiences for them. We learned that any intervention had to be consistent with the authorities and practices of their society.[7]

Avraham's recovery after therapeutic intervention was consistent with his tradition: reading the Psalms, trusting in God's promises, and dyadic fidelity in the shape of the father-son relationship. Therapeutic interventions were structured within this world, placing great importance upon healing as defined within Avraham's virtue grammar.

A Thin Self

The thin self, in contrast to Avraham's thick ethnic self, is communally unencumbered, assumes a position of distance from particular communities, takes a universalist perspective, and makes freedom a primary virtue. MacIntyre comments that

> . . . the specifically modern self, the self that I have called emotivist, finds no limits set to that on which it may pass judgment for such limits could only derive from rational criteria for evaluation, and as we have seen, the emotivist self lacks any such criteria. Everything may be criticized from whatever standpoint the self has adopted, including the self's choice of standpoint to adopt. It is in this capacity of the self to evade any necessary identification with any particular contingent state of affairs that some modern philosophers, both analytical and existentialist, have seen the essence of moral agency. To be a moral agent, on this view, is precisely to be able to stand back from any and every situation in which one is involved, from any and every characteristic that one may possess, and to pass judgment on it from a purely universal and abstract point of view that is totally detached from all social particularity. Anyone and everyone can

thus be a moral agent, since it is in the self and not in social roles and practices that moral agency has to be located.[8]

For Michael Walzer a thin view of the self is linear and hierarchical. One voice dominates. At the top stands a single critical "I." In the thin self, the other voices are either repressed or not listened to. In thin descriptions, Walzer asserts, the upper layers of the human psyche determine lower layers: reason over will over passion, culture over personality over biology, and so forth.[9]

Thin descriptions of the self tend to assume that personality traits are universal, that the essential structure of human nature is unchanged across time and space. Examples abound in the psychological literature. Freud assumed his model of the self (superego, ego, and id) was universal,[10] as did Jung with his notion of the collective unconscious.[11] Behaviorists assume that the "laws" which shape behavior operate in any culture.[12] Thin constructions are evident in transcultural stages of moral development. Lawrence Kohlberg generalized his stages of moral development to all cultures,[13] as did Piaget when theorizing about stages of cognitive development.[14] Although he was willing to speak the language of religion in the public square, a thin, universalist view of religion is apparent in William James's Gifford Lectures. His argument is that there are common emotions underlying all religions which include the

> feelings, acts, and experiences of individual men in their solitude, so far as they apprehend themselves to stand in relation to whatever they may consider the divine. Since the relation may be either moral, physical, or ritual, it is evident that out of religion in the sense in which we take it, theologies, philosophies, and ecclesiastical organizations may secondarily grow.[15]

It appears that there is a pervasive universalism implicit in American psychology's view of nature as regular, and human nature as a reflection of nature's structure. American psychology has manufactured and exported models of the thin self.[16]

Thin Therapy

Thin identity and thin therapy reflect each other. Thinner modes of therapy tend to be more cross-cultural and generic in their linguistic forms, while thicker modes of therapy are more tradition-sensitive, shaped by the language of a particular community and determined by their views of healing. Therapeutic discourse may be confused in the absence of self-conscious reflection on the nature of the resources clients bring to therapy.

In thin psychotherapy, the clinician, as a scientist-practitioner, would presumably make no commitment to a preexisting theoretical or communal perspective. The goal is objectivity and neutrality. Knowledge based on corre-spondence to reality is more reliable than knowledge based on common sense, opinion, or belief. The clinician assumes a universal standard of knowledge to which all rational persons in a therapeutic setting can agree. While there are differences in the problems that clients bring to the therapeutic setting, the method of addressing them remains the same, namely, a framework larger than the ethnic particularity of the client's community.

We will examine thin therapy in several ways. First, we consider therapy as a response to the emptiness of the thin self. Second, we suggest that thin therapies emerge from thick cultural backgrounds; and, finally, thin therapy may reinforce a thin internal community. We end this section with an illus-tration of a morally sensitive psychotherapy which is nonetheless thin in its construction of morality.

First, Philip Cushman has argued persuasively that the construction of what we have called a thin psychotherapy is evident in the social construction of an "empty self," or identity without faces.[17] The empty self is an evolution of market-driven consumption, where the latter is likewise advised by modern psychology, perpetuating a circle of vacuous materialism that is "resolved" only with the application of the therapeutic. Empty selves require thin thera-pies in order to maintain economies of scale—a carefully scripted symbiosis. Purpose and meaning are relegated to the acquisition of material items and self-referencing experiences of relationship.

Second, psychologists emerging out of thick ethno-religious communities have tended to develop models for the larger public that may implicitly build on ethnic narratives but in public are shorn clean of ethnic and religious particularity. David Bakan cites Freud as an example of a psychologist whose Jewish roots were in Eastern Europe but who developed a universal theory.[18] Raised in a Jewish home, Freud encountered considerable discrimination in Vienna as a Jewish doctor. These experiences, placed as they were within the particularity of the European perspective on Jewishness, became the context for meaning later expressed in Freud's general theories and postulates. While the language of Freud is singularly scientific, it is shaped by the doctor's internal struggles with social marginalization. Thin discourse is dependent upon the thick roots of community and other elements of thick culture that provide the context that serves as the basis for group identity. A similar case can be made for the departure of Carl Jung and Carl Rogers from their thick Protestant backgrounds. Thin psychologies are thick psychologies in disguise.

Third, thin therapy has a particular perspective on the internally plural voices that is related to our earlier discussion of democratic liberalism. Of concern to us is the argument that inner plurality may reflect cultural atti-tudes toward ethnic pluralism and that the private inner community reflects the neutrality of the public square. The plurality of voices in public debate

may be mirrored internally in the constellation of the self. The implications
of Richard Rorty's model of public debate for the nature of inner dialogue
are clearly outlined by Walzer:

> In the psychoanalytic tradition, it is the instincts that are universal, while the
> critical standards by which the instincts are judged are always the standards
> of a particular culture. The superego, by contrast, is a human artifact, a
> social creation, different in different times and places, enforcing different
> rules and regulations, with different degrees of rigor and zeal. But these dif-
> ferences make only a marginal difference, for the function of the superego
> is determined not by its own particularist content but by the universal id,
> which is always there and always in need of repression. The philosophical
> view reverses the terms of this argument. Now it is the castigated self that
> is various in form and parochial in content, the product of this or that local
> history, while the critical "I" is in touch or at least aspires to be in touch with
> universal values. Self-criticism for the philosopher is much like social criticism
> (for the philosopher); it is a kind of reflection in tranquility, a scrutiny of the
> self *sub specie aeternitatis*. I step back, detach myself from my self, create a
> new moral agent, let's call him superagent, who looks at the old one, me, as
> if I were a total stranger. Superagent studies me as one among the others, no
> different from the others, and applies to all of "them," including me, objective
> and universal moral principles.[19]

It is possible for one voice (e.g., democratic liberalism or the Moral Majority)
to dominate the internal discussion. Modern psychotherapists may give priority
to the thin discourse of democratic morality. We would not deny a voice to the
therapist or the internalized therapist who takes a universal perspective. Such
a voice is concerned about the effects of an agent's actions on all humanity.
However, an internalized voice as powerful as that of the clinician may serve
to undermine the voices of ethno-religious particularity within the client's
self. Following Stephen Carter's description of the nature of conversation in
the public square, the inner voice that speaks for particularity may well feel
inferior and need encouragement to speak. A model of public debate that
allows for the legitimacy of thick discourse in the public square would imply
that all the particular reasons of a specific tradition for an action would also
be considered and given voice within.

Walzer rightly points out that in psychoanalysis the analyst may be critical of
the overly strict, provincial superego. Insofar as therapy is successful, one arrives
at a historically and morally departicularized self. One wonders then about
the consequences for a thick client when he or she introjects a thin therapist!
Modern psychotherapy is a practice of healing that loosely promotes integration of the self, reducing internal ambivalence where the individual must daily
navigate uncharted waters of social context and cultural ethos. One might
suggest that therapy is itself a language of integration, an attempt to build

bridges between fragmented, alienated parcels of our internalized experiences and feelings and between ethnically diverse communities.

Therapists have the option of beginning therapy with what they consider a thin or thick cultural perspective. In any case, psychotherapy is a moral enterprise.[20] If the therapist's discourse is thin and the clients' discourse is thick, the therapist may seek to build a bridge to the client across the chasm of their cultural and moral differences. If the discourse of the therapist and the client is similarly thick, the therapist may assume he or she can build on their commonality.

The implications of this discussion are potentially far-reaching. So completely are we conditioned to eliminate thick particularity in therapy that the moral residue of ethno-religious conviction is easily swept beneath the rug. In a video that accompanied a standard textbook in psychopathology,[21] we found one illustration of a client's thick use of moral language to describe personal behavior and the therapist's reframing of her behavior in a way that was more publicly and linguistically acceptable but strikingly morally neutral.

Therapist: So you want to have a session without John.

Client: Yeah, there is something that's really important that I need to discuss with you that I am not ready to talk about with John yet. But I need to know that what we talk about today is going to stay confidential.

Therapist: Anything in therapy remains confidential unless somebody tells me of their intention to commit a crime.

Client: Okay, so whatever I share with you today, when John and I come back the day after tomorrow for our couple's therapy, you don't have to discuss that with him at all or feel that you need to let him know.

Therapist: It's not my prerogative to discuss it without your consent.

Client: Okay, I guess I should just get right down to it. I've been cheating on John for a couple of years.

Therapist: You mean you have been seeing someone else.

Client: Yeah . . . it's the same thing isn't it? (Laughs)

Therapist: It's the same thing without the moral twist to it. I just use descriptive language instead of moralizing language.

Client: Yeah, okay.

Therapist: But I know what you mean.

Client: I have been seeing someone else.

Therapist: How long?

Client: About two years. . . . I just felt like I was living a lie coming to you with John in therapy and presenting ourselves as this husband and wife that only have their life going in different directions without letting you in on the fact that I had another relationship.

This clip illustrates the morally charged nature of therapy where the client obliquely referenced the thick moral implications of her mother language. Certain clients bring problems to therapy clothed in moral presuppositions that are embedded in another understanding of reality. The client could have referred to the relationship she was having as adultery, an affair, an extramarital relationship, an acquaintance, a friendship, cohabitation, or, as the therapist suggested, that she was simply "seeing someone." But she didn't. She used moral language to describe not only the relationship as "cheating," but also her relationship with the therapist as a "lie." Regardless of whether this client had a religious background or not, the therapist was clearly uncomfortable with the moral language of the client's mother tongue. Somewhere she had learned that deception was inappropriate.

Given his discomfort, the therapist's response to the client was to reframe her language from his thin (but implicitly thick) perspective. With the authority of his position, he informed her that what she really meant was that she was "seeing someone." He presumed that while the client used the moral language of cheating, what she really meant was that she was simply meeting with someone. When she expressed concern that her relationship to her husband and to the therapist was a lie, the therapist made no comment.

A client can learn the language the therapist thinks appropriate to the clinical encounter. And this was exactly what this client did. She acquiesced, using a thin vocabulary to state, "I have been seeing someone else." The therapist assumed he was only being descriptive with an admittedly moralistic client. His secularese was the neutral language of the public square, while hers was the language of a thickly acquired morality. His therapeutic move was to substitute public discourse for her private moral convictions. This is psychological Constantinianism.

However, it should not be assumed that thin therapeutic discourse cannot have positive outcomes when thin therapists work with thick clients. On October 2, 2006, Charles Carl Roberts IV shot five girls in an Amish schoolhouse near Nickel Mines, Pennsylvania.[22] As a result of this violence in their midst, the Amish were no longer isolated from the larger world. But they were prepared, materially and spiritually. The close-knit community provided support for one another and was able to love Amy, the perpetrator's widow, and her children. They attended Roberts's funeral and provided her with financial support. The Amish told their children: "We shouldn't think evil of the man who did this."[23]

Though obviously sectarian, the Amish were willing to receive help from "the English," that is, outsiders. They spoke glowingly of the police. Could a religious and deeply traditioned Amish community be assisted by the more generic psychological insights of the mental health community? The Lancaster County Emergency Management Agency arrived only hours after the shooting and remained all week. They assisted the terrorized and panic-stricken, whether they were the Amish children or "the English." And they connected. One Amish official stated: "They did a great job. They told us that things will never be the same again, that we must find a 'new normal.'"[24] The Amish man kept repeating, "a new normal, a new normal." Clearly, psychological insights can travel across disparate cultures—but not always.

A Thick Self

The thickness of a person's self may be construed as plural, with many voices. This plurality includes an internalization of the various roles, names, and values that are held more publicly. In a pluralist culture, the roles (citizen, parent, professional) played on any given day are represented internally. The names for the various identities include father, mother, deacon, parishioner, man, woman, citizen, and many others, including vocational identities. Inner personalities associated with these roles may also reflect one's moral ideals, principles, and values.[25]

These multiple voices or selves are exquisitely displayed in Chaim Potok's novel *My Name is Asher Lev*,[26] in which he describes the dream of an aspiring young Jewish painter. His dream illustrates the thick plurality of the ethno-religious psyche. An ancestor comes thundering out of the past to reinforce the values and commitments of Asher's conservative Hasidic community that reject his gifts as an artist.

> And that is what it has been all along—a mystery, of the sort theologians have in mind when they talk about concepts like wonder and awe. Certainly it began as a mystery, for nowhere in my family background was there any indication that I might have come into the world with a unique and disquieting gift. My father was able to trace his family line down through the centuries to the time of the Black Death in 1347, which destroyed about half the population of Europe. My father's great-great-grandfather was in his early years the manager of the vast estates of a carousing Russian nobleman who when drunk sometimes killed serfs; once, in an act of wild drunkenness, he burned down a village and people died. You see how a goy behaves, I would be told by my father and mother. The people of the *sitra achra* behave this way. They are evil and from the Other Side. Jews do not behave this way. My father's great-great-grandfather had transformed those estates into a source of immense wealth for his employer as well as himself. In his middle years, he began to travel. Why did he travel so much? I would ask. To do good deeds and bring the Master of the Universe into the world, my father would respond. To find people in need and to comfort and

help them, my mother would say. I was told about him so often during my very early years that he began to appear quite frequently in my dreams: a man of mythic dimensions, tall, dark-bearded, powerful of mind and body; a brilliant entrepreneur; a beneficent supporter of academies of learning; a legendary traveler, and author of the Hebrew work *Journeys to Distant Lands*. That great man would come to me in my dreams and echo my father's queries about the latest bare wall I had decorated and the sacred margins I had that day filled with drawings. It was no joy waking up after a dream about that man. He left a taste of thunder in my mouth.[27]

Representations of individuals, past and present, animate Asher's internal discourse. Asher Lev's introjections are the characters of his parents, the Rebbe, his mentor Jakob Kahn, and his father's great-great-grandfather. Of interest is not only the plural internal psyche, but also that the characters can be seen to inhabit two cultural contexts. On the one hand, there is Jakob Kahn, a devotee of Picasso; and on the other there is the mythic ancestor. The former is thin, the latter is thick. Potok uses the first character to draw Asher into the universal artistic community, and the second to reinforce the values of the ethno-religious community.

The plural self is well known in psychology. Its uniqueness lies, however, in the potential conflict anticipated by those aspects of the self that embody differential aspects of the particular and the universal. Walzer states:

> The order of the self is better imagined as a thickly populated circle, with me in the center surrounded by my self-critics who stand at different temporal and spatial removes (but don't necessarily stand still). Insofar as I am receptive to criticism, ready for (a little) castigation, I try to draw some of the critics closer, so that I am more immediately aware of their criticism; or I simply incorporate them, so that they become my intimate worriers, and I become a worried self. I am like a newly elected president, summoning advisors, forming a cabinet. Though he is called commander-in-chief, his choices in fact are limited, his freedom qualified; the political world is full of givens; it has a history that pre-dates his electoral triumph. My inner world is full of givens, too, culturally bestowed or socially imposed—I maneuver among them insofar as their plurality allows for the maneuvering. My larger self, my worried self, is constituted by the sum of them all. I am the whole circle and also its embattled center. This at least is the thick view of the self.[28]

While thick descriptions of the self are more nuanced, particular, and ethnically unique, the various internal selves described by Walzer seem to be disembodied value positions rather than thickly embodied selves. Thickness applies not only to the constellation of inner selves, but also to the very character of the inner selves. We would propose that there is a gift in the thickness of the internal conversation. Often this inner conversation is filled with religious references. The potential, then, for consensus within depends upon the thick or thin nature of internally despised or idealized selves, and the individual's integration of those selves with what is actual and real in behavior. To what extent can thick and thin voices of expectation within the self be heard, understood, and integrated?

Thick Tradition in Psychotherapy

How can we understand a thick, traditioned psychotherapy? As we have seen, the ethical therapist is expected to respect the religious background of the client while remaining neutral with regard to any particularity, even her or his own. Consequently, the nature of the discourse that emerges is thin. On the other hand, a therapist who emerges out of particular ethno-religious communities, or who has had profound intercultural experiences, may experience considerable empathy with clients from different ethno-religious communities and be able to speak their language. However, given the cultural bias against particularity in public spaces, even this thicker therapist may feel strong pressure to reduce her or his thick construal of the psyche, of an emotional issue, or of treatment itself, into a thin, more generalized perspective for the client. We must consider the implications of silencing the religious voice in therapy altogether. What will happen if thinness is acceptable as an integrative therapeutic tool, positioned as a means to successfully resolving human ambivalence?

A perspective of the self as traditioned, narratively constructed, with a plurality of thick and thin internal psychological representations, makes therapy, in our view, an inescapably intercultural event, especially when the client's community is unknown by or different from that of the therapist. The therapist may have absorbed a therapeutic ideology that focuses on individual rights, freedom of personal expression and individual pursuit of happiness, the importance of differentiation and individuation, and so forth. These values may not be part of the social expectations which constitute the client's selves. The client may be Muslim, Christian, or Jewish. For each of the therapeutic values espoused by the therapist, the client may have different norms.

In thick cultures, religious rituals are a reflection of the symbols, worldview, emotional sentiments, and practical commitments of the religious community. Healing, for example, is a ritual deeply embedded in religious culture. This is most apparent in premodern shamanic rituals of healing.[29] The shaman's diagnosis and treatment take on meaning in the context of the religious perspective of the community. Religion, then, cannot be as easily separated from the self as was suggested by Richard Rorty. The reasons one gives for one's actions are related to a larger worldview. While it is possible to withhold one's personal reasons in the public square, it may occur at some psychic and social cost.

Since the client anticipates that he or she can learn from the virtue tradition of the clinician, therapeutic conversation is not a neutral dialogue. As previously noted, clients learn to speak and value the language[30] of their therapists.[31] Hence, tradition sensitivity is an honest reappraisal of the unique virtues espoused and practiced by *each* of the participants in the therapeutic conversation. Recognizing the power differential in the client–clinician relationship, tradition-sensitive therapists are sensitized to their own definitions of virtue along with potential effects they could have on their clients.

The tradition-sensitive approach to psychotherapy elaborates on the morality of the client in that clients are assisted to rediscover the craft of living from within their own moral tradition. The *telos* of the encounter is located first in the history of the client's tradition, as informed by dialogue with someone inside or outside that tradition. The client reformulates her or his own view of a problem based on an integration of what is brought to the session, in terms of their common moral tradition (therapist and client) and what transpires within the session. However, one privileges the shared meanings the client brings from his or her community. The nature of justice, truth, and the good are then local, nuanced by the client's primary community. Therapeutic conversation on this model is not a neutral dialogue.

One implication of Michael Walzer's approach is that the clinician who is cognizant of his or her own thick morality may more easily recognize the complexity of a client's thick morality. He or she may recognize the idiomatic language and relevance of specific virtues to local practices. Tradition-sensitive psychotherapy is then, first and foremost, a validation of ethnic and religious identity associated with local virtues. As such, it affirms the client's narrative with its traditions, symbols, and need to articulate differences. Tradition-sensitive therapy empowers individuals to resolve the pain of mental illness from within the shared meanings of the client's own community, consistent with local virtues and practices. Health may well include a greater discernment of, and commitment to, the virtues of one's community of origin. Where there is serious need for critique of the virtue language of the client, the therapist does not invoke moral principles transcendent to the client's community but focuses on immanent morals, those emerging from the central convictions of the community. When the client seeks to remain within the community (perhaps even rejecting parts of the majority culture), consistency with the charter of the client's community is explored.

Tradition-sensitive therapy begins with the historical reality of two or more individuals who address each other out of their particularities, each with their own list of prioritized virtues. To the extent we are nonuniversalist, the result may be a genuine conversation. However, it is not a conversation with a predetermined script or theory about how healing should occur independent of the client's world of meanings and convictions regarding critical virtues. *Commonality emerges out of the conversation, not prior to it.* Change is the hoped-for consequence of the therapeutic conversation.

The thick, tradition-sensitive clinician honors the client's particularity, his or her embeddedness in a preexisting historical community. The tradition-sensitive clinician rejects a transcendent position encouraging assessment of the client's virtues independent of tradition-engaging conversation. More often than not, the clinician and client will represent different traditions, but each should be enabled to speak from within those particularities as necessary. One of the primary goals of tradition-sensitive therapy is not to impose the clinician's particularity, but to enrich the client's tradition. The clinician seeks to learn the moral language of the client and interpret the problematic event or experience from within his or her constellation of desired virtues. Therapists would then recognize their own particularity, bracket their tendency toward universal understandings, and validate the client's unique virtue grammar. What distinguishes this kind of therapy is not the ability to transcend all traditions, but rather the ability to reach out to a client beyond one's own traditioned identity, a virtue closed communities do not develop.

Juanita

We continue now our adaptation of Juanita's story as she experiences a thicker form of therapy. Juanita represents a person with a rich ethnic heritage, a mother tongue that is Quiché and Pentecostal. Her sense of self as a woman, wife, and mother is shaped by life in Santiago, with its native and Spanish history. Juanita's depressive symptoms had persisted. A friend at her church had recommended a women's center that might help her to address the psychological and spiritual losses occasioned by the civil war. The program used Mayan religious and cultural symbols and narratives, but filled them with Christian themes, in order to facilitate the grief and trauma recovery process.[32] And it was free.

When Juanita arrived at the center she met other Guatemalan women.[33] In the work area they were doing beadwork, which held an immediate connection with her past in Santiago. She sat quietly beside one woman from Panajachel who had come to the United States some years earlier. For several weeks Juanita returned to sit with the women, eventually creating a necklace of her own.

Juanita did not have an individual therapist. All work at the center was done in a group, and the leader, herself from rural Guatemala, spoke only Quiché when they gathered. She too had experienced the trauma of war—loss of family members, leaving her home behind, and moving to another country. Juanita saw scattered around the room traditional candles, a small clay stove, corn, a mortar and pestle, a Mayan calendar, and other objects she recognized from her early years in Santiago.

Much of their time together was spent talking about the events of the week, their children, and, of course, the pain of the past. Some months after arriving, the group leader brought out a bag of corn, together with a mortar and pestle. Juanita remembered the times her mother used them to make flour for the tortillas the family loved. Sitting with others who too had experienced loss, Juanita could feel sadness creep into her body. As she ground the corn she found herself weeping. Those near her held her in their arms. Others began humming a song Juanita had not heard since she left Santiago. It was a song they had often sung as part of their celebration of the Lord's Supper. The song told of their ancestors who grew corn, plucked the ears, let them dry, and then rubbed them to release the kernels. It retold the story of Jesus's life, his nourishing love for others. Then the tune echoed the rhythmic crushing of the corn, and the lyrics told of the betrayal of Jesus and of Christ's painful death on a cross. The song closed with the rising of the dough, the smells of the baking bread, the bread broken for others to eat, and the risen Christ who brings new life. Juanita could not sing with them, but she did eat the warm tortillas; and she did not forget the event.[34]

A year after Juanita had joined the women's group, the leader raised the possibility of traveling together to Guatemala. Juanita had not returned to Santiago for a number of years. The facilitator went on to indicate that individuals from the Catholic diocese in Guatemala City were traveling to remote mountain areas to talk with villagers about what had happened during the civil war. One of Juanita's friends in the group had been on one of these trips and said that they dug up mass graves and gave the dead a proper burial. Juanita thought about her missing father. Was his name on a list somewhere? She remembered some vague details about his disappearance, but would it be enough? How would she pay for such a trip? Would her family support her? Who would go with her?

Six months later Juanita, the facilitator, and three others traveled to the Lake Atitlán area where Juanita's father had disappeared. The night before the dig was to begin, the group met in the Ecclesia del Buen Pastor for prayer and meditation. Juanita was able to reveal her fears and anxieties to the others. This was bringing back vivid memories of those dark days. The group listened and held her as Juanita once again spoke of her loss, her years of sadness, and her hope for resolution. She asked them to read the story of Lazarus. She wept when Jesus wept. She chose to read where Jesus commanded Lazarus to come forth. She was comforted. The facilitator gently reminded her that they might not find her father. Juanita remained silent.

The next day, in the chilly mountain air the group that came to exhume the bodies began their work. By mid-morning they had uncovered nothing, but just before lunch there was a shout, and the first bones, those of a young boy, were discovered. Juanita felt a pang of fear. Continuing with the help of candles, they worked on until late evening, carefully removing, tagging, and bagging the scattered remains. Juanita knew that it would take some time for the forensic experts to identify her father's body. Nevertheless, something had changed inside her.

Some months later, Juanita received a letter indicating that her father's body had been among those exhumed. Would she wish to return for the reburial? She decided that she would. When she returned to Santiago for the funeral, the entire extended family she had left behind was there to grieve with her. After the burial they returned to the church. A picture of her father surrounded by candles was displayed at the front. Tears, hugging, and singing followed. Older persons who remembered Juanita's father told stories of quieter and more joyous times in Santiago. They remembered the march to the garrison, the martyred, the disappearances, and the glimmerings of peace. At the end of the service, Juanita herself praised her father for the example he had been, for his love of God and the community of believers. Juanita returned to Los Angeles a different person. There was still sorrow, but the paralyzing depression had lifted.[35]

Tradition-Sensitive Peacemaking and Therapy

The importance of being tradition-sensitive is relevant not only in therapy but also in conflict-transformation and reconciliation. We close this chapter with an example of thick, indigenous peacemaking and its relation to therapeutic work. John Paul Lederach is internationally recognized for his experience in the field of conciliation and mediation. He has provided consultation and conciliation in a range of situations, from the Miskito/Sandinista negotiations in the 1980s to peace-building efforts in Somalia, Northern Ireland, Colombia, Spain's Basque region, the Philippines, Tajikistan, and Nepal. He has considerable experience in resolving conflicts involving inter-ethnic, cross-cultural, and religious issues, and in working with indigenous peoples. He has helped design and conduct training programs in twenty-five countries across five continents. Currently he is Professor of International Peacebuilding at the University of Notre Dame.[36]

In 1984 he was in Guatemala giving a workshop on conflict resolution. He tells how carefully he had prepared, hoping not to impose a North American model of peacemaking on the participants. The workshop and role-plays were conducted in fluent Spanish. After illustrating a conflict between a Guatemalan father and adult daughter, with Lederach acting as mediator, a participant commented directly to the Guatemalan actors: "You two looked like gringos." It stopped Lederach in his tracks. How had the actors picked up the nature of the conflict that had a North American texture and resolution? "What was there in this process," Lederach kept asking himself, "that could take two Guatemalans and turn them into *gringos*?"[37] He came to two conclusions. First, while he had hoped to be contextually sensitive to the Guatemalan situation, he had not spent sufficient time reflecting on the assumptions implicit in his North American model of conflict resolution. Second, he had to admit that embedded in his approach was the unintended residue of imperialism.

After this experience, Lederach changed his approach. He examined his own language and spent more time listening carefully to the language the Latin Americans used when talking about conflict. Consistent with our tradition-sensitive model of therapy, he spent more time understanding the thick nature of culture and how conflict emerges from within the culture. He focused on common-sense understandings of everyday conflicts. He sought to understand indigenous experience with conflicts, and how it was managed. More universal knowledge about conflict that emerges from research was secondary.

Building on the work of the Brazilian priest, Paulo Freire,[38] Lederach refers to his own approach to conflict resolution as elicitive. He distinguishes between two approaches: prescriptive and elicitive. Prescriptive approaches simply transfer their knowledge and skills from one cultural setting to another. The conflict mediator is seen as an expert, his or her knowledge as universal, and techniques as neutral. Assistance is content-oriented, the mediator is the model, and the mood is didactic.

Lederach utilizes the elicitive approach. He assumes a position of ignorance regarding the nature of the problem, the meaning of critical terms in the language, the strategy for resolving the problem, and the criteria for resolution. The non-Westerner assumes the role of facilitator, with the goal of empowering individuals indigenous to the culture to come to resolution or transformation. Local members have a much richer understanding of their cultural milieu than does the outside consultant. Their more culturally implicit knowledge is a form of common sense.[39] Hence, the approach to change is to experiment in the client's cultural setting. Lederach states:

> The participants and their knowledge are seen as the primary resource for the training, whether or not they initially see themselves as such. By knowledge-as-resource I refer to the often implicit but rich understandings people have about their setting. Included is their knowledge about how conflict emerges and develops among them and about how people try to handle and manage that conflict. Also included are their understandings about what things mean; that is, how language, perception, interpretation, and meaning are constructed around events and interactions in their context. Simply put, the foundation of this approach is that this implicit indigenous knowledge about ways of being and doing is a valued resource for creating and sustaining appropriate models of conflict resolution in a given setting.[40]

As he sat with members of the Puntarenas community in Costa Rica (and sits with indigenous people elsewhere), Lederach discovered that the word "conflict," as academics use it, seldom occurs in everyday conversation. He relates the following:

> I remember an enlightening conversation I had one evening in Puntarenas, with one of the participants in our workshop, about a neighborhood problem. They

were in a real *clava*, a nail, she explained. After she had finished, I remarked that people in Puntarenas do not frequently use the word conflict to describe these situations. "Ah no," she replied, "here we do not have conflicts. Conflicts [wars] are what they have in Nicaragua. In Puntarenas we have *pleitos*, *lios*, and *enredos* (fights, messes, and entanglements)."[41]

Lederach began collecting words for conflict; he was able to develop a list of over two hundred words used in everyday Latin conversation. In one workshop in Mexico, a participant suggested the word *desmadre* (without a mother) as equivalent to conflict. What Lederach realized was that Latin understandings of conflict were viewed less as individual than as relational. A common phrase in Central America for conflict is "*Estamos bien enredados*" (We are all entangled). In addition to individual words and phrases for conflict, Lederach tapped the indigenous proverbs and stories which addressed conflict. This approach affirms what psychiatrist Milton Erickson modeled:

> Take what the patient brings you. This rule stands in sharp contrast to the teaching of most schools of psychotherapy, which either tend to apply mechanically one and the same procedure to the most disparate patients, or find it necessary first to teach the patient a new language, and then to attempt change by communicating in this language. By contrast, reframing presupposes that the therapist learn the patient's language, and this can be done much more quickly and economically than the other way around.[42]

Transformation in therapy with ethnic and religious clients might then require the following. The therapist would begin with a genuine discovery phase in which he or she learns the thick culture and language of ethno-religious clients. Not only is the problem identified, but questions are asked. How is this problem generally addressed in their ethnic and religious community? Why is it a problem? What are the meanings in their community of ethical terms such as fairness and unfairness, justice and injustice, sickness and health? Further, what is the wisdom of the community? What proverbs might be relevant to this situation? Are there historical exemplars in the culture and tradition who have addressed this situation successfully?

The ethno-religious client is the best judge of whether healing and transformation have occurred. Evaluation is contextualized.

> Contextualized evaluation simply means that participants in a given setting evaluate their own action and behavior according to the standards and values of that setting, rather than judging their approaches according to outside criteria.[43]

This approach is highly participatory and circular, moving back and forth between discovery, experimentation, and contextual evaluation.

What Lederach names as the prescriptive approach is similar to what we have identified as thin, universalizing models of the person, religion, and psychotherapy. Since they assume universality, prescriptive approaches move quickly to techniques and strategies for change. Culture is then simply an adaptation of universal rules to the local situation. The elicitive approach, however, *begins* with culture as the foundation for change.

> Cultural context and knowledge about conflict-in-setting make up the foundation through which the model development happens. Participants' natural knowledge, their way of being and doing, their immediate situation, their past heritage, and their language are seen as the seedbed in which the training and model building will be rooted.[44]

Validating and eliciting these cultural elements as resources is fundamental for therapeutic transformation.

Lederach notes that this approach would not exclude more generalist approaches, but they are bracketed, secondary, and introduced later in the process if appropriate. In our model, general knowledge is actually particular to the therapist's world; hence, what is being shared is wisdom from the therapist's native culture. This would be construed as a cross-cultural dialogue in which the client and therapist both contribute from their ethnic, and possibly religious, heritage.

Tradition-sensitive therapists are carriers of a narrative of implicit virtues that may be both similar to and different from that of their clients. Tradition-sensitive therapy avoids the charge of imposition of values, if client and therapist agree in advance that healing takes place in an encounter between two or more virtue narratives. To flourish, tradition-sensitive therapy requires that the virtue traditions of both the therapist and client will be viewed as resources for change. A misogynist ethnic client who is engaged in conflicted heterosexual relationships may well learn from a clinician's narrative that is less hierarchical. A guilt-ridden, Christian fundamentalist client may find therapeutic healing in the notion of a God of grace who already exists within his or her own Christian narrative. The meaning of "relationship" and "peace," as defined from within the client's community, may differ from the therapist's understanding, even when these words obviously exist within both language communities.

If tradition-sensitive therapy accepts the radical otherness of the client, then it is more peaceable than approaches that violate the client's particularity by assuming the universality of human nature. It may even be more personally transformative than the application of thinner interventions. A therapy that accesses the social network of the client and his or her thick cultural heritage will enable the client to manage the pain of human experience from within local narratives to which the client is committed.

We have attempted to locate thick and thin virtue in psychotherapy, outlining a posture of tradition sensitivity for the contemporary clinician that no doubt has parallels in other forms of applied behavioral science. Such a perspective holds the client accountable to his or her own virtues. As a moral enterprise, therapy requires particular attention to local virtue traditions, and it avoids beginning with or assuming universalized models of virtue. However, we are not assuming that therapists will discount wholesale the value of thin discourse for building rapport when client and therapist emerge from disparate communities. Tradition-sensitive psychotherapy will require more effort on the part of the clinician to create a sense of community and shared language while respecting fundamental differences. But it will also require the therapist to encounter the thickness of his or her own virtue tradition as a hedge against the imposition of liberal universalism on the client. In a tradition-sensitive therapy, we might hope for ethnically and religiously indigenous virtue traditions that intersubjectively influence the other. It is just such a therapy that is in fact able to be inclusive of marginal and underrepresented groups. This ability, our key concern, is obtained as it focuses on the interpretation of virtues within a cultural context, sensitizing client and clinician to a range of qualities reflecting positive therapeutic outcomes.

7

Morality

Abstract and Traditioned

■ ■ ■ ■ ■ ■ ■ ■ ■ ■

We remain unconscious of the prodigious diversity of all the everyday language-games because the clothing of our language makes everything alike.

Wittgenstein, *Philosophical Investigations*

In the HBO series entitled *In Treatment*, the therapist sees a young man named Alex, an air force pilot.[1] In the first session he exuded confidence, challenged the therapist at every point, and then ended with a request for advice. He reported he was the one who completed the mission in which sixteen children were killed in a madrassa (school) outside Baghdad. He felt no remorse. They hit the target within two seconds of the appointed time, and he said "he slept like a baby." While jogging back in the United States, he challenged his running partner to keep going, but the partner, a medical doctor, said it was not wise to get one's heart rate up too high. Alex continued, and at mile twenty-two of his run had a heart attack. He was put into a freezer bag and was unconscious for two days, but he lived. He smiled as he told the story. Paul, the therapist, was nonplussed. Here is his response.

> Paul: You know what I find interesting? That shortly after you complete this mission, you go on leave, and against the best advice of your friend who happens to be a medical doctor, you work yourself up into state of extreme exertion. It's as if you were avoiding going back to active duty.

143

> Alex: No, I have no problem flying again. In fact, I am dying to get back in action.
>
> Paul: Hm. You don't see a connection between your collapse and what went before? I know you say you don't have any guilt feelings. But don't you think there is a strong desire there to atone for your actions?
>
> Alex: [Silence] You have any coffee around here? A guy could use a good cup of coffee.
>
> Paul: [Pause] Our time is up, I am afraid.

Paul uses the moral language of atonement and appears to make a connection for Alex between past and present actions. Many communities share the language of atonement, even though there are particular meanings in each community. Moreover, here the language of atonement clarifies and intensifies the clinical issues. In all probability Alex came from a religious tradition that used the language of guilt and atonement, though he largely rejected it.

If clinicians do not think one should ever feel guilty, even after bombing a school, then raising the issue of atonement is a distraction. If there is a moral issue here, then using the spiritual language the client understands is clinically and ethically wise. An appropriate role for spiritual language in therapy is to make residual moral sensibilities conscious in the therapeutic moment.

The pre-Socratic poet and philosopher, the tribal shaman, and the ancient sage spoke to moral issues from their villages without being concerned about the need to speak for or to a wider world. Their world was the only one they knew; there was no other place from which to speak. It is only the geographically mobile modern who can imagine speaking to and for a plurality of communities from a place beyond history, a God's-eye perspective. The modern therapist faced with a plethora of ethnically and religiously diverse clients survives by assuming a generalized view of human nature and/or a principled morality. The first we already have critiqued; the second is our concern now.

In this chapter we look at the nature of foundationalist knowledge and abstract principles of morality. We explore the nature of morality embedded in communal convictions and practices. Foundationalism was originally a strategy for peace, but we now wonder whether that is still the case. In this chapter we point to Wittgenstein's view of language communities as a critique of foundationalism and recommend MacIntyre's perspective on coherent traditions as a correction. We contrast a thin epistemology with a more thick, communitarian view of knowledge and morality, granting there is a place for both.

What is foundationalism? With the demise of the medieval world and the raging religious wars that decimated a large portion of the population of Europe (1618–1648), the need surfaced for self-evident truths upon which a new worldview could be constructed. Modernists replaced what they perceived to be a superstitious medieval worldview with a foundation, indubitable beliefs on which to construct a social consensus. War created a problem not only for the unity of society, but also for the unity of knowledge. Modern foundation-alism resulted from challenges to the perceived authoritarianism of religion and the superstitious nature of premodern beliefs. How does one create unity where there is violent diversity? Foundationalism was originally a strategy for creating peace between warring factions of the Christian church!

Not surprisingly, then, modernity has been obsessed with discovering knowl-edge that is certain, beyond doubt. Stephen Toulmin, in his book *Cosmopolis: The Hidden Agenda of Modernity*, has argued that Descartes's search for foundations emerged during thirty years of religious war. What could replace warring traditions and create a unifying foundation? One needed only to look at the effect of religious ideologies on society—fragmentation. As long as one catholic church ordered society, epistemological issues remained hidden. If traditions war with one another, the situation is ripe for creating an overarch-ing ideological resolution.[2] Toulmin makes the point that major shifts in the seventeenth century served as the context for Descartes's reflections.[3] These shifts, which were reflected in Descartes's solution to the conflict of religious traditions,[4] included a move from oral to written communication, from the particular to the universal, from the local to the general, and from what is timely to the timeless.

Descartes sought knowledge that was indubitable. He believed that if one could perceive something "clearly and distinctly" in one's mind, one could be certain of its veracity and build the rest of one's knowledge upon it. For Descartes, a system of beliefs (i.e., knowledge) could be conceived of as a building. This system of beliefs, like any stable construction, needed a foun-dation. Descartes felt a need to replace the unstable foundation of religion and tradition in the old building with the more stable foundation of indubi-table beliefs. One thing beyond doubt was the fact that we are able to doubt everything except that we are doubters. Since doubting is a form of thinking, reason became the new foundation. *Cogito ergo sum*—I think, therefore I am. According to Toulmin, modernity emerged from Renaissance humanism and Descartes's plea for "decontextualized rationalism."

From Descartes onward, a foundation was assumed on which one could build a superstructure of knowledge. Rationality was our common human heritage, our universal resource. Such an approach, referred to as foundationalism, as-sumes that there is a point in the regress of explanations that leads to a class of beliefs that is beyond question.[5] So Descartes could begin with the indubitable belief that he was a thinking being, move on to prove the existence of God, and go from there to a certain knowledge of the external world. Foundation-alism is an epistemology that assumes a bedrock of unquestionable beliefs is available to all rational individuals. Common reason rather than conflicting religious ideologies will be the final court of appeal.

Alasdair MacIntyre makes a distinction between two versions of inquiry: the Encyclopaedic and the Tradition-sensitive.[6] The Encyclopaedic paradigm of knowledge is a descendent of Descartes's position. As a model for the Encyclopaedic mode of inquiry, MacIntyre points to the ninth edition of the *Encyclopedia Britannica*. Just as the British Empire had one code of civility, the encyclopedia assumed one standard of rationality. Given such a faith in rationality, any educated person presumably could be brought to agreement with other educated persons. The methods and goals of this rationality can be equally applied to any distinctive subject matter, whether theology or astronomy. What distinguished entries was the subject matter, not the method.

What is precluded in the Encyclopaedic view is any commitment to a prior and particular theoretical standpoint. MacIntyre comments:

> Descartes symbolized for the nineteenth-century Encyclopaedist a declaration of independence by reason from the particular bonds of any particular moral and religious community. It is on this view of the essence of rationality that its objectivity is inseparable from its freedom from the partialities of all such communities. It is allegiance to reason as such, impersonal, impartial, disinterested, uniting, and universal, that the Encyclopaedist summons his or her readers and hearers.[7]

In this tradition the data must speak for themselves. The encyclopedia uses as its standard of inclusion the scientific verifiability of the material reported.

The progress of science assumes that knowledge is cumulative and the fundamental regularity of nature becomes ever more evident. It is a small step then to apply this to other disciplines as well—psychology, theology, economics, and anthropology. States MacIntyre:

> The Encylopaedist's conception is of a single framework within which knowledge is discriminated from mere belief, progress towards knowledge is mapped, and truth is understood as the relationship of our knowledge to the world, through the application of those methods whose rules are the rules of rationality as such.[8]

In the Encylopaedist's perspective, problems arise and are also resolved from within the paradigm. It is a public, objective paradigm.

Abstract and Minimalist Morality

A foundationalist epistemology generates an abstract morality. MacIntyre's description of the Encyclopaedic tradition is the basis of one of his versions of moral inquiry. Morality in this tradition is a distinct subject matter that can be the object of study like any other object. Morality is then a matter of rules that guide behavior. Further, morality requires that ordinary persons in all places agree regarding the duties necessary for the survival of society. And lastly, morality is independent of particular religious beliefs. The former is more universal, and the latter adds nothing to what is already known. In fact, moral theory can presumably correct the corruptions and distortions of particularist and provincial religions. Non-Western moral traditions are derided as superstitious, primitive, and based on taboos. MacIntyre states:

> Correspondingly in ethics there is on the Encylopaedist's view a set of conceptions of duty, obligation, the right, and the good which have emerged from and can be shown to be superior to—in respect both of title to rational justification and of what is taken to be genuinely moral conduct—their primitive, ancient, and other pre-Enlightenment predecessors.[9]

Moral minimalism means that a moral rule "serves no particular interest, expresses no particular culture, regulates everyone's behavior in a universally advantageous or clearly correct way."[10] A thin abstract morality emerges as minimalist when a situation requires mutual recognition across cultures. Michael Walzer gives the example of watching a televised report on people in Prague marching for justice. To the extent that we understand their placards, there is a transcultural morality of justice, namely, an end to arbitrary arrests and the privileges of the party elite.[11] Minimal morality is not the result of persuasion as much as it is the result of mutual recognition among members of different thick cultures.

Moral philosophy has sought to provide a foundation for moral minimalism and to build an ethical superstructure on this foundation. Minimalism, it was hoped, would supply the few generative rules we could all share that would guide the construction of complex moral structures. MacIntyre, however, repeatedly states that the Enlightenment and subsequent theorists have been unable to agree on what these moral universals are.[12] A thin view of equality, though useful, is, however, incapable of addressing the problem of distributing social goods in a particular society.

Walzer argues that a thin morality is simply one that reiterates the common features of some thick moralities. The hope that universal morality will apply to all cultures fails to reflect our moral experience and pays too high a price for its imposition on thick local cultures. Walzer comments:

> The hope that minimalism, grounded and expanded, might serve the cause of a universal critique is a false hope. Minimalism makes for a certain limited, though important and heartening, solidarity. It doesn't make for a full-blooded universal doctrine. So we march for a while together, and then we return to our own parades. The idea of a moral minimum plays a part in each of these moments, not only in the first. It explains how it is that we come together; it warrants our

separation. By its very thinness, it justifies us in returning to the thickness that is our own. The morality in which the moral minimum is embedded, and from which it can only temporarily be abstracted, is the only full-blooded morality we can ever have. In some sense, the minimum has to be there, but once it is there, the rest is free. We ought to join the marchers in Prague, but once we have done that, we are free to argue for whatever suits our larger moral understandings. There is one march, and there are many (or, there are many marches, and sometimes there is one).[13]

Minimalism is a simplified and single-minded morality. It works with an elementary and undifferentiated understanding of society and self, abstracted from all the actual and elaborated understandings. A minimalist view is a view from a distance or a view in a crisis, so that we can recognize injustice only writ large. "Minimalism gives us no access to the range of social meanings or the specific forms of distributive complexity. We can deal justly, as agents of distribution and as critics-in-detail, only from the inside of a maximalist morality."[14]

Foundationalism in psychology assumes that reason can determine principles of morality. Perhaps one might avoid the language of moral neutrality so common in theorists of psychotherapy and begin with a view of therapy shaped by moral principles. We could assume the existence of a moral foundation that would serve as the positive objectives of psychotherapy. Mary Nicholas posits five such principles or virtues: justice, egalitarianism, honesty, altruism, and responsibility.[15] She identifies scientific materialism, individualism, and positivism as factors that militate against taking these virtues seriously in therapy.[16]

Nicholas opens her book with a case example. A client pays for his sessions with large wads of cash. Nicholas, the therapist, suspects he is a drug dealer, and her supervisor suggests she confront him about his unethical behavior. To her surprise, the client accepts Nicholas's concern about his drug dealing. He replies:

> Now that I have a kid, I cannot respect myself for doing this—I never did, really. How would I feel if someone sold my kid drugs? It's a lousy thing to be doing. I guess I needed you to say something. I'm going to stop.[17]

And he did. Nicholas predicates her intervention on the belief that this client violated the principles listed above. Unethical behavior and mental health are antithetical.

Nicholas argues that the therapist is a moral beacon. Building on the work of Viktor Frankl, Gordon Allport, Eric Fromm, Perry London, and Rollo May, she advocates that we see the therapist as a moral guide, and therapy as the creation of goodness. For most contemporary therapists, the highest priority for clients in treatment is the improved expression of feelings, the exercise of freedom and autonomy, and the development of coping skills, self-awareness, and growth.[18] However, for Nicholas, therapy is a process of *remoralizing* clients. It can help them understand the difference between appropriate and inappropriate guilt. To take responsibility for one's actions while in therapy may occasion guilt if one has violated some personal or community standard. This may lead to asking for forgiveness and then making reparation.

Nicholas reports on a program offering Vietnam veterans opportunities to address the effects of the war by asking them to engage in public acts of service. Group therapy, for example, inherently encourages the development of egalitarianism, altruism, and honesty. Therapy "changes the client's virtue profile for the better—increasing virtues that are neglected and evening out the imbalances among the virtues and their level of operation in the private and public domains."[19] Failure to take growth seriously in these moral domains implicates the therapist. Moral outrage is for Nicholas an appropriate response to a client who is HIV positive and engaging in unprotected sex.[20]

Nicholas is troubled by the possibility that therapists see issues in therapy as primarily psychological, rather than also as possible moral violations. Imagine a mother who changes her will after her daughter wishes to marry a man she does not approve of. Nicholas sees the mother as violating a tacit promise she in fact made to her daughter regarding the inheritance. That is a moral issue. The therapist would do well to encourage the client to take moral responsibility for unjust actions.

Nicholas believes that there are moral issues related to various pathologies but does *not* argue that ethical failures cause pathologies. She grants the contribution of biological and cultural factors, but then goes on to suggest that in depression, for example, nascent narcissism must also be addressed. Borderline clients who vacillate between idealizing and denigrating others do so after years of fearing abandonment or feeling controlled. Symptoms may include dissociation, rage, paranoia, and phobic anxiety. All of these tendencies and symptoms render goodness difficult for the individual with borderline personality disorder, who is prone to unfairly blaming others for his or her own problems (justice), is totally unaware of the feelings and needs of others (altruism), reneges on commitments (responsibility), acts superior to and humiliates others (egalitarianism), and presents radically contradictory and inaccurate information (honesty).[21]

To the extent that therapy fosters free and equal relationships, Nicholas maintains, it can also foster goodness. Therapy can empower the oppressed client to address oppression. Therapy must be a search for truth, a pursuit of life, and a growing courage to love. Moral therapists are openly delighted when clients engage in goodness. The therapist seeks not to be morally neutral but to be fair, compassionate, morally sensitive, and encouraging. He or she can assist clients in not making their mental illness an excuse for immoral behavior. Nicholas quotes psychiatrist Richard Rubin:

I hold as a jumping off point two assumptions: that ultimately the currency of love is a higher order of interaction than the currency of power; and that living in harmony and balance with the universe is better than trying to live separately from and/or trying to control the universe.

I don't proselytize that. It influences how I interact, and I just keep questioning. For example, if someone says, "My goal is power and money," I say, "Why do you want power? What will it give you? What do you want power over? Why?" Over and over and over until their beliefs fall apart, and what they realize they really want is that higher order of interaction—love. If they are struggling to win, to control, to gain revenge, I always find, upon questioning, that what they really want is the harmony that comes after the struggle.

I use my beliefs to help them begin to question theirs, to help them clarify their own philosophical position; and while I rarely tell them my philosophy, inevitably their ideas seem to move in the direction I have described. I don't believe that this is because I lead them there, but because these conclusions are more or less inescapable when we struggle with our goals and purposes in life.[22]

Nicholas makes an important contribution. She models how morality can play a significant role in understanding pathology and directing psychotherapy. We agree with her argument that virtues exist on a continuum from private to public. She maintains that the virtues must be consistently practiced at personal, relational, familial, social, and global levels. Moreover, she sees this moral framework as an integral part of personality theory. We concur, and would add that this consistency between public and private morality applies to the therapist as well.

Although there is then much in Nicholas's argument with which we agree, we do have some reservations. Moral imperatives in modern societies (as in thin therapy) take the form of rules that are context-independent and unrelated to religious particularities. The client's religiosity, then, is assessed from a foundationalist moral point of view that is assumed to correct the provincial morality of the client—and sometimes it does. Moral minimalism is all that is possible in this model of therapy. Justice is the moral average of the two communities represented in the client–therapist dyad. This thin form of morality—minimalism—may have its roots in some form of moral maximalism resident in the therapist's own community, or in the culture in which both client and therapist exist. It may be utilized in times of crisis and confusion. Granted, a thin foundationalist morality may sometimes be all that a therapist has available to leverage change.

In her approach, Nicholas simply *posits* the five virtues. One wonders if there is consensus on their meaning in our culture and whether indeed they carry the same meaning in different ethno-religious groups. The legitimacy of these moral principles is grounded in standard Kantian moral philosophy. In so doing, her approach reflects the method of resolving moral conflicts in liberal societies, namely, stating rights and responsibilities any rational person can discover and endorse. She concurs with Lawrence Kohlberg's claim that justice as a moral principle is cross-cultural but criticizes him for failing to include the other virtues she emphasizes, for neglecting emotionality in the social context of moral development, and for missing the importance of narrative in understanding morality.[23] Her principled morality reflects a thick morality, that of liberal democracies in the Enlightenment tradition. Thin-principled therapy disguises thick moral and cultural assumptions embedded in Western liberal ideology. While we applaud her concern to make therapy ethical, it is not apparent that consensus about the morality emerges out of dialogue with the client. It appears the moral principles are given, a priori.

As a result, when moral exemplars are described in some developmental theories (e.g., Kohlberg), a person like Martin Luther King Jr. is viewed as exhibiting the highest level of moral reasoning, but there is no mention of King's African-American heritage, Christian faith, or theological training. The particularity of his moral community is forgotten.[24]

Charles Taylor argues it is precisely in the particularities that we find the sources of morality and what sustains us in being moral.[25] High moral standards require strong sources. When morality is abstracted from normative traditions that give them substantive meaning, and from contexts that make them concrete, what is left are "values" that are little more than sentiments, expressions of personal preference. James Davidson Hunter refers to this as Romantic modernism, itself a translation of traditional Christian theology. Hunter comments:

> In their most basic contours, the philosophy and literature of Romantic modernism derived from traditional theology. The movement sought to sustain the inherited cultural order of Christianity but without its dogmatic understructure. The problem, of course, was that orthodox theology was no longer tenable in an age dominated by speculative rationality and progressive humanism. Among the urban, well-educated classes, traditional dogma and its assorted pieties had to be abandoned. Yet the moral ideals that Christendom had bequeathed to the late eighteenth and nineteenth century—ideals such as benevolence, civility, and justice—all retained a deep existential relevance. The task, then, was to reconstitute moral philosophy to make it intellectually acceptable as well as emotionally and spiritually fitting to the times. To do this, the traditional Christian narrative and its central concepts were demythologized and reconceived. . . . Particularly in the nineteenth century, Romanticism evolved into a Neoplatonized Christianity in which all of the core concepts of biblical theology were transformed into ethical universals. God "the Father" was displaced by a notion of an impersonal first principle—variously understood as "mind" or "spirit." Divine perfection was equated with the notion of a natural, self-sufficient, and undifferentiated unity in the cosmos. Likewise, traditional concepts of evil, represented by rebellion against a holy deity, were transmogrified into notions of a "division" and "estrangement." In this, Romantic modernists did not so

much discard the old myths as translate them into the conceptual framework of an agnostic and intuitive humanism.[26]

Tradition-Sensitive Epistemology

The moment one experiences another culture as truly different, the question of relationship to one's own origins becomes salient. The new culture may be different not only in language and custom, but also in morality and normative myths. As we have pointed out in the previous sections, given the diversity of cultures one can find commonality in ideas which override the differences. However, Plato's distillation of ideas from "mere" appearance is a process that occurs within a language whose words were presumed to be univocal. Socrates' definition of the person who is just occurs within a particular language located in a particular culture that valued justice in terms of honor (*arête*).[27]

There are a number of voices that counter the prevailing Cartesian rationalist foundationalism. All are skeptical of the received tradition that assumes rational inquiry can build on an indubitable foundation. Their point of departure is the historical community that precedes the individual. We begin with Wittgenstein's view of language and then proceed to MacIntyre's tradition-oriented view of knowledge.

An important step toward a tradition-sensitive knowledge or psychotherapy is the recognition that language emerges out of communities. Wittgenstein's analysis of language is a thick analysis and hence useful in understanding the difference in languages between cultures. Standard language theories assume sentences take on meaning if we know what the individual words refer to. In his *Philosophical Investigations*, Wittgenstein assumes that words do indeed refer to a reality.[28] But he points out that we request, report, speculate, role-play, and so on, using language. The meaning of a word is a function of context, of usage in a community of language users. Language was for Wittgenstein no private affair; it was a communal practice. Language and its applications are rule-governed in a community of language users who implicitly agree on the rules. Sentences take on meaning depending on the circumstances in which they are uttered. Meaning and action are closely related to the context and community in which a statement is made.

Wittgenstein refers to this contextuality in terms of "language games." He suggests that each language game is complete in itself, like a tribal language. It is difficult to engage in conversation across language communities because there is no standpoint beyond the language communities from which one can engage conversation. The rules (or grammars) that shape language games differ from one language community to the next. One cannot know in advance the commensurability of two language games.

Wittgenstein described language as referential in his first major work, the *Tractatus Logico-Philosophicus*.[29] After detailing the nature of referential language, he concluded that whereof one cannot speak, one must remain silent—that other reality was a mystical reality. These two realities were incommensurable. But in his later work, Wittgenstein argued for the importance of understanding language and meaning from within a given language community. These language games are, for Wittgenstein, a form of life. By extension, tradition-sensitive psychotherapy functions as a form of life.

Tradition is not a popular basis for reflecting on the nature of inquiry, conversation in the public square, moral inquiry, or an understanding of the self. After all, an obsession with tradition has resulted in bigotry, ethnic cleansing, and religious wars. Nevertheless, Alasdair MacIntyre wishes to refurbish the notion of tradition. As we have already seen, he sets forth the case that Encyclopaedia and Tradition represent different modes of rationality.[30]

The tradition-sensitive approach points out that for any event there is more than one interpretation. How does the Encyclopaedist decide which data are to be included and which excluded? That, the Traditionalists argue, is a function of pretheoretical and theoretical commitments. Tradition-oriented rationality seeks continuity with the past within a tradition. Reason, MacIntyre argues, requires membership in a prior community, a tradition.

For MacIntyre, the goal of encyclopedic knowledge is a singular basis for all knowledge, available to everyone through a common application of reason. From the Encylopaedist's perspective, problems arising from within the paradigm are also resolved from within, via a consensus-driven application of rules that are universal in scope. MacIntyre notes that this is problematic where decisions must be made regarding which data to include in a particular domain of knowledge. Worse, the Encyclopaedist may be confronted by contradictory data that cannot be resolved via internal consensus alone.

MacIntyre argues that the purposive basis for knowledge is better understood in terms of its membership in a tradition. Rationality in a tradition seeks as its *telos* vital continuity with its own living, breathing history. The medieval lecturer, for example, shared with his audience a background of beliefs and assumptions with the general understanding that his material was authoritative because its authority was derived from the storied legacy of its tradition.

MacIntyre takes his stand as follows: "A prior commitment is required and the conclusions which emerge as enquiry progresses will of course have been partially and crucially predetermined by the nature of this initial commitment."[31] The nature of this prior commitment is the willingness to apprentice oneself to a craft and to submit to the wisdom and authority of a master teacher who embodies the tradition.

> The apprentice has to learn to distinguish between the kind of excellence which both others and he or she can expect of him or herself here and now and that

ultimate excellence which furnishes both apprentices and master craftsmen with their *telos*. . . . So the apprentice learns what it is about him or herself that has to be transformed, that is, what vices need to be eradicated, what intellectual and moral virtues need to be cultivated.[32]

(Such reliance on authority is anathema in the Encyclopaedist tradition, where to think for oneself is the primary virtue.) Following Aristotle, MacIntyre adds that learning the skills of a craft is not sufficient. Desire informed by reason must be directed to some end; that end is the *telos* as defined by the moral community. Furthermore, the history of the tradition is used to interpret and critique the present. MacIntyre uses Aquinas to illustrate that the tradition-sensitive approach is not a closed paradigm. Aquinas's integration of Aristotle and Augustine led to the grand structure of the *Summa,* a work Aquinas viewed as incomplete.

Maximal and Minimal Moralities

Given our earlier review of Michael Walzer, it is not surprising that we also turn to him for a more communitarian reading of morality.[33] Following Clifford Geertz,[34] Walzer utilizes the thick–thin distinction as a way of construing moral inquiry. Thick morality is "richly referential, culturally resonant, locked into a locally established symbolic system or network of meanings."[35] The notion of justice is in Walzer's perspective embedded in a network of social meanings (i.e., thick).

> But any full account of how social goods ought to be distributed will display the features of moral maximalism: it will be idiomatic in its language, particularist in its cultural reference, and circumstantial in the two senses of that word: historically dependent and factually detailed. Its principles and procedures will have been worked out over a long period of time through complex social interactions.[36]

Such a process does not begin with a single comprehensive and universal principle. Nor does it assume the isolated self makes a rational decision that considers others from a position where their particularities are irrelevant. Rather, Walzer begins with the community that already has a history and a set of shared meanings. "Justice requires the defense of difference—different goods distributed for different reasons among different groups of people—and it is this requirement that makes justice a thick or maximalist moral idea, reflecting the actual thickness of particular cultures and societies."[37] Minimalism does not work, because it assumes that a simple good can be generalized across what Walzer calls different spheres. Any social good is enclosed within boundaries, fixed by the principles of that sphere such that application outside of it creates problems. Money, for example, is appropriate for market exchange, but not as a political bribe.

As important as it is to distinguish thick and thin moralities, it is just as important to know their relationship to each other. Corresponding to thick and thin are Walzer's terms: moral maximalism and minimalism. Their relationship can be summarized as follows. Maximalism precedes minimalism in time and substance. Minimalism assumes that we all have the same ultimate values in common; maximalism does not. Referring to the dualism of thick and thin morality, Walzer comments:

> This dualism is, I think, an internal feature of every morality. Philosophers most often describe it in terms of a (thin) set of universal principles adapted (thickly) to these or those historical circumstances. I have in the past suggested the image of a core morality differently elaborated in different cultures. The idea of elaboration is better than adaptation, it seems to me, because it suggests a process less circumstantial and constrained, more freely creative: governed as much by ideal as by practical considerations. It accounts better for the actual differences that anthropology and comparative history reveal. But both these descriptions suggest mistakenly that the starting point for the development of morality is the same in every case. Men and women everywhere begin with some common idea or principle or set of ideas and principles, which they then work up in many different ways. They start thin, as it were, and thicken with age, as if in accordance with our deepest intuition about what it means to develop or mature. But our intuition is wrong here. Morality is thick from the beginning, culturally integrated, fully resonant, and it reveals itself thinly only on special occasions, when moral language is turned to specific purposes.[38]

Minimalism and maximalism are both helpful, depending on the context and purposes. We return to the example mentioned earlier, the people in Prague marching for justice. To the extent that we understand the message their placards proclaim, to that extent there is a transcultural morality of justice—namely, an end to arbitrary arrests and the abolition of privileges of the party elite. However, when Czech citizens debate their health-care system, the meaning of justice will be less universal and more a reflection of their history and culture. The latter comes first in time; the former builds on it.

Minimalism is inherent in maximalism. The relationship of thin to thick moralities is for Walzer such that within every thick particularist morality there are the makings of a thin morality.

> Minimalist meanings are embedded in the maximal morality, expressed in the same idiom, sharing the same (historical/cultural/ religious/political) orientation. Minimalism is liberated from its embeddedness and appears independently, in varying degrees of thinness, only in the course of a personal or social crisis or political confrontation.[39]

Definitions of justice for Chiapas Indians in Mexico, Kosovar Albanians in the Balkans, and Soweto blacks in South Africa are necessarily thicker than in the United Nations, or other international interests with a stake in those struggles. The Hebrew definition of justice may be more accessible to the Jew or Christian than it will be to others. On the other hand, the moral minimalism that emerges may be as close as possible to the core morality of a group. Thickness only tends to qualify, compromise, complexify, and disagree.

Minimalism cannot replace maximalism. Walzer would eschew the external imposition of values or principles on a thicker group. He also assumes that the morality of no one group in a society should determine the distribution of goods in a particular society. However, every maximalist community stands in relation to its own society, and that relationship of dialogue may be descriptive or critical. Its ethic is thick and its idealism unique to its social meanings and ideals. A thin view of equality, though useful, is incapable of addressing the complexity of distributing goods within that community

Walzer disagrees with those who suggest that a thin transcultural morality has no role to play. Minimalism can critique particularism. Here it plays primarily a critical or negative role. Walzer believes that a general sense of justice can emerge out of a community that serves as a critique and qualification of other thick moral communities. A person who justifies suicide on the maximalism of his or her community may be criticized on the basis of moral principles of the value of life.

Finally, minimalism is not the foundation for maximalism. Minimalist morality is hastily constructed, on the fly, like the marchers' placards—and that only alludes to the thick morality in the background. Minimalism can facilitate the encounter between maximalist cultures and moralities. When a form of justice that crosses cultures is necessary, then moral minimalism is invoked; but when the justice needed is local, then a more thickly nuanced morality can be the basis of discussion.

MacIntyre's distinction between Encyclopaedic and Traditioned knowledge places the problem of foundations and tradition in a frame that is relevant to our own Christian commitments. The resources of Encyclopaedic knowledge are limited as an adequately reconciling and healing force. Ironically, tradition might also end as an exercise in idolatry, and worship its own legacy apart from any appeal to external validation. The difference is in MacIntyre's insistence that authentic tradition is placed *under* authority. Moreover, the human quest for universal foundations is an idolatrous attempt to usurp God's prerogative to create unity around the cross of Jesus Christ. A Christian psychology recognizes near total hegemony of foundationalism which obscures God's prerogatives in the ultimate ends of knowledge. We believe that these ends, revealed in the biblical narrative, are unavoidably christological.

8

Sacred Order and a Prozac God

■ ■ ■ ■ ■ ■ ■ ■ ■ ■

> It is a very dangerous inversion to advocate Christianity, not because it is true,
> but because it might be beneficial.
>
> T. S. Eliot, *Christianity and Culture*

Apart from William James, who thought religion was a proper subject of study for psychologists, most of the past century followed the lead of Sigmund Freud, for whom religion was an illusion, a compensation for instinctual sacrifices, and the psychological residue of harsh religion.[1] But by the end of the century there seemed to be a thaw, such that even a hard-core behaviorist like Albert Ellis changed his mind. He had initially regarded religious beliefs as irrational and emotionally harmful but adopted a more moderate position where religion might be useful for psychological health.[2]

In recent years there has been renewed interest by research psychologists on the role of religion in human behavior.[3] Contrary to the modernist argument that religion was a seedbed for psychopathology, current studies have obtained very different results. Religion is correlated to health across a variety of measures. In fact, the research suggests that on some variables religious people are healthier than nonreligious individuals; hence, psychologists are encouraged to use spirituality as an important intervention in therapy.

At face value this development seems positive. The hidden issues, however, should give us pause. How is religion defined and understood in this research literature? Are we referring to the dogmatic statements of religious bodies slightly adapted for therapy? Or is religion the all-embracing arms of acceptance that turn out to be ethically anemic? Is religion inclusive or exclusive? Is

157

it a feeling? A system of beliefs? Public or private? Is religion simply a social habit that a client brings to therapy? Is religion an abstract, universal conceptualization of what all religious groups have in common? How is health defined? Is it possible that the meaning of spirituality and religion has changed once it is imported into the framework of research designs? Now that the profession of psychology is taking religion more seriously, these questions become increasingly important.

In earlier chapters we proposed that there is an inextricable link between culture, religion, and language. We emphasized that in therapy the religious client should be empowered to speak in his or her mother tongue. In this chapter we will be first critical and then constructive. After a sample of studies of religion and health, we will argue that the "religion" of these research studies is a very thin version of what passes for spirituality in many particular religious communities. We have allowed a secular society to define religion in ways suitable to its purposes, a domesticated religiosity. We think that the generic label "religion" is a social construction that does not reflect the reality of particular faith traditions.

Next we address the fact that religion and spirituality are now considered useful: they promote health. Given the popularity of mood-altering medication, the American public looks to science to solve emotional and spiritual issues. Just as Prozac alters moods, so God becomes the dispenser of health, if only one faithfully engages in personal acts of piety. Religion and spirituality are still primarily viewed from the perspective of a psychology of individuals. Healing, apparently, is not something that occurs in the context of a community. This may be a grave error, particularly given Wendell Berry's argument that community is the smallest unit of healing.[4] In the second half of this chapter, we call for a traditioned religion as part of therapy. In particular we explore the recent work of Philip Rieff on sacred cultures, a profound contrast to the religion of a Prozac god.

Religion and Health

We begin with a brief sampling of the literature which examines the relationship between religion and health. In one study, African-American inpatients who suffered from schizophrenia were less likely to be rehospitalized when their families encouraged them to continue religious worship in the hospital, and patients were more likely to be readmitted if their families had no religious affiliation.[5] In another study, patients with higher intrinsic religious motivation remitted faster (70%) from depression than those with extrinsic religious motivation. In another setting, two-thirds of patients studied indicated that religion helped them cope with medical problems and life crises.[6] Being religious is correlated with reduced alcoholism.[7] Religiously oriented therapy treating anxious and/or depressed clients had significantly better short-term outcomes.[8] Religious populations have lower rates of suicide and live longer.

An early and well-known study on the beneficent effect of religion on therapy was conducted by Rebecca Propst and her colleagues.[9] They utilized two versions of cognitive-behavioral therapy—one religious and the other nonreligious. Patients were all diagnosed as having nonpsychotic, nonbipolar depression, and all fifty-nine patients were religious, divided between a control group and a group that received standard pastoral counseling. The results indicated that those patients receiving religious cognitive therapy or pastoral counseling scored lower than the control group on measures of depression, a difference that persisted when measured again after three months, and again after two years. Furthermore, there was greater social adjustment and reduced general symptomatology for religious individuals receiving religious cognitive therapy. Also, individuals in the pastoral-counseling treatment condition significantly improved as measured by the Beck Depression Inventory. Propst and her group reasoned that there might be a clash in cultural values between traditional cognitive therapy that associates personal autonomy with self-efficacy and religious individuals who value dependence on a divine being.

So what can we conclude? Does religion facilitate the process of healing? Certainly we cannot conclude that just because religious language was used that God was then directly involved in the healing process. Minimally, we can conclude that the inclusion of religious language is not necessarily harmful to the client. It may be that using the language of faith helps to create a therapeutic alliance and helps the client to access deeply held values and beliefs. If the move toward embracing religion means that psychology and medicine are relinquishing a positivist view of the body and psyche, we think this is a move in the right direction. If this shift to understanding the role of religion in the life of the individual means we will respond more holistically to clients in terms of their religious convictions, practices, and communities, we could affirm this development.

But what does this connection between religion and health mean? Does the research reinforce the notion that devotion to God or respect for divine forces is the immediate cause of health?[10] This may not be the assumption of those who conducted the research, but in a cultural ethos in which correlation equals causation, it follows that personal devotion leads to God's intervention. After all, some may assume that worship of a Prozac god is rewarded with healing and health.

The deeper issue relates to the nature of the religion that is being advocated as therapeutic. The religion that emerges from the research on faith and health may not be the God of the scriptures. We have been theologically uncritical of the rapprochement between religion and mental health. We agree with Shuman and Meador:

As theologians and practitioners, we believe that there is much to be commended about the rediscovery of religious faith by scientific medicine, but we remain suspicious of the shape taken by that discovery to this point. . . . In spite of what empirical studies show about the correlation between religion and health, it is from the perspective of faithful Christian discipleship fundamentally wrong-headed to suggest—as our colleagues sometimes seem to do—that religious belief or behavior is in some sense the efficient cause of better health.[11]

It is one thing to take religion into account. It is yet another to propose that religion serves as an instrument of healing.[12] The research assumes that a scientific perspective is neutral with regard to any particular religion. Is this possible? To portray the individual desire for individual health as an end in itself, do we not unwittingly give expression to a particular religion? Is that expression different from orthodox Christianity?[13] The view of religion implicit in this research literature is instrumental, private, and commoditized.

Religion from a Secular Perspective

As we have stated earlier, religion and secularism are two diverging traditions in the modern world. So the first issue is, which community will define religion? Is it the secular researcher or the religious community? Is "religion" even the best term to use? The problem is that to speak of a faith tradition as a religion may already bias us toward secularity. To speak of religions in general assumes that one can take a bird's-eye view of all religions and then objectively compare them. Note how abstract and general religion becomes in this definition: ". . . beliefs, actions and institutions predicated on the existence of entities with powers of agency (that is, gods) or impersonal powers or processes possessed of moral purpose (the Hindu notion of karma, for example), which can set the conditions of, or intervene in, human affairs."[14]

In secular academic culture it is possible to refer to the literature of a religious group as a sacred language. Yet, as Asad points out, in classical Islamic discourse the Arabic language of the Qur'an is never called "a sacred language" as it is in modern secular discourse.[15] The idea of a sacred language presupposes an abstraction called "language" and that it can then be combined with a contingent quality called "sacredness."

Consistent with our emphasis on indigeneity, we begin with the discourse of a particular faith tradition, Christianity, rather than that of religion in general. We begin with the ordinary language that particular individuals use to describe their faith. However, in social-science research religion is usually defined as privately held beliefs or attendance at religious events. It is assumed that religion is a sacred entity that is in decline with the rise of secularism. When the secularist defines religion, it becomes a universal essence, a universal but hidden quality. The sacred becomes a mysterious mythical quality. We follow Asad in arguing that there is no universal essence which defines sacred language or sacred experience. To the extent that theology uncritically adopts the secular rationality of modern psychologies, the latter will shape the former. John Milbank takes a hard line: twentieth-century theology has capitulated to the autonomy of secular reason. The Christian scholar would argue for the priority of a Christian meta-discourse, "a persuasion intrinsic to the Christian logos itself."[16] It is possible that we too easily connect our knowledge of God with some immanent field of knowledge. According to Milbank:

> There is a perceived need to discover precisely how to fulfill Christian precepts about charity and freedom in contemporary society in an uncontroversial manner, involving cooperation with the majority of non-Christian fellow citizens. Purportedly scientific diagnoses and recommendations fulfill precisely this role.[17]

Milbank cautions against a theology which assumes that the social sciences provide a significant reading of religion which theology must "take account of." Rather, secular discourse is a heresy in relation to orthodox Christianity. Scientific social theories are anti-theologies in disguise. Writing about sociology in particular, Milbank suggests that "theology encounters in sociology only a theology, and indeed a church in disguise, but a theology and a church dedicated to promoting a certain secular consensus."[18]

We are sympathetic to Milbank's argument and agree that the social sciences are fully secularized. It is important to understand what that means and how it affects the way a discipline functions in society. We agree that it is imperative that we juxtapose to secular understandings a Christian understanding of the self. Does that require a complete dismissal of secular disciplines? We think not. The secular can be construed as that which we share in common.[19] We are simply suggesting that a theology of the person need not begin with a secular tradition. When we begin with our confessional convictions we can then incorporate from other traditions and discourses that which is consistent and helpful, a notion well articulated by Karl Barth.[20] This will, however, require that we understand the vocabulary and syntax of secular discourse as argued in an earlier chapter.

Religion as Generic

If one can develop categories to describe the flora and fauna of nature, one presumably can do the same when comparing religions. We are concerned about the consequences for religion and health research given this assumption. While there are some clear differences between religions, it is assumed that there are nevertheless overarching common categories such as belief in a deity or ultimate force, sacred scriptures, exemplary figures, and so forth. Since reality is fundamentally and metaphysically homogeneous, all religions are at a basic level similar but with some historically accidental differences. However, we argue that religion as a category is the fabrication of the idealist.

The religion and health research assumes that more important than what is believed is the very act of believing itself. Says Herbert Benson,

> I describe "God" with a capital "G" in this book but nevertheless hope readers will understand I am referring to all the deities of the Judeo-Christian, Buddhist, Muslim, and Hindu traditions, to gods and goddesses, as well as to all the spirits worshipped and beloved by humans all over the world and throughout history. In my scientific observations, I have observed that no matter what name you give the Infinite Absolute you worship, no matter what theology you ascribe to, the results of believing in God are the same.[21]

We have created a Prozac god, reducing knowledge of the deity to attributes rather than focusing on the redeeming actions of God in history. Is it possible that the god referenced in religion and health studies is not the God of Jesus Christ? Can one simply plug any god into the salubrious equation of religion and health?

Religion is assumed in this research literature to be a comprehensive and neutral category. Religion is a more determinative category than is Islam, Judaism, or Christianity. The focus is not the object of belief, but simply the willful act of believing. Shuman and Meador comment:

> A religious faith that is understood primarily as a function of universal human subjectivity is necessarily theologically neutral with respect to any particular religious tradition. Because the contemporary rapprochement has its origins at least partly in recent social scientific and epidemiological research, it is directed by the canons of that research toward a broader, more generic understanding of religion and of faith than any one tradition would ordinarily permit. Since the act of believing is transcultural and transhistorical, the capacity of faith to influence health exceeds any limitations placed on it by any particular historical religious tradition.[22]

So "the primal act of belief, because it is thought to be a scientifically demonstrable part of human being, is more significant and more inherently 'truthful' than the content of any particular belief."[23]

In contrast to the religion studied by the researchers, the faith practiced by many Americans is much more historically particular. In fact, faithfulness is usually interpreted as consistency with an account of the world offered by the religious tradition. However, the definition of religion in the religion and health reasearch is radically individualized. In a culture that emphasizes the autonomous individual, religion is a private way of achieving personal mental health. In a technological culture, a sense of entitlement to a physically and emotionally problem-free world emerges, and religion becomes a backup strategy. It seems the larger culture, more than a particular tradition, is shaping the definition of religion. Is it empirical research that demonstrates what leads to wholeness and health, or is that a matter to be decided by the theology of a particular religious tradition? For most historic religions, it is the tradition that shapes the meaning of truth, goodness and health.

Religion as Instrumental

Increasingly, in both the pulpit and consulting room religion is seen as useful. If medical and psychological interventions fail, one can always pray. Religion and science can be partners. If psychological science and psychopharmacology are reliable interventions, then it is possible that the Prozac god becomes simply the "god of the gaps." This is an instrumental view of religion. If religion is good for your health, the prescription is logical—practice religion! If certain religious beliefs are empirically demonstrated to result in bad health, they should be discouraged; but if they lead to health, obviously they should be reinforced.

However, historic religions have been concerned less with teaching their adherents how to live long than with how to live faithfully. Following T. S. Eliot, to value religion for its usefulness, viewed theologically, may be a form of idolatry.[24] It is one thing to affirm that persons with shared religious beliefs and practices live longer or spend less on health care, but it is quite another matter to argue that *for those reasons* one should adopt the beliefs of a particular religious group. When the findings of the connection between religion and health are made the basis of clinical interventions, ethical, theological, and moral issues emerge. Here the logic is that *because* epidemiological data indicate religious persons are healthier, religious behavior can be advocated as a salutary clinical intervention.

The psychological consequences of believing in a Prozac god are considerable. For those clients who come to therapy with thick religious construals, instrumental versions of religiosity may well undermine their belief in the truth of their own faith apart from its usefulness. Implicit to the religion of the religion–health equation is an obsession with controlling the course of history. However, Shuman and Meador point out that the Christian can "live hopefully, with the certainty that the ultimate meaning of history—including each individual's personal history of sickness and of health—is determined not by scientific or religious cause and effect but by the cross and the resurrection of Christ."[25]

Religion and physical/mental health have been shaped by a consumerism in which health is the commodity, the practitioners are the purveyors, and the HMOs are the brokers. The meaning of health is then separated from the communities and their hierarchy of goods in which sickness and health are located. In a consumerist ethos, religion is simply one commodity among many, a commodity one can select, purchase, and exchange. A pragmatic American culture wants a religion that is helpful, especially when one is in crisis. For HMOs, religious interventions are a cost-effective way of addressing rising health-care costs.

When religion is domesticated, God becomes an element in an exchange.[26] If one engages in particular kinds of devotional behaviors, such as regular church attendance, meditation, or prayer, the result will be increased health. The religious life is then reduced to techniques that can produce results. In this contractual relationship God is bound to fulfill an obligation to reward devotion with health.

But this approach comes at great cost. What is lost is the social context in which these religious practices take on meaning. What if the suffering is a consequence of unjust acts the client has engaged in? Do we simply help the counselee remove the pain of suffering the consequences? There are those who suffer because of their religious convictions, but that does not seem to get factored into the religion and health formula.

The Privatization of Religion

Related to the notion of a Prozac god is the belief that religion is a private affair. The privatization of religion means that religious language, religious assumptions about the world, and religiously justified moral principles belong to a committed minority with these inner beliefs. And yet most cultures of the world do not share these assumptions. Millions of people practice their faith publicly, structuring their daily routines around spiritual practices. Dress, careers, eating habits, gender relations, and spending all unfold beneath a sacred canopy. In many cultures of the world, politics and civil society are suffused with religion. To separate public character from religious norms is anathema in Christianity, Judaism, and Islam. For many the center of their social world is the church, the synagogue, or the mosque. How then can one argue that religion must remain private?

As we have been arguing, a minimalist view of religion's public role will have negative consequences for clients and therapists who are avowedly religious. The implications of the withdrawal of religion from the public square are serious for the clinical encounter. If religion is an issue of character, we are wise to consider how religion functions in maintaining that character, not as a private phenomenon but rather as a public interface. We have seen that Richard Rorty assumes the religious aspect can be sifted out and silenced in public.[27] Clients who have absorbed the cultural bias against religion in public will be reluctant to bring their religious self to the therapeutic situation. Should these individuals enter therapy, only part of their personhood is present and available for treatment.

From the perspective of a cultural anthropologist, Clifford Geertz makes a case for religion as a preeminent integrative force in human experience, potentially the most important single aspect in an appropriation of what it means to be human. Religion, Geertz argues, is not simply one characteristic of cultural beings. It is integral to culture. Religion synthesizes a person's ethos and worldview. Religion binds together reason and practice, emotion and relationship, public and private. Geertz explains:

> In religious belief and practice a group's ethos is rendered intellectually reasonable by being shown to represent a way of life ideally adapted to the actual state of affairs the world view describes, while the world view is rendered emotionally convincing by being presented as an image of an actual state of affairs peculiarly well-arranged to accommodate such a way of life. This confrontation and mutual confirmation has two fundamental effects. On the one hand, it objectivizes moral and aesthetic references by depicting them as the imposed conditions of life implicit in a world with a particular structure, as mere common sense given the unalterable shape of reality. On the other, it supports these received beliefs about the world's body by invoking deeply felt moral and aesthetic sentiments as experiential evidence for their truth. Religious symbols formulate a basic congruence between a particular style of life and a specific (if, most often, implicit) metaphysic, and in so doing sustain each with the borrowed authority of the other.[28]

Religion serves to interpret the chaos of events that threaten to overwhelm the individual, to help transcend personal ignorance, weakness, and moral confusion. Religion addresses big questions of ignorance, pain, and justice. Religious rituals are a reflection of the symbols, worldview, emotional sentiments, and practical commitments of the religious community.[29]

Our primary concern is to take seriously the communal dimensions of a client's religion—to validate, nourish, and affirm it. To assume religion is something generic or universal seems to be the most prevalent perspective. Our commitment to the communal religious expression of an ethnic client emerges out of our prior faith convictions. Religion is for us not an invisible entity common to all humanity. It is the expression of a particular confession made by a visible, historical community.

If a client has an intact religious community, values it highly, and finds comfort and support there, why would a clinician not affirm the client's involvement for its own sake, rather than simply for instrumental reasons? This does not mean the therapist agrees with the ideology of the religious community, but only that he or she recognizes that the religious community is what the client has chosen as integral to his or her life. If a client and therapist discover they have in common a religious tradition, it would be important to explore together the meaning of an illness or stressor from the religious tradition's view of health, flourishing, and sickness. We think it important to advocate for exploring fully the particularity of a client, rather than advocating a particular version of religion that is individual, instrumental, and commoditized.

We do not think a Prozac god can deliver on its promises. Religion does not necessarily bring health. For many people, to be religious includes the possibility of suffering. Unfortunately for the instrumental view of religion, not all religious convictions and practices have the positive effects. Violation of a deeply held belief may (appropriately, if we may say so) occasion depression.[30] A prophet may pay with his or her life for taking a specific stance. Ignacio Martín-Baró, the Catholic psychologist martyred in El Salvador, once quipped, "In the US if one does not publish one will perish. Here it is not publish or perish but publish and perish." For sixteenth-century Anabaptists like Conrad Grebel, Felix Manz, and Georg Blaurock, confessing Christ meant being drowned or burned at the stake, or having one's tongue cut out. Had there been a Surgeon General's warning at the time regarding religion and health, it should have read, "Practicing religion can be hazardous to your health." For some contemporary religionists, practicing their radical faith in public has resulted in more depression, not less, in which case religion did not pay off with good mental health.

Health in many religious communities is not a commodity but a gift. Since capitalist cultures tend to take on the character of an exchange of merchandise, religion becomes then simply a private commodity one can select, purchase, and exchange without all the institutional religious baggage.[31] But is not physical and mental health a gift rather than the result of a physical contract in which the Prozac god is bound to fulfill an obligation to reward devotion with health?

Religion as Traditioned

Throughout this book we have advocated for a more cultural and communal understanding of religiosity. In part, to be religious is to learn the language of a particular religious culture and live a life consistent with the grammar of the language learned.[32] Religion in this vein is more about reshaping desire than fulfilling it. Given the myriad of ways religion is practiced, we have not worked with a range of religious perspectives, but with the particular convictions that shape our point of departure. We have not assumed a religion in general because we do not believe religions function "in general." They have histories, memory, rituals, and symbols that differ among them. And so we have begun with particular religious confession, commitments, convictions, and practices. John Caputo writes:

Any book entitled *On Religion* must begin by breaking the bad news to the reader that its subject matter does not exist. "Religion," in the singular, as just one thing, is nowhere to be found; it is too maddeningly polyvalent and too uncontainably diverse for us to fit it all under one roof. . . . Indeed the uncontainable diversity of "religion" is itself a great religious truth and a marker of the uncontainability of what religion is all about.[33]

A comparative approach to religions claims that all religions have themes in common. It may be said that all aim at some form of salvation. For example, salvation is a movement from self-centeredness to other-orientedness. And to say that all religions seek salvation means also that no one religion can claim a unique or normative status. Thus we avoid giving offense to persons of other faiths, and we make available to all the positive contribution of all religions.

We take a decidedly different tack. We think that particularity is not an offense as much as it is a condition of genuine respect for other religious or nonreligious persons. We agree with J. Augustine Di Noia that inter-religious dialogue often fails to consider sufficiently the radical particularity of religiosity.[34] Not all religions define their essential core as salvation. Christianity may, but animism does not. To say that salvation is the core of what it means to be religious may be a Christian reading of other religions. For many Christians, salvation in Christ is a new relationship with God the Creator, Redeemer, Sustainer, a transformation into a godly character on earth, and a membership in a new public and visible community of the Spirit. Such a construal is highly particular.

If a person from another religion maintains another way of salvation (e.g., the Buddhist eightfold path, the Islamic prayers, or Hindu deities), one may choose to follow, or not to follow, their communal practices. But if I have no desire to do so, then in their eyes I will not achieve salvation. This is as it should be, and we need not be offended. Each religious tradition develops a community with an all-encompassing worldview and a set of practices that move one toward transformation into the community's ideals. Each tradition develops a unique answer to a critical question. Di Noia quotes a rabbinic friend as saying, "Jesus Christ is the answer to a question I have never asked."[35] Salvation in the Christian sense is not what this rabbi seeks.

However, if one is Christian, then the questions and answers the Christian community proffers become salient. A client seeking to be shaped into the ideals of his or her chosen community is not being imposed upon when the therapist draws on that tradition and holds the client accountable to his or her professed convictions. For the Christian client, the language of the Triune God, the death and resurrection of Christ, and the continuing work of the Holy Spirit in the life of the church are usually viewed as part of the narrative charter, the mother tongue. The centrality of love and forgiveness, the love of enemies, and the nurturing of gifts in the life of the community become salient.

It is not clear to us why such a tradition-specific view of religion should give offense in a public setting. By virtue of their concrete historicity and particularity, religious groups are exclusive. Transformation is conditioned on identification with the communities' ideals, language, convictions, and beliefs. If a person has not chosen to be part of a religious tradition, his or her life will not be impacted by the life of faith as practiced by those who identify with that particular religion. If a Buddhist thinks that we will not attain nirvana apart from their community, we would agree. If a Muslim thinks we will not achieve salvation as a worshipper of Allah unless we live the life of a Muslim, we would understand. Their road to salvation is as historically particular as is ours. To recognize the radical differences between religions is then an act of respect even as we hope for a significant conversation. It is the foundation of hospitality.[36]

The assumption made by the religion and psychotherapy researchers that one can begin with religion in general is one we understand and may accept at times as a thin intervention, but one we will continue to critique for its lack of particularity. We own our particularity and seek to explore the role of religion in therapy from its sense. We believe that our Anabaptist tradition has a contribution to offer to the discussion of religion in psychotherapy. Ours is a tradition that takes seriously the public nature of faith, but with a commitment to peace. Good news is not good if it comes with coercion, whether from the state or from a therapist.

Anabaptism was a response to the sixteenth century reformers. It emerged out of protest to Martin Luther and Ulrich Zwingli, who were committed to a greater marriage of church and state—as the Anabaptists discovered when they chose to dissent by baptizing adults upon their confession of faith. The Constantinian alliance of religion with the government of the day resulted in persecution and death. The Anabaptists were committed to a public faith, but not by coercion. Hence, it is not difficult for us to make a case for the appropriateness of religion in therapy on the one hand, and to reject its imposition on the other. The Christian's role in the world is one of witness, not crusade.[37]

With all this emphasis on particularity, there is nonetheless a clear sense of universality in the Judeo-Christian tradition. Christians believe that there is one justice that is universal because God is one. If God is the God of all peoples, then this justice applies to all people. The justice of God transcends cultural constructions of justice and peace (Mic. 4:2–4; Isa. 2:2–4). That justice is not a prescription; it is a hope. Each nation has its own god with its own view of justice. And it will be God who judges the nations, not us, and so we can only hope to determine provisionally the differences between what we perceive to be God's justice and the justice of the nations. Christians, after all, stand within a particular culture, with their view of justice shaped by that particularity. The church sees itself as a potentially universal community, not a religious ghetto or safe haven for the chosen few. The gathered community is a catholic community. Inside the particularity of the church is a universal, but peaceable, vision. In the eschatological reign of God we have the creation of a single people of God from every tribe and nation (Rev. 7:9). Again, such a gathering comes not by coercion but by open invitation.

It must also be pointed out that Yahweh relativizes all traditions.[38] The apostle Paul envisions the emergence of a distinct people who make no distinctions between Jew and Gentile, male or female, master or slave (Gal. 3:28). Paul's solution to the tension between universality and particularity is to point to the oneness of God that requires God's universality. God's universality entails human equality, and human equality implies equal access to God's blessings, regardless of genealogy.

This, however, is not a rejection of particularity. Abraham's journey is the creation of a pilgrim people whose character is to reflect their God. Paul viewed Abraham as laying the foundation for a multiethnic community in which all the nations of the earth would be blessed (Gal. 3:8). Douglas John Hall and Rosemary Reuther have pointed out that:

> The implementation of the universal age of God necessarily entails particularity. Particularity is always a "scandal," but it is also the only way of getting to the universal.[39]

Devi

In their book *Encountering the Sacred in Psychotherapy*, James and Melissa Griffith illustrate the importance of entering their client's religious and ethnic world.[40] In a highly pluralist culture, it is almost inevitable that at some point one will have a client like Devi with her mother. The case exemplifies the concerns in this chapter regarding the particularity of religious traditions and how they can be honored in the context of psychotherapy. It is an act of hospitality.

> When Devi first arrived, she had to check to see if her pager was on. She explained that we might be interrupted because her husband required that she respond immediately if he called to ask her whereabouts. Her request was for help in leaving this marriage. While she had not married for immigration reasons, her pending citizenship would be at risk if she divorced. Though she was successful in her studies and her work and was fluent in three languages, Devi had come to believe her husband's insults that she was stupid and inept. She said she had lost her appetite for eating, and almost for living. "I feel that I am disappearing," she said, and this was reflected in the thinness of her body and the vagueness in her eyes. I (Melissa) was the third therapist she had seen. The couple had attempted marital therapy, and Devi had tried to change herself in many ways to please her husband, but she could no longer endure his degradation and threats.

Devi and her mother had journeyed from their homeland of India to the United States to obtain an American education for Devi. She had excelled in school and spoke nearly flawless English. Midway through one of her sentences she paused, apologizing for a minor linguistic mistake. I had not noticed. I marveled at her fluency, but I wondered what our conversation might be like if she were able to speak about the entrapment in her marriage in her native tongue. It was then that she told me that her husband would not permit her to speak in her own language, not even when talking with her mother on the phone. He considered her to be culturally and racially inferior and wanted her to disguise as much of her ethnicity as possible. I offered to search for a therapist who could communicate with her in Hindi. Devi did not want to see a different therapist. She didn't mind speaking English in therapy, but she did long to speak Hindi with her mother on the telephone in her own home.

Two weeks later Devi came to see me again. She still felt trapped. Although her situation had worsened at home, she was still unable to leave. She had secured a safe place in case of an emergency, but insisted that she presently was in no physical danger. The danger, she said, was that she might give up. She was sustained only by her friends and her mother. They were worried about her and called daily, begging her to leave.

I asked that she invite her mother to our next meeting. Her mother, Ms. Chowdry, arrived dressed in a sari with her head lowered, who, after a long period of silence, made only one pleading comment in a soft and deferential tone. I could not understand all of her words, a mixture of Hindi and English, but I needed no translation to hear the intense love, helplessness, and fear in her voice as she entreated her daughter to leave her husband, to come home with her that very day. "My mother is saying that she doesn't want me to become another Nicole Brown Simpson," Devi explained. Ms. Chowdry nodded and again addressed her daughter in Hindi. Devi gently reprimanded, "speak English." At this moment, I became acutely aware of Devi's earlier description of her husband requiring that she and her mother converse in English.

"Please," I said, "speak in your own language. You don't need to translate for me unless you want to. I will ask questions that may be helpful, and the two of you can use them as you wish. I have confidence that you will find a way to talk with each other about what is most important, and that your talk will be more comfortable and fruitful if you talk in your own language."

The conversation seemed to flow well and I became optimistic that Devi was unified with Ms. Chowdry in the decision to put her safety first. I was surprised and worried when, near the end of the session, Devi confessed that she was still confused. She said she would stay in the marriage a bit longer until she achieved more financial and immigration security. Ms. Chowdry bent down, hiding her face in her hands. I inquired about her sadness and her worries, expecting her to speak of her sorrow for her daughter. She spoke plaintively in Hindi and Devi translated: "My mother says to tell you that she is sad because she is homesick."

"What would she do with such a serious problem if she were at home?" I asked.

"If she had a serious problem, she would go to the temple," replied Ms. Chowdry. They conversed a bit more in Hindi. Then Devi turned to me and said, "My mother says the temple is what she misses most about home. She went to pray there every day."

I asked Ms. Chowdry to describe the temple and what it was like to be there. "Peaceful," she answered. I wondered aloud what it would be like to be in the temple together now: "Would the peacefulness bring answers to Devi?" Ms. Chowdry and Devi became quiet. I sensed the sacredness of this moment and felt that more questions would be an intrusion. Then I thought that even my presence might be an intrusion, much like it might be if I were a guest at their temple, present when their need was to pray, undistracted by attention to their guest. I slipped out my office door, telling them I would give them privacy for a while, and requesting that they open the door when they finished talking.

In about ten minutes they invited me back. Devi and her mother seemed peaceful, and her mother no longer looked sad. Devi had resolved to leave her husband. We set up our next appointment. Devi called the next day to let me know that she had left my office with her mother, never to sleep in her husband's home again. She expressed gratitude to me for holding the meeting, for encouraging them to speak in Hindi, and for leaving the room so that she and her mother could pray. She identified these acts as different from anything that had happened in her previous therapies. It was different for me, too, I thought to myself. We chatted a while about our shared admiration for the gentleness and wisdom of her mother.

Relatively quickly, with the help of Indian and American friends and immigration lawyers, Devi was able to obtain a divorce. When I last spoke with her, she was interested in starting a group for immigrant women trapped in abusive relationships.[41]

The Griffiths observe that Devi was able to act when she and her mother entered the peacefulness of their spiritual tradition. Notice that the therapist does not instrumentalize religion. She honors it as part of the client's world. Note the nature of Devi's religion; it is not private but relational. It is connected to Devi's culture. It is not the spiritual tradition of the Griffiths, and yet Melissa, the therapist, was able to create a sacred space in which healing could take place. Our twin concerns about religion and ethnicity are echoed in Devi's reflections on the session: "It is good that we spoke in our own language," she said, "and good that my mother and I could pray."

Religion as Sacred Order

We have examined religion as instrumental for health, as generic, as privatized, and as traditioned. As the story of Devi illustrates, not only is religion traditioned for its adherents, it is also hallowed. So also argued Philip Rieff, in his *My Life among the Deathworks*. Rieff is a Jew and a sociologist who wrote in a style that is a cross between prophecy and lament. Rieff's critique of modernity was in the tradition of Peter Berger, Christopher Lasch, Charles Taylor, and Peter Gay.[42] Psychological homelessness, unbridled narcissism, toxic secularity, and heretical modernity are the usual suspects in critiques of modernity. Rieff predates them all and, in some cases, is their progenitor. In the 1960s he stormed onto the scholarly stage with his critical analysis of Freud and the psychologization of American culture. Therapy socializes clients, he insisted, into a new culture freed of the starched collar of tradition. Rieff warned us of the emergence of the therapeutic individual and culture in his two books *Freud: The Mind of the Moralist*, and *The Triumph of the Therapeutic*.[43] Many cultural observers would agree that his dire predictions have come true.[44]

Religion, Rieff laments, has become little more than self-fulfillment.[45] In a recent interview with the *Guardian* he scolded psychologized religionists:

> I think the orthodox are role-playing. You believe because you think it's good for you, not because of anything inherent in the belief. I think that the orthodox are in the miserable situation of being orthodox for therapeutic reasons. . . . So Christianity becomes, therapeutically, "Jesus is good for you." I find this simply pathetic.[46]

After some three decades of relative silence, we hear him again. Acerbic as always, this time the voice has an element of lament—a Jewish lament.

What constitutes Rieff's lament? It is for him the passing of sacred cultures, those cultures that emanated from Abraham: Jewish, Muslim, and Christian. In sacral cultures life is lived in response to the command, grace, and love of God. This culture understands that God is above human authority and that God's revelation makes a demand on us. Rieff reminds us that Jesus says to the rich young ruler, "Keep the commandments." Personal identity in sacral culture is a function of one's response to the command of God, and the needs of the "not-I," the other. In his view, the range of possibilities my personality can take is constrained by my relationship to a sacred authority. Happiness means right living, not the freedom from constraint. Personality is shaped by the interdictions obeyed and the remissions graciously extended. When Augustine, at a child's injunction, takes up the scriptures to read, he reads an interdictory passage. To quote Abraham Heschel, "To be is to obey."[47] That our relationship to sacred authority has been marginalized by destructive forces in modern culture comprises a major element of Rieff's critique.

The creation of culture is the process of world-making, suggests Rieff, and at its best it inculcates the common values of society in nonviolent ways. What organizes culture is authority, a particular authority. Like Freud's conflicted individual, culture is about the struggle to survive, to supersede other cultures by disarming or eliminating them. Cultures are missional civilizations whose task is the transliteration of sacred visions into visible social orders. That cultures clash—*Kulturkampf*—should not come as a surprise. "Cultures are the habitus of human beings universal only in their particularities symbolically inhabited."[48] He states: "Culture is the form of fighting before the firing actually begins. Every culture declares peace on its own inevitably political terms."[49] What war will this be?

> The war that will emerge is between those who assert that there are no truths, only readings, that is, fictions (which assume the very ephemeral status of truth for negational purposes) and what is left of the second culture elites in the priesthood, rabbinate, and other teaching/directive elites dedicated to the proposition that the truths have been revealed and require constant rereading and application in the light of the particular historical circumstance in which we live.[50]

Though grand typologies are no longer de rigueur, Rieff boldly proposes three cultures in conflict. Primordial first cultures are characterized by the raw power of nature, shaped by fate, and ruled by capricious gods who are passionate, but not moral or good. The sacral second world culture materializes, Rieff suggests, in response to divine command. Fictive third culture lives parasitically on sacral cultures, by negation of the sacred. We live in all three worlds simultaneously: animist, sacral, and modern/postmodern. They are polytheistic, monotheistic, and atheistic respectively. Morality is shaped by social taboos in the first, divine revelation/commands in the second, and humanly constructed rules in the third. The shift from second to third world cultures is epitomized in an exchange between Benjamin Franklin and Thomas Jefferson over the opening words in the Declaration of Independence. Jefferson had originally written: "We hold these truths to be sacred." At Franklin's insistence, he changed "sacred" to "self-evident."[51]

We focus here on that second culture Rieff posits as sacral by nature. This culture understands that God is above human authority, and that God's revelation makes a demand on us. Rieff refers to this culture with an acronym, *VIA* (i.e., vertical in authority). At the apex is the "I am that I am" (Exod. 3:14), a God who acts by commandment and grace. Identity in second culture is a function of one's response to the command of God. The sacred self cannot be communicated; it is more than identity.

What is new in our world today, Rieff suggests, is that never before has such a barbaric culture emerged as third culture postmodernity. "Every world, until our third, has been a form of address to some ultimate authority."[52] But this third culture denies the sacred and assumes a central authority is unnecessary. Its ruling elites are virtuosi of deconstructing the verities of second cultures. Truth is traded for fiction in this fundamentally anti-sacral culture with no coherent identity, a culture in which unrepressed libido has permeated society. Rieff again:

> The third world successor to the sacred messenger is the artist, who knows he has nothing to say but clever mystifications of the transgressive nothing. The

comedy of third world is that the sacred primordial is nothing. The artist is a bridge to nowhere. Third world sacred messengers do not suffer; they laugh.[53]

The third culture rejects sacral cultures and hopes to do so with impunity. Is that possible? Rieff says no. There are profound social, psychological, and cultural consequences. Because it rejects the commanding truth of God, it produces more insanity. It creates a world culture of narcissism in which the boundaries between self and world are blurred. Happiness is freedom from commanding truth. Dispossessed of sacred order, like Hamlet, third culture individuals can engage in endless creativity and entertainment. Without the truth that humans are made in the image of God, they can enslave blacks, consume women, and annihilate the enemy. Third culture trusts nature rather than the Word (John 1). "In what I call second culture, there is no such thing as chance, not even in the fall of a sparrow. Chance is a third culture pseudo-primordiality, an empty god term to be filled with deceits, embodied in the character Chance Gardner in the film *Being There* (1979)."[54] Third culture is the colonizer; the second culture is the colonized.

Third cultures are replete with "deathworks" (Rieff's neologism). If the second culture lives by faith and obedience, one is nourished in the third culture by fiction and imagination that take pleasure in caricatures and absurdities. Their works of art are deathworks, in that they undermine sacral cultures. Rieff's list of such transgressive works is very long. Among them we find Freud's masterpiece of deconstruction of morality and religion, *Moses and Monotheism*, in which the most authoritative figure in the Jewish tradition "is reinvented as an enlightened Egyptian put to death by 'the savage Semites' who 'took fate into their own hands and rid themselves of their tyrant.'"[55] We also find Wallace Stevens's poetry declaring the commandments amount to "Just one more truth, one more / Element in the immense disorder of truths."[56] For Rieff, James Joyce's *Finnegans Wake* is a comic assault on Jewish God-terms, a "negation of the Jewish recognition that the world creator [. . .] is not one and the same as that creation."[57] Another "great artist of deathworks," Picasso, in his painting *Les Demoiselles d'Avignon*, creates a regressive representation through which he disarms Christian images of the world woman (Mary) by using "images of the woman as a threatening transgressor."[58] The painting depicts, from Rieff's perspective, the figure of a defecating female prostitute that appears as both lying down and standing up.

Third-world works, such as Andres Serrano's *Piss Christ*, are also characterized by an anti-sacramental theme as well as vulgarity and contempt for their viewers. "Sacred messengers of second worlds, who, operating under the authority of highest authority, deliver a message that will bring the world into saving obedience; the third world messengers deliver a message of subjectivity that amounts to self-hatred."[59] For example, in Robert Mapplethorpe's homoerotic *Self-Portrait*, he poses with a whip extending from his buttocks;

or Piero Manzoni's *Artist's Shit, no. 31*, with its picture of a can containing the artist's excrement. In contrast to second-world sacred messengers (Moses, Jesus, Augustine, Bach, Lincoln, and Jefferson), third-world messengers are a scourge of second cultures. Rieff lists as the ultimate third-world deathwork one that is both a symbol and a reality of the soul's death and the stripping of the sacred self: the Nazi death camps.

If we are paranoid of the ways of this third culture, Rieff says, we should be. Repeating an argument he has made previously, he points out that third cultures are inherently remissive, incapable of a "Thou shalt not." This culture has no experience of genuine guilt, because there are no commands that might produce guilt. Essentially they are anti-culture, for "where there is nothing sacred, there is nothing. Third cultures are nullities, anti-cultures."[60] Third culture is left with humanly constructed, abstract moral rules. It is a fictive world of free imagination. For Rieff, this culture can envision nothing but terrifying emptiness, a gradual loss of memory of sacred history and of acquired knowledge of commanding truths. In this third culture, "the earth has become again without form and void."[61]

Therapists in third cultures are its high priests, helping émigrés from second culture make the transition to third culture. In this sense, therapists are the champions of a third culture devoid of sacred references. They assist clients from sacral culture to reinterpret their guilt as false guilt, to understand their feelings of alienation as symptoms, and to deconstruct the demand of revelation as arbitrary and fictive, a social construction. Psychologists like Jung recycle first-world mythologies as a new canon, since third cultures can provide no absolute truth. Commenting on the shift in self-description as one moves from second to third cultures, Rieff states: "Identity changes constitute the new idolatry."[62] And again:

> No one understands himself or anyone else. What can be understood is where one is in the vertical in authority and where others are, themselves always on the move. This understanding of where we are makes every psychology radically moral, as well as sociological. We only know where we are in relation to others and to those inviolate commands (however arbitrary we may now think them) that warrant our sense of self and of others. Wherever we find ourselves is what we are. Our own motions in sacred order are locatable once each of us has restored to himself the notion of sacred order. . . . Identity must accept a certain canonicity: the commanding truths are known. Identity is no mere assertion: it is linked to a canon, which does allow for some remissive passages as it is addressed to the world, in all its vicissitudes and revolts.[63]

Rieff's association of repression with numinosity is particularly insightful; repression is the psychological price for rejecting sacred truths. In the famous case of "Miss Lucy R.," who is plagued with the smell of burnt pudding, Freud told her that "really you are in love with your employer, the Director, though perhaps without being aware of it yourself."[64] The woman agrees and explains that the reason she did not tell him was that she knew, and did not want to know, at the same time. Freud called it repression. Rieff sees it otherwise: "Repression is the unconscious last and negational playing out of the authority that once belonged consciously to revelation."[65] Similarly, in Freud's famous case of Dora, Rieff points out, the moral and ethical issues of her father's affair and Dora's attractions are not on the table.[66] Freud thereby de-creates sacral culture rather than remembering it (Eccles. 12). Self-esteem therapy cannot undo the effects of failing to respond to the commanding truths.

Repression is Freud's word for lying to oneself without really knowing it. Guilt and its correlative, forgiveness, are not part of third-world therapeutic cultures. However, in sacred second cultures "what is suppressed is kept conscious and renunciation is not paid in neuroses but in a realization of guilt. The discipline of inwardness becomes a public and shared condition of inadequacy to the terms of the covenant."[67] Contrary to Rieff, forgiveness is increasingly part of the armamentarium of therapeutic interventions of which contemporary clinicians are apprised. If there is little consensus over what is worth feeling guilty about in the absence of commanding truths, forgiveness becomes facile. Clearly it would be an overstatement to argue that all symptoms are the price of repressed revelation, traumatic events that are buried to reduce the pain. Nevertheless, Rieff has with clarity identified parts of psychology's complicity with a dangerous anti-sacred project.

We do have concerns with aspects of Rieff's argument. Rieff credits sacral cultures with a sense of reality, and critiques third cultures as fictive. In fact, there are realists in Rieff's third world, and constructivists in sacral cultures. Barbara Held makes the case that we have too easily dismissed the notion of reality, and that many postmodern therapists implicitly adopt a modest realism.[68] Why does sacrality demand realism and exclude constructivism? Is there no appropriate fictive dimension in sacral cultures? Is there not a place for a chastened imagination in the context of second-world commanding truths? Is all art a violation of the prohibition against graven images? Why marshal the forces of a sacral culture to support realism? Rieff's emphasis on reality is a corrective, but an overstated one.

Some will find Rieff's sectarianism objectionable. His distinction between second and third worlds is so dichotomous one wonders whether good is possible in worlds other than sacral cultures shaped by the Decalogue. Given the lens of sacrality, can one not discern when a father loves a son in third cultures (Luke 11:11–12)? Is it not possible that, after millennia of coexistence, sacral cultures have left at least a pale imprint on pagan culture? And is that goodness not worth affirming?

At times it is not clear whether Rieff reflects the lamentations of Jeremiah or the residue of a disenchanted sociologist. Sometimes his judgment of social issues emerges out of his analysis of sacral and fictive cultures, and we hear echoes of a lament. Rieff's writing is characterized by a plethora of poignant and incisive reflections, but also, occasionally, he is more fatalistic, judgmental, and pessimistic. The latter feature is evident in his repetitive ramblings, colicky tone, and various brash and arbitrary criticisms of homosexuals, feminists, and even abolitionists.[69] However, while the reader may dismiss him at times for being bitter, discontented, and eccentric, one cannot but feel his deep concern for, as well as the sense of incredible loss of, a sacral culture in the face of the current cultural depletion.

In other words, Rieff has given us a Jewish critique of culture that Christians do well to consider. It will require a reconsideration of notions of personality, identity, fulfillment, aesthetics, authority, and constructionism. The present culture wars are explicable, in part, as a flight from sacral identity into self-constructed, theatrical roles. What is deemed as progress and enlightenment on the third-world cultural stage is replete with tragic implications. The destruction of transcendent reality, the "not-I," the mysterious and sacred other, is both a product and a consequence of an emergent culture driven by endless life-affirming consumption and by ever-increasing obsession with overthrowing all authorities except the contemporary man or woman. It is a culture of immanence rather than transcendence, a society of narcissists, and, as Rieff argues, a culture that departs from true democracy, one that replaces sacred truths with self-evident truths. "True democracy must perpetually republish its declarations of dependence on something suprapolitical: its predicative sacred order, the vertical in authority."[70] Rieff recognizes that true democracy cannot be built on ontological principles (self-evident truths) that originate within human constructions, but only on ethical grounds, on conceptions of the human within a sacred order.

Rieff, a Jew, believed that Christianity supplied the best possibility for a sustainable culture, but, as he stated in an interview, that is not to be.[71] He does not think an authentic religious culture can be resurrected. Rieff's argument is enormously unsettling for Christians who happen to be therapists and clinicians. Without public attention given to our own sacred reference points, we unwittingly support and encourage the construction of a third culture that actively opposes the sacred order. Worse, we do our work with a mantle of advocacy and self-righteousness, ordained to a ministry of instrumental religion that removes the client from sacred frameworks that make healing a morally significant possibility. If we are unable to recognize the signs of complicity with third-culture priorities, ours becomes a Prozac god whose sole purpose is to support the flourishing of our own idolatrous designs.

9

A Peaceable Psychology

■ ■ ■ ■ ■ ■ ■ ■ ■ ■

You know that the rulers of the Gentiles lord it over them, and their great ones are tyrants over them. It will not be so among you; but whoever wishes to be great among you must be your servant, and whoever wishes to be first among you must be your slave.

Matthew 20:25–27

For many of us the march from Selma to Montgomery was both protest and prayer. Legs are not lips, and walking is not kneeling. And yet our legs uttered songs. Even without words, our march was worship. I felt my legs were praying.

Abraham Joshua Heschel, "Our Generation's Teacher"

We move now from instrumental religion to portrayals of psychologists and psychotherapists deeply shaped by a sacral culture committed to peace. We begin with an example of a peaceable psychologist, one whose life demonstrates that God chooses what is weak in the world to shame what is strong (1 Cor. 1:27). He is an emerging Central American psychologist concerned about reconciliation. José[1] grew up in grinding poverty, living with some five thousand others who eked out an existence on the city dump in Guatemala City.[2] Competing with vultures and dogs for food, he worked for five years amid toxic gasses and glue-sniffing addicts. When a family offered to help him obtain an education, he worried about the survival of his parents and siblings—but they offered to pay his family the lost income. They taught him, he says, that he was a human being. For the next three years he was at school in the morning and at the dump in the afternoon. At age sixteen he attended a conservative evangelical church that interpreted his emotional condition as demon possession and recommended exorcism. They were oblivious to his simple need for food.

When his Honduran-born father was abducted, tortured, and deported by the police, José became the sole supporter of his family. The Guatemalan militia harassed him repeatedly because of his Honduran papers, and at one point he was kidnapped, stripped, and left to die. He survived, but only barely. Some time later, while playing with close friends, a car without license plates or lights roared down the street with machine guns blazing. Six of José's friends were killed. Watching his friends die, he was overcome with anger and considered joining the guerillas to avenge their deaths. At the invitation of a pastor, however, he attended a Mennonite church and heard a gospel of peace and justice. He discovered that God is preoccupied with those who suffer and those who are poor. He learned of a person named Jesus.

In the years that followed, he has defended the innocent—at a price. A bomb exploded outside his home, and both he and his family were repeatedly threatened at gunpoint. Each day he asked himself—"Is this the day they are going to kill me?" But after reading the stories of Anabaptist martyrs, he said: "Death is not the last word. And just as Jesus was raised from the dead, someday too I will be resurrected. This is what gives me my confidence and my hope." José went on to complete college. During his undergraduate days one hundred sixty students entered the school's history program, but only two graduated. The rest were forced into exile, assassinated, or dropped out because they experienced their studies at the university as too dangerous. But José pressed on, and as a graduate student he focused on the psychological effects of trauma; in the process he discovered he was the only Christian in his program. When his class once again listened to the story of a family traumatized by the war, the instructor wondered who could speak a word of hope. The class pointed toward José. He graduated from his program and is now working as a psychologist for peace in a country that still wrestles with violence.

In this chapter we propose that there are ways Christian psychologists can embrace peace. It is imperative that if we encourage an increased openness to religion in therapy, there be a correlative emphasis on the relinquishment of power. Otherwise, we fear that a powerful Constantinian psychotherapy will engulf the client.

We begin with an exploration of Constantinianism and a view of God as one who comes to us not as a monarch, but in the form of the crucified Christ. We turn to Augustine and wonder whether he was able to transcend the Constantinianism of his day. We then introduce you to other psychologists who embody a commitment to peace and justice as part of their faith by the way they conduct research, the questions they ask, and the changed culture they hope for. As therapists, they model self-surrender, vulnerability, and weakness. In response to the power of psychologists, we argue for the relinquishment of power, whether internationally or in the consulting room. In the former we encourage the empowerment of indigenous psychologists. In the context of psychotherapy, a peaceable psychologist will be self-emptying and more transparent.

The Power of Weakness

In this section we continue the earlier discussion of the problematic collaboration of religion with power as a way of creating culture. Constantinianism occurs when the power of the state is used to homogenize culture in religious ways. The imposition on local peoples of a presumably universal psychology has striking similarities. Constantinian religion effectively spawned inquisitions, crusades, pogroms, and wars. Religion with theocratic ambition engendered colonial expansion under missionary pretenses. English Puritans carried the crusading mentality to the New World. Oppressive regimes seduced religionists in condoning, if not actually blessing, their violence, whether by the Russian Orthodox Church in the Stalin/Leninist era, the German church during the Third Reich, American ecclesial support of slavery, domination of women, or the two Gulf wars.

To legitimate their actions, kings and presidents have invoked the image of a potent deity, a Constantinian god, who was called upon to reinforce the authority of men over women, the rich over the poor, armed nations over weak nations. This was the god of Jesus's disciples, whose implicit image of authority was the Roman emperor. When the kingdom arrived they hoped to sit to the right and left of the conqueror. This was the god of Augustine when he relied on the power of the emperor to resolve the problem of the heretical Donatists. This was the god of Luther, who felt the church must still serve the will of the magistrates. This is the god in whose name we have refused to talk with those of differing religious perspectives. It is the god American presidents call upon in campaign and inaugural speeches.[3]

We started this book with the accounts of suffering of Guatemalans and wondered whether there was comfort in knowing that God suffers. John Howard Yoder comments:

> We remember that the initial shape of the classical problem [of theodicy] was provoked by the notion of divine monarchy. If anything happens that should not, it must be God's fault. The corrective for that might be the conviction that God, out of His own graceful nature, may have chosen to qualify his omnipotent control, not (or not merely, or not primarily) in order to create freestanding wills able to talk back to him, but in order to share in the suffering of finite existence.[4]

The good news of the gospel is not about a Constantinian god. The Gospel of Mark tells the story of the Son of Man inaugurating a kingdom characterized by Jesus's loss of power ending with his death. In the midst of a Roman occupation, Jesus announces the reign of God, an empire without royal power or a regal army. In his empire we are not engaged in political machinations or masterminding the future.

The scandal of the cross is that God's strength is incarnated in weakness. It is scandalous for powerful nations that this God is revealed in lowly nations (Israel, not Rome), in lesser tribes (Benjamin over Judah), and in little towns (Bethlehem rather than Jerusalem). For the mighty it is embarrassing that this God marks Israel's faithfulness by how they respond to the stranger, the widow, and the orphan in their midst. Unlike the Mesopotamian creation account in the Enuma Elish, Yahweh notices peoples in exile and oppression. In the empire of God the first are last, the favored son has no home, and a king hangs on a cross. This sovereign God calls, but does not overpower, invites rather than coerces. This God confuses language when people seek power, goes to prison with Joseph, hides in caves with David, whispers to Elijah, and weeps with his people in exile, and when this God fully appears, it is as a nobody from Nazareth. This is a peaceable God who comes to us in weakness.

The New Testament points to weakness rather than the exercise of power. It suggests that when our God is defined as strong, we need to redefine strength in terms of voluntary powerlessness. It is the nothings (*me onta*) of this world who are used to serve God's purposes. The message of the cross, of suffering of and weakness, is foolishness to the Greeks. Perhaps we have become the modern Hellenists.

Augustine's Constantinianism

Augustine, the Bishop of Hippo (354–430), was entangled with his sociopolitical context in a manner not unlike our earlier discussion of a psychology embedded in the military. Augustine lived and wrote during the shift toward Constantinianism, at the beginning of a formal marriage between church and state that frames contemporary fears about the relation of religion with violence, oppression, and imposition.

An early father of contemporary psychology, Augustine dissected his motivations, desires, and inner demons. He is the ultimate apostle of interiority. While he provided us with a profound understanding of the depth of the human soul, we wonder if his psychology is peaceable. Our question is whether he avoided the Constantinian synthesis of religion with power. Reluctantly, we would say no. His marriage of religion and state became prototypical for future presidents and professions who minimize difference and glorify sameness, eschew particularity and valorize universality. After we have reflected on Augustine, we examine how psychotherapy and cross-cultural psychology may reflect or resist the Constantinian temptation.

What psychology might emerge in a Constantinian political framework?[5] We would like to test the thesis that Augustine's vision for ecclesial homogeneity by political means correlates with a psychology unable to hear internal dissenting voices. The Constantinian political world in which he lived was reflected in Augustine's understanding of the psyche. Inner and outer reinforced one another; the psychological reflected the political. Aberrant religious believers and delinquent inner urges were similarly outlawed. We consider this failure to honor internal psychological and external public differences a form of Constantinianism, psychological Constantinianism. It is not peaceable.

Until 405 CE, Augustine battled the Donatists for the unity of the church without the help of the emperor. In the end, Augustine reluctantly justified the use of force by the state in the interest of ecclesial unity. Augustine thought that the God of the Old Testament chastised those who wandered from the law. Following this idea, teaching and discipline were useful for softening up errant individuals in preparation for gospel truth. The law had deterred them from the sin of polytheism. Augustine assumed that without the pressure of the law, social chaos would result.

Augustine then became the dispenser of justice to the wayward Donatists. He argued that war was tragic but justified in certain cases; war was a means to address sin, righting a wrong. The Donatists were a present hazard to the unity of Christian thought and belief. In their disobedience to the law they risked the integrity and ongoing vitality of the church. So violence was justified.

The interiority of Augustine's theology becomes evident in his reflections on the Donatist problem. In the midst of contentious, real-world problems such as these, Jesus's teachings did not necessarily call for literal obedience. Regarding Jesus's injunction, "If anyone strikes you on the right cheek, turn the other also" (Luke 6:29), Augustine believed he could inwardly contain the responsibility for peace even when externally it proved impossible.[6] In the end, we would argue, it occurred in neither venue.

In public, then, Augustine utilized the power of the state to enable the church to control dissidents. Given the interiority of Augustine's theology, it is not a stretch to consider his response to the Donatists in relation to his own psychology. Phillip Cary proposes that Augustine's self is not one he discovers as much as constructs.[7] Influenced by Plato and Plotinus, Augustine created a private self out of reflection and confession. What then is the role of the "other"? Romand Coles's analysis of the neglected other suggests that Augustine's psychology directly contributed to his coercive stance in the Donatist controversy.

Augustine's inner self reflects the larger culture—the external and the internal mirror each other. In public life the pagan self is characterized by conceit, lust, dispersion, forgetting, regression to evil, and nothingness. By contrast, the Christian self is humble, yearning for depth, remembering, and progressing toward being. Internally, these two selves are both present, and Augustine represented them as being intertwined and in opposition. The confessing self is one that is continually aware of willful struggle and seeks to rout out pagan fallenness. Coles states:

> The confessing self is fastened to the imperative to discover and embrace God's truths deep within. This imperative means that everything within and outside the self should be revealed in God's light, and what does not shine forth should, one way or another, be transformed or silenced and reduced to the nothing it really is.[8]

When Augustine writes, "Help me so that I may see the truth about myself," his wish is ultimately to hear one voice within and to snuff out other voices in his experience of the world, an echo of his political response to the Donatists. As the confessing self is deepened, it moves incrementally closer to the elimination of otherness. For Augustine, the Christian self is constituted by the one true voice within which all selves are to be ordered. What space is there for other voices within the self that choose not to listen to or be ordered by this one true voice?

Augustine's self seems to permit no space for an undeveloped other beyond the core self. His confessing self unifies itself according to God's truth and, as in public, extirpates all that is discordant. This reflects his political stance toward the Donatists. In public settings, the inner psychology is played out. Can one engage in conversation with the inner "Donatist" voices to hear their complaint, rather than simply eradicating them? Coles comments:

> Within the self, God's voice meets the voice of the other as it confronts impure desires, thoughts, and pleasures. But that this meeting bears little resemblance to dialogue is indicated by the "nothing" to which all that is not in agreement with God is assigned. The confessing self is characterized more accurately as a site of inner confrontation than one of inner conversation (albeit often discordant), for the encounter in depth between God's light and what is not is marked by the aim of absolute hegemony of God's voice. Within the multiple manifestations of God's light is a dialogue in which the various dimensions of God commingle to give birth to deeper truth. Yet with respect to what lies beyond his Word, there is only a monological polemic—a ceaseless attempt to silence the other—and no possibility of a dialogue in which God is illuminated in the critical light of his other.[9]

Coles maintains that Augustine could not hear the pagans given his suppression of the pagan inner voice.

> Obedience isn't simply suggested, it is demanded by a textual *tour de force* that
> mobilizes responsibility, guilt, and death in a manner that aims at thoroughly
> extirpating others—the non-Christians within and without—which are consti-
> tuted as "evil," "ignorant," and "vanity."[10]

Augustine's psychology and his politics both endorse coercion as a way of
subduing the other. The Augustine who is so trenchant in his critique of Roman
imperialism engages in religious hegemony through his administration as the
Bishop of Hippo. Peter Brown goes so far as to suggest that "Augustine may
be the first theorist of the Inquisition."[11]

Augustine's psychology is a Constantinian psychology in that it reflects the
politics of his day. His project becomes a totalizing narrative in its treatment
of the internal and external enemy by extirpation. We would maintain that
the corollary is also true; love of the enemy politically and the honoring of
multiple voices psychologically are parallel. To love enemies is not to kill them,
but to hear them. To address the internal enemy requires not simply extirpation,
but careful listening, compassion, understanding, and firm limits. Automatic
excommunication does not make for a peaceable psychology. Augustine's
perspective forces countervailing beliefs and traditions underground.

Augustine's failure was the inability to accept the difference posed by the
other. We argue that in contrast to psychological Constantinianism, a peaceable psychology honors differences, respects other traditions, and recognizes
God's presence in religious confessions other than one's own. A peaceable
psychology is non-Constantinian; it does not create change through violent
means internally or externally.

Peace is ultimately achievable not through a universalizing ethic of democratic plurality, tolerance, or relativism, but rather in the deepest commitment
to follow Christ's example. In the famed Johannine account of the encounter
with a Samaritan woman of questionable repute, Christ transcends cultural
and gendered barriers, risking his public reputation in affirming the woman
as "other," with transformative results. Accordingly, a peaceable psychology
will be non-Constantinian in ethos and practice. Reconciliation and healing
are forged through the radical affirmation of the other, by the grace of a Christ
victorious over the vicissitudes of psychological Constantinianism.

Martín-Baró: A Peaceable Postcolonial Psychologist

Is it possible that a discipline like Western psychology can avoid being Constantinian and colonialist? We move now from a concern about the suppression of
religious groups and emotionally troubled internal parts to the disempowerment of native psychologies. Here again we will argue for the relinquishment
of power.

From an international and domestic perspective, the role of psychology as a scientific discipline with generalizable knowledge is increasingly under critique. Critics are recognizing that in a postcolonial world there lurks still the mind-set of the colonizer. That attitude is clearly depicted in the now infamous—but then celebrated—"Macaulay minute," which stated with imperial confidence that "we [the British] must at present do our best to form . . . a class of persons, Indian in blood and color, but English in taste, in opinions, in morals and in intellect."[12] Thomas Babington Macaulay (1800–1860), a British statesman, essayist, and policy reformer, made a strong argument for the establishment of English education and culture in India for Indians.

Postcolonial thinkers assume that we now live in an era that critiques colonialism and assumes that colonial ideas and practices should no longer be reflected in academia. Their writings consider the problems of colonialism and its effects on marginalized peoples.[13] A postcolonial psychology would then be most sensitive to the possibility of its own theories being hegemonic; but more importantly, it would reform its own theory and practices based on what it has learned from other cultural traditions. With the exception of Jung, it is not apparent to us that the West has changed its assumptions based on the contributions of non-Western psychologies.[14]

Before we turn to a more theoretical analysis of indigenous psychologies, we introduce you to a contemporary example of an indigenous and peaceable psychologist. The legacy of Latin liberation theology is perhaps best known by its call for a Christianity freed from the status quo.[15] The influence of the liberation movement eventually impacted psychological theory and reflection among indigenous Latin psychologists. Ignacio Martín-Baró was educated in social psychology at the University of Chicago in the 1960s but came to El Salvador amid escalating violence there.[16] Over some thirty years he wrote passionately about a psychology that could be liberating, that was just,[17] and not a servant of violent government. Martín-Baró critiqued the academic work in El Salvador noting that:

> Latin American psychology, save for a few exceptions, has not only remained servilely dependent when it has needed to lay out problems and seek solutions, but has stayed on the sidelines of the great movements and away from the stresses of the people of Latin America.[18]

The critical exception, he noted, was the work of a Brazilian priest, Paulo Freire, whose purpose in the education of indigenous peoples was to raise consciousness against the wholesale "banking" of information in passive student-learners.[19] For Freire, the personal was dialectically related to the political. Martín-Baró pointed out that the current Latin psychology, as a Western import, served the status quo by neglecting and subjectivizing the political.

Instead of helping tear down the edifice of common sense that in our culture both obscures and justifies the interests of the powerful by representing their techniques of control as character traits, Latin American psychology subscribes to the reigning psychologism either by action or by omission.[20]

This servitude was furthered by a partiality to quantitative data, and by a concern with understanding the individual rather than transforming individuals along with society. Martín-Baró traced this bias to a history of colonial dependence, a fascination with technology, and the imitation of Western science. Essentially, Latin psychologies hoped to attain legitimacy as a science and compete with Western psychology. As a result, Latin psychological theories and practice were unabashedly American. Orthodox behaviorism, methodological individualism, and, more recently, cognitive psychology were all implicated in the Latin context. However, the problems chosen for study in the United States were potentially alien to the Latin setting or mind: a scientific psychology vs. one with soul, secular psychology vs. Christian anthropology, a materialistic psychology vs. a humanistic psychology, and a reactionary vs. a progressive psychology.

Martín-Baró's response was to design theoretical and practical tools from the standpoint of the lives of the suffering, from the aspirations and struggles of Latin people. However, in order to do so Latin psychology had to be liberated from its enslavement to a North American psychological paradigm.

A liberated psychology stated positively would, Martín-Baró posits, require three elements: a new horizon, a new epistemology, and a new praxis. The new horizon would focus more on service to the needs of oppressed people, and less on achieving scientific and social status. A revised epistemology would begin from below, from the experiences recounted by the oppressed, and from the subsequent knowledge emerging from these forgotten voices; that knowledge would critically revise the existing fund of psychological insight. A novel praxis would focus not simply on gathering data from a position of power, but rather on transforming reality by direct participation in local culture and society. However, Martín-Baró did not reject empiricism.[21] One of his controversial studies involved gathering data that contradicted a government public opinion report, demonstrating that science can serve a liberating psychology.

For Martín-Baró, these changes point to three urgent tasks. First, they require the recovery of historical memory. The Latin American wars and related suffering have precluded open conversation. History is neutralized in the vacuum precipitated by violence and conflict. Unless history is recovered, Martín-Baró suggests, the result of prolonged conflict will include the internalization of oppression, the incorporation of violence into the human spirit, and an emergence of conformist fatalism. Second, it is necessary to de-ideologize everyday experience—that is, to retrieve the original experience of groups and persons and return it to them as objective data. People can then use the data to formally articulate a consciousness of their own reality, and by so doing verify the validity of the acquired knowledge.[22] Third, it is necessary for a liberating psychology to draw on the virtues of a people. Referring to his own Salvadoran context, Martín-Baró points to virtues alive in popular religious traditions and cultural practices, such as solidarity with those who suffer, an ability to sacrifice for the common good, a faith in the possibility of change, and hope for a better tomorrow.

What does Martín-Baró's work as a psychologist teach us about being peaceable? Here is a person whose life work is dedicated to common good. He seeks liberation for an oppressed people. He is vulnerable, passionate about justice, and deeply insightful about the role of psychology in society.

A Peaceable Indigenous Psychology

A peaceable psychology is one that recognizes its own particularity and empowers psychologists in other cultures who wish to do the same. We begin with some reflections on indigeneity and then examine ways in which a commitment to particularity and indigeneity emerges in international settings and can counter psychological Constantinianism.[23]

Martín-Baró's model resonates with Kenneth Gergen's contention that psychology abroad (and also at home) must begin with the local or particular, rather than the universal:

> In effect, the richly variegated traditions must be explored, articulated, and celebrated for the range of resources they can bring to the practice of psychology as a global cooperative. In our view, the most positive forms of professional interchange occur not when one attempts to improve or enlighten the other, but when the fascinating, the novel, and the practical from one context are made available for others to appropriate selectively as their local circumstances invite. It is to the practical means of achieving such dialogue that attention is now required.[24]

This indigenization of psychological theory and practice must, in the end, remain relevant to local interpretations of healing. Gergen continues:

> By placing culture in the vanguard of our concerns, we are finally drawn to the enormous global need for a psychology of practical significance. Western psychology has had the luxury of devoting most of its research to questions of abstract theory and viewing application as a second-rate derivative. However, not only do we find such theories largely parochial (even when purporting universality), but very little of the research has practical payoff.[25]

The purpose of cultural analysis in a modern perspective is to promote a nonevaluative alternative to ethnocentrism (suspending judgment in research, viewing a culture from a distance, being critical of one's own culture). It furthers the humanistic project of social criticism: assessing the cost and benefits of human behaviors. However, the study of culture as a whole may become the exclusive privilege of the modern psychologist's superior perspective. The idea of culture as a whole may help the colonizer to "manage" the people as a whole. A colonizing psychology is not a peaceable psychology.

An indigenous psychology that emerges locally is for us more peaceable. However, it will require that North American psychologists place their own psychologies in brackets. Since the publication of Uichol Kim and John Berry's book more than a decade ago,[26] indigenous psychology as a discipline is growing. They defined indigenous psychology as "the scientific study of human behavior or mind that is native, that is not transported from other regions, and that is designed for its people."[27] Uichol Kim, Kuo-shu Yang, and Kwang-Kuo Hwang, in the opening chapter of their book *Indigenous and Cultural Psychology: Understanding People in Context*, begin with this definition:

> Indigenous psychology is an emerging field in psychology. It attempts to extend the boundary and substance of general psychology. Although both indigenous and general psychology seek to discover universal facts, principles, and laws of human behavior, the starting point of research is different. General psychology seeks to discover decontextualized, mechanical, and universal principles and it assumes that current psychological theories are universal. Indigenous psychology, however, questions the universality of existing psychological theories and attempts to discover psychological universals in social, cultural and ecological context.[28]

Indigenous psychology emphasizes a descriptive understanding of human functioning in a cultural context.

In response to Kim, Yang, and Hwang, we would ask a number of questions. Who decides the substance of a local psychology? Whose indigeneity is honored? Where is the primary location of power and control? Whose epistemology or methodology is privileged?

First, we would agree with Kim, Yang, and Hwang that an indigenous psychology would emphasize examining psychological phenomena in their native context, whether those contexts are familial, social, political, historical, religious, cultural, or ecological. However, in the past, culture has been construed as monolithic and insufficiently pluralistic. A peaceable indigenous psychology can be a discipline that embraces multiple voices. Like the arts and sciences, which are plural and diverse, indigenous psychology does not need to find a unified voice to validate its existence. We expect that since cultures and their religions are pluralistic, indigenous psychologies would reflect local understandings, whether they are mystical, animist, or religious, instead of uprooting those traditions and replacing them with secular Western ideology. Hence, we disagree with Kim, Yang, and Hwang when they posit that indigenous psychology is part of a scientific tradition that advocates multiple *perspectives*, but not multiple *psychologies*. The current volume uses the singular form of indigenous psychology rather than the plural form. Indigenous psychology is a part of scientific tradition in search of psychological knowledge rooted in cultural context. This knowledge can become the basis of the discovery of psychological universals and can contribute to the advancement of psychology and science.[29]

Why not encourage multiple psychologies? To live in a highly pluralist, global community in which we recognize ethnic diversity, why might there not be multiple psychologies that undergird local identities? And it is not the prerogative of the Western psychologist to decide which psychological paradigm is chosen locally.

A related issue is the relationship of culture to religion in indigenous psychologies. Is the normative view of culture secular or religious? Except for a few chapters on morality in the text by Kim, Yang, and Hwang, one would think that the world's population was not religious and that religion is not integral to indigenous psychologies. Rieff has argued cogently that culture is not neutral but prescriptive.[30] It makes demands on its members. The narrative of a community invites members to live in accordance with its implicit charter. Does indigenous psychology include a narrative of a people's sacred texts, self-explanations, aesthetics, and poetry?[31] How do the more archetypal themes in the literature of a people shape their character?

We believe a peaceable and indigenous psychology acknowledges the religiosity of a given culture. Some of the authors in the text by Kim, Yang, and Hwang separate indigenous psychology from philosophical and religious considerations. How is that possible when a high percentage of individuals living in non-Western settings construe their personal worlds religiously? Approximately 73 percent of the world's population self identify themselves as an adherent to a particular religion.[32] Kim, Yang, and Hwang suggest that we need to translate these ancient texts into operationalizable terms and then validate them with empirical research. For example, they state: "Philosophical and religious texts are [sic] developed for a specific purpose several thousand years ago. In order to utilize these texts, we need to translate these ideas into psychological concepts and empirically verify their validity."[33] Further, they state: "In psychology, empirical analysis is necessary to verify whether philosophical or indigenous ideas actually influence the way people think, feel, and behave."[34] We suggest that it is critical to consider how the ancient texts themselves, not their modern translations, serve to empower the individual to flourish and a society to prosper consistent with its own cultural mandate. We suggest the amoral perspective of the authors belies their universalistic ideological commitments.

A peaceable, indigenous psychology endorses a variety of methods and epistemologies and affirms that the choice of method is locally determined.

Although some advocate for a new methodology for indigenous psychology, such as constructive realism and Confucian relationalism,[35] or Filipino *pakapakapa*,[36] the hegemony of scientific empiricism is still evident in much of the field. Kim, Yang, and Hwang dismiss local religious traditions as follows: "These analyses are speculative philosophy and they have yet to be supported by empirical evidence. Although they provide a wealth of information and the basis of development of formal theories, they need to be empirically tested and validated."[37]

Why not consider methodological pluralism as suggested by Imre Lakatos and Alan Musgrave,[38] or even the radical epistemological pluralism of Paul Feyerabend?[39] Is the privileged epistemology locally determined?[40] In terms of epistemology, we feel strongly that local leaders and their communities should decide what constitutes knowledge, what is relevant to the local setting, and how it is best augmented.[41] Methodologies should be determined by local researchers, and they may be multiple and nonscientific. Indigenous psychology may well include nonlocal wisdom (e.g., scientific and Western), but members of the host culture decide what should be imported or contextualized in the local culture. Indigenous psychology might build not only on the collaboration between anthropologist, psychologist, historian, and sociologist, but also on a relationship of mutual respect and empowerment between the researchers and the lay leaders of local communities.

A peaceable psychology is comfortable with multiple approaches, including hermeneutic and symbolically sensitive approaches. Hermeneutic perspectives have a long history in Continental philosophy and psychology,[42] and take with utmost seriousness the interpretive and constructive aspects of meaning creation. Instead of privileging psychology as an empirical science, a methodology clearly emerging out of the West, why not include a place for interpretive epistemologies?[43] Why not a more visible role for the symbolic? We argue that we need both hermeneutic *and* scientific epistemologies. The goal of the hermeneutical method is to work out an interpretation applicable to human discourse. It can (and must) work directly at the level of local language speakers and their immediate and historical context. As it has developed, the hermeneutic approach has provided a way of rethinking the underlying assumptions of social science. Hermeneutic theories have influenced the areas of anthropology,[44] history of science,[45] and political theory,[46] and have gradually transformed the practices of psychotherapy in the last decade.[47] The hermeneutic approach seems potentially appropriate in indigenous settings, but that is a local decision.

A peaceable and non-Constantinian psychology addresses the issues of power and local autonomy in that an indigenous psychology begins with the articulations of local practitioners—whether formally trained psychologists or local community leaders—about the nature of their implicit or explicit "psychology" and "culture." Indigenous psychology as an international discipline is not a model to be imposed on a local culture. The input of an exogenous psychologist would be given when requested. An indigenous psychologist would be empowered to research matters most relevant to the local people, rather than what matters to the international professional association or editors of publications.

To avoid psychological Constantinianism, we must ask a number of questions about knowledge construction. Who is requesting the research? What issues are being addressed? Are they pressing local questions or questions that concern the discipline? Who will collect the data or interview the participants? Who will ultimately use the data? Do locals think their intuitive, native psychology has already made a positive contribution to their society; or has it failed them, and hence more research is necessary?

The development of indigenous psychology might look quite different in a country that has been colonized, traumatized, and populated by the West than in one that was not. We must consider the sociopolitical backdrop in each country before assuming homogeneity in the discipline of indigenous psychology across different cultures. We would argue that it is the local psychologist who decides what research and insights from other indigenous psychologies (most notably Euro-American) might be helpful. We wonder if the empowerment of a colonized people who seek to be indigenous is not more important than creating a homogeneous discipline. Of course, whether a local community seeks to be indigenous or to accommodate to Western psychologies is their decision. In an age of global travel and communication, local communities are seldom "pure" or untouched by other cultures. A certain level of hybridity emerges. This complexifies the issue of indigenization and highlights the importance of local decision-making about the nature of the cultures the local community wishes to embrace. A peaceable North American psychologist leaves behind a small footprint.

Virgilio Enriquez: An Indigenous Psychologist

Universalizing our research findings may well be a form of cultural violence when, in point of fact, there are hidden cultural differences.[48] These differences will require of us that we be sensitive to historical development and the social construction of reality. For example, the evolution of the self involves a dynamic relationship with the social world. If it is true that discourse about the self is embedded in the larger political arena, then we must deconstruct the political subtext of Western psychology before we can engage in researching indigenous psychology in any other part of the world. If we export to other cultures a Western configuration of the self as an objective, ahistorical, and universal self, the unintentional political consequences may well be imperialism, racism, cultural chauvinism, and the disempowerment of indigenous psychologists like

Filipino Virgilio Enriquez. It appears that modern Western psychologists often function like missionaries of yesteryear. Wearing pith helmets and netting, they bring the Western gospel of psychology to the uncultured natives.[49]

The Philippine nation has had a long history of colonization, from the Spaniards (1565–1898) to the Americans in the twentieth century. After the Spanish-American War, Americans pursued a war against the Philippines when they refused to submit immediately to the United States. More than one hundred thousand Filipinos were killed by the United States, which then established a governmental and educational system reflecting American values and culture. Children under the American rule learned to sing the American national anthem before their own. The first psychologists in the country were trained in American universities and hoped to transfer knowledge from the United States to the Philippines. These psychologists returned to their country armed with Western models and theories.[50] They lectured in English and used American textbooks.

Enriquez began teaching psychology at the University of the Philippines in 1963. As early as 1965, he was teaching psychology in Filipino, which was unheard-of and even looked down upon. He left for the US in 1966 to pursue a master's and then a doctorate from Northwestern University. However, back home there was considerable unrest because of what came to be called the First Quarter Storm. Student activists denounced the deteriorating political and social situation of the country. A wave of nationalism swept through the campus at the University of the Philippines, where professors debated the merits of teaching in the national language.

Enriquez witnessed the unshackling of the Filipino mind and decolonization of the Filipino psyche as the first steps in establishing a *sikolohiyang malaya*, or liberated psychology. In analyzing how this decolonization was accomplished, he proposed stages of cultural domination.[51] The first is denial by the colonizer of a local culture (indigenous law, religion, literature, science, and technology) and devaluation of the minority culture while promoting the culture of the colonizers. Included here is the suppression of the indigenous language. The colonizers make the local people believe that because they live in a multilingual setting, they need one language that can unite them; and the adoption of the superior language of the colonizer will help them achieve that. However, by controlling the language of the people—what happened in the Philippines where the Americans imposed English as the medium of communication and instruction—foreigners wielded greater power to influence the values and beliefs of the Filipino people to suit their own needs and interests.

A second stage involves destroying elements of indigenous culture such as through the burning of indigenous manuscripts and desecration of ancestral burial grounds. A third stage involves denigrating local people themselves, with the consequent feelings of marginalization. Indigenous religious practices are labeled as pagan. In a fourth stage, indigenous culture is tolerated by allowing a few songs and ceremonies into the mainstream culture, but there is only a surface appreciation of indigenous beliefs. In a fifth stage, the dominant culture now selectively recasts theoretical, methodological, and practical elements of the minority culture into the colonizer's mold (e.g., use of indigenous belief system in healing diseases). The concept of *hiyang*, which literally means "compatible" or "suited," refers to the indigenous medical notion of the compatibility of the treatment and medicine with the particular individual. This was dismissed earlier as nonsensical but now is reinvented in terms of personal validation. American corporations in the Philippines use the notion of *hiyang* in promoting their soap products. In a final stage, the dominating culture commercially exploits the profitable elements of the indigenous culture. This is not peaceable.

Enriquez used various metaphors to depict the way Western psychology had been imposed on the Filipino: "*malapustisong paglalapat ng teorya at metodolohiya*," which literally means "the denture-like imposition of theory and method." Western psychologies, like dentures, come after the teeth have been removed, may be ill-fitting, and make speaking and eating more difficult. He also likened the cultural imposition to the wearing of the "Americana," which is the way Filipinos refer to a formal American jacket—again, ill-fitting and uncomfortable considering the warm weather in the tropics, but still considered fashionable and desirable because it is from America. Yet another term that he used to refer to cultural imposition is "*angat-patong*" (literally, "lift and place or thrust"), which he defined as "uncritical acceptance of methodologies and theories developed in impersonal and industrialized countries."[52]

Concerned about the Americanization of psychology in the Philippines, Enriquez proposed the development of a postcolonial, indigenous Filipino psychology.[53] This local psychology was taught in Tagalog, the research participants were local Filipinos, and the methodology was adapted to local conditions. *Sikolohiyang Pilipino* (Filipino psychology) was seen as part of the search for national identity, and hence was a rejection of the imported etic psychology. It is often assumed that the development of an indigenous psychology is propaedeutic to a universal psychology, but Enriquez strenuously opposed the collecting of data in a Third World country to validate a Western theory.

Enriquez returned to the Philippines in 1971 and immediately established what later came to be called the Philippine Psychology Research and Training House (PPRTH). In 1975 he chaired the first national conference on Filipino psychology, where he articulated the ideas and concepts of *Sikolohiyang Pilipino*. Rogelia Pe-Pua and Elizabeth Marcelino indicate that Filipino psychology is the legacy of Enriquez.[54] "Doc E," as he was affectionately called by his students, started a movement that affected not only the practice of psychology in the Philippines, but the social sciences more generally.[55] He established a psychology that was "born out of the experience, thought and orientation of the Filipinos, based on the full use of Filipino culture and language."[56]

Enriquez was adamant about developing a psychology that represented systematic and scientific study, appreciation, and application of indigenous knowledge for, of, and by Filipinos. This psychology would pertain to their own psychological makeup and would be rooted in their rich history. He saw this as imperative because of the extreme reliance on Western models as a basis for analyzing Philippine social realities. He advocated for local psychologies that are neither neutral nor indifferent, and he protested against psychologies fostering colonialism with a pervasive influence on Filipinos. He identified three primary areas of protest: first, against psychologies that perpetuate the colonial status of the Filipino; second, against the imposition, in a Third World country like the Philippines, of psychologies developed in industrialized countries; and third, against psychologies oriented toward the elite in society that are used to exploit the masses.[57]

The contributions of Enriquez to the development of a Filipino psychology include the following. First, it was he who defined Filipino psychology as a psychology that is anchored in Filipino thought and experience understood from a Filipino perspective. He articulated its major characteristics—an emphasis on identity and national consciousness, social awareness and involvement, the study of language and culture, and the importance of applications to health issues, agriculture, art, mass media, religion, and other key areas.[58] Enriquez avoided the colonial mentality of overgeneralization by recognizing the linguistic and cultural complexity of the Filipino cultures. There was no single Filipino culture.

The second major contribution Enriquez made was the development of a number of indigenous concepts and theories. He made every effort to correct the distorted image of the Filipino created through years of research on what was supposedly the "Filipino character" and value system, which foreign researchers printed in textbooks and bandied about as definitive and authoritative. One of the key concepts in Filipino psychology is *kapwa.* "In the Philippine value system, *kapwa* is at the very foundation of human values. This core value then determines not only a person's personality but his or her personhood or *pagkatao*. Without *kapwa*, one ceases to be a Filipino. One also ceases to be human."[59] An inclusive term connoting interrelatedness, *kapwa* emphasizes a unity of the self with others that arises from the awareness of shared identity with others.

There are other examples where Enriquez forged local understandings of personality. Bostrom, a Western researcher, had proposed that the concept of *bahala na* was akin to "American fatalism."[60] He described this as the Filipinos' attitude that makes a person accept sufferings and problems, leaving everything to God. Enriquez cited the work of Alfredo V. Lagmay,[61] another prominent Filipino psychologist, who commented on the improvisatory personality of the Filipino, which allowed him or her to be more comfortable with unstructured, indefinite, and unpredictable situations. *Bahala na* is a phrase with roots in the pre-Hispanic concept of God, or *Bathala*. It is used by Filipinos when they have done everything in their power to prepare for or remedy a situation, and then acknowledge that the rest is all in the hands of God, *Bathala*. Contrary to what Bostrom argued, Enriquez countered that *bahala na* is actually determination and courage in the face of uncertainty, rather than a passive, fatalistic attitude.

Enriquez was also instrumental in developing indigenous personality measures. He lamented the fact that most of what passes as indigenization in this area were mere modifications of test items in psychological inventories developed in America in what he called a "change-apples-to-papayas" approach. There have been several indigenous personality measures developed, including Enriquez's *Panukat ng Ugali at Pagkatao* (Measurement of Character and Personality), that uses personality dimensions relevant to Filipino psychology.

Another contribution was the utilization of indigenous research methods. Many of Enriquez's students answered the challenge he posed to develop indigenous research methods and came up with *Pakapa-kapa* (*"groping"*—an approach characterized by searching and probing into an unsystematized mass of social data), *Pagtanung-tanong* (improvised informal, unstructured interview), and *Pakikipagkuwentuhan* (storytelling or informal conversations).[62]

Finally, as Enriquez and his students spent more time in the barrios and rural areas of the Philippines studying indigenous language and culture, it was inevitable for them to encounter concepts about the Filipinos' spirituality, which they found were an integral part of Filipino life and identity.[63] In fact, they discovered that the first Filipino "psychologists" were healers and priestesses from different ethnic groups—the *babaylan* from the Visayas, the *catalonan* from Central Luzon, and the *baglan* from northern Philippines. They found that the *dalangin* (prayer) and *bulong* (whisper) of these priestesses were a rich resource for Filipino sacred knowledge and psychology. Based on studies about these and other ethnographic accounts, historian and ethnologist Zeus Salazar proposed that Filipino personhood has two fundamental elements: *kaluluwa* (spirit) and *ginhawa* (vital principle).[64] *Kaluluwa* is the essence of a person, that part of himself or herself that will not die and is concerned with things moral, while *ginhawa* is related to feelings of health, wellness, and living a good life.

One of Enriquez's students, Melba Maggay, has incorporated the work of Enriquez in her own theorizing about Filipino spirituality.[65] Maggay applied Enriquez's concept of indigenous psychology to the contextualization of Christianity. She points to two concepts in Filipino personhood that are key in the task of contextualization—the Filipinos' idea of a mediator, *tagapamagitan*, and the value that Filipinos place on connectedness. She observes that in Filipino culture the concept of mediator serves several functions: the *tagapamagitan* stands in our place and pleads for us, especially when we need some favor from the powers, delicately setting forth our case when negotiating or when healing ruptured relationships, and speaking for us when we need help in advancing our cause during courtship or when expressing sensitive feelings that are best sent indirectly. She suggests that Jesus's role as a go-between, one who mediates the presence and power of God, has to be emphasized in light of the need in the culture to make God more accessible to humans.

Second, Maggay noted that Filipinos feel a sense of connectedness even to one's ancestors. This is evident in the rich ritual surrounding burial, and the remembrance of loved ones who have gone before. In such a culture it is good to emphasize themes like being surrounded by a great cloud of witnesses or being a part of great community of faith that stretches through generations (Heb. 12:1). She calls for the incorporation of Christian concepts in Filipino rituals. She says: "The *loob* (innermost being) is the place where we return for healing and recovery of identity. It is where genuine conversion takes place, the stage upon which our own Damascus experience as a people happens. It is there that we truly turn from idols to the living God."[66]

A Peaceable Psychotherapy

We began this chapter with Augustine and hoped for a peaceable approach to one's inner community. Then we explored ways psychologists can be peaceable as they empower indigenous psychologists to develop their own anthropology, should they so desire. We end this chapter with reflections on peaceable psychologists who seek healing in the face of violence, and who are willing to surrender power.

As was evident from José, it is in Guatemala that we encountered visible examples of a peaceable psychology that brought reconciliation and healing. Another example of a reconciling therapeutic is the work of the Catholic Church in Guatemala City. It has played a major role in gathering data so that the memory of the war is not lost, precisely as Martín-Baró had envisioned. Their efforts (known as the RHEMI Project) are now published in a four-volume report.[67] The objective was to underline the reality of the war and help reconstruct the memory of the people affected by the violence. They recorded the abuses perpetrated by the militia and guerrillas. Many indigenous families lost members without understanding why the war was even fought. Under the leadership of Monsignor Gerrardi, archbishop of the diocese of Guatemala City, conversations were conducted with local people regarding the atrocities. Using something akin to what North American clinicians would call the TAT (Thematic Apperception Test), they created their own indigenous cards and asked the people what had happened. The TAT technique presents to participants an evocative picture that asks them to describe what they see in the picture. Therapy was conducted in groups, mirroring the communal structure of the local context. To help process the pain of their losses, they used skits, group exercises, and storytelling. They explained why the war was fought and used fingerpainting to help express their pain. They exhumed bodies from mass graves, identified them, and assisted the community in giving them a proper burial. They discovered that 90 percent of the deaths were initiated by militia. In a tragic and bitter turn of events, Monsignor Gerrardi was assassinated two days after the report was released.

Ernestina,[68] a Guatemalan-trained psychologist, lived through the violence of the 1980s while a student at the university. She was also part of a solidarity group that spoke out against the war and lived in fear of being arrested. After she was picked up by the police for a day of questioning, she realized she could no longer safely go home to visit her parents. Nightmares followed in which her parents were abducted. There were hours of weeping. Her friends in the university disappeared. She came to the realization that she could not depend on the government, but only on God. In the small group that gathered in her apartment for support, there were both Catholics and Protestants whose theological differences were forgotten.

Though the peace accords were signed in 1996, the violence did not stop. When Bishop Gerrardi was assassinated in 1998, all the old fears returned. In 1999 Ernestina's former teacher in the department of psychology disappeared. Even after the peace accords it seemed little had changed. Ernestina felt great anger toward the military, but says she had to remember that they were puppets. She is a licensed psychologist who works today using her own experience to help other trauma victims of the war. Her clinic conducts group therapy with a focus on reconciliation and healing from a Christian perspective. The group members include former militia members, the police, and war widows. She gives them space to talk about their pain, to draw it, and to share it. She explains to them that they knew a different god then, one that permitted violence, that hurt them and destroyed others. She hears adult men weep over being poor, indigenous, and deceived. They close their sessions with prayer, thanking God for the opportunity they now have to find nonviolent ways of living. Ernestina also prepares materials on forgiveness and reconciliation to be used when she visits schools to talk with teachers and train them to work in their communities.

The Kenotic Therapist

It is as a therapist listening to the suffering other that I (AD) am overwhelmed by the suffering face of God. I listen to the weak: the woman fondled by her uncle, the African American husband scarred by the violence of his home community, the gay adolescent considering suicide. In their faces I see the face of our suffering God. Indeed, I am held hostage by my clients' suffering. Their face places an ethical claim on me because as a fellow human I am systemically responsible for their suffering.

As therapists, ours is a position of vulnerability. There is no need here for power tactics. We believe that conversation and humility are more effective in fostering change than manipulation and status. The client invites us to empty ourselves, to create a space within for him or her. The late Randall Lehmann Sorenson, a clinical psychologist and psychoanalyst, was trained at Fuller Theological Seminary's School of Psychology. He spoke eloquently of a kenotic therapist, a self-emptying healer.

In his book *Minding Spirituality*,[69] Sorenson tells of a Christian client who was incredibly articulate about her inner life. She told the story of her mother, who adored her brothers but ignored her. As a result she spent much of her childhood in the basement playing with her favorite stuffed animal, a worm. As therapy progressed, it became apparent that the client had the unique ability of alienating just about everyone she met. She seemed unaware that others had an interior life other than their desire to hurt her.

After a number of years of work, Sorenson recounted how in a particular session he became strangely angry with her. The intensity of his feelings surprised him. When he chose to share with her his feelings, the room went silent. After a long pause, the client remembered a time when her mother had slapped her, and that at that moment the client said she knew for sure that she existed—she even felt close to her mother. Randall worked with her to develop healthier ways of experiencing identity and intimacy. He took a risk for the sake of the other. Rather than being distant, he had been transparent. Randall critiqued the neutral (withholding, even) stance of the dispassionate therapist. He invited healers to consider a more fully alive and accessible posture of loving openness, mutual curiosity, and committed trust. He too believed in love as the transformative elixir. Randall's position was one of weakness, of vulnerability. Might this count as laying down one's life for a client (John 15:13)?

The "weakness" of God predisposes me not to see my clients first of all as guilty, but as suffering. After all, as Christians we are the people of God with a memory for suffering. Johann Metz suggests, in his recent book *Memoria Passionis*,[70] that the gift of the church to society is that it will not forget suffering. The suffering of the mentally ill sensitizes us to the suffering of God, the God whose strength is made manifest in our weakness. Is this the peaceable God in whose name we are instruments of healing?

It has been our intention that the ethics emerging within the clinical relationship be understood as more than an accessory to the "real business" of therapy. It is the clinical relationship itself that is ethical. The ethical aspect of the relationship is evidenced in powerlessness and vulnerability, in simple acts of civility, hospitality, kindness, and politeness. Civility includes learning and validating the language of the ethno-religious client. It is polite to defer to the meaning framework of a client. A peaceable psychology does not require the client to sacrifice his or her moral sensibilities for the sake of a public morality. As a result, the moral sensibility of the therapist is awakened by the other. The transcendence of the other creates an earthquake in the clinician's being. Emmanuel Lévinas argues it is not the voice of Being but that of the other who faces me that disrupts my life. In response to the criticism that religion is disrupting, Lévinas would say it should be.[71]

Lévinas's work implies that therapy involves substitution and sacrifice. This is not a new idea. Freud thought of psychoanalysis as the sacrifice of the therapist's personal ego and interests in order for the client's ego to emerge. Although not immediately concerned with therapy, Lévinas was profoundly interested in the unity and transformative potential of human relationships, using the biblical theme of substitution to characterize interactions. Substitution entails bringing comfort by associating ourselves with the essential weakness and finitude of the other. The sacrifice of our lives before God is a gift (Rom. 12:1–2). Voluntary effacement by the therapist mirrors the face of God.

Peaceably speaking, ethics means questioning the freedom and spontaneity of the therapist's ego in relationship with the other. Therapists do not usually speak of being responsible for the client. The client is to take responsibility for change. The therapist is responsible to be consistently present, to care for and facilitate the healing process. For Lévinas, the "other" poses an infinite responsibility for me. The client truly appears only if he or she pierces my egocentrism and disrupts my horizon, as a stranger capable of surprising me. The deepest relationship with the other is one of vulnerability, openness, and responsibility.[72] Therapy is not necessarily a matter of enabling freedom (the usual therapeutic mantra), but of circumscribing arbitrary freedom in the service of the other. This is deeply countercultural in a society where democratic virtue principles dictate that individuals should never limit their freedom for the sake of others. Modeling this posture of restraint means the therapist will sacrifice herself or himself for the sake of the client. When I carry the pain of the other I sacrifice myself.

The peaceable psychologist, we have proposed, is one with deep commitment to peace and justice. This commitment would be apparent in one's willingness to lay down one's power. While Augustine is celebrated as an apostle of introspection, we stumbled over his psychological and political Constantinianism, his willingness to use force to ensure truth. It was in people like José, Ernestina, and Enriquez that we encountered the beauty of healers who were willing to give up their power so that others could be empowered. We move now to ask the question of what difference the life of Jesus makes for psychotherapy.

10

What Difference Would Jesus Make?

■ ■ ■ ■ ■ ■ ■ ■ ■ ■

According to the grace of God given to me, like a skilled master builder I laid a foundation, and someone else is building on it. Each builder must choose with care how to build on it. For no one can lay any foundation other than the one that has been laid; that foundation is Jesus Christ.

1 Corinthians 3:10–11

The Russian war with the Japanese in 1904–5 was not going well. In the Ukrainian city of Sevastopol some demanded an explanation; others sought a scapegoat. The Jews became the target of public frustrations. The newspapers were filled with inflammatory articles. Pogroms were actively organized while the police remained passive.

Peter Friesen was the first chronicler of Mennonite Brethren denominational history.[1] He was living in Sevastopol at the time and was highly cognizant of the political situation. Peter had been seriously ill for several weeks, so when he told his wife, Susannah, that he must go out, she was astonished. "Why?" she queried. His response was simple. "During the night, I have realized I must make public intercession on behalf of the Jews." Susannah knew full well the possible consequences of such an act. She tearfully pleaded with him to remain at home. Peter was adamant. They prayed together and he left.

His opportunity to intervene came soon enough. When Peter arrived at the marketplace, an angry crowd had gathered. In the center stood a wagon, jammed by the mob. He began elbowing his way through the crowd. When he finally arrived at the center, he clambered to the driver's seat. Then the German Mennonite began speaking in fluent Ukrainian, recalling the love of Christ for all. Could they extend the same love to the Jews? Surely no one present would want their hands soiled by the blood of another's death.

Standing beside the wagon was a burly dockworker, dusty with dirt and soot. Without warning Friesen pulled the man onto the wagon. In full view of the crowd, he kissed him, comrade style, on both cheeks. Then, with a firm voice, he sent them all home. And the crowd simply obeyed. That day in Sevastopol not a single Jew was harmed.

How was it possible that this ethnic German could communicate with these angry Ukrainians? After all, they spoke different languages, came from very different cultures, had radically different religious and political histories, and apparently different convictions. Why wasn't there that spring day simply the confusion of Babel instead of a kind of modern-day Pentecost, a Pentecost marked by cross-cultural understanding, a focus on Jesus, a change in behavior, and a momentary sense of community? This story of courage, hope, and peace suggests that understanding across languages and cultures is possible.

In this chapter we propose that a peaceable psychology is constructed on a sure foundation: the life and message of Jesus. However, that may conflict with other foundations that shape our conversation about healing. In our approach we do not begin with a bedrock of beliefs with which anyone can agree, beliefs that are beyond question and upon which one can construct the edifice of our theories, whether in religion or in psychology. Following the apostle Paul, we affirm that our foundation is in Christ, and in doing so our peaceable psychology is less about a rational system of beliefs and more about the concrete life of the Christian community. We think that in the body of believers, the continuing presence of Christ, we have a foundation from which to function in ad hoc ways in the world and in our work as therapists. We admit we have no detailed blueprint for how a peaceable psychotherapy should be conducted. Whether in life or in therapy, we are epistemological pilgrims. Although we have provided snapshots in the various chapters of peaceable psychotherapy, we have no manual. Though we think therapists might take more seriously their own thick religious heritage, we are tentative in our therapeutic strategies for the sake of our clients.[2]

Theological Foundations

Western theologies have clearly been shaped by the foundationalism described in a previous chapter. Nancey Murphy has argued that a modern foundationalism can be found in both conservative and liberal theologies.[3] Conservatives have emphasized God's transcendent intervention into the world of natural and human affairs, while liberal theologians have focused on God's immanence in human experience. For the conservative theologian, revelation is a representational account of heavenly realities. For the liberal theologian, revelation correlates to human discovery; God is disclosed through genuine human means. According to Murphy, the conservative's use of scripture is an attempt to provide unassailable foundations from which to begin constructing the theological edifice. Conservatives treat scripture as foundational "acts of God, not of human discovery, and emphasize the factual character of their contents." Further, for the conservative, "Scripture provides precise and true accounts of supernatural realities."[4] On the other hand, liberals, Murphy asserts, view "Scripture as belonging to a class of writings that express, with different degrees of aptness, insights regarding God and human life that arise from religious experience."[5] So liberals take religious experience as foundational, while conservatives turn to scripture. Both treat their foundations as sources of universal truth.

Murphy has argued that the epistemology of conservative theologians is "outside-in." It begins with an agreed-upon external reality. For the conservative, theology is the science of God.[6] The objective fact of revelation is the ground of theology. Scripture becomes an inerrant, indubitable foundation for theological construction.[7] The role of human experience is then secondary to the primary role of scripture in the theological enterprise.

The epistemology of the liberal theologian, on the other hand, is "inside-out," Murphy suggests. She uses Friedrich Schleiermacher as an example.[8] He began his theological construction on the foundation of "awareness of absolute dependence." Theological constructions such as doctrines were then tested by this experience.[9] In this approach we begin with experience as described in ordinary language. The test of adequacy is the acceptability of the theological construction in the larger public, rather than in a particular religious body.

The nature of religious language for the conservative tends to be propositional, while that of the liberal is expressivist. Like the scientist, the conservative hopes that theory will match or correspond to reality. The liberal assumes a consensus on reality is impossible, but that we can begin with our common human experiences.

Thus it can be argued that both modern conservative and liberal theologians are foundationalist in their approach. The theological language that emerges from each of these foundations perceives God's activity in the world differently. The conservative discourse focuses on the God who intervenes in nature and history from the outside (transcendentalism). The liberal discourse emphasizes how God acts in and through nature (immanentism). The dilemma we are left with is how to get from inward experience to the God beyond human experience, or from God as objective to inner human experience. When rational and expressive foundationalisms are primary, the test of truth may have less to do with Jesus's life, death, and resurrection.

What might be the implications of seeing Jesus as foundation (1 Cor. 3:10–11)? To make Jesus foundational means we begin with the confession that God is known to us in a particular person, Jesus Christ. We know who the person of Christ is from a written record of his life as a human being living his life within a particular cultural group at a specific point in history. This person Jesus was killed under the rule of a historically real person, Pilate, and according to the witness of his disciples, rose again. In the Spirit, a community continues which seeks to embody in the present the character of God revealed in the person of Jesus.

In contrast to liberal foundationalism, we are not simply beginning with the experience of Jesus or the conservative foundationalism with its belief in Jesus. Rather we begin with a commitment to follow Christ in life and deed. To begin with Jesus means that his character is the test for what it means to be human. To say one is a follower is to focus on the narrative and practices that emerge from Christ's life. Our hermeneutic does not view the Scriptures in a flat manner but from a Christological center in the context of a discerning Christian community.

Psychological Foundations

American psychology is incontrovertibly a foundationalist discourse.[10] Here are some foundationalist beliefs. First, an objective psychological reality is assumed, which researchers in any culture can measure and manipulate experimentally. Second, while some variation is admitted, the meanings of such fundamental psychological constructs as environment, consciousness, self, behavior, or emotion are assumed to be commensurable across cultures. Third, psychological reality is presumed to be sufficiently stable over time to permit meaningful manipulation and assessment of subsequent changes. Fourth, psychological language can be mapped onto an objective psychological reality. Fifth, the isolated, rational individual is the primary unit of psychological analysis. Sixth, psychological and spiritual realities are independent, and hence it is possible to make changes in one without reference to the other. While there are variations in psychological paradigms, to the extent that the above are present, psychology moves toward modernism and foundationalism.[11]

Since the beginning of the last century, the academic discipline of psychology has been constructed on the sure foundation of an objective reality that can be rationally comprehended. On the one hand, with its emphasis on a falsificationist research design that uses random samples, operationally defined variables, and statistical analysis, psychology is clearly positivist. As a result, an area of psychology like psychoanalysis cannot claim to have scientific status, because it is not genuinely predictive.[12] Psychoanalytic theories, by their nature, are insufficiently precise to have negative implications, and so are immune from experimental falsification. Nevertheless, psychoanalysis has its own foundational principles and its own verificational procedures. It does not escape the problems of foundationalism.

On the other hand, there is in modern psychologies the romanticist's commitment to firsthand personal experience. Like nature, one can trust the inner
core of the human nature. What is needed for change to occur is the removal
of the shackles of tradition and the encouragement of personal expression
and imagination.[13]

Consistent with the ethos of modernity, much of current clinical psychology
depends on a scientist-practitioner model as a significant foundation for the
competencies, values, and progress of the profession. Following the Boulder
Conference on Graduate Education in Clinical Psychology,[14] some psychologists called for a greater emphasis to be placed upon directly integrating science and practice.[15] The clinician was to function scientifically. This emphasis
has been reflected in the American Psychological Association's interest in
promoting the awareness and use of empirically supported treatments as
part of a broader movement initially known as evidence-based medicine.[16]
Increasingly, clinical psychology emphasizes the use of validated methods of
assessment or treatment. In situations where validated assessments are lacking,
the modern clinician applies a systematic approach to observation, hypothesis
formation, hypothesis testing, and hypothesis evaluation to the individual
patient. In a foundationalist-oriented psychology, there is an emphasis upon
evidence-based approaches, in which formal evidential criteria are employed
to draw up lists of empirically supported treatments.[17] Modern foundationalist psychology carefully outlines the therapeutic procedures in the form of a
treatment manual.[18]

Charisma and Jesus's Character

From theological and psychological foundationalism, we turn to Jesus. Jesus,
we submit, is a model for what it means to be human, whether therapist or client. First we focus on the character of the therapist. Earlier, Philip Rieff helped
us understand the nature of sacral cultures. We turn to him again because we
believe that Rieff makes a major contribution in helping us understand thick
therapy from within a christological frame. It is in his book *Charisma: The
Gift of Grace, and How It Has Been Taken Away from Us*, that Rieff points
to the positive role of charisma in sacral cultures.[19] Far from contemporary
notions of charisma as celebrity, Rieff understands charisma as the inspira-
tion that comes to a person or persons who enter into a covenant with God.
Charisma, Rieff asserts, is ultimately embodied in the personhood of Jesus.
Rieff's work becomes a boxing ring where he clashes with the great sociologist
Max Weber, whose view of charisma is utterly emptied of substantial religious
meaning. It is because of Weber's legacy that charisma is now perceived as
the exclusive talent of celebrities, artists, and politicians who are worshipped
by a third-culture public.

206 A Peaceable Psychology

Rieff's call for a rehabilitated charisma, we suggest, is a template for the sacral therapist working in a third culture that continues its all-out effort to undermine sacred cultures. Rieff suggests that the charismatic figure is one who embodies the interdicts of sacred culture in such a way that his or her life becomes exemplary.

> Holy terror is rather fear of oneself, fear of the evil in oneself and in the world. It is also fear of punishment. Without this necessary fear, charisma is not possible. To live without this high fear is to be a terror oneself, a monster. . . . All holy terror is gone. The interdicts have no power. . . . A great charismatic does not save us from holy terror, but rather conveys it.[20]

Charisma is the consequence of a life so lived. Herein lies both the authority for, and the source of, healing for Rieff.

> Certainly, we have stunning numbers of people who copy the outward features of the charismatic. They insist on wearing sandals. But there is a great new perplexity in an anticredal order such as our own, because being therapeutics now there is no correlation between soul and body. All is body. Nothing material now emanates from the spiritual. We are mirrors still, but not mirrors of some spiritual or inner reality from which our appearance is derived. Rather, our world is as a theater, and in that theater, rather than the world as church, the program announces the end of all sacramental action; wearing sandals itself must be put in quotation marks—it is a role, a put-on, one of the many costumes that may be worn, one of the transformations and adjustments for which the therapeutic more or less consciously can prepare himself.[21]

Rieff intends to go beyond Weber to establish what a charismatic person or therapist may be, in direct contrast to therapeutic character in third cultures. He offers a devastating critique of the therapeutic in non-sacred orders.

> Therapeutic and charismatic are proposed in this book as ideal anti-types. Thus, for Weber, the charismatic leader proposes a radical breakthrough, a transformation of those transgressive motifs proposed by him in his Protestant pathos as shadowing of a new normative order. The therapeutic, on the other hand, also proposes a radical transformation of transgressive motifs, but not as foreshadowings of a new normative order. Indeed, the key to understanding the therapeutic as the successor ideal anti-type of the charismatic is that he hopes for, as his own lifestyle proclaims, a society in which there is no normative order.[22]

In stark opposition to this trend, charisma for Rieff arises in the lives of those whose gift of healing reflects close alignment with the sacred order. He states: "I understand the charismatic as somehow in truth an innovative resolver of ambivalences by the introduction of new interdicts, a transgressive figure."[23]

Rieff notes that Christ offers a charisma that reinstates the legitimacy of guilt for moderns by raising expectations for social obligation and fidelity. Rieff reminds us of our own theological narrative, that of the covenantal nature of God's revelation in Christ. This covenant grants us the hope of reconciliation and healing through his person, an incarnational hope imbued with honest appraisal of human limitation, suffering, disease, and disobedience. This knowledge changes the role of therapist from third-culture priest to second-culture theologian. The peaceable therapist as Christian is witness to the covenantal work of Christ, who mediates healing.

What Difference Would Jesus Make?

Not only is Jesus the model for therapists, his life narrative is healing for clients as well. So, in terms of therapy, "What earthly difference can Jesus make here?" So begins David Kelsey's account of Sam.[24] The story begins over twenty-five years ago, just before Sam turned eight. The turning point in his life came one evening when his father found Sam's breathing was labored and his face was turning blue. Unconscious, Sam was rushed to the hospital, where he was given oxygen; for the next three months he remained in a coma. He was diagnosed with Guillain-Barré syndrome, an ascending paralysis. During this time his parents took turns sitting at his bedside, reading to him in case he could hear them. Upon regaining consciousness, Sam was not the old Sam; his personality had changed radically. After a full year of hospitalization, Sam was discharged.

Upon returning home Sam was enormously irritable and angry. He was constantly antagonistic and unmanageable with other children, his sisters, and his parents. He was so disruptive in school that he was transferred to a private day school for children with serious neurologically based behavior problems. With severe short-term memory loss, Sam was unable to learn basic mathematical and reading skills. Despite more than three years of work with a child psychiatrist, there was no improvement in his ability to interpret others' responses to him.

Family dynamics changed such that Sam's father withdrew emotionally, and his sisters disappeared into their rooms and into their friends' lives. When Sam was approximately twelve, his mother suffered a severe psychotic break and was hospitalized with depression and paranoia. Unable to cope with his wife, daughters, and Sam, Sam's father agreed to place him in a residential facility. What earthly difference can Jesus make here?

Although the system of institutional assistance was confusing, Sam's family received considerable help from professionals and the state's department of children and youth services. Thanks to his strong identity in a local congregation, Sam's father had a framework for understanding what was happening spiritually to his family, though at times he was overwhelmed with guilt, wondering whether it would have been better if Sam had died. A neurologist whom Sam's father had not met asked to speak with him. They conversed in a leisurely manner, and the doctor shared from his Buddhist background practices (breathing and exercise), which he thought might be helpful to the family. Sam's father found himself calmer after the conversation and to his amazement discovered several days later that the doctor was also an ordained Christian minister. He was moved by the fact that a complete stranger would take that amount of time to talk with him.

Sam's father's pastor had sought him out in the hospital in order to find out how he and the family were doing. In the process of their conversation, the pastor hit the wall, saying, "I don't know about you. If it were my kid, I'd be so mad at God I'd pound my fist into this wall." Sam's father wondered if he was too passive, an emotionally inadequate father. Then he realized that he differed from his pastor, in that he had not thought that God was responsible for Sam's condition. It did jolt him, though, into realizing that he did have considerable free-floating anger.

The situation worsened. Sam began to suffer seizures at the residential school he was now attending. He was placed permanently on anticonvulsant medication, but the medical staff could not establish any consistent correlation between anomalies in the brain tests and Sam's seizure episodes. Eventually, Sam trusted his therapist enough to admit that at times he faked his seizures. (The therapist worked with Sam to end the practice, but it continued into adulthood.) Several weeks after his mother returned from the hospital her depression lifted, she found work, and she continued to see her psychiatrist. But then, tragically, she committed suicide. Sam thought it was his fault, became suicidal himself, and was hospitalized over the next three years. What earthly difference can Jesus make here?

If Jesus is our foundation, then that is where we begin. Sam's concrete situation cries out for redemption, the language of the church. How does God in Christ relate redemptively to Sam? Kelsey's response to the question is simple. God redeems in and through what Jesus did and underwent. Kelsey points out that the question he is asking is raised

> in the midst of the common life of one Christian congregation and about practices that are central to the common life of all communities of Christian faith— practices of preaching; practices of living with Scripture in study, prayer, and liturgy; and practices of worship of God.[25]

Kelsey wants to think about redemption "Christianly" and chooses not to do so from a transcendent perspective but from a particular context, the church and Sam's concrete situation. And there is not simply one Christian perspective on redemption. "Accordingly, what members of communities of

Christian faith say about God, the world, and themselves is said not from some comprehensive, systematic Christian 'point of view,' but from the context in which they live."[26] Moreover, there may be similarities and differences in the ways the word "redemption" is used in the Christian community and in the linguistic space of a larger world. In the latter, redemption often means: (1) making up for a bad performance, (2) redeeming from alien control, and (3) making good on a promise. Instead Kelsey proposes the following with respect to historical Christian dialogue on redemption:

1. Christians tend to speak of redemption in terms of an act of relating that makes a difference to the person or situation being related to. In this case it was to Sam.
2. Christians view redemption in terms of the character of the one who actively relates redemptively, and not some god in general—"the great divine whatever." In Christian talk, the God who relates redemptively to Sam is explicitly understood in terms of the story of Jesus.
3. Christians tend to assume that what God relates to redemptively are concrete human beings (Sam and his father) in concrete circumstances (the disability and the sequelae) that are in need of redemption, not to humanity in general.
4. We stand in need of redemption in two general situations: (a) when we actively sin and (b) are in situations of horrific evil that befall us. The latter is the primary issue in Sam's life.
5. Redemption tends to be understood temporally. God's work of redemption takes time. Sam's positive changes are small and emerge over a quarter century.[27]

It is these thick, redemptive assumptions that Kelsey brings to Sam's situation.

One could say that Sam's situation was redeemed because his family received help from the church. That is, the church was a "redemptive community." Kelsey is cautious about such talk. Redemption is more than receiving assistance. Moreover, he asserts that "Christianly speaking, it is only God, definitively described by the story about Jesus, who can redeem; the church and the helping professions cannot."[28] Their task is to minister, help with coping, and give comfort.

Kelsey suggests that redemption involves imagination, and such imagining does not come easily. For example, he invites us to imagine that God has made a promise to humankind of a new creation, in spite of what befell Sam and his family. The hoped-for world of Sam's family was dashed on the rocks of the reality of Sam's disease and its effects on their family. Jesus entered a world just as unpromising, but his coming was the beginning of the fulfillment of God's promise.

It is precisely this temporally extended *fact* of God's making that promise about the future that can be imagined as one way in which God relates to humankind redemptively. The very fact of Jesus' living with Sam's family—seen as God's act of making them a promise—can be imagined as a way that God redeems what Sam's family has undergone.[29]

It is not so much that Jesus makes up for their losses and returns them to the state before they suffered losses—only insurance companies promise that.

Rather, redemption in Sam's world is based on God's power to create new lifeworlds in the midst of a living death. "If Jesus' presence *is* God's act of promise making, it is *his* presence, not the terrible series of situations that Sam's family has undergone that defines the context they all share."[30] Initially, Sam and his parents learned to *define* themselves in terms of the horrendous things that happened to them. Whether they live by this new context of Jesus's presence depends on their willingness to live into God's promise. If they do, "they may have a lived-world marked by a genuinely open future that they could not have imagined in the living death of the old world they had constructed for themselves."[31] This will require a moment of insight of seeing the connection between Jesus and their situation. It does not simply happen in some mystical, gnostic fashion. Redemption is earthy and everyday, giving new meaning to Paul's words to the Philippians:

> Work out your own salvation with fear and trembling; for it is God who is at work in you, enabling you both to will and to work for his good pleasure. (Phil. 2:12b–13)

Kelsey notes that there are forms of imagined redemption that are not entirely adequate. The focus of redemption is not on some sin committed by Sam or his family, but rather on the evils that befell them. What happened to Sam and his family was not punishment (John 9:1–3). Neither was it God's purpose to send suffering as part of the process of either redemption or perfection. C. S. Lewis seems to have subscribed to this view when he says: "The redemptive effect of suffering lies chiefly in its tendency to reduce the rebel will."[32] But does that describe Sam's self? Suffering may be the occasion for change, but it is not suffering *as such* that is inherently redemptive. Further, to be redemptive is more a matter of imagining God as one who understands our suffering. Redemption is beyond giving comfort; Jesus must make a difference in the situation.

What Jesus can do is liberate Sam and his family from that which distorts their personal identities into a living bondage. Continuing at school, Sam won sympathy from his peers with his story of victimization by a disease and abandonment by his mother's suicide. Sam learned to define himself in terms of the terrible things that had happened to him. He was able to get some part-time jobs, but when he faked his seizures he was asked not to return. His father, overwhelmed by responsibilities as a single parent and Sam's dependence, began to view himself simply as the man whose son had Guillain-Barré syndrome, whose wife committed suicide, and who alone was left to manage his son for the remainder of their lives. Even though there was a support network for Sam, his father continued to organize his life so as to be endlessly responsible for Sam.

Since one of the ways Sam gained respect was to define himself as a victim, his future was defined by past events. Given this story line, Sam felt compelled to remain dependent on others and to sabotage employment and social relationships. Kelsey points out that it is only a profound sense of God's suffering love in Jesus that could help Sam and his father move beyond a bondage to the past. Rather than an identity shaped by victimage, our personal narrative is changed by the story of Jesus.

But redemption is also public, the creation of a new heaven and a new earth. Transformation is not only a change in inward disposition. The presence of Jesus in history is God's performative utterance.[33] That is, in some speech there is an implicit observable action, such as saying "I do" in response to marriage vows. In who he is, Jesus is the promise of God that new things are already happening; namely, a visible community emerges around those who accept this promise.

> In sum, making a promise is a public act that enacts a practice that is one part of the common life of a society and its culture. It results in a change in that society and its culture: the creation of a new community within it, an institution with its own distinctive structure of various sorts of power. The act of promise making and its consequences are part of the public realm.[34]

Transformation for Sam's family carries public import. Both Sam and his father lived their lives in vicious cycles of relationship to powerful institutions: teaching and research hospitals and the department of children and youth services. Sam had no comprehension of how these systems worked, and his father was at times overwhelmed and passive. In his world, Sam acted out his needs for attention, to which institutions responded with more behavioral control. Jesus's role in their lives is to break this vicious cycle as they learn to live into what it means to be loved persons; and that is also the role of the Christian community.

The church community continued to support Sam and his family with prayer and a steady stream of hot meals. The faith of the community upheld them at a time when their own faith was at low ebb. Once, while attending another congregation, Sam's father heard Sam prayed for by name. One of Sam's physicians was apparently a congregant there.

At age twenty-one, Sam earned his high school certificate. Incredibly proud of his achievement, Sam realized he was able to learn and to grow. He relocated nearer to his father, and was able to live on his own in a small apartment with the help of a well-organized social and medical support system. Sam's father came to delight in his son's thoughtfulness, his intense but fleeting empathy for others, and his sense of humor.

The Body of Christ

We included Sam's story because it illustrates how central Jesus's presence is for redemption. Moreover, it is the body of Christ, in the continuing presence of Christ, that envelops Sam. In the body of believers we have a foundation from which to function, to discern ways we can be faithful to the narrative of Jesus.

A number of theologians have pointed the way for us.[35] Stanley Grenz and John Franke ask rhetorically whether we must "finally appeal to some court beyond the Christian faith itself, some rational 'first principle' that supposedly carries universality."[36] Together with other theologians, they argue that propositional systems of truth based on universal reason are coming to an end. They focus on the centrality of the church as the context for the nurturing of faith, rather than faith as final product of doubting.[37] Theologians such as George Lindbeck argue that we should approach religion, church, and doctrine by locating theology's roles within its community and narrative contexts.[38] Miroslav Volf explores the relationship between persons and community in theological discourse, with the focus upon the "community of grace."[39] The church provides the lens through which faith is interpreted.

The church is an ethical community of discernment.[40] Since we have no manual for how a peaceable psychotherapy works, we need the wisdom of the Christian community. Hence, we function in an ad hoc manner. Just because we are Christian does not mean we have a blueprint for effective therapy with persons who suffer from schizophrenia, depression, or autism. We proceed by taking help from wherever we can find it, whether in science, literature, folk wisdom, conventional wisdom, scripture, history, the church, or traditions. However, in the end the church is called upon to test the consistency of our strategies against how Jesus is represented to us in scripture.

A peaceable psychology requires a corresponding ecclesial epistemology. Chris Huebner writes the following:

> Christian pacifism is thus not to be understood merely as a conclusion to some ethical theory which legitimizes and prohibits various activities and justifies particular political structures. It is also—at the same time, in the same place—a particular style of thinking or mode of discourse. . . . Christian pacifism also involves a distinct epistemology.[41]

A pacifist epistemology tends to travel "nomadically, or diasporically, holding no territory, and moving in an *ad hoc* manner."[42] Monological discourse is violent in the social sciences, because it makes inquiry invulnerable to critique; it speaks as if the other does not exist. An ecclesial epistemology assumes that there are many voices, and that all should be heard. Rather than assuming a common foundation from which conversation can begin, Christian psychologists can affirm that conversation between disparate communities or therapists with clients will be a more ad hoc affair.[43] One simply begins the conversation in the hope that in the end healing consistent with our confession of Jesus as Lord will occur. That is, on the basis of conversation we can discover points of agreement about what is true or just, and then enlarge on these agreements. William Werpehowski points out that

> An "ad hoc apologetics" would make a case for the reasonableness of Christian belief not by referring to some putatively neutral datum of experience to which the Christian religion conforms but, rather, through the skillful demonstration of how our common and everyday world in its variety really conforms to the biblical world.[44]

Philosopher, theologian, and therapist James Olthuis reflects a mosaic of themes that reinforce Werpehowski's point. First, Olthuis sees the task of psychotherapy as an act of hospitality, of welcoming and blessing of those who come for counsel. He is more concerned that those who come for therapy are cared for and blessed than cured. Thus, the relationship between therapist and client is viewed less as expert and novice than as coach and fellow sufferer.[45] Second, Olthuis eschews the modernist emphasis on control and technique. "Psychotherapy is modernism's therapeutic arm, the method designed to extend our mastery of the external world into mastery of the internal one."[46] Third, he argues that in a postmodern context psychotherapy must honor and nourish difference. He points out that the unity of truth has been purchased through violence. Fourth, in contrast to the individualism of modernity, his approach is relational and covenantal. Following Lévinas, he calls for a psychology that is interconnected, that begins with responsibility rather than freedom. Fifth, in terms of integration of psychology and spirituality, Olthuis calls for a psychology that is sensitive to mystery. Olthuis is prepared to think of psychological disorders not only as pathology, but also in terms of evil and its dynamics.

A peaceable psychology is more confessional, assuming that there is no conviction-free place from which to evaluate the disciplines of theology and psychology. We can state confessionally our point of departure is the life, death, and resurrection of our Lord.[47] This commitment permits us to affirm the Christian tradition and community which shapes the grammar of our language and praxis as psychologists. Randall Lehmann Sorenson, whom we met in the previous chapter, illustrated this by being explicit about his theological and personal confessional starting point.[48] He wrote as a clinical psychoanalyst who encouraged his fellow analysts to mind spirituality in their practice. Unabashedly, he proposed that as therapists we "take an interest in our patients' spirituality that is respectful but not diffident, curious but not reductionistic, welcoming but not indoctrinating."[49] Sorenson wrote as a confessing Christian, not only because that was his tradition and what he knew best, but also because belonging to a tradition was a precondition for dialogue (rather than, as modernity presupposes, a "biased" impediment to dialogue). He stated:

> I also suspect that my being an analyst influences what kind of Christian I am. But—and this is my point—I also suspect that my being Christian influences what kind of analyst I am. It is my impression that years of participation in communal spiritual practices (liturgy, meditation on sacred texts, social service, etc.) partially shape and influence my character. And my character, for better or worse, impacts the work I do.[50]

Our point in this chapter has been to ask which foundation we affirm, and how that foundation shapes our work as therapists. To say that there is no other foundation but Jesus means other foundations are relativized. However, it does not follow that if Jesus is our point of departure, we know in advance the therapeutic trajectory, and that any conversation is thereby precluded. Our clinical and ethical obligation is to participate in what God is already doing in the life of the client. We embrace an incarnational reign of God that is present but not fully known through the thickest and most particular experiences of our client. We are stating confessionally that Christ is our point of departure, and that our dialogue with clients will thereafter be influenced in an ad hoc way. In so doing we hope the reign of God will be more visible in our broken world.

Conclusion

A Western brochure described David Livingston as having "discovered" the Victoria Falls in Zambia, Africa in October 1855. Discovered? On the one hundred fiftieth anniversary of his "discovery," a bronze-colored statue of Livingstone was erected near the falls. The plaque was more sensitive. David Livingston was hailed as the first European to "describe" the falls. However, the name "Victoria Falls" remains, rather than the indigenous "Mosi-oa-Tunya," which means "smoke which thunders."

We close this book with a restatement of our argument. It has been our hope that those whose race, religion, or ethnicity has been slighted by the dominant Euro-American cultures would discover their voice. We have been preoccupied with what may appear to be disparate themes: the impact of empire, globalization, the loss of ethnic identity, the thickness of indigenous cultures, secularism, thick discourses, thin therapists, instrumental religion, religion in therapy, and the centrality of Jesus. We seek to make these themes as concrete as possible in this conclusion with examples of indigenous Christian therapy in Africa.

Dr. Gladys Mwiti and I (AD) were commissioned by the School of Psychology at Fuller Theological Seminary to write a book on African indigenous Christian counseling.[1] Mwiti had provided counseling for pastors in Rwanda after the genocide there, and later in the aftermath of the bombing of the American embassy in 1998 she coordinated counseling for the traumatized. She completed a clinical psychology degree at Fuller, and from the beginning of her studies we had dreamed of writing a book for therapists in Africa. It was a profound experience to support and collaborate with an African Christian psychologist as she articulated what she clinically intuited, below layers of Western psychologies. I served as amanuensis and editor. The book and the accompanying DVD illustrate many of the themes we have discussed. Our clinical approach was constructed on an African three-legged stool: African

Christian traditions, African indigenous resources, and Western research and practices—in that order of importance. The books and DVDS were distributed exclusively to African seminaries and churches.[2]

People like Dr. Mwiti reinforce the convictions that animate this book, as well as the beliefs native to our respective Christian communities. Her reflections add considerably to our response to the following questions. Can a peaceable psychology interpret suffering within an ethical, political, and cultural context? Can psychologists take seriously the suffering of the other? Can therapists adapt themselves radically to the ethnicity and religiosity of their clients? Will clients experience the freedom to use their native ethnic and religious voices in therapy? Would clients experience greater freedom if in society there were a greater affirmation of a diversity of languages? Is it possible that therapists who hope for neutrality harm their ethno-religious clients? What difference would Jesus make in therapy? In her indigenous African approach to healing, Mwiti addresses many of these questions:

> African counseling that is truly Christian emerges out of the life of a people, is consistent with the spirit of Christian teaching, and seeks healing where there is suffering. It does not deny culture but affirms what is good in it. It takes myths and stories (African and Western), and interprets them through both the Hebrew Scriptures and the practices of the New Testament community. Rituals are practiced in such a way that they reflect the culture of the Reign of God. Healing takes place in the context of the community, with an eye on larger political realities.[3]

Suffering versus Symptoms

We began our journey in the first chapter by recounting the suffering of Guatemala, a country racked by civil strife for more than three decades. We introduced the reader to Juanita, who was our companion in this book. Like Soheil, she suffered. We worried about a reductionism that viewed Juanita's suffering simply as symptoms, when perhaps what is more important is the meaning of her suffering. We proposed that Christ's innocent suffering at the hands of the Roman Empire gives meaning and dignity to her suffering. Throughout, we have maintained that a peaceable psychology begins with Jesus, the Prince of Peace. His response to violence was to absorb it and to propose an alternative system not based on domination. A peaceable psychology will not forget that Jesus was a political scapegoat, that his death was a gift to God and provided forgiveness of his enemies. Given this narrative, Juanita is not reduced to a bundle of symptoms; she is honored as one who seeks meaning for her suffering.

After the genocide in Rwanda, Mwiti tells Faustina's story, a story similar to Juanita's. We cannot simply reduce her to a trauma victim; we must view her as one seeking to understand what happened to her.

I remember when life was happy in my village in Cyangugu, in southwest Rwanda. When the harvest was good, there was always plenty to share with everyone, and the village lay in peace and harmony. At 18, I was the favorite of my father, a Tutsi. My mother was Hutu, but this difference did not matter to anyone. There were many other such marriages all over Rwanda. People spoke the same language, ate the same food, and married each other. However, by the beginning of 1994, there was tension in the air, and some families started leaving to live with relatives in areas reputed to be safer. My father decided to stay. He argued that the south was safer and that little would happen there. However, this was not to be. A week later, killers came by night and the village was surrounded. My family was under attack. The killers seemed to have a list of who would be eliminated. I remember fleeing through the cornfield, and coming to a stop only after miles and miles of running and stumbling in the darkness. I dared not call out for fear of getting caught, because I was sure I heard footsteps behind me in the darkness. Finally, I was too tired to run anymore. I stumbled into a hole in the bushes, and lay there, panting. Tired and spent, I drifted off to sleep. When I awoke the next morning I was hungry and thirsty, so I decided to sneak back to my house. What I saw turned my stomach. Our home was a total mess. Blood was all over the place. One by one, I discovered the bodies. My father lay spread-eagled, with a huge gash over his head. My big brother, with a slit throat, lay in his own pool of blood. My two female cousins who had come to visit were in the bedroom. The way their bodies were spread showed that they had been raped, then cut up with machetes. I ran out again, and kept running and running, with inner screams of horror. I thought I was in a dream. . . . All this time, I kept asking myself, "God, are you really there? Then why do you not deliver me?" Where was he? Where was God?[4]

As Faustina shared her story in a support group led by Mwiti, an older man began to speak. His name, Bizimungu, means "He sees me." Mwiti describes the old man as tall and gaunt, with a lined face and grey hair. One fateful night in his city of Butare, a mob had set his home on fire, stolen all his vehicles, and killed his entire family. Only two teenage sons escaped, and even now Bizimungu did not know their whereabouts. Perhaps they were dead or in some refugee camp in a foreign nation. He did not know. Yet in his confusion, Bizimungu hung onto his faith: "Where was God, we ask. I believe that God was always there in each of our villages, situations, and conditions. He was weeping with us and holding us to himself."[5]

Colonialism and Empire

Both Juanita and Faustina sought meaning in their suffering. With Bizimungu, we think that in Christ God suffers with us. However, the suffering of Soheil, Juanita, and Faustina is explicable given the historical context: American expansionism and European colonialism. The anticommunist rhetoric of the

1950s spilled over into Guatemala. And American psychology, which reflected American cultural and political interests, was hardly a neutral profession in relation to this process. It has been complicit in American political, capital, and cultural expansionism that has undermined local cultures. Psychologists colluded with the American government's foreign policy in Project Camelot in the 1960s, a project that involved American psychologists' assessment of Third World countries, their risk for revolution, and whether the United States should intervene militarily. Psychologists have been involved in interrogations in Guantánamo and Iraq that have brought down international condemnation. Then there is that silent form of violence that occurs when American psychology exports its paradigms uncritically, thereby displacing local psychologies.

Africa has been scarred by empire. In Rwanda Colonialism robbed Africa of its physical resources and undermined its indigenous values. Africa has been dismembered and needs to be re-membered, says Mwiti. She laments the fact that there are Africans who are ashamed of being African. What is left is a palimpsest in which the original African narratives were overwritten by those of the colonists.

> When one is not fully human, that person's culture and indigenous value system is declared inferior and put aside, to be replaced by something labeled as superior. His dance and music is called primitive, as are his traditions and rituals. Her poetry is replaced with what is considered more elegant, and it is determined that his proverbs cannot be so wise. Africa ended up with a subsumed culture and an attempt to write over her traditions that were unacknowledged and subtly denied.[6]

Western culture is aggressive and competitive, influenced as it is by a Euro-American worldview that holds such beliefs as "rugged individualism, competition, mastery and control over nature, a unitary and static conception of time, religion based on Christianity, and separation of science and religion."[7] These values have built world economies, conquered and ruled, and succeeded in making the world more Western through media and communication. But Western culture has been used as a tool of colonialization, such that leading indigenous peoples to accept Western culture was seen as developing them. Local "lifestyles, customs, and practices were seen as uncivilized and attempts were made to make over the 'heathens.'"[8] Mwiti comments that:

> Today, post-colonial Africa is waking up. For decades, Africans have been memorizing Shakespeare, singing Celtic ballads, and learning the steps of Scottish dances. Africans have been baking French bread to perfection in villages, when there is nothing wrong with African yams and sweet potatoes.[9]

Several days after the beginning of a workshop in Kenya, a therapist asked me (AD), with tears welling up in her eyes, "You mean that, truly, we can use our own proverbs in therapy? We have only learned Rogerian and Freudian models of counseling, and our own African tradition was looked down upon." Perhaps the winds are changing—learning Swahili is now mandatory in Kenyan schools.[10]

As a result we ask the question, as psychologists, how our work furthers an empire mentality. A peaceable psychology will need greater political sensitivity, as evidenced in Paul's letters to the Romans and to the Philippians. The gospel is political. To say Jesus is Lord means there are no other sovereigns.

Diversity and Difference

We have maintained, as vigorously as we can, that in the context of Western democratic liberalism, ethnic and religious groups should flourish. However, historic liberalism is itself a thick tradition enshrining individual rights above communal distinctives. It can therefore contest and displace local, minority cultures. This is reflected in the press toward acculturation and the absence of religious language in the public square. We need a "politics of difference" rather than of sameness in our response to the needs of ethnic groups. Such groups need not simply toleration, but legitimation and encouragement to survive and flourish. Difference is a gift. A public square that recognizes and honors ethnic and religious differences will not necessarily result in chaos. Rather, we argued, it will enrich the larger culture and also will empower clients to use their religious dialects in the context of therapy. Religious language has been trivialized in the public square. Implicitly, our clients have learned only too well that spiritual language is best left at home. We argued for a public square—and, correlatively, a therapeutic space—in which many languages could be spoken. After all, Pentecost is our model—there each person present heard the gospel in his or her own voice.

Mwiti argues that African and Western cultures differ in their understanding of personhood and community. These similarities and differences dramatically affect how people understand illness, create contexts for healing, involve a counselee's community, and provide counseling. Mwiti is following an indigenous Meru view of the self, where the other gives one identity and a sense of worth. African cultures have a holistic perspective on life, and they value interdependent relationships. They seek balance and harmony among the various aspects of the universe. The survival of the family and the community is more important than individual fulfillment.

Sacred and Secular

In Western cultures, the language of the land, the lingua franca, is secularese. It is a language shorn of all religiosity so as to make it possible for anyone to speak it in the public square—if they have learned the language. The lingua franca is a trade language used to communicate between communities. It is more contractual, matter-of-fact, and universal. We argued that secularity is a social project, and not simply a neutral language for communicating across traditions. It is a tradition that replaces traditions. As such, it is capable of violence. A secular psychology reflects a secular culture and serves as an agent of socialization into secular culture. However, a major problem for the secularist is the rise of religiosity in the past century, despite the prediction that secularity would make religion obsolete. The American clientele is more religious than that of professional mental-health practitioners. A peaceable psychology recognizes this fact and is open to a religion-accommodating psychotherapy.

Mwiti recognizes that much of Western psychology is constructed on the basis of secularity. As such it may not be appropriate in some African contexts. Simon Maimela speaks eloquently of the effects of colonization on African identity. He notes that colonial "humiliation was calculated to highlight the relative uselessness of our African cultures, religions, and gods, which failed to protect us against European military assault, our eventual subjugation and consequent oppression."[11] The challenge now, he says, is to reconstruct African identity and theology. Maimela envisages the emergence of indigenous Christian theologies and observes that degradation and domination made "South Africans suspicious of the inculturation approach in the reconstruction of African theology."[12] He defines African theology as an attempt that "tries to marry the essential core of the Christian message with the African worldview, so that Christianity could at last speak with an African *idiom* and *accent*."[13] Africa is not, Mwiti insists, the "dark continent," as it has sometimes been called; God has been present all along. African stories, sages, communities, and traditions have often communicated God's presence in his world, and served as a gift to humanity in preserving community welfare.

A Spiritual Mother Tongue

If we wish not to violate the other by expecting the other to speak our language, then a peaceable psychology must be multilingual. A peaceable therapist is a linguist; he or she recognizes differences between languages and honors them by learning them. Our mother tongue is the language of one's chosen or native community. It is often spoken with passion, replete with spirituality, wisdom, some foolishness, and innuendo. However, if I shift from one language to another, my identity seems to change as well. It makes a difference if therapy is conducted in the language of the land or in the client's mother tongue. A peaceable psychology does not impose a narrative on the suffering individual but engages in a conversation that is profoundly sensitive to local grammars. Faith traditions and psychological communities have different discourses, and they may not be entirely commensurate. One operates with a logic of giving reasons for one's actions, and the other with the logic of causes to explain motivation and change. We advised peaceable psychologists to become polyglots, discerning which language to use when appropriate.

Spirituality, communal responsibility, and cooperation are some of the most basic African values, Mwiti suggests. African people are notoriously religious and spiritually minded. Nthamburi observes: "It is almost natural for Africans to take for granted the presence of God in every situation."[14]

Mwiti points out that it should *not* come as a surprise that some African clients in need also seek the help of the wise village elder—and sometimes the medicine men—even when Western psychological and medical help is available. There are physically sick Africans who run to the diviner when Western medicine seems to fail. There are African believers who hop between two worlds, with one leg in the Christian faith, while the other leg is set in superstitions, in an attempt to explain strange happenings in their lives. Many people with troubled marriages leave behind the city's Western-trained counselors and travel to villages to find comfort from their mothers, and to seek the wisdom of elders in order to settle a marital dispute. This does not mean that the practice of secular Western psychology is irrelevant. It may serve as a reminder, though, that perhaps something is missing, and that African people may feel disconnected from the Western therapist. Mwiti comments:

> Appreciating people's indigenous cultural value systems, speaking in a language they can understand, discovering and using their metaphors, and planting seeds of change by using biblical practices that build on people's traditions—all these will build up a practice of psychology and counseling in Africa that resonates with people's identity. This way, healing will be sustainable over time and will become a ripple of positive change over generations.[15]

Thick and Thin

A peaceable psychology recognizes thin discourse in therapy and, where appropriate, affirms a recovery of thick discourses. We made a distinction between thick and thin construals of the self within culture and moral traditions. "Thickness" referred to the rich heritage of beliefs, symbols, traditions, and practices in communal traditions. Its ethic tends to be maximalist. "Thinness" referred to the cross-cultural generalizations and ethical injunctions that are minimalist. In turn, therapy can reflect one's commitment to thick or thin moralities. The danger in so-called value-neutral therapy is that thin therapies mask a thick tradition that is unconsciously imposed on clients. A peaceable psychology honors thin moral discourses but seeks to empower persons who wish to recover their thick cultural and moral traditions.

Mwiti admits that when counselors mention the word "indigenous," some clients are immediately frightened. They ask:

> Are scholars asking us to dig up our traditional goblets and imbibe from animal horns? How can we sing traditional songs anymore? Did we go to school to learn in the city only to come back and sit with the old people in the village? What wisdom does my unschooled father have on how I should raise my children in modern Africa? I left him behind and studied in America, and when I came back, I still find him seated on his three-legged stool![16]

Mwiti grew up in the Meru tribe and draws extensively on traditions, stories, and proverbs.[17] She maintains that counseling in Africa requires accessing tribal wisdom and proverbs. Here are some examples from the Meru of Kenya:

Uume bwa muntu umwe ni gacigo
- Translation: "One man's wisdom is only a small part of the whole."
- Moral: Do not rely on your knowledge only; seek the validation of others in community.

Tonga mwanka ugaire ngaara
- Translation: "May you be so rich as to have enough to share with the field mice."
- Moral: Riches are never worth having until the whole community benefits, and that community includes even the animals in the wild.

Ruri itara rutithekagira ruri mwikano
- Translation: "The firewood up in the drying rack should not laugh at the one by the fireside."
- Moral: Never laugh at anyone in any unfortunate situation, for you never know when you, too, will experience the same.

Then there is the rich store of tribal stories that are a resource for healing. Imagine the wisdom gained by listening to this Meru folktale:

> One day, an old man saw a boy standing at the riverside. He asked, "What are you doing standing alone at the river bank?" Answered the boy, "I am waiting for the river to pass by so that I can cross over to the other side." On hearing this, the old man was surprised and answered, "My son, if you will not put your feet into the water, you'll never be able to cross the river for the rest of your life."[18]

The moral is that those who are afraid of "getting their feet wet" in taking risks will never move ahead into unknown areas of their lives.

Mwiti reflects also on indigenous understandings of human development and personality. Intelligence is not the recall of byte-sized information, or the cognitive skill of seeing patterns; rather, it is wisdom to know how to live. She wonders whether the Western *Diagnostic and Statistical Manual of Mental Disorders* is appropriate in the African setting.

Jean Masamba ma Mpolo and Daisy Nwachuku state categorically that mental-heath services, psychotherapy, and pastoral counseling in Africa "have to take into account the African dynamic interpretations of illness and health."[19] We agree. They advise that diagnosis and treatment should incorporate the patient's worldview, including any mention of the influence of evil forces. Raised with belief in the connectedness of all of life, Africans will perceive mental illness as arising from spiritual or relational factors: bewitching, anger from neglected or offended spirits, possession, or broken relationships.

The Ewondo of Cameroon and the Ba-Kongo of Zaire begin with the diagnosis of the patient by the healer or diviner. This expert brings the members of the patient's group together in a therapeutic palaver to diagnose the cause of the problem in terms of broken relationships, and to plan the goals of treatment. The palaver is a tribal conference or council gathered to assist an individual member or to deal with a community or group need.[20] After communicating hope, the healer plays the role of intermediary between the patient and the clan, utilizing directive therapy to help restore broken relationships.

Traditioned Religion

If religion and morality are to play a significant role in therapy, the issue is what kind of morality will it be: abstract rule-governed or more communal, traditioned? The former, constructed on the foundation of idealism, Descartes, and the Enlightenment tradition is thinner, more rational. The latter is more historical and sociological. We made the case that epistemology and ethics seem to mirror each other. There is a place for moral considerations based on abstract moral principles in therapy; but we have wondered whether such abstract reflection is as transformative as the socialization which comes in a community of moral convictions and practices. All this emphasis on a thick moral tradition was preparation for the argument that religious therapists honor their own and their clients' moral traditions in therapy in peaceable, clinically sensitive ways. However, we would emphasize that honoring tradition is not a romantic move. Tradition can harbor destructive as well as constructive impulses. What is needed is discernment of the best of a tradition based on its ethical charter.

Christian culture, as we see it, is shaped by Jesus's message of the reign of God. It transcends color, race, and gender, and celebrates cultural heritage. The Christian message, Mwiti argues, is cooked and presented within calabashes of culture. The late Ghanaian theologian Kwame Bediako says it well. Christianity can be "one song sung in many tongues."[21] Because of this, Christian counselors live with the imperative to be students of the culture within which they work.

Africans celebrate the fact that each individual's survival is linked to the other's, with God as the center of life, and everything else in cosmic relationship to the order that his presence creates. You can hear a passionate hope for a respect of difference in Mwiti's words:

> Discerning alternatives; rediscovering meaningful symbols, proverbs, rituals, and myths; reclaiming the lost; and legitimizing African experience through the Christian faith—these are the tools with which we can rebuild and reclaim. These are the vitalities still alive in Africa waiting to be reclaimed so that after re-membering the broken, African vitality can be restored. Christian counselors within the Church in Africa will play a significant role in filling the vacuum and bringing restoring life to the people and families of Africa.[22]

Instrumental Faith

Arguing that religion is good for your health is quite popular these days. The question then becomes what religion is affirmed in psychological research and in psychotherapy. We indicated that this "religion" was individualist, consumer-oriented, instrumental, and private. The contours of this religion are shaped by a secular paradigm. It is generic; its features apply to any faith tradition. We called this the religion of a Prozac god. In contrast, with the help of Philip Rieff, we explored the textured nature of sacral cultures, where religion is not instrumentalized and where the sacred is not repressed but obeyed. Life lived in sacred cultures responds to the command, grace, and love of God. Personal identity in sacred cultures is not the object of scientific psychological research.

One can imagine in the African context that religion too can become the magic that creates healing. However, Mwiti embodies a faith that focuses on simple obedience, on faithfulness to a call. She functions within a sacral culture.

> The year before, the United Nations had asked me to work with the expatriate staff they had evacuated from Rwanda five days after the onset of the genocide. For three months, with a team of four other professionals, we completed the job, and then presented our final report. However, while I worked with U.N. staff, my heart broke for the Rwandan people. I kept asking everyone, "What about the horror and trauma of the Rwandan people themselves? Who is helping them to deal with their loss and grief?" I was referred to many groups:

the United Nations High Commissioner for Refugees, relief agencies, and church groups. No one seemed to have a mental health intervention plan in place. All they were doing was what they knew best: providing food, shelter, and medicine.

Finally, my husband said to me, "You keep asking others what they are doing about Rwanda. What are you doing yourself?" "Me!" I responded, "I have nothing. Oasis Africa Counselling Centre is a small indigenous organization. I am also an African woman. What can I do?" He looked at me and responded, "I thought that you were a Christian before all those other things." It was then that I took the challenge. Getting on my knees with my faithful, prayerful staff, I began preparing myself, believing that soon God would open the door into Rwanda. And he did. I had already researched and written a crisis counseling training manual for lay counselors, so I translated it into Kinyarwanda and printed it. Then I sat back and waited.

Peaceful Healing

In international settings where Western psychology has been exported, we proposed that the Christian psychologist would seek to empower local practitioners who wish to explore the contours of a psychology sensitive to their culture, in terms of the nature of mental illness and health, stories of healing, wisdom encased in proverbs, and folk stories that narrate the best values of a culture. We rejected the Constantinian impulse to universalize our psychology and encouraged mental-health practitioners to take a more humble position. We now have numerous contemporary examples of indigenous psychologists to emulate, including José, Ernestina, Martín-Baró, Gladys Mwiti, and Virgilio Enriquez. We think their psychology is more peaceable.

Making peace, we have suggested, is at the heart of the reconciling mission of Jesus. Therapists who seek to be Christian are sensitive to issues of peace and justice, not simply self-fulfillment. In discussing the relationship between the Bible, peace, and development, Nlenanya Onwu, New Testament professor at the University of Nigeria in Nsukka, writes that humanity needs three types of peace: individual peace, community peace, and peace in the midst of conflict.[23] Mwiti writes:

> With so much conflict in Africa, peacemaking cannot be assumed—be it at the individual, community, or church level. Indeed, the Church has often been blamed for preparing people for heaven but ignoring the truth that life on earth is supposed to be abundant and enriching. . . . Such peace begins with Yahweh, the source of Shalom. To communicate this peace, the Israelite prophets became God's voice in the community and aroused the conscience of the Hebrew nation. The author [Onwu] notes that these prophets were not professionals, but because of their relationship with God, they could call the nation to order, stressing that real covenant with Yahweh must find expression through moral

action and upright living. Living at a time of rapid change and yet rooted in the here and now, the prophets became the voice of the voiceless and the advocates of the orphan, the widow, the refugee, the poor, and the disadvantaged. . . . All this means that the Christian counselor in Africa has the role of becoming God's voice for community wholeness, a voice springing from a heart committed to righteousness which seeks the wholeness of the city, not just the wholeness of individuals in the city. The strength of the cry for peace in Africa cannot be overstated. Archbishop Desmond Tutu, renowned African theologian and leader, has said on many occasions that peace is cheaper than repression.[24]

A New Foundation

If a peaceable psychology is tradition-sensitive, then the foundation that will shape the Christian mental-health worker is the person of Jesus Christ. No other foundations are adequate. There are no universal, absolute truths that can substitute for the truth of Jesus's life in shaping our imagination, our convictions and our actions. The church as an emerging sign of God's reign is where, through its practices, our character as therapists is shaped. It is where we discern what it means to be followers of Jesus. There is no manual available for Christian models of therapy, whether when working with a suicidal client, a borderline personality disorder, or a grieving parent. However, we are convinced that the narrative of the gospel of our Lord heals now, as it did then.

Central to our approach in African Christian counseling is the person of Jesus as healer. The story of Jesus coming to the Samaritan woman at the well is paradigmatic. He begins with where the woman is experiencing life. Jesus addresses the deeper issues, of meaning rather than water to slake thirst. He addresses her in terms of her history. Mwiti states:

> Jesus earned the rights of an elder, not because he was elected but because he was an *opinion leader*. Opinion leaders are respected elders who are listened to because they command respect by their very lifestyles and characters. Jesus was linked to the supernatural. What he said happened. And so, with deep spirituality, an authentic lifestyle, and a proven track record, this Elder with a difference addressed the needs of the villagers wherever he went. Some were blind and needed to see. Others ran out of wine at a wedding and he met their need. Still others were children who needed his touch. Even a woman caught in sin, judged and sentenced as a sinner by fanatically religious men, found safety at his feet. Such was this village Elder—a safe place for all.[25]

Mwiti exudes a deep sense of hope that African uniquenesses will be honored. There is still an oral tradition filled with wisdom. Africans view the psyche holistically, as inseparable from the larger universe. There are tribes that care for the environment. Africans understand deeply the nature of the collective self, as evidenced in their commitment to *umuntu* (i.e., "I am because we are"). The focus for Africans is not self-actualization but is other-oriented. African indigenous Christian counselors might view their work as similar to the African forest twine that links and holds up weak twigs, interlocking them with the everlasting forest oaks. In the same way, African counselors seek to link a thirsting humanity with a loving Creator.

We end with the story of a Zairian woman who suffered incredibly and is now helping others. It is another story of hope and transformation capturing themes with which we hope to inspire our readers as they pursue a peaceable psychology.

When the war broke out, I was in Kidaho commune. We heard that the presidential plane had crashed, that the president had died, and that after his death, the killings had immediately started. Because we lived far from the place where killings began, it took two months before our place was affected. When the war finally reached our area, my parents, brothers, and sisters were scattered. Amidst many problems, I joined the crowds walking miles and miles to Zaire as we ran away from the war. I thank God that by God's grace I was eventually reunited with my family in the refugee camps.

After three weeks in Zaire, seeing many die from cholera and exhaustion, a missionary with whom we worked told us that he was going back to Rwanda, and that whoever wanted to could go with him. Although I was very afraid to go back home, I welcomed the opportunity to leave the misery of the camp, where people were dying in great numbers because of hunger and illness. After crossing the Zaire border, I made my way to Kigali. I was a troubled person with all the memory of suffering that I had experienced and witnessed. There were so many sad people around me.

Finally, I got work with a Christian organization, trying to help people. However, as I shared God's word, I was always afraid because of the insecurity around us. Fear was all over because we thought that people would be arrested or killed. I could not sleep well, and was always anxious with all sorts of physical problems. Most of my colleagues at work were also in the same state. We had no peace of mind. I kept seeing images of dead or dying people all around me. Then I was appointed by my organization to attend the Oasis Africa trauma counselors training in 1996.

During the first seminar, I was helped by what Dr. Mwiti taught us. As I listened to her, I realized that I was emotionally traumatized. Later on, in the debriefing groups, I was able to tell my story for the first time since the onset of the genocide. Among a caring group of other traumatized people, I related what had happened to me. I emptied my heart of all the many months of pain. It was as if a heavy burden was lifted off my heart. God healed me and my heart was free. My fear was gone, my illnesses taken away, and horror was replaced with hope and a quiet assurance of his presence in me. What God has done for me has stimulated me to seek to help others in my community.

Before I attended the first Oasis Africa seminar, some of us in our church had set up a reconciliation program because we were concerned about the anger and bitterness in our community. However, all of us were sick people, the blind trying to lead the blind. Fortunately, three of us from my community came to the Oasis Africa training seminar, and God touched all of us. We sat together during that week and made a plan about how to take the message of change and hope back to our church and community. Our goal was inner healing and reconciliation. With the help of some Christian organizations, we began a series of similar seminars in all areas where our church operates. Using the Oasis Africa manual, we trained more people to help us. After taking them through the healing process, they, too, joined us in our work. Together, we reached more than 1,500 persons through seminars and church groups and those people, also, are helping others, beginning with members of their own families. We have also set up a permanent committee, which has responsibility for coordinating both training and follow-up in our church. The committee members travel from region to region, overseeing the effectiveness of this work of healing and transformation, as well as training more trainers and counselors.[26]

Acknowledgments

■ ■ ■ ■ ■ ■ ■ ■

This book was written as much by the spiritual communities we love as by ourselves. Those communities nurtured us in the stories of the faith, gave us unforgettable exemplars and writers who encouraged us to put our convictions on paper as well.

A great many individual people have earned our gratitude in the conceptualization and writing of this book. We would be remiss if we did not mention individuals who have been so helpful to us over the past seven years. First, we are grateful to those who, through the tears of their suffering, told us their stories. We are indebted to Stanley Hauerwas, Don Browning, Steven Sandage, Craig Boyd, Paul J. Watson, John D. Friesen, John E. Toews, James Pankratz, Peter Hill, Theresa Tisdale, Marv Erisman, Robert Welsh, Mark Baker, Joy Bustrum, Valerie Rempel, F. LeRon Shults, Rodney Clapp, Britt-Mari Sykes, Marie Hoffman, David Goodman, and Nancey Murphy who provided us with invaluable comments on various drafts. Kathryn Streeter, Daniel Groot, Scott Grover, and Adam Ghali copyedited various versions. We are grateful to our students from integration classes at Fuller Theological Seminary's School of Psychology and the Mennonite Brethren Biblical Seminary over the past years. These students listened carefully to the main ideas from this book and offered valuable feedback from the trenches of psychotherapy and pastoral ministry.

Finally, we are grateful to the publishers of earlier versions of articles that are referenced in this book, and who have given us permission to adapt them for use in this book: Christian Scholar's Review, Pastoral Psychology, Journal of Psychology and Christianity, Christian Counseling Today, International Journal of Existential Psychology and Psychotherapy, Guilford Press, and the American Behavioral Scientist.

Alvin Dueck
Kevin Reimer
Pasadena, California

229

Bibliography

Ali, Ramón K. "Bilingualism and Systemic Psychotherapy: Some Formulations and Explorations." *Journal of Family Therapy* 26 (2004): 340–57.

Allport, Gordon W. *The Individual and His Religion: A Psychological Interpretation.* New York: Macmillan, 1950.

Anderson, Bernard. "The Babel Story: Paradigm of Human Unity and Diversity." In *Ethnicity.* Edited by A. Greeley and G. Baum, 63–70. New York: Seabury, 1977.

APA Public Affairs. "APA Members Approve Petition Resolution on Detainee Settings." September 17, 2008. www.apa.org/releases/petition0908.html.

Aristotle. *The Works of Aristotle.* Translated by W. D. Ross, B. Jowett, and J. A. Smith. Oxford: Clarendon, 1921.

Aron, Lewis. *A Meeting of Minds.* Hillsdale, NJ: Analytic Press, 1996.

———. "Analytic Impasse and the Third: Clinical Implications of Intersubjectivity Theory." *International Journal of Psychoanalysis* 87 (2006): 349–68.

Asad, Talal. *Formations of the Secular: Christianity, Islam, Modernity.* Stanford, CA: Stanford University Press, 2003.

Asociación Utz K'aslemal Salud Mental Comuntaria El Quiché. *Construyendo una buena vida.* Noruega: Save the Children, n.d.

Augsburger, David. "Sermon on the Mount and Honor versus Shame." Unpublished paper. Fuller Theological Seminary, Pasadena, May 14, 2008.

Aulén, Gustaf. *Christus Victor: An Historical Study of the Three Main Types of the Idea of Atonement.* Eugene, OR: Wipf and Stock, 1998.

Austin, J. L. *How to Do Things with Words*. Cambridge: Harvard University Press, 1962.

Avram, Wes. *Anxious about Empire: Theological Essays on the New Global Realities*. Grand Rapids: Brazos, 2004.

Azhart, M. A., S. L. Varma, and A. S. Dharap. "Religious Psychotherapy in Anxiety Disorder Patients." *Acta Psychiatric Scandinavica* 90 (1994): 1–3.

Babington, Charles. "Clinton: Support for Guatemala Was Wrong." *Washington Post*, March 11, 1999. www.washingtonpost.com/wpsrv/inatl/daily/march99/clinton11.htm.

Bakan, David. *Sigmund Freud and the Jewish Mystical Tradition*. Princeton, NJ: Van Nostrand, 1958.

———. *Disease, Pain, and Sacrifice: Toward a Psychology of Suffering*. Chicago: University of Chicago Press, 1968.

Bakhtin, Mikhail. *Problems of Dostoyevsky's Poetics*. Translated by Caryl Emerson. Minneapolis: University of Minnesota Press, 1984.

Barclay, John M. G. "Neither Jew nor Greek." In *Ethnicity and the Bible*. Edited by Mark G. Brett, 197–214. New York: E. J. Brill, 1996.

Barna, George. *Church Attendance*. Barna Research Online, 2000. www.barna.org.

Barth, Karl. *Church Dogmatics*. Edited by G. T. Thompson. Edinburgh: T&T Clark, 1949.

Bediako, Kwame. *Jesus and the Gospel in Africa: History and Experience*. New York: Orbis, 2004.

Bellah, Robert Neelly. *The Broken Covenant: American Civil Religion in a Time of Trial*. New York: Seabury, 1975.

Benjamin, Ludy T., and David B. Baker. "History of Psychology: The Boulder Conference." *American Psychologist* 55 (2000): 233–54.

Benson, Herbert. *Timeless Healing*. New York: Scribner, 1996.

Berger, Klaus. *Identity and Experience in the New Testament*. Translated by Charles Muenchow. Minneapolis: Fortress, 2002.

Berger, Peter. *The Desecularization of the World: Resurgent Religion and World Politics*. Washington, DC: Ethics and Public Policy Center, 1999.

Berger, Peter, Brigitte Berger, and Hansfried Kellner. *The Homeless Mind: Modernization and Consciousness*. New York: Random House, 1973.

Bergin, Allen. "Mental Health Values of Professionals: A National Interdisciplinary Survey." *Professional Psychology: Research and Practice* 3 (1988): 290–97.

Berry, Wendell. *Life Is a Miracle: An Essay against Modern Superstition*. Washington, DC: Counterpoint, 2000.

———. "Healing Is Membership." In *The Art of the Commonplace: The Agrarian Essays of Wendell Berry*. Edited by Wendell Berry and Norman Wirzba, 144–58. Washington, DC: Counterpoint, 2002.

Bilu, Yoram, Eliezer Witztum, and Onno Van der Hart. "Paradise Regained: Miraculous Healing in an Israeli Psychiatric Clinic." *Culture, Medicine & Psychiatry* 14 (1990): 105–27.

Bloesch, Donald G. *Essentials of Evangelical Theology: God, Authority, and Salvation*. San Francisco: Harper & Row, 1978.

Bogert-O'Brien, Daniel. "Against Global-Speak." *Encounter* 17 (2004): 9–13.

Bonhoeffer, Dietrich. *Letters and Papers from Prison*. New York: Macmillan, 1953.

Braght, Thieleman J. van. *The Bloody Theater: or, Martyrs Mirror of the Defenseless Christians, Who Baptized Only upon Confession of Faith, and Who Suffered and Died for the Testimony of Jesus, Their Saviour, from the Time of Christ to the Year A.D. 1660*. Translated by Joseph F. Sohm. Scottdale, PA: Mennonite Publishing House, 1938.

Brandt, Lewis. "American Psychology." *American Psychologist* 25 (1970): 1091–93.

Brierley, Peter. *Religious Trends: 2000/01*. London: Christian Research Association, 2000.

Brock, Adrian C., ed. *Internationalizing the History of Psychology*. New York: New York University Press, 2006.

Brown, Joanne Carlson, and Rebecca Parker. "For God So Loved the World?" In *Christianity, Patriarchy and Abuse: A Feminist Critique*, edited by Joanne Carlson Brown and Carole R. Bohn, 1–30. New York: Pilgrim, 1989.

Brown, Laura S. *Subversive Dialogues: Theory in Feminist Therapy*. New York: Basic Books, 1994.

Brown, Peter. *Augustine of Hippo: A Biography*. Berkeley: University of California Press, 1967.

Bruce, Steve. *God Is Dead: Secularization in the West*. Oxford: Blackwell, 2002.

Brueggemann, Walter. *Genesis*. Atlanta: John Knox, 1982.

———. "The Legitimacy of a Sectarian Hermeneutic: 2 Kings 18–19." In *Education for Citizenship and Discipleship*. Edited by Mary Boys, 3–34. New York: Pilgrim, 1989.

Bryan, Christopher. *Render to Caesar: Jesus, the Early Church, and the Roman Superpower*. Oxford: Oxford University Press, 2005.

Burck, Charlotte. "Living in Several Languages: Implications for Therapy." *Journal of Family Therapy* 26 (2004): 314–39.

———. *Multilingual Living*. Basingstoke: Palgrave Macmillan, 2005.

Burston, Daniel, and Roger Frie. *Psychotherapy as a Human Science*. Pittsburgh: Duquesne University Press, 2006.

Calvin, John. *Commentaries on the Book of Genesis*. Translated by John King. Grand Rapids: Eerdmans, 1948.

Canadian Psychological Association. *Canadian Code of Ethics for Psychologists*. Ottawa: The Association, 2000.

Caputo, John D. *On Religion*. New York: Routledge, 2001.

———. *The Weakness of God: A Theology of the Event*. Bloomington: Indiana University Press, 2006.

Carroll, James. *Constantine's Sword: The Church and the Jews: A History*. Boston: Houghton Mifflin, 2001.

Carter, Stephen L. *The Culture of Disbelief: How American Law and Politics Trivialize Religious Devotion*. New York: Anchor, 1994.

———. *The Dissent of the Governed: A Meditation on Law, Religion, and Loyalty*. Cambridge: Harvard University Press, 1999.

———. *God's Name in Vain: The Wrongs and Rights of Religion in Politics*. New York: Basic Books, 2000.

Cary, Phillip. *Augustine's Invention of the Inner Self: The Legacy of a Christian Platonist*. Oxford: Oxford University Press, 2000.

Catholic Institute for International Relations and Latin America Bureau. *Guatemala, Never Again!* New York: Orbis, 1999.

Cattori, Silvia. "Sami Al-Haj, Al Jazeera Journalist, Tells His Story." Interview with Silvia Cattori. www.silviacattori.net/article491.html.

Cavanaugh, William T. *Theopolitical Imagination*. London: T&T Clark, 2002.

Chambless, Diane L., and Thomas H. Ollendick. "Empirically Supported Psychological Interventions: Controversies and Evidence." *Annual Review of Psychology* 52 (2001): 685–716.

Charry, Ellen. "Understanding Saint Augustine's Theological Anthropology." Lecture 2 at the Integration Symposium. Fuller Theological Seminary's School of Psychology, February 19, 2007.

Chesterton, G. K. "What I Saw in America." In *The Collected Works of G. K. Chesterton*, vol. 21, 41–45. San Francisco: Ignatius, 1990.

Chu, Chung Chou, and E. Helen Klein. "Psychosocial and Environmental Variables in Outcome of Black Schizophrenics." *Journal of the National Medical Association* 77 (1985): 793–96.

Coles, Romand. *Self/Power/Other: Political Theory and Dialogical Ethics*. Ithaca: Cornell University Press, 1992.

Collins, Randall. *The Sociology of Philosophies: A Global Theory of Intellectual Change*. Cambridge: Belknap Press of Harvard University Press, 1998.

Cone, James. *God of the Oppressed*. Maryknoll, NY: Orbis, 1997.

Connolly, William E. *Why I Am Not a Secularist*. Minneapolis: University of Minnesota Press, 1999.

Costanzo, Mark, Ellen Gerrity, and M. Brinton Lykes. "Psychologists and the Use of Torture in Interrogations." *Analyses of Social Issues and Public Policy* 7 (2007): 7–20.

Covar, C. "Foreword." In *Pagbabagong Dangal: Indigenous Psychology and Cultural Empowerment*. Edited by Virgilio Enriquez. Quezon City: PUGAD Lawin, 1994.

Cushman, Philip. "Why the Self Is Empty: Toward a Historically Situated Psychology." *American Psychologist* 45 (1990): 599–611.

———. *Constructing the Self, Constructing America: A Cultural History of Psychotherapy*. New York: Addison-Wesley, 1995.

Deputy Inspector General for Intelligence. *Review of DoD-Directed Investigations of Detainee Abuse, Report No. 06–INTEL10*. www.fas.org/irp/agency/dod/abuse.pdf.

Descartes, René. *Discourse on Method and Meditations on First Philosophy*. Translated by Donald A. Cress. Indianapolis: Hackett, 1998.

Dillard, Annie. *For the Time Being*. New York: Vintage Books, 2000.

Di Noia, J. Augustine. "Jesus and the World Religions." *First Things* 54 (1995): 24–28.

Driver, Juan. *Understanding the Atonement for the Mission of the Church*. Scottdale, PA: Herald, 1986.

Dueck, Alvin. *Between Jerusalem and Athens: Ethical Perspectives on Culture, Religion, and Psychotherapy*. Grand Rapids: Baker Books, 1995.

———. "Babel, Esperanto, Shibboleths, and Pentecost: Can We Talk?" *Journal of Psychology and Christianity* 21 (2002): 72–80.

———. "Anabaptism and Psychology: Personal Reflections." In *Mennonite Perspectives on Pastoral Counseling*. Edited by Daniel Schipani, 3–16. Elkhart, IN: Institute of Mennonite Studies, 2007.

Dueck, Alvin, and David Goodman. "Substitution and the Trace of the Other: Lévinasian Implications for Psychotherapy." *Pastoral Psychology* 55 (2007): 601–17.

Dueck, Alvin, and Cameron Lee. *Why Psychology Needs Theology: A Radical-Reformation Perspective*. Grand Rapids: Eerdmans, 2005.

Dueck, Alvin, and Thomas Parsons. "Integration Discourse: Modern and Postmodern." *Journal of Psychology and Theology* 32 (2004): 232–47.

Dueck, Alvin, and Kevin Reimer. "Retrieving the Virtues in Psychotherapy: Thick and Thin Discourse." *American Behavioral Scientist* 47 (2003): 427–41.

Dueck, Alvin, Kevin Reimer, Joshua Morgan, and Steve Brown. "Let Peace Flourish: Descriptive and Applied Research from the Conflict Transformation Study." In *Peace-building by, between, and beyond Muslims and Evangelical Christians*, edited by Mohammed Abu-Nimer and David Augsburger, 233–54. Lanham, MD: Lexington Books, 2009.

Dueck, Alvin, Sing-Kiat Ting, and Renee Cutiongco. "Constantine, Babel, and Yankee Doodling: Whose Indigeneity? Whose Psychology?" *Pastoral Psychology* 56 (2007): 55–72.

Dueck, Alvin, and Sherry Walling. "Theological Contributions of Bishop K. H. Ting to Christian/Pastoral Counseling." *Pastoral Psychology* 56 (2007): 143–56.

Dunn, James D. G. *The Theology of Paul's Letter to the Galatians*. Cambridge: Cambridge University Press, 1993.

Dworkin, Ronald. "Liberalism." In *Public and Private Morality*. Edited by Stuart Hampshire, 113–43. Cambridge: Cambridge University Press, 1978.

Eliade, Mircea. *Shamanism: Archaic Techniques of Ecstasy*. Princeton, NJ: Princeton University Press, 1964.

Eliot, T. S. *Christianity and Culture: The Idea of a Christian Society and Notes Towards the Definition of Culture*. New York: Harcourt Brace, 1968.

Ellis, Albert. "Can Rational Emotive Behavior Therapy (REBT) Be Effectively Used with People Who Have Devout Beliefs in God and Religion?" *Professional Psychology: Research & Practice* 31 (2000): 29–33.

Ellul, Jacques. *The Technological Society*. New York: Knopf, 1964.

Enriquez, Virgilio G. *From Colonial to Liberation Psychology: The Philippine Experience*. Manila: De La Salle University Press, 1994.

———. *Pagbabagong Dangal: Indigenous Psychology and Cultural Empowerment*. Quezon City: PUGAD Lawin, 1994.

Fanon, Frantz. *The Wretched of the Earth*. Translated by Constance Farrington. New York: Grove, 1965.

Ferenczi, Sandor. *First Contributions to Psycho-analysis*. Translated by E. Jones. New York: Brunner/Mazel, 1952.

Feyerabend, Paul. *Against Method: Outline of an Anarchistic Theory of Knowledge*. London: Humanities, 1975.

Fink, Bruce. *Fundamentals of Psychoanalytic Technique: A Lacanian Approach for Practitioners*. New York: W. W. Norton, 2007.

Fish, Stanley. *The Trouble with Principle*. Cambridge: Harvard University Press, 1999.

Flynn, Patricia, dir. *Discovering Dominga*. Encino, CA: Jaguar House Films, 2002.

Ford, Bárbara, Roberto Cabrera, and Virginia Searing. *Buscando una buena vida: tres experiencias de salud mental comunitaria*. Guatemala: Redd Barna, 2000.

Frankl, Viktor E. *Man's Search for Meaning: An Introduction to Logotherapy*. New York: Holt, Rinehart, and Winston, 1963.

Freire, Paulo. *Pedagogy of the Oppressed*. New York: Seabury, 1970.

Freud, Sigmund. *Future of an Illusion*. London: Hogarth, 1961.

Gabrenya, William K. Jr. "A Sociology of Science Approach to Understanding Indigenous Psychologies." In *Ongoing Themes in Psychology and Culture*, edited by B. N. Setiadi, A. Supratiknya, W. J. Lonner, and Y. H. Poortinga, 131–45. Jakarta: International Association for Cross-Cultural Psychology, 2004.

Gantt, Edwin. "Lévinas, Psychotherapy, and the Ethics of Suffering." *Journal of Humanistic Psychology* 40 (2000): 9–28.

Garcia, Rodrigo. "Alex." *In Treatment*. Season 1, episode 2. HBO, 2008.

Gay, Craig. *The Way of the (Modern) World*. Grand Rapids: Eerdmans, 1998.

Gay, Peter. *Modernism: The Thrill of Heresy*. New York: W. W. Norton, 2007.

Geertz, Clifford. *The Interpretation of Cultures: Selected Essays*. New York: Basic Books, 1973.

Gergen, Kenneth, Aydan Lock, Andrew Gulerce, and Girishwar Misra. "Psychological Science in Cultural Context." *American Psychologist* 51 (1996): 496–503.

Ghali, Adam. "The Ethics of Interrogation." Poster presented at the Christian Association for Psychological Studies in Phoenix, Arizona, April 2008.

Glenn, David. "Prophet of the 'Anti-Culture.'" *Chronicle of Higher Education* 52 (November 11, 2005): A14–A17. http://chronicle.com/free/v52/i12/12a01501.htm.

Gorsuch, Richard L. "Religious Aspects of Substance Abuse and Recovery." *Journal of Social Issues* 5 (1995): 65–83.

———. *Integrating Psychology and Spirituality?* Pasadena, CA: Fuller Seminary Press, 2007.

Gray, John. *Al Qaeda and What It Means to Be Modern*. New York: New Press, 2003.

Green, Joel, and Mark Baker. *Recovering the Scandal of the Cross: Atonement in New Testament and Contemporary Contexts*. Downers Grove, IL: InterVarsity Press, 2000.

Greenberg, David, and Eliezer Witztum. *Sanity and Sanctity: Mental Health Work among the Ultra-Orthodox in Jerusalem*. New Haven: Yale University Press, 2001.

Greenson, Ralph R. "The Mother Tongue and the Mother." *International Journal of Psycho-Analysis* 31 (1950): 18–23.

Grenz, Stanley J., and J. R. Franke. *Beyond Foundationalism: Shaping Theology in a Postmodern Context*. Louisville: Westminster John Knox, 2001.

Griffith, James, and Melissa Griffith. *Encountering the Sacred in Psychotherapy: How to Talk with People about Their Spiritual Lives*. New York: Guilford, 2001.

Gutierrez, Gustavo. *A Theology of Liberation: History, Politics, and Salvation*. New York: Orbis, 1984.

Hall, Douglas John, and Rosemary Radford Ruether. *God and the Nations*. Minneapolis: Fortress, 1995.

Hardt, Michael, and Antonio Negri. *Empire*. Cambridge: Harvard University Press, 2000.

Hart, David Bentley. *The Beauty of the Infinite: The Aesthetics of Christian Truth*. Grand Rapids: Eerdmans, 2003.

Hauerwas, Stanley. *The Peaceable Kingdom: A Primer in Christian Ethics*. Notre Dame, IN: University of Notre Dame Press, 1983.

———. "The State of the Secular: Theology, Prayer, and the University." In *The State of the University: Academic Knowledges and the Knowledge of God*. Oxford: Blackwell, 2007.

Hauerwas, Stanley, and Romand Coles. *Christianity, Democracy, and the Radical Ordinary: Conversations between a Radical Democrat and a Christian*. Eugene, OR: Cascade Books, 2008.

Hauerwas, Stanley, Nancey Murphy, and Mark Nation. *Theology without Foundations: Religious Practice and the Future of Theological Truth*. Nashville: Abingdon, 1994.

Heine, Steven, Shinobu Kitayama, and Darrin Lehman. "Cultural Differences in Self-Evaluation: Japanese Readily Accept Negative Self-Relevant Information." *Journal of Cross-Cultural Psychology* 32 (2001): 434–43.

Held, Barbara S. *Back to Reality: A Critique of Postmodern Theory in Psychotherapy*. New York: W. W. Norton, 1995.

Herman, Ellen. *The Romance of American Psychology: Political Culture in the Age of Experts, 1940–1970*. Berkeley: University of California Press, 1995.

Heschel, Abraham. *Who Is Man?* Stanford, CA: Stanford University Press, 1965.

Hiebert, Theodore. "The Tower of Babel and the Origin of the World's Cultures." *Journal of Biblical Literature* 126 (2007): 29–58.

Hofgaard, Tor Levin. "Letter Written to the American Psychological Association President Dr. Alan E. Kazdin on Behalf of the European Psychological Association in Preparation for a Meeting in Berlin with APA representatives." www.psysr.org/about/committees/endtorture/Nordic%20Committee%20Letter%20on%20Torture.pdf.

Hollinger, David. "The Enlightenment and the Genealogy of Cultural Conflict in the United States." In *What's Left of Enlightenment?* Edited by Keith Michel Baker and Peter Hanns Reill, 1–32. Stanford, CA: Stanford University Press, 2001.

Horsley, Richard A. "1 Corinthians: A Case Study of Paul's Assembly as an Alternative Society." In *Paul and Empire*, 242–52. Harrisburg, PA: Trinity Press International, 1997.

———. *Jesus and Empire: The Kingdom of God and the New World Disorder.* Minneapolis: Fortress, 2002.

Huebner, Chris. *A Precarious Peace: Yoderian Explorations on Theology, Knowledge, and Identity.* Waterloo, ON: Herald, 2006.

Hunter, James Davidson. *The Death of Character: Moral Education in an Age without Good or Evil.* New York: Basic Books, 2000.

Hwang, Kwang-Kuo. "Constructive Realism and Confucian Relationalism: An Epistemological Strategy for the Development of Indigenous Psychology." In *Indigenous and Cultural Psychology: Understanding People in Context.* Edited by Uichol Kim, Kuo-shu Yang, and Kwang-Kuo Hwang, 73–107. New York: Springer, 2006.

International Federation of Social Workers. *Ethics in Social Work Statement of Principles.* 2004. www.ifsw.org/en/p38000324.html#top.

Jaeger, Werner Wilhelm. *Paideia: The Ideals of Greek Culture.* New York: Oxford University Press, 1965.

James, William. *The Principles of Psychology.* New York: Mentor, 1958.

———. *The Varieties of Religious Experience: A Study in Human Nature.* New York: Modern Library, 2002.

Jaschik, Scott. "Not So Godless after All." *Inside Higher Ed*, October 9, 2006. http://insidehighered.com/news/2006/10/09/religion.

Jefferson, Thomas. "A Bill for Establishing Religious Freedom." *Daedalus* 132 (2003): 15–19.

Jenkins, Philip. *The Next Christendom: The Coming of Global Christianity.* Oxford: Oxford University Press, 2002.

Jersak, Brad, and Michael Hardin. *Stricken by God? Nonviolent Identification and the Victory of Christ.* Grand Rapids: Eerdmans, 2007.

Johnson, Chalmers A. *The Sorrows of Empire: Militarism, Secrecy, and the End of the Republic*. New York: Metropolitan Books, 2004.

Johnson, Eric L. "Sin, Weakness, and Psychopathology." *Journal of Psychology and Theology* 15 (1987): 218–26.

———. *Foundations for Soul Care: A Christian Psychology Proposal*. Downers Grove, IL: InterVarsity Press, 2007.

Johnson, Glen. "For Bush, 'Bob Jones' May Spell T-R-O-U-B-L-E." *Black Issues in Higher Education* 17 (March 16, 2000): 9. http://findarticles.com/p/articles/ mi_m0DXK/is_2_17/ai_61573625.

Johnson, Luke Timothy. *The Real Jesus: The Misguided Quest for the Historical Jesus and the Truth of the Traditional Gospels*. San Francisco: HarperSanFrancisco, 1996.

Jones, Charisse, and Kumea Shorter-Gooden. *Shifting: The Double Lives of Black Women in America*. New York: HarperCollins, 2003.

Jordan, Augustus, and Naomi Meara. "Ethics and the Professional Practice of Psychologists: The Role of Virtues and Principles." *Professional Psychology: Research and Practice* 21 (1990): 107–14.

Jordan, Merle. *Taking on the Gods: The Task of the Pastoral Counselor*. Nashville: Parthenon, 1986.

Jung, Carl G. *Psychology and Religion: West and East*. Vol. 11, *The Collected Works of C. G. Jung*. Princeton: Princeton University Press, 1977.

Jung, Carl, and Aniela Jaffe. *Memories, Dreams, Reflections*. New York: Vintage Books, 1963.

Kasonga, Kasonga Wa. "African Palaver: A Contemporary Way of Healing Communal Conflicts and Crises." In *The Church and Healing: Echoes from Africa*, edited by Emmanuel Lartey, Daisy Nwachuku, and Kasonga wa Kasonga, 49–65. New York: Peter Lang, 1994.

Katsavdakis, Kostas, Mohamed Sayed, Anthony Bram, and Alice Brand Bartlett. "How Was This Story Told in the Mother Tongue? An Integrative Perspective." *Bulletin of the Menninger Clinic* 2 (2001): 246–65.

Kaufman, Gordon. *God, Mystery, Diversity: Christian Theology in a Pluralistic World*. Minneapolis: Fortress, 1996.

Kelly, Timothy, and Hans H. Strupp. "Patient and Therapist Values in Psychotherapy: Perceived Changes, Assimilation, Similarity, and Outcome." *Journal of Consulting & Clinical Psychology* 60 (1992): 34–40.

Kelsey, David H. *Imagining Redemption*. Louisville: Westminster John Knox, 2005.

Kendall, Philip C., and Diane L. Chambless. "Empirically Supported Psychological Therapies." *Journal of Clinical and Consulting Psychologies* 66 (1998): 3–167.

Kendall, Philip C., Brian Chu, Andrea Gifford, Clair Hayes, and Maaike Nauta. "Breathing Life into a Manual: Flexibility and Creativity with Manual-Based Treatment." *Cognitive Behavior Practice* 5 (1998): 177–78.

Kim, Uichol, and John Berry, eds. *Indigenous Psychologies: Experience and Research in Cultural Context*. Newbury Park, CA: Sage, 1993.

Kim, Uichol, Kuo-shu Yang, and Kwang-Kuo Hwang. "Contributions to Indigenous and Cultural Psychology: Understanding People in Context." In *Indigenous and Cultural Psychology: Understanding People in Context*, 3–25. New York: Springer, 2006.

———, eds. *Indigenous and Cultural Psychology: Understanding People in Context*. New York: Springer, 2006.

Kimelman, Reuven. "Abraham Joshua Heschel: Our Generation's Teacher." *Religion and Intellectual Life* 2 (1985): 9–18.

King, Martin Luther Jr. "Keep Moving from This Mountain." A sermon delivered at Temple Israel of Hollywood, February 26, 1965.

Kitayama, Shinobu, Hazel Rose Markus, Hisaya Matsumoto, and Vinai Norasakkunkit. "Individual and Collective Processes in the Construction of the Self: Self-Enhancement in the United States and Self-Criticism in Japan." *Journal of Personality & Social Psychology* 72 (1997): 1245–67.

Kleinman, Arthur. *The Illness Narratives: Suffering, Healing, and the Human Condition*. New York: Basic Books, 1988.

———. *Social Origins of Distress and Disease: Depression, Neurasthenia, and Pain in Modern China*. Ann Arbor: University of Michigan Press, 1998.

Koenig, Harold, ed. *Handbook of Religion and Mental Health*. San Diego: Academic Press, 1998.

Koenig, Harold, Linda K. George, and Bercedes L. Peterson. "Religiosity and Remission from Depression in Medically Ill Older Patients." *American Journal of Psychiatry* 155 (1998): 536–42.

Koenig, Harold, Michael E. McCullough, and David B. Larson, eds. *Handbook of Religion and Health*. London: Oxford University Press, 2001.

Kohlberg, Lawrence. *Stages of Moral Development as a Basis for Moral Education*. Cambridge: Center for Moral Education, Harvard University, 1971.

Kolodiejchuk, Teresa, and Brian Kolodiejchuk. *Mother Teresa: Come Be My Light: The Private Writings of the "Saint of Calcutta."* New York: Doubleday, 2007.

Koontz, Ted. "Thinking Theologically about the War in Iraq." *Mennonite Quarterly Review* 77 (2003): 93–108.

Kory, Deborah. "Psychologists Aiding and Abetting Torture." *Tikkun* 31 (2007): 60–64.

Krapf, E. Eduardo. "The Choice of Language in Polyglot Psychoanalysis." *Psychoanalytic Quarterly* 24 (1955): 343–57.

Kraybill, Donald B., Steven M. Nolt, and David Weaver-Zercher. *Amish Grace: How Forgiveness Transcended Tragedy*. San Francisco: Jossey-Bass, 2007.

Kuhn, Thomas. *The Structure of Scientific Revolutions*. Chicago: University of Chicago Press, 1962.

Kymlicka, Will. *Liberalism, Community and Culture*. Oxford: Clarendon, 1989.

———. *Multicultural Citizenship: A Liberal Theory of Minority Rights*. New York: Clarendon, 1995.

Lakatos, Imre, and Alan Musgrave. *Criticism and the Growth of Knowledge*. Cambridge: Cambridge University Press, 1970.

Lake, Frank. *Clinical Theology*. London: Darton Longman and Todd, 1986.

LaMothe, Ryan. "Pastoral Care of Political Discourse: Shepherding Communication." *Pastoral Psychology* 56 (2008): 467–81.

———. "What Hope Is There? The Enthrallment of Empire Stories." *Pastoral Psychology* 56 (2008): 481–97.

Lasch, Christopher. *The Culture of Narcissism: American Life in an Age of Diminishing Expectations*. New York: Warner Books, 1977.

Leahey, Thomas H. *A History of Psychology: Main Currents in Psychological Thought*. 2nd ed. Englewood Cliffs, NJ: Prentice Hall, 1987.

Lederach, John Paul. *Preparing for Peace: Conflict Transformation across Cultures*. Syracuse, NY: Syracuse University Press, 1996.

———. *Building Peace: Sustainable Reconciliation in Divided Societies*. Washington, DC: U.S. Institute of Peace Press, 1997.

Lehr, Elizabeth, and Bernard Spilka. "Religion in the Introductory Psychology Textbook: A Comparison of Three Decades." *Journal for the Scientific Study of Religion* 28 (1989): 366–71.

Lévinas, Emmanuel. *Otherwise than Being: Or, Beyond Essence*. Translated by Alphonso Lingis. Boston: M. Nijhoff, 1981.

Levison, John, and Priscilla Levison-Pope. *Return of Babel: Global Perspectives on the Bible*. Louisville: Westminster John Knox, 1999.

Lewis, Clive S. *The Problem of Pain*. London: Geoffrey Bles, 1940.

Lindbeck, George. *The Nature of Doctrine: Religion and Theology in a Post-liberal Age*. Philadelphia: Westminster John Knox, 1984.

Lindbeck, George, and James J. Buckley. *The Church in a Postliberal Age*. London: SCM, 2002.

ma Mpolo, Jean Masamba, and Daisy Nwachuku, eds. *Pastoral Care and Counselling in Africa Today*. Frankfurt am Main: P. Lang, 1991.

Macaulay, Thomas Babington. "Minute on Indian Education." In *Selected Writings*. Edited by J. Clive, 237–51. Chicago: University of Chicago Press, 1972.

MacIntyre, Alasdair. *After Virtue: A Study in Moral Theory*. Notre Dame, IN: University of Notre Dame Press, 1984.

———. *Whose Justice? Which Rationality?* Notre Dame, IN: University of Notre Dame Press, 1988.

———. *Three Rival Versions of Moral Enquiry: Encyclopaedia, Genealogy, and Tradition*. Notre Dame, IN: University of Notre Dame Press, 1990.

Maggay, Melba P. "Towards Contextualization from Within: Some Tools and Culture Themes." www.mpmaggay.blogspot.com/2005/04/towards-contextualization-within.html.

Maimela, Simon S. "Cultural and Ethnic Diversity in Promotion of Democratic Change." In *Democracy and Development in Africa: The Role of Churches*. Edited by J. N. K. Mugambi, 112–20. Nairobi: All Africa Conference of Churches, 1997.

Marcos, Luis R., and Leonel Urcuyo. "Dynamic Psychotherapy with the Bilingual Patient." *American Journal of Psychotherapy* 33 (1979): 331–38.

Marian, Viorica, and Ulrich Neisser. "Language-Dependent Recall of Autobiographical Memories." *Journal of Experimental Psychology: General* 129 (2000): 361–68.

"Marital Stress and Extramarital Relationships." Chap. 20, DVD accompanying text by Comer, Ronald J. *Abnormal Psychology*, 3rd ed. New York: W. H. Freeman, 1998.

Markus, A. Robert. *Christianity and the Secular*. Notre Dame, IN: University of Notre Dame Press, 2006.

Markus, Hazel Rose, and Shinobu Kitayama. "The Cultural Construction of Self and Emotion: Implications for Social Behavior." In *Emotion and Culture: Empirical Studies of Mutual Influence*, edited by Shinobu Kitayama and Hazel Rose Markus, 89–130. Washington, DC: American Psychological Association, 1994.

Marsden, George. *The Soul of the American University: From Protestant Establishment to Established Nonbelief*. New York: Oxford University Press, 1994.

Marsden, George, and B. J. Longfield. *The Secularization of the Academy*. New York: Oxford University Press, 1992.

Martín-Baró, Ignacio. *Writings for a Liberation Psychology*. Cambridge: Harvard University Press, 1994.

McAdams, Dan. *The Stories We Live By: Personal Myths and the Making of the Self*. New York: Morrow, 1993.

————. *The Redemptive Self: Stories Americans Live By*. New York: Oxford University Press, 2006.

McAdams, Dan, Ruthellen Josselson, and Amia Lieblich. *Identity and Story: Creating Self in Narrative*. Washington, DC: American Psychological Association, 2006.

McClelland, David. *The Achievement Motive*. New York: Appleton-Century-Crofts, 1953.

McClendon, James Wm. Jr. *Ethics*. Vol. 1 of *Systematic Theology*. Nashville: Abingdon, 1986.

————. *Biography as Theology: How Life Stories Can Remake Today's Theology*. Philadelphia: Trinity Press International, 1990.

————. *Doctrine*. Vol. 2 of *Systematic Theology*. Nashville: Abingdon, 1994.

————. *Witness*. Vol. 3 of *Systematic Theology*. Nashville, Abingdon, 2000.

McCoy, Alfred W. *A Question of Torture: CIA Interrogation, from the Cold War to the War on Terror*. New York: Metropolitan Books, 2006.

Mead, George Herbert. *Mind, Self, and Society*. Chicago: University of Chicago Press, 1934.

Mead, Walter Russell. "God's Country?" *Foreign Affairs* 85 (October 16, 2006). www.foreignaffairs.org/20060901faessay85504/walter-russell-mead/god-s-country.html.

Meador, Keith G. "My Own Salvation: The Christian Century and Psychology's Secularizing of American Protestantism." In *The Secular Revolution: Power, Interests, and Conflict in the Secularization of American Public Life*. Edited by Christian Smith, 269–305. Berkeley: University of California Press, 2003.

Meara, Naomi, Harold B. Pepinsky, Joseph W. Shannon, and William A. Murray. "Semantic Communication and Expectations for Counseling across Three Theoretical Orientations." *Journal of Counseling Psychology* 28 (1981): 110–18.

Meara, Naomi, Joseph W. Shannon, and Harold Pepinsky. "Comparison of the Stylistic Complexity of the Language of Counselor and Client across Three Theoretical Orientations." *Journal of Counseling Psychology* 26 (1979): 181–89.

Menchu, Rigoberta. *I, Rigoberta Menchu*. Translated by A. Wright. London: Verso, 1984.

Menninger, Karl. *Whatever Became of Sin?* New York: Hawthorn Books, 1973.

Metz, Johann Baptist. *Memoria Passionis*. Freiburg, Germany: Herder Verlag, 2006.

Milbank, John. *Theology and Social Theory: Beyond Secular Reason*. Oxford: Blackwell, 1990.

Miller, Ronald B. *Facing Human Suffering: Psychology and Psychotherapy as Moral Engagement*. Washington, DC: American Psychological Association, 2004.

Miller, Vincent Jude. *Consuming Religion: Christian Faith and Practice in a Consumer Culture*. New York: Continuum, 2004.

Mohanty, Chandra T. "Under Western Eyes: Feminist Scholarship and Colonial Discourses." *Feminist Review* 30 (1998): 65–88.

Moltmann, Jürgen. *The Crucified God: The Cross of Christ as the Foundation and Criticism of Christian Theology*. New York: Harper & Row, 1974.

———. *The Spirit of Life: A Universal Affirmation*. London: SCM, 1992.

Mowrer, O. Hobart. *The Crisis in Psychiatry and Religion*. Princeton, NJ: Van Nostrand, 1961.

Murphy, Nancey C. *Beyond Liberalism and Fundamentalism: How Modern and Postmodern Philosophy Set the Theological Agenda*. Valley Forge, PA: Trinity Press International, 1996.

Mwiti, Gladys, and Al Dueck. *Christian Counseling: An African Indigenous Perspective*. Pasadena, CA: Fuller Seminary Press, 2006.

———. *Christian Counseling: An African Indigenous Perspective, A Video Series*. Pasadena, CA: Fuller Seminary Press, 2006.

Myers, Ched. *Binding the Strong Man: A Political Reading of Mark's Story of Jesus*. Maryknoll, NY: Orbis, 1997.

Narvaez, Darcia, and Daniel Lapsley. "The Psychological Foundations of Everyday Morality and Moral Expertise." In *Character Psychology and Character Education*, edited by D. Lapsley and F. Clark Power, 140–65. Notre Dame, IN: University of Notre Dame Press, 2005.

Neuhaus, Richard John. *The Naked Public Square: Religion and Democracy in America*. Grand Rapids: Eerdmans, 1984.

Neyrey, Jerome H. *Honor and Shame in the Gospel of Matthew*. Louisville: Westminster John Knox, 1998.

Ngugi wa, Thiong'o. *The River Between*. London: Heinemann, 1965.

Nicholas, Mary W. *The Mystery of Goodness and the Positive Moral Consequences of Psychotherapy*. New York: W. W. Norton, 1995.

Nicholson, Ian. "Gordon Allport, Character, and the 'Culture of Personality,' 1897–1937." *History of Psychology* 1 (1998): 52–68.

Nthamburi, Zablon J. "Ecclesiology of African Independent Churches." In *The Church in African Christianity: Innovative Essays in Ecclesiology*, edited by J. N. K. Mugambi and Laurent Magesa, 43–56. Nairobi: Initiatives Ltd, 1990.

Nyomoo, Ngono cia. *Meru Animal Tales*. Meru, Kenya: Meru Bookshop, Methodist Church, 1975.

Okorodudu, Corann, William J. Strickland, Judith L. Van Hoorn, and Elizabeth C. Wiggins. "A Call to Action: APA's 2007 Resolution against Torture. *Monitor on Psychology* 38 (July 2, 2008), 22–24. www.apa.org/monitor/nov07/calltoaction.html.

Olson, Brad, Stephen Soldz, and Martha Davis. "The Ethics of Interrogation and the American Psychological Association: A Critique of Policy and Process." *Philosophy, Ethics, and Humanities in Medicine* 3 (February 19, 2008). www.peh-med.com/content/3/1/3.

Olson, Bruce. *Bruchko*. Carol Stream, IL: Creation House, 1978.

Olthuis, James. *The Beautiful Risk*. Grand Rapids: Zondervan, 2001.

Onwu, Nlenanya. "Biblical Perspectives for Peace, Development and Reconstruction. Its Socio-Religious Implications for the Churches in Africa." In *The Role of Christianity in Development, Peace and Reconstruction: Southern Perspectives*, edited by Isobel Phiri, Kenneth Ross, and James Cox, 32–48. Nairobi: All Africa Conference of Churches, 1996.

Ownby, R. L. *Psychological Reports: A Guide to Report Writing in Professional Psychology*. New York: Wiley, 1997.

Paranjpe, Anand C. *Self and Identity in Modern Psychology and Indian Thought*. New York: Kluwer Academic, 2002.

Peachey, J. L. "Anabaptism on the Line in Guatemala." *Gospel Herald*, Nov. 15 (1992): 1–4.

Peck, M. Scott. *The Road Less Traveled*. New York: Simon and Schuster, 1978.

Pe-Pua, Rogelia. *Sikolohiyang Pilipino: Teorya, Metodo at Gamit* (Filipino Psychology: Theory, Method and Application). Quezon City: Philippine Psychology Research and Training House, 1982.

———. "From Decolonizing Psychology to the Development of a Cross-Indigenous Perspective in Methodology: The Philippine Experience." In *Indigenous and Cultural Psychology: Understanding People in Context*. Edited by Uichol Kim, Kuo-shu Yang, and Kwang-Kuo Hwang, 109–37. New York: Springer, 2006.

Pe-Pua, Rogelia, and Elizabeth Marcelino. "Sikolohiyang Pilipino (Filipino Psychology): A Legacy of Virgilio G. Enriquez." *Asian Journal of Social Psychology* 3 (2000): 49–71.

Pettifor, Jean. "Respect Is More than Autonomy: Implications for International Psychology." In *IUPS Global Resource CD-ROM Edition 2008*, edited by M. J. Stevens and D. Wedding. Hove, UK: Psychology Press, forthcoming.

Piaget, Jean. *The Language and Thought of the Child*. Translated by M. Warden. London: Kegan Paul, 1926.

Placher, William C. *Narratives of a Vulnerable God: Christ, Theology, and Scripture*. Louisville: Westminster John Knox, 1994.

Popper, Karl. *The Logic of Scientific Discovery*. London: Hutchinson, 1959.

Potok, Chaim. *My Name Is Asher Lev*. New York: Fawcett Crest, 1973.

Prilleltensky, Isaac, and Dennis R. Fox. "Psychopolitical Literacy for Wellness and Justice." *Journal of Community Psychology* 35 (2007): 1–13.

Propst, Rebecca, Richard Ostrom, Phillip Watkins, and Terry Dean. "Comparative Efficacy of Religious and Nonreligious Cognitive-Behavioral Therapy for the Treatment of Clinical Depression in Religious Individuals." *Journal of Consulting and Clinical Psychology* 60 (1992): 94–103.

Rawls, John. *A Theory of Justice*. Cambridge: Harvard University Press, 1972.

———. *The Law of Peoples*. Cambridge: Harvard University Press, 1999.

Raybon, Patricia. *My First White Friend: Confessions on Race, Love, and Forgiveness*. New York: Viking, 1996.

Reimer, Kevin. "Agape, Brokenness, and Theological Realism in L'Arche." In *Visions of Agape*. Edited by C. Boyd, 85–102. Aldershot, United Kingdom: Ashgate, 2008.

Reimer, Kevin, and Alvin Dueck. "Inviting Soheil: Narrative and Embrace in Christian Caregiving." *Christian Scholars Review* 35 (2005): 205–20.

Reporters without Borders. "Call for Sami Al Hajj's Release from Guantanamo after Lawyer Provides New Information." April 19, 2006. www.rsf.org/article.php3id_article=17217.

Richardson, Frank, Blaine Fowers, and Charles Guignon. *Re-Envisioning Psychology: Moral Dimensions of Theory and Practice*. San Francisco: Jossey-Bass, 1999.

Rieff, Philip. *Freud: The Mind of the Moralist*. New York: Viking, 1959.

———. *The Triumph of the Therapeutic: Uses of Faith after Freud*. New York: Harper & Row, 1966.

———. *My Life among the Deathworks: Illustrations of the Aesthetics of Authority*. Charlottesville: University of Virginia Press, 2006.

———. *Charisma: The Gift of Grace, and How It Has Been Taken Away from Us*. New York: Pantheon Books, 2007.

Roberts, Robert C. "Outline of Pauline Psychotherapy." In *Care for the Soul: Exploring the Intersection of Psychology & Theology*, edited by Mark McMinn and Timothy R. Phillips, 134–63. Downers Grove, IL: InterVarsity Press, 2001.

———. *Spiritual Emotions: A Psychology of Christian Virtues*. Grand Rapids: Eerdmans, 2007.

Rorty, Richard. *Philosophy and the Mirror of Nature*. Princeton, NJ: Princeton University Press, 1979.

———. *Philosophy and Social Hope*. London: Penguin Books, 1999.

———. "Religion as Conversation Stopper." In *Philosophy and Social Hope*, 168–74. London: Penguin Books, 1999.

Rosenthal, David. "Changes in Some Moral Values following Psychotherapy." *Journal of Consulting Psychology* 19 (1955): 431–36.

Ross, Michael, Elaine Xun, and Anne Wilson. "Language and the Bicultural Self." *Personality and Social Psychology Bulletin* 20 (2002): 1040–50.

Ryle, Gilbert. *The Concept of Mind*. London: Hutchinson's University Library, 1949.

Sackett, David L., W. S. Richardson, W. Rosenberg, and R. B. Haynes. *Evidence-Based Medicine*. New York: Churchill Livingstone, 1997.

Sacks, Jonathan. *The Dignity of Difference: How to Avoid the Clash of Civilizations*. New York: Continuum, 2002.

Said, Edward. *Orientalism*. London: Routledge and Kegan Paul, 1978.

Salazar, Zeus. "Ang Kamalayan at Kaluluwa: Isang Paglilinaw Ng Ilang Konsepto Sa Kinagisnang Sikilohiya." In *Sikolohiyang Pilipino: Teorya, Metodo at Gamit*. Edited by R. Pe-Pua, 83–92. Quezon City: University of the Philippines Press, 1989.

Samuels, Andrew. *The Political Psyche*. London: Routledge, 1993.

———. *Politics on the Couch: Citizenship and the Internal Life*. New York: Other Press, 2001.

Sandage, Steven, Kaye Cook, Peter Hill, Brad Strawn, and Kevin Reimer. "Hermeneutics and Psychology: A Review and Dialectical Model." *Review of General Psychology* 12 (2008): 344–64.

Sanford, John A. *The Kingdom Within: A Study of the Inner Meaning of Jesus' Sayings*. Philadelphia: Lippincott, 1970.

Schleiermacher, Friedrich. *The Christian Faith*. Philadelphia: Fortress, 1976.

Segovia, Fernando. *Decolonizing Biblical Studies: A View from the Margins*. New York: Orbis, 2000.

Shapiro, Monte B. "Clinical Psychology as an Applied Science." *British Journal of Psychiatry* 113 (1976): 1039–42.

Shults, LeRon, and Steven J. Sandage. *The Faces of Forgiveness: Searching for Wholeness and Salvation*. Grand Rapids: Baker Academic, 2003.

Shuman, Joel James, and Keith G. Meador. *Heal Thyself: Spirituality, Medicine, and the Distortion of Christianity*. Oxford: Oxford University Press, 2003.

Shweder, Richard A., Martha Minow, and Hazel Markus, eds. *Engaging Cultural Difference: The Multicultural Challenge in Liberal Democracies*. New York: Russell Sage Foundation, 2002.

Skinner, Burrhus F. *Science and Human Behavior*. New York: Macmillan, 1960.

Sloan, Richard, Emilia Bagiella, and Tia Powell. "Religion, Spirituality, and Medicine." *Lancet* 353 (1999): 664–67.

Sloan, Richard P., Emilia Bagiella, Larry VandeCreek, Margot Hover, "Should Physicians Prescribe Religious Activities?" *New England Journal of Medicine* 342 (2000): 1913–16.

Smith, Christian. *The Secular Revolution: Power, Interests, and Conflict in the Secularization of American Public Life*. Berkeley: University of California Press, 2003.

Sorenson, Randall Lehmann. *Minding Spirituality*. Hillsdale, NJ: Analytic Press, 2004.

Stanton, Graham. *Jesus and Gospel*. Cambridge: Cambridge University Press, 2004.

Stark, Rodney, and Roger Finke. *Acts of Faith: Explaining the Human Side of Religion*. Berkeley: University of California Press, 2000.

Stassen, Glen, and David P. Gushee. *Kingdom Ethics: Following Jesus in Contemporary Context*. Downers Grove, IL: InterVarsity Press, 2003.

Steele, Richard. "Narrative Theology and the Religious Affections." In *Theology without Foundations: Religious Practice and the Future of Theological Truth*, edited by Stanley Hauerwas, Nancey C. Murphy, and Mark Nation, 163–79. Nashville: Abingdon, 1994.

Stendahl, Krister. *Paul among Jews and Gentiles, and Other Essays*. Philadelphia: Fortress, 1976.

Stout, Jeffrey. *Democracy and Tradition*. Princeton, NJ: Princeton University Press, 2004.

Strong, Augustus H. *Systematic Theology*. Philadelphia: Judson, 1907.

Sue, Derald W., and David Sue. *Counseling the Culturally Different: Theory and Practice*. New York: Wiley, 1999.

Sugirtharajah, R. S. *Voices from the Margin: Interpreting the Bible in the Third World*. Maryknoll, NY: Orbis, 1991.

Sutherland, John. "The Ideas Interview: Philip Rieff." *Guardian,* December 5, 2005. www.guardian.co.uk/ideas/story/0„1657860,00.html#article_continue.

Tacitus. "Life of Cnaeus Julius Agricola," c. 98 CE, *Ancient History Sourcebook*. www.fordham.edu/halsall/ancient/tacitus-agricola.html.

Tan, Siang-Yang. "Training in Professional Psychology: Diversity Includes Religion." Paper presented at the National Council of Schools of Professional Psychology, January 19–23, 1993.

————. "Religion in Clinical Practice: Implicit and Explicit Integration." In *Religion and the Clinical Practice of Psychology*. Edited by Edward P. Shafranske, 365–390. Washington, DC: American Psychological Association, 1996.

Taubes, Jacob. *The Political Theology of Paul*. Stanford, CA: Stanford University Press, 2004.

Taylor, Barbara Brown. *Speaking of Sin: The Lost Language of Salvation*. Cambridge, MA: Cowley, 2000.

Taylor, Charles. *Sources of the Self: The Making of the Modern Identity*. Cambridge: Cambridge University Press, 1989.

————. "Peaceful Coexistence in Psychology." In *The Restoration of Dialogue: Readings in the Philosophy of Clinical Psychology*. Edited by Ronald B. Miller, 70–84. Washington, DC: American Psychological Association, 1992.

————. "The Politics of Recognition." In *Multiculturalism:Examining the Politics of Recognition*, edited by A. Gutman, 25–73. Princeton: Princeton University Press, 1994.

————. Modes of Secularism. In *Secularism and Its Critics*. Edited by Rajeev Bhargava, 31–53. Delhi: Oxford University Press, 1998.

————. *Varieties of Religion Today: William James Revisited*. Cambridge: Harvard University Press, 2002.

————. *Modern Social Imaginaries*. Durham, NC: Duke University Press, 2004.

————. *A Secular Age*. Cambridge: Belknap Press of Harvard University Press, 2007.

Teo, Thomas. *The Critique of Psychology: From Kant to Postcolonial Theory*. New York: Springer, 2005.

Theissen, Gerd. *Psychological Aspects of Pauline Theology*. Translated by John P. Galvin. Philadelphia: Fortress, 1987.

Thiessen, Franz. *Peter M. Friesen*. Winnipeg, Manitoba: Christian Press, 1974.

Tilley, Terrence W. *The Evils of Theodicy*. Washington, DC: Georgetown University Press, 1991.

Ting, Rachel Sing-K. *Who am I Talking to? The Effect of Language on Bilingual Chinese Expression of Self-concept and Depressive Emotion*. Saarbrücken, Germany: VPM Verlag Dr. Mueller e.K., 2008.

Tjelveit, Alan. "The psychotherapist as Christian ethicist: Theology applied to practice." *Journal of Psychology & Theology* 20 (1992): 89–98.

————. Ethics and Values in Psychotherapy. London: Routledge, 1999.

Toews, John E. *Romans* (Believers Church Bible Commentary). Scottdale, PA: Herald, 2004.

———. "The Politics of Romans." Paper presented at the Edmund Janzen Lectureship, in Fresno, California, March 27, 2008.

Toulmin, Stephen. *Cosmopolis: The Hidden Agenda of Modernity.* New York: Free Press, 1990.

Tracy, David. *Blessed Rage for Order: The New Pluralism in Theology.* New York: Seabury, 1978.

———. *The Analogical Imagination: Christian Theology and the Culture of Pluralism.* London: SCM, 1981.

Volf, Miroslav. *Exclusion and Embrace: A Theological Exploration of Identity, Otherness, and Reconciliation.* Nashville: Abingdon, 1996.

Walzer, Michael. *Spheres of Justice: A Defense of Pluralism and Equality.* New York: Basic Books, 1983.

———. *Thick and Thin: Moral Argument at Home and Abroad.* Notre Dame, IN: University of Notre Dame Press, 1994.

Watson, Paul J. "After Postmodernism: Perspectivism, a Christian Epistemology of Love, and the Ideological Surround." *Journal of Psychology and Theology* 32 (2004): 248–61.

Watts, Fraser N., ed. *Jesus and Psychology.* Philadelphia: Templeton Foundation Press, 2007.

Watzlawick, Paul, John Weakland, and Richard Fisch. *Change: Principles of Problem Formation and Problem Resolution.* New York: W. W. Norton, 1974.

Wentz, Richard. "The Domestication of the Divine." *Theology Today* 57 (2000): 24–34.

Werpehowski, William. "Ad Hoc Apologetics." *Journal of Religion* 66 (1986): 282–301.

West, Cornel. *Democracy Matters.* New York: Penguin, 2004.

Whorf, Benjamin Lee. *Language, Thought, and Reality: Selected Writings.* Cambridge: Technology Press of Massachusetts Institute of Technology, 1956.

Wihak, Christine. "Psychologists in Nunavut: A Comparison of Principles Underlying Inuit Qaujimanituqangit and the Canadian Psychological Association Code of Ethics." *Pimatisiwin: A Journal of Aboriginal and Indigenous Community Health* 2 (2004): 29–40.

Williams, Delores S. *Sisters in the Wilderness: The Challenge of Womanist God-Talk.* Maryknoll, NY: Orbis, 1993.

Williams, Glanmor. *The Welsh and Their Religion.* Cardiff: University of Wales Press, 1991.

Winch, Peter. *The Idea of a Social Science and Its Relation to Philosophy.* New York: Humanities, 1958.

Wink, Walter. *The Powers That Be: Theology for a New Millennium.* New York: Doubleday, 1998.

Wittgenstein, Ludwig. *Tractatus Logico-Philosophicus.* London: Routledge & Kegan Paul, 1922.

————. *Philosophical Investigations.* Edited by G. E. M. Anscombe. New York: Macmillan, 1953.

Wolin, Sheldon S. *Politics and Vision: Continuity and Innovation in Western Political Thought.* Princeton, NJ: Princeton University Press, 2006.

Wolterstorff, Nicholas. *Lament for a Son.* Grand Rapids: Eerdmans, 1987.

————. "The Role of Religion in Decision and Discussion of Political Issues." In *Religion in the Public Square: The Place of Religious Convictions in Political Debate*, edited by Robert Audi and Nicholas Wolterstorff, 67–120. New York: Rowman and Littlefield, 1997.

————. *Justice: Rights and Wrongs.* Princeton: Princeton University Press, 2008.

Wood, Ralph. "Performing the Faith: An Interview with George Lindbeck." *Christian Century* 28 (2006): 28–35.

Worthington, Everett, Taro A. Kurusu, Michael E. McCollough, and Steven J. Sandage. "Empirical Research on Religion and Psychotherapeutic Processes and Outcomes: A 10-Year Review and Research Prospectus." *Psychological Bulletin* 119 (1996): 448–87.

Wright, N. T. "Paul's Gospel and Caesar's Empire." In *Paul and Politics: Ekklesia, Israel, Imperium, Interpretation: Essays in Honor of Krister Stendahl*, edited by Richard A. Horsley, 160–83. Harrisburg, PA: Trinity Press International, 2000.

————. "Kingdom Come: The Public Meaning of the Gospels." *Christian Century* (2008): 29–34.

Wuthnow, Robert. *The Restructuring of American Religion.* Princeton, NJ: Princeton University, 1988.

Yoder, John Howard. "But We Do See Jesus: The Particularity of Jesus and the Universality of Truth." In *The Priestly Kingdom: Social Ethics as Gospel*, by John Howard Yoder, 46–62. Notre Dame, IN: University of Notre Dame Press, 1984.

————. *The Politics of Jesus: Vicit Agnus Noster.* Grand Rapids: Eerdmans, 1992.

————. "Trinity versus Theodicy: Hebraic Realism and the Temptation to Judge God." Unpublished manuscript, 1996.

———. "Patience as Method in Moral Reasoning: Is an Ethic of Discipleship 'Absolute'?" Unpublished paper, 1997.

———. *Body Politics: Five Practices of the Christian Community before the Watching World*. Scottdale, PA: Herald, 2001.

———. *Preface to Theology: Christology and Theological Method*. Grand Rapids: Brazos, 2002.

Yong, Amos. *Hospitality and the Other: Pentecost, Christian Practices, and the Neighbor*. Maryknoll, NY: Orbis, 2008.

Zehnle, Richard. *Peter's Pentecost Discourse: Tradition and Lukan Reinterpretation in Peter's Speeches of Acts 2 and 3*. Nashville: Abingdon, 1971.

Notes

Introduction

1. Soheil (sô'heel), a pseudonym, is a composite description of children who suffer in war-torn nations, such as Afghanistan, the Democratic Republic of Congo, and Iraq. This case study is drawn from Kevin Reimer and Alvin Dueck, "Inviting Soheil: Narrative and Embrace in Christian Caregiving," *Christian Scholars Review* 35 (2005): 205–20. See also the following essay, which attempts to address the character of Christian and Muslim peacemakers: Alvin Dueck, Kevin Reimer, Joshua Morgan, and Steve Brown, "Let Peace Flourish: Descriptive and Applied Research from the Conflict Transformation Study," in *Peace-building by, between, and beyond Muslims and Evangelical Christians,* ed. Mohammed Abu-Nimer and David Augsburger, 233–54 (Lanham, MD: Lexington Books, 2009).

2. In his *Politics* Aristotle states that a person by nature is a political animal, an animal whose nature is to live in relationships in the context of the city. From *The Works of Aristotle*, trans. W. D. Ross, B. Jowett, and J. A. Smith (Oxford: Clarendon, 1921), 1252 b30–1253 a3.

3. Our theological understanding of politics is very much influenced by William T. Cavanaugh. Cavanaugh analyzes the state, civil society, and globalization as three ways of imagining space and time. Each has deep theological assumptions and metaphors. The modern state, for example, is built on a soteriology of rescue from violence. To view politics as imagination is hopeful in that to imagine something is to recognize its historical contingency and that the current state of political affairs could be otherwise. The eucharistic community is a venue for imagining and embodying a different politics. See William T. Cavanaugh, *Theopolitical Imagination* (London: T&T Clark, 2002), together with Stanley Hauerwas and Romand Coles, *Christianity, Democracy, and the Radical Ordinary: Conversations between a Radical Democrat and a Christian* (Eugene, OR: Cascade Books, 2008). See also Sheldon S. Wolin, *Politics and Vision: Continuity and Innovation in Western Political Thought* (Princeton, NJ: Princeton University Press, 2006). For a political understanding of the psyche from a Jungian perspective see Andrew Samuels, *The Political Psyche* (London: Routledge, 1993) and Andrew Samuels, *Politics on the Couch: Citizenship and the Internal Life* (New York: Other, 2001).

4. Richard A. Shweder, Martha Minow, and Hazel Markus, eds., *Engaging Cultural Difference: The Multicultural Challenge in Liberal Democracies* (New York: Russell Sage Foundation, 2002); Arthur Kleinman, *Social Origins of Distress and Disease: Depression, Neurasthenia, and Pain in Modern China* (Ann Arbor: University of Michigan Press, 1998).

5. Indeed there may be neuropsychological research that is more generalizable, but that is less the case in social and personality research.

6. Philip Rieff, *The Triumph of the Therapeutic: Uses of Faith after Freud* (New York: Harper and Row, 1966).

7. Alvin Dueck, "Anabaptism and Psychology: Personal Reflections," in *Mennonite Perspectives on Pastoral Counseling,* ed. Daniel Schipani (Elkhart, IN: Institute of Mennonite Studies, 2007), 3–16; Alvin Dueck, *Between Jerusalem and Athens: Ethical Perspectives on Culture, Religion, and Psychotherapy* (Grand Rapids: Baker Books, 1995), conclusion.

8. See Dueck, *Between Jerusalem and Athens*, pt. 1.

9. See Philip Rieff for his view of culture which we will discuss in chapter 8. Philip Rieff, *My Life among the Deathworks: Illustrations of the Aesthetics of Authority* (Charlottesville: University of Virginia Press, 2006), 2.

10. See the work of Robert C. Roberts, Eric Johnson, and Paul J. Watson for a renewed effort to be more explicitly Christian as psychologists. Robert C. Roberts, *Spiritual Emotions: A Psychology of Christian Virtues* (Grand Rapids: Eerdmans, 2007); Robert C. Roberts, "Outline of Pauline Psychotherapy," in Mark McMinn and Timothy R. Phillips, eds., *Care for the Soul: Exploring the Intersection of Psychology & Theology* (Downers Grove, IL: InterVarsity Press, 2001), 134–63; Eric L. Johnson, *Foundations for Soul Care: A Christian Psychology Proposal* (Downers Grove, IL: InterVarsity Press, 2007); Paul J. Watson, "After Postmodernism: Perspectivism, a Christian Epistemology of Love, and The Ideological Surround," *Journal of Psychology and Theology* 32 (2004): 248–61. Johnson and Watson are also editors of a new journal entitled, *Edification: The Journal of the Society for Christian Psychology.*

11. Craig Gay, *The Way of the (Modern) World* (Grand Rapids: Eerdmans, 1998). Gay makes extensive use of Kierkegaard's notion of practical atheism in a review of secularization in Western culture. See also John Howard Yoder, *Body Politics: Five Practices of the Christian Community before the Watching World* (Scottdale, PA: Herald, 2001).

12. Annie Dillard, *For the Time Being* (New York: Vintage Books, 2000), 187.

13. Thieleman J. van Braght, *The Bloody Theater: or, Martyrs Mirror of the Defenseless Christians, Who Baptized Only upon Confession of Faith, and Who Suffered and Died for the Testimony of Jesus, Their Saviour, From the Time of Christ to the Year A.D. 1660*, trans. Joseph F. Sohm (Scottdale, PA: Mennonite Publishing House, 1938).

Chapter 1 Suffering, Symptoms, and the Cross

1. These stories of Guatemala are inspired by a program developed by Al Dueck (AD) at Fuller Theological Seminary's School of Psychology. The student immersion program, part of the seminary's clinical integration (psychology and theology) curriculum, involves exposure to indigenous Guatemalan psychologists and healers.

2. Antonio Marco Garavito, personal communication with AD, 1999.

3. There may be those who assume that if we address the meaning of suffering, we would tackle the traditional topic of theodicy. That is, how can a God who is all-powerful and good allow the suffering of the innocent? Having answered that question, we would then be able to provide a meaningful response to our clients. We have chosen not to go that direction. We think it best to remain silent on that issue. To explain the ways of God is for us presumptuous. Besides, what would count as a defense? Is the notion of "defending" God not intrinsically incoherent? John Howard Yoder asks the following critical questions: "a) Where do you get the criteria by which you evaluate God? Why are the criteria you use the right ones? b) Why do you think you are qualified for the business of accrediting Gods? c) If you think you are qualified for that business, how does the adjudication proceed?" Given the impossibility of answering these questions, he argues that theodicy is a form of idolatry. John Howard Yoder, "Trinity versus Theodicy: Hebraic Realism and the Temptation to Judge God," unpublished manuscript, 1996. Terrence W. Tilley argues that to seek to justify God in the face of human suffering has the potential to legitimize the very evils of which it seeks to exonerate God. Our approach will be to look to Jesus to understand our suffering God. Terrence W. Tilley, *The Evils of Theodicy* (Washington, DC: Georgetown University Press, 1991).

4. See Philip Cushman, *Constructing the Self, Constructing America: A Cultural History of Psychotherapy* (New York: HarperCollins, 1995). Granted, the American Psychological Association has published a spate of books on religion and psychotherapy in the past decade. However, religious students in secular placement sites and university programs are routinely perceived as aggressive fundamentalists who will impose their religion on their clients.

5. A pseudonym.

6. Adapted from the story of Concepción Sojuel, as told to a Self-Help study tour in March, 1995. Available from Semilla, 26 Calle 15–56 Col., Las Charcas, Z. 11, Guatemala City, Guatemala. Reprinted with her permission.

7. This spontaneous prayer emerged (AD) after having read Juanita's story many times.

8. Ronald B. Miller, *Facing Human Suffering: Psychology and Psychotherapy as Moral Engagement* (Washington, DC: American Psychological Association, 2004).

9. Kleinman makes a distinction between illness, disease, and sickness. Illness is how the client and his or her community perceive an emotional issue. Disease is what the practitioner defines in terms of a theory of disorder, and sickness is the generic sense of a disorder in relation to macro social forces. Often it is only the client who uses the language of suffering. In Arthur Kleinman, *The Illness Narratives: Suffering, Healing, and the Human Condition* (New York: Basic Books, 1988), 3–6.

10. Edwin E. Gantt, "Lévinas, Psychotherapy, and the Ethics of Suffering," *Journal of Humanistic Psychology* 40 (2000): 9.

11. Viktor E. Frankl, *Man's Search for Meaning: An Introduction to Logotherapy* (New York: Holt, Rinehart, and Winston, 1963).

12. M. Scott Peck, *The Road Less Traveled* (New York: Simon and Schuster, 1978), 15.

13. David Bakan, *Disease, Pain, and Sacrifice: Toward a Psychology of Suffering* (Chicago: University of Chicago Press, 1968).

14. See Emmanuel Lévinas, *Otherwise than Being: Or, Beyond Essence,* trans. Alphonso Lingis (Boston: M. Nijhoff, 1981); Alvin Dueck and Thomas Parsons, "Ethics, Alterity and Psychotherapy: A Lévinasian Perspective," *Pastoral Psychology* 55 (2007): 271–82; Bruce Fink, *Fundamentals of Psychoanalytic Technique: A Lacanian Approach for Practitioners* (New York: W. W. Norton, 2007), chap. 1.

15. We are dependent on Latin American theologians such as Juan Driver, *Understanding the Atonement for the Mission of the Church* (Scottdale, PA: Herald, 1986).

16. See the following for an attempt to do so in the African context: Gladys Mwiti and Alvin Dueck, *Christian Counseling: An African Indigenous Perspective* (Pasadena, CA: Fuller Seminary Press, 2006); Gladys Mwiti and Alvin Dueck, *Christian Counseling: An African Indigenous Perspective: A Video Series* (Pasadena, CA: Fuller Seminary Press, 2006).

17. *Pistis* is usually translated anemically as faith, i.e. assent. This is much too cognitive. Faith as loyalty makes the political options clearer. Are we loyal to the rulers or to God?

18. Richard A. Horsley, *Jesus and Empire: The Kingdom of God and the New World Disorder* (Minneapolis: Fortress, 2002).

19. David Augsburger, "Sermon on the Mount and Honor versus Shame," unpublished paper, Fuller Theological Seminary, Pasadena, May 14, 2008. See also Jerome H. Neyrey, *Honor and Shame in the Gospel of Matthew* (Louisville: Westminster John Knox, 1998).

20. Glen Stassen and David P. Gushee, *Kingdom Ethics: Following Jesus in Contemporary Context* (Downers Grove, IL: InterVarsity Press, 2003), 37.

21. Quoted in Gustaf Aulén, *Christus Victor: An Historical Study of the Three Main Types of the Idea of Atonement,* trans. A. G. Hebert (Eugene, OR: Wipf and Stock, 1998), 19.

22. Ched Myers, *Binding the Strong Man: A Political Reading of Mark's Story of Jesus* (Maryknoll, NY: Orbis, 1997).

23. Miroslav Volf, *Exclusion and Embrace: A Theological Exploration of Identity, Otherness, and Reconciliation* (Nashville: Abingdon, 1996); Timothy Luke Johnson, *The Real Jesus:*

The Misguided Quest for the Historical Jesus and the Truth of the Traditional Gospels (San Francisco: HarperSanFrancisco, 1996).

24. Joel James Shuman and Keith G. Meador, *Heal Thyself: Spirituality, Medicine, and the Distortion of Christianity* (Oxford: Oxford University Press, 2003).

25. John Howard Yoder, "'Patience' as Method in Moral Reasoning: Is an Ethic of Discipleship 'Absolute'?" Unpublished paper, 1997.

26. William C. Placher, *Narratives of a Vulnerable God: Christ, Theology, and Scripture* (Louisville: Westminster John Knox, 1994).

27. Joel B. Green and Mark D. Baker, *Recovering the Scandal of the Cross: Atonement in New Testament and Contemporary Contexts* (Downers Grove, IL: InterVarsity Press, 2000).

28. John Howard Yoder, *The Politics of Jesus: Vicit Agnus Noster* (Grand Rapids: Eerdmans, 1992).

29. Jürgen Moltmann, *The Crucified God: The Cross of Christ as the Foundation and Criticism of Christian Theology* (New York: Harper and Row, 1974).

30. David Bentley Hart, *The Beauty of the Infinite: The Aesthetics of Christian Truth* (Grand Rapids: Eerdmans, 2003), 392–94.

31. Johann Baptist Metz, *Memoria Passionis* (Freiburg, Germany: Herder Verlag, 2006).

32. John Howard Yoder, *Preface to Theology: Christology and Theological Method* (Grand Rapids: Brazos, 2002), 310–11.

33. John D. Caputo, *The Weakness of God: A Theology of the Event* (Bloomington: Indiana University Press, 2006).

34. Nicholas Wolterstorff, *Lament for a Son* (Grand Rapids: Eerdmans, 1987), 81.

35. Dietrich Bonhoeffer, *Letters and Papers from Prison* (New York: Macmillan, 1953), 361.

36. Jürgen Moltmann, *The Spirit of Life: A Universal Affirmation* (London: SCM, 1992).

37. See Brad Jersak and Michael Hardin, *Stricken by God? Nonviolent Identification and the Victory of Christ* (Grand Rapids: Eerdmans, 2007); Joanne Carlson Brown and Rebecca Parker, "For God So Loved the World?" in *Christianity, Patriarchy and Abuse: A Feminist Critique,* ed. Joanne Carlson Brown and Carole R. Bohn (New York: Pilgrim, 1989), 1–30; Delores S. Williams, *Sisters in the Wilderness: The Challenge of Womanist God-Talk* (Maryknoll, NY: Orbis, 1993), 161–67.

38. Stanley Hauerwas, *The Peaceable Kingdom: A Primer in Christian Ethics* (Notre Dame, IN: University of Notre Dame Press, 1983).

39. James Cone, *God of the Oppressed* (Maryknoll, NY: Orbis, 1997), 211–12.

40. Aulén, *Christus Victor.*

41. See here the relevant work of Walter Wink, *The Powers That Be: Theology for a New Millennium* (New York: Doubleday, 1998).

42. See the work of a theologian and a psychologist as they address the issue of satisfaction theories of atonement: LeRon Shults and Steven J. Sandage, *The Faces of Forgiveness: Searching for Wholeness and Salvation* (Grand Rapids: Baker Academic, 2003).

43. Yoder, *Preface,* 281–327.

44. In Revelation (chap. 12) the battle between the forces of God and of Satan are depicted in terms of the Roman Empire with its seven heads, ten horns, and seven crowns. Here Jesus is confronting the evil in the world as empire, a conflict that continues as the church encounters the powers. However, the victory of the church over Rome will occur nonviolently.

45. James Wm. McClendon Jr., *Doctrine,* vol. 2 of *Systematic Theology* (Nashville: Abingdon, 1994). See chap. 5.

46. Yoder, *Preface,* 304.

47. Moltmann, *Spirit of Life,* 137.

48. Ibid., 125–38.

49. Hart, *Beauty of the Infinite,* 392–94.

50. On March 10, 1999, then-president Clinton apologized to the people of Guatemala, stating that the US involvement in Guatemalan affairs was wrong. He did so on the basis of the conclusion of an independent commission that US-backed security forces committed the vast majority of human-rights abuses during the war. "It is important that I state clearly that support for military forces or intelligence units which engaged in violent and widespread repression of the kind described in the report was wrong. . . . And the United States must not repeat that mistake. We must, and we will, instead continue to support the peace and reconciliation process in Guatemala." Charles Babington, "Clinton: Support for Guatemala Was Wrong" (March 11, 1999), www.washingtonpost.com/wp-srv/inatl/daily/march99/clinton11.htm (accessed September 6, 2008).

51. Pedro, personal communication with AD, August 30, 2003.

Chapter 2 Constantine, American Empire, and "Yankee Doodling"

1. See James Carroll, *Constantine's Sword: The Church and the Jews: A History* (Boston: Houghton Mifflin, 2001).

2. Michael Hardt and Antonio Negri, *Empire* (Cambridge: Harvard University Press, 2000). The authors remind readers that the book was written midway between the Gulf War and the beginning of the war in Kosovo, but the events which have transpired since have only supported their observations on the nature of empire. See also Chalmers A. Johnson, *The Sorrows of Empire: Militarism, Secrecy, and the End of the Republic* (New York: Metropolitan Books, 2004); Wes Avram, *Anxious about Empire: Theological Essays on the New Global Realities* (Grand Rapids: Brazos, 2004). See the excellent work of Ryan LaMothe: "Pastoral Care of Political Discourse: Shepherding Communication," *Pastoral Psychology* 56 (2008): 467–81, and "What Hope Is There: The Enthrallment of Empire Stories," *Pastoral Psychology* 56 (2008): 481–97. For a very different view of the response to empire in Jewish and early Christian communities, see Christopher Bryan, *Render to Caesar: Jesus, the Early Church, and the Roman Superpower* (Oxford: Oxford University Press, 2005).

3. Tacitus, "Life of Cnaeus Julius Agricola," c. 98 CE, *Ancient History Sourcebook*, www.fordham.edu/halsall/ancient/tacitus-agricola.html.

4. Hardt and Negri, *Empire*.

5. John Gray, *Al Qaeda and What It Means to Be Modern* (New York: New Press, 2003).

6. It is estimated that the US has military bases in thirty-eight foreign countries, with a total replacement value of $118 billion (Johnson, *Sorrows of Empire*, 154).

7. Hardt and Negri, *Empire*, 11, xi, xii–xiii (italics original).

8. Gray, *Al Qaeda*, 86.

9. Lewis Brandt, "American Psychology," *American Psychologist* 25 (1970): 1091–93.

10. Philip Cushman, *Constructing the Self, Constructing America: A Cultural History of Psychotherapy* (New York: Addison-Wesley, 1995).

11. The second author (KSR) recently served on a doctoral dissertation committee in forensic psychology. Consistent with changes in forensic practice, the therapeutic clientele was referred to as "consumers." The implication is somewhat startling, that therapy represents a service commodity subjected to the same economic principles of exchange as qualified auto repair.

12. Alfred W. McCoy, *A Question of Torture: CIA Interrogation, from the Cold War to the War on Terror* (New York: Metropolitan Books, 2006), 32.

13. Thomas H. Leahey, *A History of Psychology: Main Currents in Psychological Thought*, 2nd ed. (Englewood Cliffs, NJ: Prentice Hall, 1987).

14. Ellen Herman, *The Romance of American Psychology: Political Culture in the Age of Experts, 1940–1970* (Berkeley: University of California Press, 1995).

15. Quoted in Herman, *Romance of American Psychology*, 77.

16. David McClelland, *The Achievement Motive* (New York: Appleton-Century-Crofts, 1953).

17. Quoted in Herman, *Romance of American Psychology,* 145.

18. Ibid., 150.

19. Ibid.

20. Ibid., 155.

21. Ibid., 162.

22. Walter Russell Mead, "God's Country?" *Foreign Affairs* 85 (October 16, 2006), www .foreignaffairs.org/20060901faessay85504/walter-russell-mead/god-s-country.html (accessed October 16, 2006).

23. We wish to acknowledge the research assistance of Adam Ghali, a doctoral student in Fuller Theological Seminary's Graduate School of Psychology. See Adam Ghali, "The Ethics of Interrogation," a poster presented at the Christian Association for Psychological Studies, Phoenix, April 5, 2008.

24. www.supremecourtus.gov/opinions/05pdf/05–184.pdf (accessed June 20, 2008).

25. "Call for Sami Al-Haj's Release from Guantanamo after Lawyer Provides New Information," April 19, 2006, www.rsf.org/article.php3?id_article=17217 (accessed August 25, 2008).

26. Silvia Cattori, "Sami Al Haj, Al Jazeera Journalist, Tells His Story," interview with Silvia Cattori, www.silviacattori.net/article491.html (accessed August 25, 2008). On April 16, 2009, President Barack Obama released four formerly classified memos which detailed acceptable torture procedures in the Bush administration (www.aclu.org/safefree/general/olc_memos. html). The memos were addressed to John A. Rizzo, General Counsel, CIA, and came from either John Bybee or Steve Bradbury in the Attorney General's Office of Legal Counsel. The memos reveal the veracity of Al-Haj's report. Psychologists played a central role in the interrogations, providing justification for the interrogation methods, designing the interrogations, and monitoring implementation.

27. Stephen Soldz, "Letter to President Brehm," www.ipetitions.com/petition/BrehmLetter/ (accessed June 12, 2007).

28. Deputy Inspector General for Intelligence, "Review of DoD-Directed Investigations of Detainee Abuse," Report No. 06–INTEL10, August 26, 2006, p. 25. Available at: www.fas.org/ irp/agency/dod/abuse.pdf.

29. Deborah Kory, "Psychologists Aiding and Abetting Torture," *Tikkun,* August 31, 2007, pp. 60–64.

30. Brad Olson, Stephen Soldz, and Martha Davis, "The Ethics of Interrogation and the American Psychological Association: A Critique of Policy and Process," *Philosophy, Ethics, and Humanities in Medicine* 3 (2008): 3, www.peh-med.com/content/3/1/3 (accessed February 19, 2008).

31. See ibid.

32. Corann Okorodudu, William J. Strickland, Judith L. Van Hoorn, and Elizabeth C. Wiggins, "A Call to Action: APA's 2007 Resolution against Torture," *Monitor on Psychology* (2007), www.apa.org/monitor/nov07/calltoaction.html (accessed July 2, 2008).

33. Mark Costanzo, Ellen Gerrity, and M. Brinton Lykes, "Psychologists and the Use of Torture in Interrogations," *Analyses of Social Issues and Public Policy* 7 (2007): 7–20.

34. See the letter written to the American Psychological Association president Dr. Alan E. Kazdin by Tor Levin Hofgaard, on behalf of the European Psychological Association (two hundred twenty thousand members from thirty-four countries) in preparation for a meeting in Berlin with APA representatives, www.psysr.org/about/committees/endtorture/Nordic%20 Committee%20 Letter%20on%20Torture.pdf.

35. Ibid.

36. APA Public Affairs, "APA Members Approve Petition Resolution on Detainee Settings," September 17, 2008, www.apa.org/releases/petition0908.html.

37. APA Public Affairs, "APA Members Approve Petition Resolution on Detainee Settings," Sept. 17, 2008. www.apa.org/releases/petition0908.html. However, at this point the referendum

has not been implemented though the American Psychological Association (APA) board did issue an open letter on June 18, 2009 on the subject of psychologists' involvement in abusive national security interrogations. The letter was the first formal acknowledgments from APA leadership that psychologists were involved in torture and inhuman treatment of detainees. www.apa.org/releases/kazdin-to-bush1008.pdf (accessed October 2, 2008) (italics original).

38. Kenneth Gergen, Aydan Gulerce, Andrew Lock, and Girishwar Misra, "Psychological Science in Cultural Context," *American Psychologist* 51 (1996): 496–503. The point here is that engaging culture is vital for legitimate scientific study of psychological issues. We are committed to a psychology of scientific integrity engaged in conversation with local traditions.

39. Ibid., 496.

40. Ibid., 497.

41. See Adrian C. Brock, *Internationalizing the History of Psychology* (New York: New York University Press, 2006); Uichol Kim and John Berry, *Indigenous Psychologies: Research and Experience in Cultural Context* (Newbury Park, CA: Sage, 1993); *Indigenous and Cultural Psychology: Understanding People in Context,* ed. Uichol Kim, Kuo-shu Yang, and Kwang-Kuo Hwang (New York: Springer, 2006).

42. Gergen et al., "Psychological Science," 501.

43. Ibid., 497.

44. Chandra T. Mohanty, "Under Western Eyes: Feminist Scholarship and Colonial Discourses," *Feminist Review* 30 (1988): 65–88. See also the work of Thomas Teo, *The Critique of Psychology: From Kant to Postcolonial Theory* (New York: Springer, 2005).

45. Gergen, et al., "Psychological Science," 498.

46. Ibid., 501.

47. We are aware that our critical attitude toward universalism may be criticized as endorsing relativism. That is not our intent. We do not argue for a relativist psychology in response to Western universalism. Instead, our purpose is to amend the modernist psychological project with a tradition-sensitive alternative. See Alasdair MacIntyre, *Three Rival Versions of Moral Inquiry: Encyclopedia, Genealogy, and Tradition* (Notre Dame, IN: University of Notre Dame Press, 1990).

48. See John Howard Yoder, "'But We Do See Jesus': The Particularity of Jesus and the Universality of Truth," in *The Priestly Kingdom: Social Ethics as Gospel* (Notre Dame, IN: University of Notre Dame Press, 1984), 46–62; Jonathan Sacks, *The Dignity of Difference: How to Avoid the Clash of Civilizations* (London; New York: Continuum, 2002). See also Sheldon Wolin for an emphasis on localism in contrast to universalism in political theory. Sheldon S. Wolin, *Politics and Vision: Continuity and Innovation in Western Political Thought* (Princeton, NJ: Princeton University Press, 2006).

49. Steven Heine, Shinobu Kitayama, and Darrin R. Lehman, "Cultural Differences in Self-Evaluation: Japanese Readily Accept Negative Self-Relevant Information," *Journal of Cross-Cultural Psychology* 32 (2001): 434–43. See also Anand C. Paranjpe, *Self and Identity in Modern Psychology and Indian Thought* (New York: Kluwer Academic, 2002), and Virgilio Enriquez, *From Colonial to Liberation Psychology: The Philippine Experience* (Manila: De La Salle University Press, 1994).

50. See Rachel Sing-K. Ting. *Who am I Talking to? The Effect of Language on Bilingual Chinese Expression of Self-concept and Depressive Emotion.* (Saarbrücken, Germany: VDM Verlag Dr. Meuller e.K., 2008).

51. Alvin Dueck, "Babel, Shibboleths, Esperanto and Pentecost: Can We Talk?" *Journal of Psychology and Christianity* 21 (2002): 72–80. This section is adapted with permission of the publisher.

52. Glen Johnson, "For Bush, 'Bob Jones' May Spell T-R-O-U-B-L-E," *Black Issues in Higher Education,* March 16, 2000, http://findarticles.com/p/articles/mi_m0DXK/is_2_17/ai_61573625.

53. Bernard Anderson, "The Babel Story: Paradigm of Human Unity and Diversity," in *Ethnicity,* ed. A. Greeley and G. Baum (New York: Seabury, 1977), 63–70.

54. John Levison and Priscilla Levison-Pope, *Return of Babel: Global Perspectives on the Bible* (Louisville: Westminster John Knox, 1999).

55. Miroslav Volf, *Exclusion and Embrace: A Theological Exploration of Identity, Otherness, and Reconciliation* (Nashville: Abingdon, 1996), 226.

56. John Calvin, *Commentaries on the Book of Genesis,* trans. John King (Grand Rapids: Eerdmans, 1948), 332.

57. Walter Brueggeman, *Genesis* (Atlanta: Westminster John Knox, 1982), 98.

58. Quoted in Volf, *Exclusion and Embrace,* 227.

59. For a different reading of this text, see Theodore Hiebert, "The Tower of Babel and the Origin of the World's Cultures," *Journal of Biblical Literature* 126 (2007): 29–58.

60. Graham Stanton, *Jesus and Gospel* (Cambridge: Cambridge University Press, 2004), 51.

61. John E. Toews, "The Politics of Romans," Address given at the Edmund Janzen Lectureship, Fresno, CA, March 27, 2008, 4. See also John E. Toews, *Romans,* Believers Church Bible Commentary (Scottdale, PA: Herald, 2004).

62. N. T. Wright, "Paul's Gospel and Caesar's Empire," in *Paul and Politics: Ekklesia, Israel, Imperium, Interpretation: Essays in Honor of Krister Stendahl,* ed. Richard Horsley (Harrisburg, PA: Trinity Press International, 2000), 164–65.

63. Jacob Taubes, *The Political Theology of Paul* (Stanford, CA: Stanford University Press, 2004), 16.

64. Toews, *Romans,* 24.

65. Wright, "Paul and Caesar," 182–83.

66. Richard Horsley, "1 Corinthians: A Case Study of Paul's Assembly as an Alternative Society," in *Paul and Empire* (Harrisburg, PA: Trinity Press International, 1997), 242–52.

67. See Alvin C. Dueck, *Between Jerusalem and Athens: Ethical Perspectives on Culture, Religion, and Psychotherapy* (Grand Rapids: Baker Books, 1995), chaps. 4–7.

68. We will take up this point again in chap. 9.

69. Dueck, *Between Jerusalem and Athens,* chap. 2.

70. Laura S. Brown, *Subversive Dialogues: Theory in Feminist Therapy* (New York: Basic Books, 1994).

71. Ibid., 17.

Chapter 3 Boutique Multiculturalism

1. In the conference other religious communities (Native American and Hawaiian) were similarly invited to share from their traditions and even to preface APA sessions with invocational prayers.

2. We recognize that there appears to be a thaw in resistance regarding the role of spirituality in therapy. We will address that issue more directly in chap. 8.

3. Richard John Neuhaus, *The Naked Public Square: Religion and Democracy in America* (Grand Rapids: Eerdmans, 1984).

4. Richard Rorty, *Philosophy and Social Hope* (London: Penguin Books, 1999).

5. Ibid., 173.

6. Ibid., 171.

7. John Rawls, *A Theory of Justice* (Cambridge: Harvard University Press, 1972); John Rawls, *The Law of Peoples* (Cambridge: Harvard University Press, 1999).

8. See the excellent article on a public Christianity by N. T. Wright, "Kingdom Come: The Public Meaning of the Gospels," *Christian Century,* June 17, 2008, 29–34.

9. MacIntyre, *Whose Justice? Which Rationality?*

10. Ibid., 335.

11. Ibid., 345.

12. Alvin Dueck and Kevin Reimer, "Retrieving the Virtues in Psychotherapy: Thick and Thin Discourse," *American Behavioral Scientist* 47 (2003): 427–41.

13. This felicitous phrase is borrowed from Stanley Fish, *The Trouble with Principle* (Cambridge: Harvard University Press, 1999), 56–72.

14. Ronald Dworkin, "Liberalism," in *Public and Private Morality*, ed. Stuart Hampshire (Cambridge: Cambridge University Press, 1978), 113–43.

15. Will Kymlicka, *Liberalism, Community and Culture* (Oxford: Clarendon, 1989); and *Multicultural Citizenship: A Liberal Theory of Minority Rights* (New York: Clarendon, 1995).

16. Jean Pettifor, "Respect Is More than Autonomy: Implications for International Psychology," in *IUPS Global Resource CD-ROM Edition 2008*, ed. M. J. Stevens and D. Wedding (Hove, UK: Psychology, forthcoming).

17. International Federation of Social Workers, *Ethics in Social Work Statement of Principles,* 2004, www.ifsw.org/en/p38000324.html#top (accessed July 6, 2008).

18. Canadian Psychological Association, *Canadian Code of Ethics for Psychologists* (Ottawa: The Association, 2000), 1–32.

19. Christine Wihak, "Psychologists in Nunavut: A Comparison of Principles Underlying Inuit Qaujimanituqangit and the Canadian Psychological Association Code of Ethics," *Pimatisiwin: A Journal of Aboriginal and Indigenous Community Health* 2 (2004): 29–40.

20. Charles Taylor, "The Politics of Recognition," in *Multiculturalism: Examining the Politics of Recognition,* ed. A. Gutman (Princeton, NJ: Princeton University Press, 1994), 25–73.

21. Ibid., 25.

22. George Herbert Mead, *Mind, Self, and Society* (Chicago: University of Chicago Press, 1934).

23. Mikhail Bakhtin, *Problems of Dostoyevsky's Poetics*, trans. Caryl Emerson (Minneapolis: University of Minnesota Press, 1984).

24. Taylor, "Politics of Recognition," 43.

25. Stanley Fish, *Trouble with Principle.*

26. Taylor, "Politics of Recognition," 58.

27. Ibid., 40.

28. Ibid., 37.

29. Ibid., 66.

30. See Jeffrey Stout, *Democracy and Tradition* (Princeton, NJ: Princeton University Press, 2004).

31. Nicholas Wolterstorff, "The Role of Religion in Decision and Discussion of Political Issues," in *Religion in the Public Square: The Place of Religious Convictions in Political Debate,* ed. Robert Audi and Nicholas Wolterstorff (New York: Rowman and Littlefield, 1997), 67–120.

32. Michael Walzer, *Spheres of Justice: A Defense of Pluralism and Equality* (New York: Basic Books, 1983), 314.

33. Stephen L. Carter, *The Culture of Disbelief: How American Law and Politics Trivialize Religious Devotion* (New York: Anchor, 1994).

34. James Wm. McClendon Jr., *Biography as Theology: How Life Stories Can Remake Today's Theology* (Philadelphia: Trinity Press International, 1990).

35. While we are critical of the Enlightenment legacy, it should be remembered, as David Hollinger points out: "The Enlightenment recognized the limits and fallibility of knowledge to a degree that pre-Enlightenment regimes of truth simply did not. This Enlightenment project brought under devastating scrutiny the prejudices and superstitions that protected slavery and a virtual infinity of other injustices. It created the historical and social scientific inquiries that enable us to speak with such confidence about the social dependence of the self. The Enlightenment promoted religious tolerance against the imperialist ambitions of conflicting

absolutisms. Above all, the Enlightenment was subversive of traditional political authority, and ultimately it gave us democracy." David Hollinger, "The Enlightenment and the Genealogy of Cultural Conflict in the United States," in *What's Left of Enlightenment?* ed. Keith Michel Baker and Peter Hanns Reill (Stanford, CA: Stanford University Press, 2001), 8. It was in the context of modernity that authoritarian regimes were denounced, patriarchy was condemned, and personal liberties were extolled. We are grateful for the gifts of modernity while critical of its shortcomings.

36. Stephen L. Carter, *The Culture of Disbelief: How American Law and Politics Trivialize Religious Devotion* (New York: Anchor, 1994), 230–31.

37. See Stout, *Democracy*, 3 (italics original).

38. Ibid.

39. See Wolterstorff, "Role of Religion," 94 (italics original).

40. Ibid., 105 (italics original). Consistent with his convictions about speaking publicly from a perspective of faith, Nicholas Wolterstorff recently wrote a most scholarly treatise on justice for a wide readership. He argues that justice is based on natural human rights and that the worth of a human being is bestowed on us through God's love. Secular defenses of human rights he finds inadequate, because they need a necessary theism to ground human rights. See Nicholas Wolterstorff, *Justice: Rights and Wrongs* (Princeton: Princeton University Press, 2008).

41. Stout, *Democracy*, 10 (italics added).

42. Ibid., 73 (italics original).

43. Wolterstorff, "Role of Religion," 109.

44. Stephen L. Carter, *God's Name in Vain: The Wrongs and Rights of Religion in Politics* (New York: Basic Books, 2000).

45. We continue to be amazed by the fact that 75 percent of Americans describe themselves as Catholics or Protestants, but as we read hundreds of therapy transcripts in our research projects religious language seldom appears. See http://religions.pewforum.org/affiliations.

46. The past decade includes a burgeoning literature on religion and health/therapy. However, the incorporation of religion-accommodating approaches in therapy is still widely suspect in clinical psychology. This is the case inspite of the fact that the APA code of ethics expects therapists to take religion into account like any other issue of diversity. See the insightful work of Siang-Yang Tan, "Religion in Clinical Practice: Implicit and Explicit Integration," in *Religion and the Clinical Practice of Psychology*, ed. Edward P. Shafranske (Washington, DC: American Psychological Association, 1996), 365–90; Siang-Yang Tan, "Training in Professional Psychology: Diversity Includes Religion," paper presented at the National Council of Schools of Professional Psychology, Jan. 19–23, 1993.

47. Richard Zehnle, *Peter's Pentecost Discourse: Tradition and Lukan Reinterpretation in Peter's Speeches of Acts 2 and 3* (Nashville: Abingdon, 1971).

48. The Cuban scholar Fernando Segovia argues that biblical criticism in the past century has been dominated by one voice that is male and Euro-American. For him Pentecost means that reading the scriptures in different cultures will mean that we will hear a diversity of voices as they interpret the biblical text. See Fernando Segovia, *Decolonizing Biblical Studies: A View from the Margins* (New York: Orbis, 2000).

49. See R. S. Sugirtharajah, *Voices from the Margin: Interpreting the Bible in the Third World* (Maryknoll, NY: Orbis, 1991).

50. Volf, *Exclusion and Embrace*, 229.

51. Krister Stendahl, *Paul among Jews and Gentiles, and Other Essays* (Philadelphia: Fortress, 1976).

52. James D. G. Dunn, *The Theology of Paul's Letter to the Galatians* (Cambridge: Cambridge University Press, 1993), 28 (italics original).

53. John M. G. Barclay, "'Neither Jew nor Greek,'" in *Ethnicity and the Bible,* ed. Mark G. Brett (New York: E. J. Brill, 1996), 211 (italics original).

Chapter 4 *Secularese* as Lingua Franca

1. Charles Taylor, *A Secular Age* (Cambridge: Belknap Press of Harvard University Press, 2007).

2. John Milbank, *Theology and Social Theory: Beyond Secular Reason* (Oxford: Blackwell, 1990), 9.

3. William T. Cavanaugh, *Theopolitical Imagination* (London: T&T Clark, 2002).

4. Stanley Hauerwas, "The State of the Secular: Theology, Prayer, and the University," in *The State of the University: Academic Knowledges and the Knowledge of God* (Oxford: Blackwell, 2007), 168.

5. Christian Smith, *The Secular Revolution: Power, Interests, and Conflict in the Secularization of American Public Life* (Berkeley: University of California Press, 2003).

6. Hauerwas, "State of the Secular," 170.

7. Ellen Charry, "Understanding Saint Augustine's Theological Psychology," Integration Symposium lectures given at Fuller Theological Seminary's School of Psychology, February 19, 2007.

8. Glanmor Williams, *The Welsh and Their Religion* (Cardiff: University of Wales Press, 1991), 22.

9. Charles Taylor, "Modes of Secularism," in *Secularism and Its Critics*, ed. Rajeev Bhargava (Delhi: Oxford University Press, 1998), 31–53. See also his recent book for similarities and differences from our perspective: Charles Taylor, *A Secular Age*.

10. Peter Brierley, *Religious Trends: 2000/01* (London: Christian Research Association, 2000).

11. George Barna, *Church Attendance: 2000*, Barna Research Online: www.barna.org.

12. Steve Bruce, *God Is Dead: Secularization in the West* (Oxford: Blackwell, 2002), 205.

13. Robert Wuthnow, *The Restructuring of American Religion* (Princeton, NJ: Princeton University Press, 1988), 165.

14. Rodney Stark and Roger Finke, *Acts of Faith: Explaining the Human Side of Religion* (Berkeley: University of California Press, 2000), 53.

15. No wonder religion is seldom addressed in therapy.

16. Scott Jaschik, "Not So Godless after All," http://insidehighered.com/news/2006/10/09/religion (accessed May 26, 2006).

17. See MacIntyre on liberalism as tradition, in Alasdair MacIntyre, *Whose Justice? Which Rationality?* (Notre Dame, IN: University of Notre Dame Press, 1988).

18. Ludwig Wittgenstein, *Philosophical Investigations,* ed. G. E. M. Anscombe (New York: Macmillan, 1958).

19. Milbank, *Theology and Social Theory,* 4.

20. Bruce, *God Is Dead.*

21. Cavanaugh, *Theopolitical Imagination.*

22. Ibid., 28–29.

23. Jacques Ellul, *The Technological Society* (New York: Knopf, 1964).

24. Smith, *Secular Revolution,* 1.

25. Ibid., 2.

26. Peter Berger, *The Desecularization of the World: Resurgent Religion and World Politics* (Washington, DC: Ethics and Public Policy Center, 1999).

27. Ibid., 10 (italics original).

28. George Marsden, *The Soul of the American University: From Protestant Establishment to Established Nonbelief* (New York: Oxford University Press, 1994), 3.

29. Ibid., 9 (italics original).

30. George Marsden and B. J. Longfield, *The Secularization of the Academy* (New York: Oxford University Press, 1992), 33.

31. Marsden, *Soul of the American University,* 434.

32. Adapted from R. L. Ownby, *Psychological Reports: A Guide to Report Writing in Professional Psychology* (New York: Wiley, 1997), 178.

33. William James, *The Varieties of Religious Experience: A Study in Human Nature* (New York: Modern Library, 2002).

34. Charles Taylor, *Varieties of Religion Today: William James Revisited* (Cambridge: Harvard University Press, 2002). Charles Taylor's analysis of James's view of religion suggests there may be more continuity between the implicit assumptions and the future role of religion in psychology.

35. Elizabeth Lehr and Bernard Spilka, "Religion in the Introductory Psychology Textbook: A Comparison of Three Decades," *Journal for the Scientific Study of Religion* 28 (1989): 366–71.

36. Gordon W. Allport, *The Individual and His Religion: A Psychological Interpretation* (New York: Macmillan, 1950).

37. See Ian Nicholson, "Gordon Allport, Character, and the 'Culture Of Personality,' 1897–1937," *History of Psychology* 1 (1998): 52–68.

38. Talal Asad, *Formations of the Secular: Christianity, Islam, Modernity* (Stanford, CA: Stanford University Press, 2003), 46–47.

39. This is also an example of where secularization saved the Christian community from a simplistic theodicy.

40. See comments on kenosis by Nancey Murphy, "Theological Resources for Integration," in *Why Psychology Needs Theology: A Radical-Reformation Perspective*, ed. Alvin Dueck and Cameron Lee (Grand Rapids; Eerdmans, 2005), 42–45. A similar concern is raised in Randall Lehmann Sorenson, *Minding Spirituality* (Hillsdale: Analytic Press, 2004), 16–17.

41. Asad, *Formations of the Secular,* 52.

42. Keith G. Meador, "My Own Salvation: The Christian Century and Psychology's Secularizing of American Protestantism," in *The Secular Revolution: Power, Interests, and Conflict in the Secularization of American Public Life,* ed. Christian Smith (Berkeley: University of California Press, 2003), 269–305.

43. Milbank, *Theology and Social Theory.*

44. Asad, *Formations of the Secular,* 61–62 (italics original).

45. Walter Brueggemann, "The Legitimacy of a Sectarian Hermeneutic: 2 Kings 18–19," in *Education for Citizenship and Discipleship,* ed. Mary Boys (New York: Pilgrim Press, 1989), 3–34.

46. William E. Connolly, *Why I Am Not a Secularist* (Minneapolis: University of Minnesota Press, 1999).

Chapter 5 A Mother Tongue amid Trade Languages

1. Benjamin Lee Whorf, *Language, Thought, and Reality: Selected Writings* (Cambridge: Technology Press of Massachusetts Institute of Technology, 1956).

2. Daniel Bogert-O'Brien, "Against Global-Speak," *Encounter* 17 (2004): 9–13.

3. When we refer to languages we are not speaking literally of languages such as Spanish, Tagalo, or Cantonese. We are speaking here figuratively of religion and culture as languages with unique structures that shape communication in therapy.

4. Naomi Meara, Harold Pepinsky, Joseph W. Shannon, and W. A Murray, "Semantic Communication and Expectations for Counseling across Three Theoretical Orientations," *Journal of Counseling Psychology* 28 (1981): 110–18; Naomi Meara, Joseph W. Shannon, and Harold Pepinsky, "Comparison of the Stylistic Complexity of the Language of Counselor and Client across Three Theoretical Orientations," *Journal of Counseling Psychology* 26 (1979): 181–89.

5. Timothy Kelly and Hans H. Strupp, "Patient and Therapist Values in Psychotherapy: Perceived Changes, Assimilation, Similarity, and Outcome," *Journal of Consulting & Clinical Psychology* 60 (1992): 34–40.

6. For a creative use of first and second language categories see Ted Koontz, "Thinking Theologically about the War in Iraq," *Mennonite Quarterly Review* 77 (2003): 93–108.

7. Edward Said, *Orientalism* (London: Routledge and Kegan Paul, 1978).

8. For reasons of ethical integrity and clarity we must emphasize that the focus is placed on the first language of the client rather than the clinician. This chapter is concerned with the paradox that the clinician's mother tongue must first be known before the clinician will be able to successfully and ethically affirm the client's different mother tongue in therapy.

9. When we speak of the public nature of therapy, we mean that therapy is shaped by norms that are public. We are not suggesting that confidentiality be violated.

10. Shinobu Kitayama, Hazel Rose Markus, Hisaya Matsumoto, and Vinai Norasakkunkit, "Individual and Collective Processes in the Construction of the Self: Self-Enhancement in the United States and Self-Criticism in Japan," *Journal of Personality & Social Psychology* 72 (1997): 1245–67.

11. Hazel Rose Markus and Shinobu Kitayama, "The Cultural Construction of Self and Emotion: Implications for Social Behavior," in *Emotion and Culture: Empirical Studies of Mutual Influence,* ed. Shinobu Kitayama and Hazel Rose Markus (Washington, DC: American Psychological Association, 1994), 89–130.

12. Michael Ross, Elaine Xun, and Anne Wilson, "Language and the Bicultural Self," *Personality and Social Psychology Bulletin* 20 (2002): 1040–50.

13. Ibid., 1040.

14. Viorica Marian and Ulrich Neisser, "Language-Dependent Recall of Autobiographical Memories," *Journal of Experimental Psychology: General* 129 (2000): 361–68.

15. Charlotte Burck, *Multilingual Living* (Basingstoke: Palgrave Macmillan, 2005).

16. Charlotte Burck, "Living in Several Languages: Implications for Therapy," *Journal of Family Therapy* 26 (2004): 330.

17. Ibid., 321.

18. This was also reported by Sandor Ferenczi in 1911. Sandor Ferenczi, *First Contributions to Psycho-analysis,* trans. E. Jones (New York: Brunner/Mazel, 1952).

19. Burck, "Living in Several Languages," 322–23.

20. Ibid., 324.

21. Comment made by a bilingual speaker about speaking in a second language; Burck, "Living in Several Languages," 322.

22. Kostas Katsavdakis, Mohamed Sayed, Anthony Bram, and Alice Brand Bartlett, "How Was This Story Told in the Mother Tongue? An Integrative Perspective," *Bulletin of the Menninger Clinic* 2 (2001): 246–65.

23. Ralph R. Greenson, "The Mother Tongue and the Mother," *International Journal of Psycho-Analysis* 31 (1950): 18–23.

24. Ibid., 20.

25. E. Eduardo Krapf, "The Choice of Language in Polyglot Psychoanalysis," *Psychoanalytic Quarterly* 24 (1955): 343–57.

26. Luis R. Marcos and Leonel Urcuyo, "Dynamic Psychotherapy with the Bilingual Patient," *American Journal of Psychotherapy* 33 (1979): 331–38.

27. Katsavdakis et al., "How Was This Story Told," 252.

28. Ramón Karamat Ali, "Bilingualism and Systemic Psychotherapy: Some Formulations and Explorations," *Journal of Family Therapy* 26 (2004): 340–57.

29. Ralph Wood, "Performing the Faith: An Interview with George Lindbeck," *Christian Century*, November 28, 2006, 28–35.

30. George Lindbeck, *The Nature of Doctrine: Religion and Theology in a Postliberal Age* (Philadelphia: Westminster John Knox, 1984); George Lindbeck and James J. Buckley, *The Church in a Postliberal Age* (London: SCM, 2002).

31. Lindbeck, *Nature of Doctrine,* 23.

32. Ibid., 35.

33. McClendon makes the case that Freud's narrative gives meaning to the emotions according to the grammar of his theory; James Wm. McClendon Jr., *Ethics: Systematic Theology* (Nashville: Abingdon, 1986), 143.

34. Richard Steele, "Narrative Theology and the Religious Affections," in *Theology without Foundations: Religious Practice and the Future of Theological Truth,* ed. Stanley Hauerwas, Nancey C. Murphy, and Mark Nation (Nashville: Abingdon, 1994), 163.

35. Nancey C. Murphy, *Beyond Liberalism and Fundamentalism: How Modern and Postmodern Philosophy Set the Theological Agenda* (Valley Forge, PA: Trinity Press International, 1996).

36. Steele, "Narrative Theology," 175.

37. It is this desire for congruence between life and vision that drives the struggle recorded in the memoirs of Mother Teresa; Teresa Kolodiejchuk and Brian Kolodiejchuk, *Mother Teresa: Come Be My Light: The Private Writings of The "Saint of Calcutta"* (New York: Doubleday, 2007).

38. Walter Brueggemann, "The Legitimacy of a Sectarian Hermeneutic: 2 Kings 18–19," in *Education for Citizenship and Discipleship,* ed. Mary Boys (New York: Pilgrim, 1989), 3–34.

39. Ibid., 5–6 .

40. See Ian Nicholson, "Gordon Allport, Character, and the 'Culture of Personality,' 1897–1937," *History of Psychology* 1 (1998): 52–68.

41. Augustus Jordan and Naomi Meara, "Ethics and the Professional Practice of Psychologists: The Role of Virtues and Principles," *Professional Psychology: Research and Practice* 21 (1990): 107–14.

42. Alvin Dueck and Kevin Reimer, "Retrieving the Virtues in Psychotherapy: Thick and Thin Discourse," *American Behavioral Scientist* 47 (2003): 427–41.

43. Kevin Reimer, "Agape, Brokenness, and Theological Realism in L'Arche," in *Visions of Agape,* ed. C. Boyd (Aldershot, UK: Ashgate, 2008), 85–102.

44. G. K. Chesterton, "What I Saw in America," in *The Collected Works of G.K. Chesterton,* vol. 21 (San Francisco: Ignatius, 1990), 41–45.

45. See Eric L. Johnson, "Sin, Weakness, and Psychopathology," *Journal of Psychology and Theology* 15 (1987): 218–26; Barbara Brown Taylor, *Speaking of Sin: The Lost Language of Salvation* (Cambridge, MA: Cowley, 2000).

46. Karl Menninger, *Whatever Became of Sin?* (New York: Hawthorn Books, 1973), 48.

47. Frank Lake, *Clinical Theology* (London: Darton Longman and Todd, 1986).

48. O. Hobart Mowrer, *The Crisis in Psychiatry and Religion* (Princeton, NJ: Van Nostrand, 1961).

49. Monika is a composite characterization based on our experience.

50. See the creative work of Lewis Aron regarding a "third space" which goes beyond client and therapist and in which healing may occur; Lewis Aron, *A Meeting of Minds* (Hillsdale, NJ: Analytic Press, 1996); Lewis Aron, "Analytic Impasse and the Third: Clinical Implications of Intersubjectivity Theory," *International Journal of Psychoanalysis*, 87 (2006): 349–68.

51. The work of Frank Lake is pioneering in this regard. See Lake, *Clinical Theology.*

52. See Jones and Shorter-Gooden for an illustration from the experience of African-American women who learn to shift linguistic registers depending on the social context. Charisse Jones and Kumea Shorter-Gooden, *Shifting: The Double Lives of Black Women in America* (New York: HarperCollins, 2003).

53. To learn the language of a client takes time. How many clients can a therapist assist if reading up on the history and culture of a client is necessary, as we suggest?

54. Richard Gorsuch makes the case that there are radical differences between spirituality and psychology, making conversation between them difficult. The former valorizes unique events,

while the latter seeks replicability and generalizability. See Richard L. Gorsuch, *Integrating Psychology and Spirituality?* (Pasadena, CA: Fuller Seminary Press, 2007).

55. Winch, *The Idea of a Social Science and Its Relation to Philosophy* (New York: Humanities, 1958).

56. Ibid., 15.

57. Ludwig Wittgenstein, *Philosophical Investigations,* trans. G. E. M. Anscombe (New York: Macmillan, 1953).

58. Ibid., II, xi, 226e.

59. Winch, *Idea of a Social Science,* 72.

60. Much human behavior is habituated or unconscious. We act and then become cognizant of our actions such that cognitive or rational explanations can be subsequently applied in explanation. See Darcia Narvaez and Daniel Lapsley, "The Psychological Foundations of Everyday Morality and Moral Expertise," in *Character Psychology and Character Education,* ed. D. Lapsley and F. Clark Power (Notre Dame, IN: University of Notre Dame Press, 2005), 140–65.

61. Winch, *Idea of a Social Science,* 83.

62. Ibid., 94.

63. Ibid., 100–101.

64. Carl Jung and Aniela Jaffe, *Memories, Dreams, Reflections* (New York: Vintage Books, 1963).

65. Patricia Raybon, *My First White Friend: Confessions on Race, Love, and Forgiveness* (New York: Viking, 1996).

Chapter 6 Thick Clients and Thin Therapists

1. Geertz expands the cultural ramifications of "thick" and "thin" as descriptive modes of discourse about culture. See Gilbert Ryle, *The Concept of Mind* (London: Hutchinson's University Library, 1949); Clifford Geertz, *The Interpretation of Cultures: Selected Essays* (New York: Basic Books, 1973).

2. Geertz, *Interpretation of Cultures,* 43.

3. A pseudonym.

4. Religious academy.

5. This case was reported by Yoram Bilu, Eliezer Witztum, and Onno Van der Hart, "Paradise Regained: 'Miraculous Healing' in an Israeli Psychiatric Clinic," *Culture, Medicine & Psychiatry* 14 (1990): 105–27.

6. Ibid., 112.

7. David Greenberg and Eliezer Witztum, *Sanity and Sanctity: Mental Health Work among the Ultra-Orthodox in Jerusalem* (New Haven: Yale University Press, 2001), 9.

8. Alasdair MacIntyre, *After Virtue: A Study in Moral Theology* (Notre Dame, IN: University of Notre Dame Press, 1984), 30.

9. Michael Walzer, *Thick and Thin: Moral Argument at Home and Abroad* (Notre Dame, IN: University of Notre Dame Press, 1994).

10. Sigmund Freud, *Future of an Illusion* (London: Hogarth, 1961).

11. Carl Jung and Aniela Jaffe, *Memories, Dreams, Reflections* (New York: Vintage Books, 1963).

12. Burrhus F. Skinner, *Science and Human Behavior* (New York: Macmillan, 1960).

13. Lawrence Kohlberg, *Stages of Moral Development as a Basis for Moral Education* (Cambridge: Center for Moral Education, Harvard University, 1971).

14. Jean Piaget, *The Language and Thought of the Child,* trans. M. Warden (London: Kegan Paul, 1926).

15. William James, *The Principles of Psychology* (New York: Mentor, 1899/1958), 42.

16. See Alvin Dueck and Thomas D. Parsons, "Integration Discourse: Modern and Postmodern," *Journal of Psychology & Theology* 32 (2004): 232–47.

17. Philip Cushman, "Why the Self Is Empty: Toward a Historically Situated Psychology," *American Psychologist* 45 (1990): 599–611.

18. David Bakan, *Sigmund Freud and the Jewish Mystical Tradition* (Princeton, NJ: Van Nostrand, 1958).

19. Walzer, *Thick and Thin*, 89–90.

20. See Alan Tjeltveit, "The Psychotherapist as Christian Ethicist: Theology Applied to Practice," *Journal of Psychology & Theology* 20 (1992): 89–98; Alan Tjeltveit, *Ethics and Values in Psychotherapy* (London: Routledge, 1999).

21. "Marital Stress and Extramarital Relationships," chap. 20, DVD accompanying Ronald J. Comer, *Abnormal Psychology*, 3rd ed. (New York: W. H. Freeman, 1998).

22. Donald B. Kraybill, Steven M. Nolt, and David Weaver-Zercher, *Amish Grace: How Forgiveness Transcended Tragedy* (San Francisco: Jossey-Bass, 2007).

23. Ibid., 45.

24. Ibid., 30.

25. Alvin C. Dueck, *Between Jerusalem and Athens: Ethical Perspectives on Culture, Religion, and Psychotherapy* (Grand Rapids: Baker Books, 1995), chap. 10.

26. Chaim Potok, *My Name Is Asher Lev* (New York: Fawcett Crest, 1973).

27. Ibid., 10.

28. Walzer, *Thick and Thin*, 98–99.

29. Mircea Eliade, *Shamanism: Archaic Techniques of Ecstasy* (New York: Bollingen Foundation, 1964).

30. Naomi Meara, Harold B. Pepinsky, Joseph W. Shannon, and William A. Murray, "Semantic Communication and Expectations for Counseling across Three Theoretical Orientations," *Journal of Counseling Psychology* 28 (1981): 110–18; and Naomi Meara, Joseph W. Shannon, and Harold B. Pepinsky, "Comparison of the Stylistic Complexity of the Language of Counselor and Client across Three Theoretical Orientations," *Journal of Counseling Psychology* 26 (1979): 181–89.

31. Timothy Kelly and Hans H. Strupp, "Patient and Therapist Values in Psychotherapy: Perceived Changes, Assimilation, Similarity, and Outcome," *Journal of Consulting & Clinical Psychology* 60 (1992): 34–40; and David Rosenthal, "Changes in Some Moral Values following Psychotherapy," *Journal of Consulting Psychology* 19 (1955): 431–36.

32. The program that we use here to illustrate a peaceable ethnic and spiritual psychotherapy is adapted from the program that I (AD) encountered in San Juan del K'iche, Guatemala. It is called "Utz K'aslemal," which in the local Indian dialect of K'iche means "the good life." See Bárbara Ford, Roberto Cabrera, and Virginia Searing, *Buscando una buena vida: tres experiencias de salud mental comunitaria* (Guatemala: Redd Barna, 2000); Asociación Utz K'aslemal Salud Mental Comuntaria El Quiché, *Construyendo una buena vida* (Noruega: Save the Children, n.d.). The inclusion of Christian themes is our addition. The authors are grateful for the assistance of Steven Huett and Jenel Ramos in the research and development of this section.

33. What made the approach unique was that it did not focus on "mental health" or on a Western "psychology" but built on an indigenous Mayan understanding of the self. See Bruce Olson's indigenously sensitive approach to giving medical advice; Bruce Olson, *Bruchko* (Carol Stream, IL: Creation House, 1978).

34. Corn is central to the life and spirituality of indigenous Guatemalan people. See Rigoberta Menchu, *I, Rigoberta Menchu*, trans. A. Wright (London: Verso, 1984). In the Utz K'aslemal program, corn comes to symbolize the hardship and suffering of Quiché people. The mortar, pestle, and corn are reframed for the group. The corn is initially hard and unusable, but when ground into flour, into something soft, it becomes nourishing. "Those pains and experiences can become food for our life, just like the corn is food for our body. In order to turn all that pain into food, we must soften it, grind it and knead it, as we do with the corn. But it is not the work of a day only, but always we must return to our pains to soften them, to grind them and

to knead them in the way of our life" (Ford, Cabrera, and Searing, *Buscando una buena vida,* 69). No wonder the participants begin to weep.

35. This experience of Juanita's is adapted from the PBS documentary of Denise Becker, *Discovering Dominga,* dir. by Patricia Flynn (Jaguar House Films, 2002), www.pbs.org/pov/pov2003/discoveringdominga/.

36. John Paul Lederach, *Building Peace: Sustainable Reconciliation in Divided Societies* (Washington, DC: U.S. Institute of Peace Press, 1997); John Paul Lederach, *Preparing for Peace: Conflict Transformation across Cultures* (Syracuse, NY: Syracuse University Press, 1996).

37. Lederach, *Preparing for Peace,* 38.

38. Paulo Freire, *Pedagogy of the Oppressed* (New York: Seabury, 1970).

39. Clifford Geertz, *The Interpretation of Cultures* (New York: Basic Books, 1973).

40. Lederach, *Preparing for Peace,* 56.

41. Ibid., 74.

42. Quoted in Paul Watzlawick, John Weakland, and Richard Fisch, *Change* (New York: W. W. Norton, 1974), 104.

43. Lederach, *Preparing for Peace,* 60.

44. Ibid., 67.

Chapter 7 Morality: Abstract and Traditioned

1. "Alex," *In Treatment,* dir. Rodrigo Garcia, season 1, episode 2 (HBO, 2008).

2. See Cavanaugh for an alternative interpretation; William T. Cavanaugh, *Theopolitical Imagination* (London: T&T Clark, 2002), chap. 1.

3. Stephen Toulmin, *Cosmopolis: The Hidden Agenda of Modernity* (New York: Free Press, 1990).

4. René Descartes, *Discourse on Method; and Meditations on First Philosophy,* trans. Donald A. Cress (Indianapolis: Hackett, 1998).

5. Richard Rorty, *Philosophy and the Mirror of Nature* (Princeton, NJ: Princeton University Press, 1979).

6. Alasdair MacIntyre, *Three Rival Versions of Moral Enquiry: Encyclopaedia, Genealogy, and Tradition* (Notre Dame, IN: University of Notre Dame Press, 1990). We will not address the other (genealogical) tradition which MacIntyre discusses.

7. Ibid., 59.

8. Ibid., 42.

9. MacIntyre, *Three Rival Versions,* 42.

10. Michael Walzer, *Thick and Thin: Moral Argument at Home and Abroad* (Notre Dame, IN: University of Notre Dame Press, 1994), 7.

11. Ibid., 7.

12. Alasdair MacIntyre, *Whose Justice? Which Rationality?* (Notre Dame, IN: University of Notre Dame Press, 1988).

13. Walzer, *Thick and Thin,* 11.

14. Ibid., 39.

15. Mary W. Nicholas, *The Mystery of Goodness and the Positive Moral Consequences of Psychotherapy* (New York: W. W. Norton, 1994).

16. While this could count as a thicker form of psychotherapy, the morality is still the Kantian morality of universal principles. It appears the moral individual is not in need of a moral narrative or moral community.

17. Ibid., v–vi.

18. Allen Bergin, "Mental Health Values of Professionals: A National Interdisciplinary Survey," *Professional Psychology: Research and Practice* 3 (1988): 290–97.

19. Nicholas, *Mystery of Goodness,* 22.

20. Ibid., 82.

21. Ibid., 192.

22. Quoted in Nicholas, *Mystery of Goodness*, 225–26.

23. Lawrence Kohlberg, *Stages of Moral Development as a Basis for Moral Education* (Cambridge: Center for Moral Education, Harvard University, 1971).

24. James Wm. McClendon Jr., *Biography as Theology: How Life Stories Can Remake Today's Theology* (Philadelphia: Trinity Press International, 1990).

25. Charles Taylor, *Sources of the Self: The Making of the Modern Identity* (Cambridge: Harvard University Press, 1989).

26. James Davidson Hunter, *The Death of Character: Moral Education in an Age without Good or Evil* (New York: Basic Books, 2000), 217.

27. Werner Wilhelm Jaeger, *Paideia: The Ideals of Greek Culture* (New York: Oxford University Press, 1965).

28. Ludwig Wittgenstein, *Philosophical Investigations*, trans. G. E. M. Anscombe (New York: Macmillan, 1953).

29. Ludwig Wittgenstein, *Tractatus Logico-Philosophicus* (London: Routledge and Kegan Paul, 1922).

30. MacIntyre, *Three Rival Versions*.

31. Walzer, *Thick and Thin*, 60.

32. Ibid., 62.

33. Walzer, *Thick and Thin*.

34. Clifford Geertz, *The Interpretation of Cultures* (New York: Basic Books, 1973).

35. Walzer, *Thick and Thin*, xin1.

36. Ibid., 21.

37. Ibid., 33.

38. Ibid., 4.

39. Ibid., 3.

Chapter 8 Sacred Order and a Prozac God

1. Sigmund Freud, *Future of an Illusion* (London: Hogarth, 1961).

2. Albert Ellis, "Can Rational Emotive Behavior Therapy (REBT) Be Effectively Used with People Who Have Devout Beliefs in God and Religion?" *Professional Psychology: Research & Practice* 31 (2000): 29–33.

3. Harold Koenig, ed., *Handbook of Religion and Mental Health* (San Diego: Academic, 1998); Harold Koenig, Michael E. McCullough, and David B. Larson, eds. *Handbook of Religion and Health* (London: Oxford University Press, 2001); Everett Worthington, Taro A. Kurusu, Michael E. McCollough, and Steven J. Sandage, "Empirical Research on Religion and Psychotherapeutic Processes and Outcomes: A 10-Year Review and Research Prospectus," *Psychological Bulletin* 119 (1996): 448–87.

4. Wendell Berry, "Healing Is Membership," in *The Art of the Common-Place: The Agrarian Essays of Wendell Berry,* ed. Wendell Berry and Norman Wirzba (Washington, DC: Counterpoint, 2002), 146.

5. Chung Chou Chu and Helen E. Klein, "Psychosocial and Environmental Variables in Outcome of Black Schizophrenics," *Journal of the National Medical Association* 77 (1985): 793–96.

6. Harold Koenig, Linda K. George, and Bercedes L. Peterson, "Religiosity and Remission from Depression in Medically Ill Older Patients," *American Journal of Psychiatry* 155 (1998): 536–42.

7. Richard L. Gorsuch, "Religious Aspects of Substance Abuse and Recovery," *Journal of Social Issues* 5 (1995): 65–83.

8. M. A. Azhart, S. L. Varma, and A. S. Dharap, "Religious Psychotherapy in Anxiety Disorder Patients," *Acta Psychiatric Scandinavica* 90 (1994): 1–3.

9. Rebecca Propst, Richard Ostrom, Phillip Watkins, and Terry Dean, "Comparative Efficacy of Religious and Nonreligious Cognitive-Behavioral Therapy for the Treatment of Clinical Depression in Religious Individuals," *Journal of Consulting and Clinical Psychology* 60 (1992): 94–103.

10. We do well to remember Wittgenstein's admonition that "we must do away with explanation and description alone must take its place"; Ludwig Wittgenstein, *Philosophical Investigations*, ed. G. E. M. Anscombe (New York: Macmillan, 1953), 109.

11. Joel James Shuman and Keith G. Meador, *Heal Thyself: Spirituality, Medicine, and the Distortion of Christianity* (Oxford: Oxford University Press, 2003), 6.

12. Richard Sloan, Emilia Bagiella, and Tia Powell, "Religion, Spirituality, and Medicine," *Lancet* 353 (1999): 664–67. More recently see the editorial by Richard P. Sloan, Emilia Bagiella, and Larry VandeCreek, "Should Physicians Prescribe Religious Activities?" *New England Journal of Medicine* 342 (2000): 1913–16.

13. Shuman and Meador, *Heal Thyself.*

14. Steve Bruce, *God Is Dead: Secularization in the West* (Oxford: Blackwell, 2002), 2.

15. Talal Asad, *Formations of the Secular: Christianity, Islam, Modernity* (Stanford, CA: Stanford University Press, 2003), 55.

16. John Milbank, *Theology and Social Theory: Beyond Secular Reason* (Oxford: Blackwell, 1990), 1.

17. Ibid., 2.

18. Ibid., 4.

19. A. Robert Markus, *Christianity and the Secular* (Notre Dame, IN: University of Notre Dame Press, 2006).

20. Karl Barth, *Church Dogmatics,* vol. 3, ed. G. T. Thompson (Edinburgh: T&T Clark, 1949).

21. Herbert Benson, *Timeless Healing* (New York: Scribner, 1996), 200.

22. Shuman and Meador, *Heal Thyself,* 35.

23. Ibid., 37.

24. T. S. Eliot, *Christianity and Culture: The Idea of a Christian Society and Notes Towards the Definition of Culture* (New York: Harcourt Brace, 1940/1968), 46.

25. Shuman and Meador, *Heal Thyself,* 17.

26. Richard Wentz, "The Domestication of the Divine," *Theology Today* 57 (2000): 24–34.

27. Richard Rorty, *Philosophy and Social Hope* (New York: Penguin Books, 1999).

28. See Clifford Geertz, *The Interpretation of Cultures* (New York: Basic Books, 1973), 89–90.

29. See Mircea Eliade, *Shamanism: Archaic Techniques of Ecstasy* (Princeton, NJ: Princeton University Press, 1964).

30. See Merle Jordan, *Taking on the Gods: The Task of the Pastoral Counselor* (Nashville: Parthenon, 1986). Jordan suggests that sometimes depression results when the false gods we worship let us down.

31. Vincent Jude Miller, *Consuming Religion: Christian Faith and Practice in a Consumer Culture* (New York: Continuum, 2004).

32. George Lindbeck, *The Nature of Doctrine* (Philadelphia: Westminster John Knox, 1984), 18.

33. John D. Caputo, *On Religion* (New York: Routledge, 2001), 1.

34. J. Augustine Di Noia, "Jesus and the World Religions," *First Things* 54 (1995): 24–28.

35. Ibid., 25.

36. See Amos Yong, *Hospitality and the Other: Pentecost, Christian Practices, and the Neighbor* (Maryknoll, NY: Orbis, 2008).

37. James Wm. McClendon Jr., *Witness,* vol. 3 of *Systematic Theology* (Nashville: Abingdon, 2000).

38. This is not meant to invoke a relativist view of traditions, languages, and religious beliefs. We observe that "relativism" is a critique meaningful to individuals wishing to preserve the universality of democratic liberalism.

39. Douglas John Hall and Rosemary Radford Ruether, *God and the Nations* (Minneapolis: Fortress, 1995), 107.

40. James L. Griffith and Melissa Elliott Griffith, *Encountering the Sacred in Psychotherapy: How to Talk with People about Their Spiritual Lives* (New York: Guilford, 2001).

41. Ibid., 1–4. Reprinted by permission.

42. Christopher Lasch, *The Culture of Narcissism: American Life in an Age of Diminishing Expectations* (New York: Warner Books, 1977); Peter Berger, Brigitte Berger, and Hansfried Kellner, *The Homeless Mind: Modernization and Consciousness* (New York: Random House, 1973); Charles Taylor, *A Secular Age* (Cambridge: Belknap Press of Harvard University Press, 2007); Peter Gay, *Modernism: The Thrill of Heresy* (New York: W. W. Norton, 2007).

43. Philip Rieff, *Freud: The Mind of the Moralist* (New York: Viking, 1959); Philip Rieff, *The Triumph of the Therapeutic: Uses of Faith after Freud* (New York: Harper and Row, 1966).

44. The authors are grateful to Elizabeth Welsh, a doctoral student in Fuller Theological Seminary's Graduate School of Psychology, for her assistance on this section of the chapter.

45. Philip Rieff, *My Life among the Deathworks: Illustrations of the Aesthetics of Authority* (Charlottesville: University of Virginia Press, 2006).

46. John Sutherland, "The Ideas Interview: Philip Rieff," *Guardian,* December 5, 2005. Retrieved from www.guardian.co.uk/ideas/story/0,,1657860,00.html#article_continue.

47. Abraham Heschel, *Who Is Man?* (Stanford: Stanford University Press, 1965), 97.

48. Rieff, *Deathworks,* 2.

49. Ibid., 1.

50. Ibid., 17.

51. Ibid., 176.

52. Ibid., 4.

53. Ibid., 193.

54. Ibid., 19.

55. Ibid., 89.

56. Ibid., 71.

57. Ibid., 95.

58. Ibid., 107.

59. Ibid., 198.

60. Ibid., 1.

61. Ibid., 128.

62. Ibid., 10.

63. Ibid., 13, 17.

64. Ibid., 133.

65. Ibid., 134.

66. Ibid., 136.

67. Ibid.

68. Barbara S. Held, *Back to Reality: A Critique of Postmodern Theory in Psychotherapy* (New York: W. W. Norton, 1995).

69. A female reader may at times be puzzled by Rieff's apparently indiscriminate critique of the feminist movement. The subject emerges out of his discussion of decreational works of art that reduce gender heterogeneity and abstract it into a fused androgenic image, such as Marcel Duchamp's *The Bride Stripped Bare by Her Bachelors,* in which the artist proves himself to be indifferent to and transgressive of the reality of the distinctness of male and female identity. In response to such artistic creations of the unreal world of abstractions, Rieff argues "that generality is a fiction imposed on those irreducible identities destroyed in the reduction. As soon

as we abstract the self from others that are resisters, we destroy the very reality of the self that is resisted and turn it into a fiction. There is no self, no soul, that isn't either male or female" (Rieff, *Deathworks,* 125). Through this critique, Rieff thus appears to argue for an essentialist view of gender and against the feminist agenda to question and deconstruct gender roles. The assumption appears twofold; on the one hand, he seems to imply that sexual difference and role distinction are synonymous, and on the other that the gender roles assigned in patriarchal societies correspond to a more correct reading of sacred order than those more egalitarian and contemporary ones do.

70. Ibid., 175.

71. David Glenn, "Prophet of the 'Anti-Culture,'" *Chronicle of Higher Education,* 11 (November 2005), http://chronicle.com/free/v52/i12/12a01501.htm.

Chapter 9 A Peaceable Psychology

1. A pseudonym.

2. See J. L. Peachey, "Anabaptism on the Line in Guatemala," *Gospel Herald,* Nov. 15 (1992): 1–4.

3. Robert Neelly Bellah, *The Broken Covenant: American Civil Religion in a Time of Trial* (New York: Seabury, 1975).

4. John Howard Yoder, "Trinity versus Theodicy: Hebraic Realism and the Temptation to Judge God" (unpublished manuscript, 1996).

5. Krister Stendahl, *Paul among Jews and Gentiles, and Other Essays* (Philadelphia: Fortress, 1976).

6. Quoted in Romand Coles, *Self/Power/Other: Political Theory and Dialogical Ethics* (Ithaca: Cornell University Press, 1992).

7. See Phillip Cary, *Augustine's Invention of the Inner Self: The Legacy of a Christian Platonist* (Oxford: Oxford University Press, 2000).

8. Coles, *Self/Power/Other,* 50.

9. Ibid., 173.

10. Ibid., 174.

11. Peter Brown, *Augustine of Hippo: A Biography* (Berkeley: University of California Press, 1967), 240.

12. Thomas Babington Macaulay, "Minute on Indian Education," in *Selected Writings,* ed. J. Clive (Chicago: University of Chicago Press, 1972), 249.

13. Edward Said, *Orientalism* (London: Routledge and Kegan Paul, 1978); Ngugi wa, Thiong'o, *The River Between* (London: Heinemann, 1965); Frantz Fanon, *The Wretched of the Earth,* trans. Constance Farrington (New York: Grove, 1965).

14. Carl G. Jung, *Psychology and Religion: West and East,* vol. 11 of *The Collected Works of C. G. Jung* (Princeton: Princeton University Press, 1977).

15. Gustavo Gutierrez, *A Theology of Liberation: History, Politics, and Salvation* (New York: Orbis, 1984).

16. Ignacio Martín-Baró, *Writings for a Liberation Psychology* (Cambridge: Harvard University Press, 1994).

17. In the American context see the similar work of Prilleltensky and Fox; Isaac Prilleltensky and Dennis R. Fox, "Psychopolitical Literacy for Wellness and Justice," *Journal of Community Psychology* 35 (2007): 1–13.

18. Martín-Baró, *Liberation Psychology,* 17.

19. Paulo Freire, *Pedagogy of the Oppressed* (New York: Seabury, 1970).

20. Martín-Baró, *Liberation Psychology,* 19.

21. Neither do we.

22. Martín-Baró, *Liberation Psychology,* 31.

23. With kind permission of Springer Science and Business Media, portions of this chapter are drawn from the following article: Alvin Dueck, Sing-Kiat Ting, and Renee Cutiongco, "Constantine, Babel, and Yankee Doodling: Whose Indigeneity? Whose Psychology?" *Pastoral Psychology* 56 (2007): 55–72. We are grateful for the contribution of the last two authors to this section.

24. Kenneth Gergen, Aydan Gulerce, Andrew Lock, and Girishwar Misra, "Psychological Science in Cultural Context," *American Psychologist* 51 (1996): 502.

25. Ibid.

26. Uichol Kim and John Berry, *Indigenous Psychologies: Experience and Research in Cultural Context* (Newbury Park, CA: Sage, 1993).

27. Ibid., 2.

28. Uichol Kim, Kuo-shu Yang, and Kwang-Kuo Hwang, "Contributions to Indigenous and Cultural Psychology: Understanding People in Context," in *Indigenous and Cultural Psychology: Understanding People in Context* (New York: Springer, 2006), 3.

29. Ibid., 9 (italics original).

30. Philip Rieff, *The Triumph of the Therapeutic: Uses of Faith after Freud* (New York: Harper and Row, 1966).

31. Dan McAdams, *The Stories We Live By: Personal Myths and the Making of the Self* (New York: Morrow, 1993); Dan McAdams, *The Redemptive Self: Stories Americans Live By* (New York: Oxford University Press, 2006); Dan McAdams, Ruthellen Josselson, and Amia Lieblich, *Identity and Story: Creating Self in Narrative* (Washington, DC: American Psychological Association, 2006).

32. Philip Jenkins, *The Next Christendom: The Coming of Global Christianity* (Oxford: Oxford University Press, 2002). See www.adherents.com/Religions_By_Adherents.html.

33. Kim, Yang, and Hwang, *Indigenous and Cultural Psychology*, 9.

34. Ibid., 41.

35. Kwang-Kuo Hwang, "Constructive Realism and Confucian Relationalism: An Epistemological Strategy for the Development of Indigenous Psychology," in *Indigenous and Cultural Psychology: Understanding People in Context*, ed. Uichol Kim, Kuo-shu Yang, and Kwang-Kuo Hwang (New York: Springer, 2006), 73–107.

36. Kim, Yang, and Hwang, *Indigenous and Cultural Psychology*, chap. 5.

37. Ibid., 9. We do not impugn the importance of scientific method and research in the human sciences. Rather, we submit our empirical commitments to dialogue with local traditions in a peaceable exploration of difference. In our experience, these conversations have made us better methodologists, able to adapt empirical and qualitative methods toward a fuller and more comprehensive understanding of behavior. This approach is distinctly hermeneutical. See Steven Sandage, Kaye Cook, Peter Hill, Brad Strawn, and Kevin Reimer, "Hermeneutics and Psychology: A Review and Dialectical Model," *Review of General Psychology* 12 (2008): 344–64.

38. Imre Lakatos and Alan Musgrave, *Criticism and the Growth of Knowledge* (Cambridge: Cambridge University Press, 1970).

39. Paul Feyerabend, *Against Method: Outline of an Anarchistic Theory of Knowledge* (London: Humanities, 1975).

40. William K. Gabrenya Jr. "A Sociology of Science Approach to Understanding Indigenous Psychologies," in *Ongoing Themes in Psychology and Culture,* ed. B. N. Setiadi, A. Supratiknya, W. J. Lonner, and Y. H. Poortinga (Jakarta: International Association for Cross-Cultural Psychology, 2004), 131–49.

41. Rogelia E. Pe-Pua, "From Decolonizing Psychology to the Development of a Cross-Indigenous Perspective in Methodology: The Philippine Experience," in *Indigenous and Cultural Psychology: Understanding People in Context*, ed. Uichol Kim, Kuo-shu Yang, and Kwang-Kuo Hwang (New York: Springer, 2006), 109–37.

42. Frank Richardson, Blaine Fowers, and Charles Guignon, *Re-envisioning Psychology: Moral Dimensions of Theory and Practice* (San Francisco: Jossey-Bass, 1999).

43. Charles Taylor, "Peaceful Coexistence in Psychology," in *The Restoration of Dialogue: Readings in the Philosophy of Clinical Psychology,* ed. Ronald B. Miller (Washington, DC: American Psychological Association, 1971/1992), 70–84.

44. Clifford Geertz, *The Interpretation of Culture* (New York: Basic Books, 1973).

45. Thomas Kuhn, *The Structure of Scientific Revolutions* (Chicago: University of Chicago Press, 1962).

46. Michael Walzer, *Thick and Thin: Moral Argument at Home and Abroad* (Notre Dame, IN: University of Notre Dame Press, 1994).

47. Daniel Burston and Roger Frie, *Psychotherapy as a Human Science* (Pittsburgh: Duquesne University Press, 2006).

48. We are grateful to Renee Cutiongco, a Fuller Theological Seminary School of Psychology doctoral student, for her research on Enriquez and contribution to this section. See Dueck, Ting, and Cutiongco, "Constantine, Babel, and Yankee Doodling."

49. Alvin Dueck and Sherry Walling, "Theological Contributions of Bishop K. H. Ting to Christian/Pastoral Counseling," *Pastoral Psychology* 56 (2007): 143–56.

50. Rogelia E. Pe-Pua, *Sikolohiyang Pilipino: Teorya, Metodo at Gamit* (Filipino Psychology: Theory, Method and Application) (Quezon City, Philippines: Philippine Psychology Research and Training House, 1982).

51. Virgilio G. Enriquez, *From Colonial to Liberation Psychology: The Philippine Experience* (Manila: De La Salle University Press, 1992/1995).

52. Virgilio G. Enriquez, *Pagbabagong Dangal: Indigenous Psychology and Cultural Empowerment* (Quezon City: PUGAD Lawin Press, 1994), 70.

53. Rogelia Pe-Pua and Elizabeth Marcelino, "Sikolohiyang Pilipino (Filipino Psychology): A Legacy of Virgilio G. Enriquez," *Asian Journal of Social Psychology* 3 (2000): 49–71.

54. Ibid.

55. C. Covar, "Foreword," in Enriquez, *Pagbabagong Dangal.*

56. Pe-Pua and Marcelino, "Sikolohiyang Pilipino," 49.

57. Ibid.

58. Ibid.

59. Enriquez, *Pagbabagong Dangal,* 63.

60. Pe-Pua and Marcelino, "Sikolohiyang Pilipino."

61. Enriquez, *Pagbabagong Dangal.*

62. Pe-Pua, "From Decolonizing Psychology."

63. Enriquez, *Pagbabagong Dangal.*

64. Zeus Salazar, "Ang Kamalayan at Kaluluwa: Isang Paglilinaw ng Ilang Konsepto sa Kinagisnang Sikilohiya," in *Sikolohiyang Pilipino: Teorya, Metodo at Gamit,* ed. R. Pe-Pua (Philippines: University of the Philippines Press, 1989), 83–92.

65. Melba P. Maggay, "Towards Contextualization from Within: Some Tools and Culture Themes." See www.mpmaggay.blogspot.com/2005/04/towards-contextualization-within.html.

66. Ibid.

67. Catholic Institute for International Relations and Latin America Bureau, *Guatemala, Never Again!* (New York: Orbis, 1999).

68. A pseudonym.

69. Randall Lehmann Sorenson, *Minding Spirituality* (Hillsdale: Analytic, 2004).

70. Johann Baptist Metz, *Memoria Passionis* (Freiburg, Germany: Herder Verlag, 2006).

71. Emmanuel Lévinas, *Otherwise than Being: Or, Beyond Essence,* trans. Alphonso Lingis (Boston: M. Nijhoff, 1981).

72. See Alvin Dueck and David Goodman, "Substitution and the Trace of the Other: Lévinasian Implications for Psychotherapy," *Pastoral Psychology* 55 (2007): 601–17.

Chapter 10 What Difference Would Jesus Make?

1. See Franz Thiessen, *Peter M. Friesen* (Winnipeg, Manitoba: Christian Press, 1974).

2. We are deeply indebted to the following sources: Stanley Hauerwas, Nancey C. Murphy, and Mark Nation, eds. *Theology without Foundations: Religious Practice and the Future of Theological Truth* (Nashville: Abingdon, 1994), and William Werpehowski, "*Ad Hoc* Apologetics," *Journal of Religion* 66 (1986): 282–301.

3. Nancey Murphy, *Beyond Liberalism and Fundamentalism: How Modern and Postmodern Philosophy Set the Theological Agenda* (Valley Forge: Trinity Press International, 1996).

4. Ibid., 97.

5. Ibid.

6. Augustus H. Strong, *Systematic Theology* (Philadelphia: Judson, 1907).

7. Donald G. Bloesch, *Essentials of Evangelical Theology*: God, Authority, and Salvation (San Francisco: Harper and Row, 1978).

8. Friedrich Schleiermacher, *The Christian Faith* (Philadelphia: Fortress, 1976).

9. Gordon Kaufman, *God, Mystery, Diversity: Christian Theology in a Pluralistic World* (Minneapolis: Fortress, 1996); David Tracy, *Blessed Rage for Order: The New Pluralism in Theology* (New York: Seabury, 1978); David Tracy, *The Analogical Imagination: Christian Theology and the Culture of Pluralism* (London: SCM, 1981).

10. Portions of this chapter are drawn, with permission of the publishers, from Al Dueck and Thomas D. Parsons, "Integration Discourse: Modern and Postmodern," *Journal of Psychology and Theology* 32 (2004): 232–47.

11. We have been referring to "modernity" as if it were monolithic, while it is obviously far more complex. We agree with Charles Taylor that there are "multiple modernities." Different cultures, Western and non-Western, have modernized in their unique way. See Charles Taylor, *Modern Social Imaginaries* (Durham: Duke University Press, 2004).

12. Karl Popper, *The Logic of Scientific Discovery* (London: Hutchinson, 1959).

13. Charles Taylor, *Sources of the Self: The Making of the Modern Identity* (Cambridge: Cambridge University Press, 1989).

14. Ludy T. Benjamin and David B. Baker, "History of Psychology: The Boulder Conference," *American Psychologist* 55 (2000): 233–54.

15. Monte B. Shapiro, "Clinical Psychology as an Applied Science," *British Journal of Psychiatry* 113 (1967): 1039–42.

16. David L. Sackett, Scott W. Richardson, William Rosenberg, and R. Brian Haynes, *Evidence-Based Medicine* (New York: Churchill Livingstone, 1997).

17. Diane L. Chambless and Thomas H. Ollendick, "Empirically Supported Psychological Interventions: Controversies and Evidence," *Annual Review of Psychology* 52 (2001): 685–716.

18. Philip C. Kendall and Diane L. Chambless, "Empirically Supported Psychological Therapies," *Journal of Clinical and Consulting Psychologies* 66 (1998): 3–167; Philip C. Kendall, Brian Chu, Andrea Gifford, Clair Hayes, and Maaike Nauta, "Breathing Life into a Manual: Flexibility and Creativity with Manual-Based Treatment," *Cognitive Behavior Practice* 5 (1998): 177–78.

19. Philip Rieff, *Charisma: The Gift of Grace, and How It Has Been Taken Away from Us* (New York: Pantheon Books, 2007).

20. Ibid., 6.

21. Ibid., 4.

22. Ibid., 5.

23. Ibid.

24. David H. Kelsey, *Imagining Redemption* (Louisville: Westminster John Knox, 2005).

25. Ibid., 3.

26. Ibid., 5.

27. Ibid., 6–16.

28. Ibid., 30.

29. Ibid., 32 (italics original).

30. Ibid., 39 (italics original).

31. Ibid.

32. Clive S. Lewis, *The Problem of Pain* (London: Geoffrey Bles, 1940), 100.

33. J. L. Austin, *How to Do Things with Words* (Cambridge: Harvard University Press, 1962).

34. Ibid., 73.

35. Stanley J. Grenz and J. R. Franke, *Beyond Foundationalism: Shaping Theology in a Postmodern Context* (Louisville: Westminster John Knox, 2001); Stanley Hauerwas, Nancey C. Murphy, and Mark Nation, eds., *Theology without Foundations: Religious Practice and the Future of Theological Truth* (Nashville: Abingdon, 1994); Miroslav Volf, *Exclusion and Embrace: A Theological Exploration of Identity, Otherness, and Reconciliation* (Nashville: Abingdon, 1996).

36. Grenz and Franke, *Beyond Foundationalism*, 42.

37. Ibid.

38. George Lindbeck, *The Nature of Doctrine: Religion and Theology in a Postliberal Age* (Philadelphia: Westminster John Knox, 1984).

39. Volf, *Exclusion and Embrace*.

40. Alvin C. Dueck, *Between Jerusalem and Athens: Ethical Perspectives on Culture, Religion, and Psychotherapy* (Grand Rapids: Baker Books, 1995), pt. 2.

41. Chris Huebner, "Globalization, Theory and Dialogical Vulnerability: John Howard Yoder and the Possibility of a Pacifist Epistemology," in *A Precarious Peace: Yoderian Explorations on Theology, Knowledge, and Identity* (Waterloo, Ontario: Herald, 2006), 99.

42. Ibid., 51.

43. William Werpehowski, "*Ad Hoc* Apologetics," *Journal of Religion* 66 (1986): 282–301.

44. Ibid., 284.

45. James Olthuis, *The Beautiful Risk* (Grand Rapids: Zondervan, 2001).

46. Ibid., 30.

47. The approach recommended here differs from the traditional psychology of religion paradigm. We are exploring the implications of who Jesus was in life and death for psychologists in their work and practice. Psychologists of religion who examine the life of Christ tend to privilege their preferred psychological theory. John Sanford views the sayings of Jesus through a Jungian lens (John A. Sanford, *The Kingdom Within; A Study of the Inner Meaning of Jesus' Sayings* [Philadelphia: Lippincott, 1970]). Gerd Theissen uses cognitive, behavioral, and psychodynamic approaches to interpret biblical passages (Gerd Theissen, *Psychological Aspects of Pauline Theology,* trans. John P. Galvin [Philadelphia: Fortress, 1987]. For a recent examination of the relationship of Jesus and psychology, see Fraser N. Watts, ed., *Jesus and Psychology* [Philadelphia: Templeton Foundation, 2007]). Most helpful is the work of Klaus Berger in understanding psychological identity in the New Testament from within the ancient Near Eastern cultural context (Klaus Berger, *Identity and Experience in the New Testament,* trans. Charles Muenchow [Minneapolis: Fortress, 2002]).

48. Randall Lehmann Sorenson, *Minding Spirituality* (Hillsdale: Analytic Press, 2004).

49. Ibid., 1.

50. Ibid., 12.

Conclusion

1. We are grateful to Mr. Ron VanderPol, a member of the Fuller Theological Seminary Board of Trustees, who first envisioned such a project and then provided funding.

2. Gladys Mwiti and Al Dueck, *Christian Counseling: An African Indigenous Perspective* (Pasadena, CA: Fuller Seminary Press, 2006). The book is free to anyone interested and is available at: http://documents.fuller.edu/cio/africa_counseling/index.asp. Material borrowed from

the book was done so with permission of Fuller Seminary Press. Also, United Kingdom English spellings have been changed to American. Gladys Mwiti and Al Dueck, *Christian Counseling: An African Indigenous Perspective, Video Series* (Pasadena, CA: Fuller Seminary Press, 2006).

3. Mwiti and Dueck, *Christian Counseling,* 26.

4. Ibid., 121–22.

5. Ibid.

6. Ibid., 15.

7. Derald W. Sue and David Sue, *Counseling the Culturally Different: Theory and Practice* (New York: Wiley, 1999), 34–35.

8. Mwiti and Dueck, *Christian Counseling,* 35.

9. Ibid., 36.

10. Perhaps not in all educational contexts in Africa. My (AD) grandsons attended a school in Zambia run by Europeans. The administration insisted that only English be spoken on campus, not Bemba, the language of the Africans living in the area. Neither is Bemba taught to children of Westerners working in the copper mines or other businesses.

11. Simon S. Maimela, "Cultural and Ethnic Diversity in Promotion of Democratic Change," in *Democracy and Development in Africa: The Role of Churches,* ed. J. N. K. Mugambi (Nairobi: All Africa Conference of Churches, 1997), 106.

12. Mwiti and Dueck, *Christian Counseling,* 26.

13. Ibid. (italics original).

14. Zablon J. Nthamburi, "Ecclesiology of African Independent Churches," in *The Church in African Christianity: Innovative Essays in Ecclesiology,* ed. J. N. K. Mugambi and Laurent Magesa (Nairobi: Initiatives Ltd, 1990), 44.

15. Mwiti and Dueck, *Christian Counseling,* 85.

16. Ibid., 187.

17. In addition to the proverbs provided by Dr. Mwiti, we were able to collect proverbs from pastors and mental health professionals from a range of tribes and countries in Africa. In August 2005 we invited pastors and counselors to a retreat center at Brackenhurst, Nairobi, for the filming of the video that accompanied our book. The audience responded to the presentations by exploring the themes in small groups. The indigenous proverbs and stories they shared were incorporated in the final version of the DVD.

18. Ngono cia Nyomoo, *Meru Animal Tales* (Meru, Kenya: Meru Bookshop, Methodist Church, 1975), 1.

19. Jean Masamba ma Mpolo and Daisy Nwachuku, eds., *Pastoral Care and Counselling in Africa Today* (Frankfurt am Main: P. Lang, 1991), 27.

20. Kasonga Wa Kasonga, "African Palaver: A Contemporary Way of Healing Communal Conflicts and Crises," in *The Church and Healing: Echoes from Africa,* ed. Emmanuel Lartey, Daisy Nwachuku, and Kasonga wa Kasonga (New York: Peter Lang, 1994), 49–65.

21. Kwame Bediako, *Jesus and the Gospel in Africa: History and Experience* (New York: Orbis Books, 2004), 5.

22. Mwiti and Dueck, *Christian Counseling,* 19.

23. Nlenanya Onwu, "Biblical Perspectives for Peace, Development and Reconstruction. Its Socio-Religious Implications for the Churches in Africa," in *The Role of Christianity in Development, Peace and Reconstruction: Southern Perspectives,* ed. Isobel Phiri, Kenneth Ross, and James Cox (Nairobi: All Africa Conference of Churches, 1996), 32–48.

24. Mwiti and Dueck, *Christian Counseling,* 33.

25. Ibid., 31 (italics original).

26. Ibid., 132–33.

Index